Dedicated to My Father

Late Shri B.N. Tripathi

(01.04.1943 – 04.10.2013)

A Woman is the full circle. Within her is the power to create, nurture and transform.

— *Diane Marisechild*

Preface

Women's participation in paid workforce has increased all over the world in last few decades. More and more women are entering in various new and non-conventional spheres of workforce. This increase in women's participation in paid workforce has led to increase interest in the effects of women's employment on their well-being. The literature on work stress shows that working women are prone to the same stresses experienced by working men. Yet, women have to confront with potentially unique stresses such as discrimination, taking care of children and aging parents, sexual harassment and many more. Despite confronting such stresses, working women are found to be happier than their non-working counterparts in many researches. Studies demonstrate that paid employment had clearly beneficial health effects on some women and clearly detrimental effects on other. These effects depend on the characteristics of the individual woman, her family situation and properties of her job. Employment does not necessarily increasing women's well-being. Sometimes working women are found to be less happier than non-working women. It seems that multiple job roles of employed women produce many negative consequences too. That is why, their well-being is not increasing accordingly. Many studies report decrease in well-being of employed women. Betsey and Stevenson and Justin Wolfer (2009) have found in a study that women's happiness has declined over the past fifty years both relative to where they were and relative to men, Brigid Schmulte (2014) has described the intense time pressure that the today's women are facing. In her book "Overwhelmed: Work, Love and Play, Where No One has the Time", she explained the stress felt by the women in balancing between the multiple roles.

Women are now stucked between work and family responsibilities. American Psychological Association, says that 28 per cent women report having a great deal of stress *versus* 20 per cent of men. 49 per cent of women *versus* 39 per cent of men say their stress level has increased during the last five years. Significantly, more women are reporting physical and emotional problems than men. Although employment's role in enhancing women's status cannot be denied, but it is not always associated with women's better well-being and happiness. Therefore, it

Our Contributors

Aastha Dhingra, Consultant Psychologist, CSR, DLF Foundation.
Email: *aastha@adtrainingcoaching.edu.in*

Amit Shekhar, CSR Strategist and Development Professional.

Dr. Anubhuti Dubey, Professor & Head, Department of Psychology, D.D.U. Gorakhpur University, Gorakhpur, Uttar Pradesh.
Email: *anubhutiddu@rediffmail.com*

Dr. Chetana Pokhriyal, Associate Professor and Head, Department of English, M.K.P. PG College, Dehradun, Uttarakhand.
Email: *chetanapokhriyal@gmail.com*

Prof. C.P. Khokhar, Professor, Department of Psychology, Gurukul Kangdi University, Haridwar, Uttarakhand.
Email: *cpkhokhar @rediffmail.com*

Dr. Gaurav Kumar Rai, Assistant Professor, Department of Psychology, RGSC, BHU, Mirzapur, Uttar Pradesh.
Email: *gauravcsl@gmail.com*

Dr. G. Kumaravelu, Post Doctoral Fellow, School of Education, Pondicherry University, Puducherry-605 014.
Email: *coumaravelou@gmail.com*

Dr. Harendra Sharma, Assistant Professor (Psychology), Ma Gaytri Ram Sukh Pandey P.G. College, Masakanwa, Gonda, Uttar Pradesh.
Email: *harendrapsychology@gmail.com*

Dr. Laxmi Vajpeyi, Associate Professor & Head, Department of Humanities & Professional Ethics, Babu Banarasi Das Northern India Institute of Technology & Management, Lucknow, Uttar Pradesh.
Email: *laxmi.vajpeyi@gmail.com*

Dr. Manoj Rao, Assistant Professor, Department of Psychology, B.P.D., Government P.G. College, Kanker, Chattisgarh.

Dr. Nidhi Gupta, Assistant Professor, Department of Psychology, Vidya Bhawan Mahila College, Siwan, Bihar.
Email: *guptanidhi818 @gmail.com*

Prof. P.S.N. Tiwari, Professor & Head (Former), Department of Psychology, D.D.U. Gorakhpur University, Gorakhpur, Uttar Pradesh.
Email: *tiwaripsn@rediffmail.com*

Paramita Routh Roy, Department of English, Calcutta University, West Bengal.
Email: *routhroyparamita@gmail.com*

Pawan Kumar Mishra, Additional Director, Construction Industry Development Council (Established by the Planning Commission, Government of India), New Delhi.
Email: *pawangorakhpur @gmail.com*

Pratibha Pandey, Executive (HR), Construction Industry Development Council (Establised by Planning Commission, Government of India), New Delhi.
Email: *pratibha19pandey@gmail.com*

Dr. Preeti Tamta, Assistant Professor, Department of Psychology, Kumaun University, S.S.J. Campus, Almora, Uttarakhand.
Email: *preetiku@gmail.com*

Dr. Priyesh Kumar Singh, Department of Psychology, B.H.U., Varanasi, Uttar Pradesh.
Email: *priyeshr18@gmail.com*

Puran Chandra, Research Scholar, Department of Psychology, G.K.V. Haridwar, Uttarakhand.
Email: *puranchandra88@gmail.com*

Sakshi Seth, Research Scholar, Department of Psychology, Delhi University, Delhi.
Email: *missakshiseth@gmail.com*

Dr. Satarupa Datta, Assistant Professor in Commerce, Panchakot Mahavidyalaya.
Email: *satarupadatta10@gmail*

Shagufta Afroz, Senior Research Fellow, Department of Psychology, D.D.U. Gorakhpur University, Gorakhpur, Uttar Pradesh.
Email: *shaguftaafroz786.sa@gmail.com*

Shalini Sharma, Assistant Professor, Psychology Department, Ramanujan College, University of Delhi, Delhi.
Email: *shalinisharma_81@yahoo.com, shalini031981@gmail.com*

Dr. (Smt.) Shilpi Singh, Assistant Professor, Department of Psychology, H.R.P.G, College, Khalilabad, Sant Kabirnagar, Uttar Pradesh.
Email: *shilpikhalilabad@gmail.com*

Shoaib Hasan, Research Scholar, Department of Psychology, DDU Gorakhpur University, Gorakhpur, Uttar Pradesh.
Email: *shoaib7126 @gmail.com*

Shreosi Biswas, Research Scholar, Jadavpur University, West Bengal.
Email: *shreosi.biswas@gmail.com*

Dr. Sonali Lakhera, Assistant Professor, Department of Humanities, UPES, Dehradun, Uttarakhand.
Email: *sonalilakhera@gmail.com*

Sonam Begum, Research Scholar, Department of Psychology, G.K.V. Haridwar, Uttarakhand.
Email: *Bsonam1991@gmail.com*

Dr. (Mrs.) Sushma Pandey, Professor & Head, Department of Psychology, D.D.U. Gorakhpur University, Gorakhpur, Uttar Pradesh.
Email: *sushma_35gkp@rediffmail.com*

Dr. Tulika Anand, Research Associate, Maxi Mind Learning, ON, Canada.
Email: *tulikainbox@gmail.com*

1

Introduction

Well-being is a multi-dimensional construct (Diener, 2009; Michaelson, Abdullah, Stever Thompson & Marks, 2009; Stiglitz, Sen & Fitoussi, 2009). Bradburn (1969) has defined well-being as how excess of positive over negative affect. He highlighted how psychological well-being was the variable that stands out as being of primary importance. He referred psychological well-being as happiness many times. His idea of well-being is linked to Aristotle's idea of as eudaimonia, which is generally translated as well-being. According to Aristotle, eudaimonia is the overarching goal of human behaviours. In the same way Bradburn focuses on the difference between positive and negative effect. According the Bradburn, "An individual will be high in psychological well-being in the degree to which he has an access of positive over negative effect and will be low in well-being in the degree to which negative effect predominated over positive" (Bradburn, 1969: 9).

Diener and Suh (1997) have also emphasized on positive and negative effect model of Bradburn. According to them "Subjective well-being consists of three interrelated components: life satisfaction, pleasant affect and unpleasant affect". Affect refers to pleasant and unpleasant moods and emotions, whereas life satisfaction refers to a cognitive sense of satisfaction with life (Diener & Suh, 1977: 200). Ryff (1989,a) have identified five aspects of well-being: autonomy, environmental mastery, positive relationship will others, purpose in life, realization of potential and self-acceptance. In recent researches different models of well-being have been emphasized. Foresight mental capital and well-being project (2008) define it as ability to fulfil goals; Pollard and Lee (2003) define it as happiness; and Diener and Suh (1997), Seligman (2009) as life satisfaction.

Shin and Johnson (1978) defined well-being as "A global assessment of a person's quality of life according to his own chosen criteria". This

40 years old definition is present in many recent researches (Zikmund, 2003; Rees, Goswami & Bradslow, 2010; Stratham & Chase, 2010). There researches emphasize on quality of life in well-being. But, defining quality of life is not easy. Quality of life cannot be used as a synonym of well-being. World Health Organization (WHO) defines quality of life as an individual's perception of their position in life in the context of the culture and value systems in which they live and in relation to their goals, expectations, standards and concerns. It is a broad ranging concept affected in a complex way by the person's physical health, psychological state, personal beliefs, social relationships and their relationship to salient features of their environment.

Quality of life may be an important dimension of well-being, but it cannot be used as a synonym of well-being. In recent researches positive functioning of the individual has been emphasized for well-being (Duckworth Steen & Seligman, 2005; Linley & Joseph, 2004; Linley, Joseph, Harrington & Wood, 2006). This approach is correlated with William James's writing on healthy mindedness (James 1902). Carl Rogers (1961) also discussed well-being in terms of "The good life". According to Rogers, every person strives to become "fully functioning person". The person who is open to experience is trusting his own organism, and leads an increasingly existential life (Rogers, 1961:187-189). Ryff and Singer (2008) seem to be influenced by Rogers's conception of well-being. Their six core dimensions of well-being, i.e. self-acceptance, purpose in life, environmental mastery, positive relationship, personal growth and autonomy show Rogers's influence.

Keyes (2002, 2005) viewed mental health as a syndrome of well-being symptoms. According to him, "mental health is created when an individual shows a high level on at least one symptom of hedonic and just over half the symptoms of eudaimonia", i.e. positive functioning of life. Keyes work started the use of terms "flourishing and languishing", as scientific concepts. His work directly influenced on the formulation of "a well-being manifesto for a flourishing society" by Shah and Marks (2004). Shah and Marks (2004) defined well-being as "well-being is more than just happiness. As well as feeling satisfied and happy, well-being means developing as a person, being fulfilled and making a contribution to the community" (2004: 2).

Martin Seligman, the leader of positive psychology has outlined his new concept of well-being. According to Seligman (2011) five essential elements required for well-being are positive emotion, engagement, positive relationship, meaning and accomplishment or achievement.

Positive emotions are the element of well-being, but well-being is about more than just feeling good. It also comes from using our strength in the pursuit of meaningful activities. According to Seligman "well-being cannot exist just in your head, well-being is a combination of feeling good as well as actually having meaning good relationship and accomplishment".

While women's well-being is widely studied in recent years, but the well-being of working women remain a lesser studied area. Women here stepped into almost all conventional and non-conventional professions. But, their well-being has not been studied unlike men's well-being. Their well-being at workplace and its consequence has remained relatively under-researched area. Women in paid workforce have been increasing impressively. According to recent statistics about 43 per cent of women aged 16 and older were in labour force in 1970. This proportion has increased to about 59 per cent in 2006. In India, overall labour force participation rate for women has fallen from 37 per cent in 2004-05 to 28 per cent in 2016 (International Labor Organization, *Global Employment Trends in 2013: Recovering from Secured Jobs Dip*, 2013:79). Addressing the well-being of working women has become very relevant with this consistent increase in working women workforce. Women at work do not face the same difficulties and challenges as men do. Well-being of the women at work is very important since it is correlated with many positive outcomes. Research has shown that individuals with greater well-being have been found to have greater success in life, better health, greater career success and better relationship with others (Robertson & Cooper, 2011). Increased well-being among employees has been associated with higher customer satisfaction (Moliner *et al.*, 2008), greater productivity, higher profitability, lower employee turnover and decreased absence levels (Harter *et al.*, 2003). But, it is quite disappointing to note that as women are progressing at their workplaces, their well-being is not increasing. Cabrera, Beth (2015) says "Women have made huge strides during last several decades to achieve greater equality in education and in the workplace. But, they certainly have not figured how to have it all. "In fact striving to have it all is pushing more and more women to the breaking point".

Stevenson, Band, Wolfers, J. (2009) have found in a study that women's happiness has declined over the past fifty years both relative to where they were and relative to men. American Psychological Association (2010) report that 28 per cent of women had a great deal of stress *versus* 20 per cent of men. Forty nine per cent of women reported increase in their stress level in past five years, while only thirty nine per cent men reported increase in stress level. Women reported more physical and emotional systems of stress such as headache or upset stomach as compared to men. Working women have to undergo through a variety of stress are at time. They are under acute time pressure and multiple roles. Brigid Schulte (2014) has described the intense time pressure experience by women at work. Rising levels of role overload leads to a feeling of never ending paucity of time to accomplish the long list of responsibilities. A well-being project done by care.com (2014) found that 80 per cent of working mothers feel stressed about getting everything done with perfection. Women face a variety of newer difficulties as they proceed in their career and family life. The most contributing pressure for women's well-being seems to the pressure of performing multiple responsibilities simultaneously, that too with perfection. Although employment and economic independence has contributed to women's status and well-being. Work experience has made women more confident, enhanced their self-esteem and self-worth, but it has also created many negative consequences too. Working women's well-being and happiness is negatively affected by these factors. It, therefore, becomes very essential to address the barriers and biases affecting working women's well-being and finding ways to increase their well-being too. A review of research done the working women and their well-being suggests that many barriers and threats are influencing women's well-being. A brief description of these barriers is presented in following headings.

Balancing between Work and Family Life

Balancing work and family life is the most challenging obstacle for women's well-being. Eagly and Carli (2007), Sandberg (2013) have found this as a main obstacle responsible for women's slow career progression. Traditionally, women had the responsibility of maintaining family and children and men had the responsibility to earn and be breadwinner. But, with more and more women entering in workforce and pursuing careers, their traditional roles have started to change. Now, women do not have responsibility only in one domain that is home, rather they have to balance between the competing demands of both work and family domains. Attaining this balance is not easy. Imbalance between work and family life arises due to many factors. At home, women have to perform multiple duties, i.e. cooking, cleaning, taking care of children and elderly etc. Work-family imbalance is the result of the performing multiple roles. Household responsibilities interfere with women's ability to perform effectively in the workplace. Younkin (2010), name it "Work-Family Spillover". Many women quit their jobs because of this work-family spillover. They prefer to spend time on raising their family and quit their bright and promising careers. Men on the other hand, rarely do so. If a woman chose her career over family, she is evaluated as selfish and ambitious and not a nice woman, while men are praised for performing well at their workplace. Ignoring family responsibilities are excused for them. This dilemma pushes women back from going to higher positions at their workplace. They often forego promotions, as it will interfere with family responsibilities. Promotions may bring greater time consumption and responsibilities, so, they prefer to deny it.

Zhang (2010) has studied the source of work stress among women academicians in research universities of China. He found that women academicians perceived the demand for career development as highly stressful. The main career challenges for them include the need for renewing knowledge, lack of research productivity and slow career progress. Gender related barriers seemed to increase pressure on women academicians. Women academicians experienced more difficulty in fulfilling both academic work and roles. The main conflict situations found in research were related to performing both work and family roles very well, children's education and future and lack of time to satisfy personal interest and hobbies. In another study, Ugwu (2010) investigated the multiple role stress of female employees. He found that the "sandwich generation" (as she labelled) women that receive caregiving support either from the husbands or from house helps, experienceless stress than their counterparts without such care giving support. In similar study, Wei *et al.* (2009) on Chinese professional women, work family conflict has been found the main stream. Abdullah *et al.* (2008) assessed occupational stress, social and family difficulties and job contentment of working women in Bangladesh. Higher level of stress was found in working professionals due to imbalance between work and family. Loo (2007) has found similar results on working women in Taiwan. He too found that work-family conflict was strongly linked with lower job and family satisfaction, greater stress and more severe physical ailments.

Thus, work-family life imbalance appears to a significant barriers affecting working women's well-being.

Gender Stereotypes and Biases

Gender stereotypes types and biases present a subtle, but powerful obstacle for well-being of women. Gender stereotype is a structural set of beliefs about the personal attributes of males and females. Powell (2003) explains that this belief sees men to be high in 'masculine' trails such as independence, aggressiveness, assertiveness and dominance and women to be high in 'feminine' trails such as gentleness, sensitivity to the feelings of others and tolerant. Despite widespread coverage by media and gender friendly government policies, this gender stereotypes have remained almost unchanged. Stereotype of working women is not positive. Working women is treated as being ambitious, selfish and neglect to family. They are consistently blamed for neglecting family roles. When, women pursue a good career, they are discouraged at every level. They are stereotyped as being masculine and cursed for not behaving like a 'woman'. That is why, women are feared to proceed further in their careers. For men, family roles do not hinder in their career. For men, it is perfectly right to focus on career and overlooking family roles. It is portrayed that leading a happy family and successful career is impossible for women. Women are indirectly forced to choose between work and family.

For women, success at work brings many negative consequences. This is labelled as "Cost of Success". Successful women professional are blamed for being feminist, dominating and ambitious. Success does not bring such negative outcomes for men. Heilman and Okimoto (2007) have found that success and likability are positively correlated with men and negatively correlated with women. Sandberg (2013) named this phenomena "Punishment for Success". When a woman excels in her career, she works hard and proceeds further in career ladder. Such woman is accused for behaving like a man. She is disliked for behaving like a man. Since everybody wants to be liked, women curtail their ambitions, they willingly compromise with their careers. Famous writer Ken Auletta (2002) has summarized this phenomenon as "self-doubt becomes a form of self-defense". Women begin to suspect and underestimate their capabilities in order to be liked by others. Sandberg (2013) quotes Professor D.H. Gruenfeld for explaining this phenomenon, "Our entire cultural ideas associate men with leadership qualities and women with nurturing qualities and put women in double bind. . . ." Further, Professor Gruenfeld explains that women pay cost for their success at workplace. Men can display their abilities and accomplishments, but for women this is considered as a negative characteristic. Rudman, L.A. (1999) has found in a study that for women, taking credit comes as a real social and professional cost. When a woman explains why she is qualified or mentions previous successes in a job interview can lower her chance for getting a job. Women also lag behind men in making negotiations regarding career benefits like perks, salary hike etc. While men negotiate more than women in career advancement pursuits. Asking for oneself is not accepted as a female trail. Woman is considered to be caring, nurturing and giving. Whenever a woman negotiates on her own behalf, she violates the perceived gender norms and disliked a lot.

Discrimination at Workplace

Women face various forms of discrimination at workplace. This discrimination negatively influences women's well-being.

Although gender discrimination is banned legally, but, it is present in many indirect ways. For example, there is no gender discrimination in education and entering in jobs for women, but when women into their career and aspire to go to higher positions at their organization or workplace, they face discrimination. That is why they are badly represented at leadership position in the organization. Catalyst Survey (2015) shows that in United States of America only 5 per cent of the companies in the Standard & Poor's 500 index had female executive officers. Despite women's significant gains in education and at the workplace over the past 50 years, they are always behind men in the leadership positions, from corporate boardrooms, to the hall of congress, from universities to the courts, from religious institutions to philanthropic organizations, women leaders are not seen as men leaders. A Mckinsey survey report "Women Matter" (2015) showed that India's corporate section has only 4 per cent women at senior position compared to the average of 11 per cent average of Asia. The survey reported that number of women at entry level 25 per cent, at mid management level 16 per cent and at top management level only 4 per cent women are present. Aarti Shyamsunder *et al.* (2015) have presented the representation of gender leadership position in India. They found 24 per cent women at entry level against 76 per cent men, 21 per cent women at managerial level against 79 per cent men and only 14 per cent women at senior manager level against 86 per cent men.

It appears that something is holding women back from becoming leaders at workplace. The Glass Ceiling metaphor portrays the difficulty that women face at workplace while moving ahead to leadership positions at workplace. The glass ceiling thus constitutes an invisible barrier for women preventing them from moving up to career ladder (Weyer, 2007).

the glass ceiling phenomena has been explained in many ways, including corporate practices such as recruitment (Powell, 1987); retention, remuneration and development (Will and Nye, 1992); and behavioural causes such as stereotyping and preferred leadership. Eagly and Carli (2007) have proposed the concept of labyrinth. By using the metaphor of labyrinth, they explain that women react to senior positions in organization by negotiating within the organization. Their success and promotion is not attributed to their merit, rather, it is attributed to negotiations and compromises.

Women are undoubtedly competent and efficient as men. But at workplace men are more encouraged than women employees. Women employees are expected to behave feminine and not to supposed to be a male attribute rather. The leadership traits like independence, self-reliance, aggressiveness and assertiveness are supposed to be men's characteristics. When women leader exhibit leadership traits, the image gets conflicted with the traditional women's role. Galanoki *et al.* (2009) have found gender stereotyped perception put women leaders at a disadvantaged position.

Sandberg (2013) has elaborated this discrimination "Leadership Ambition Gap". Leadership ambition gap is a dominant factor, which refrain women from moving to leadership position at workplace. Careers progress on depends on risk taking and self-promotion. And these qualities are labelled as 'Masculine' in the society. Women are not expected to advocate for themselves and be bold and straight forward at workplace. This is perhaps the main reason for absence of women on leadership positions. Sandberg says "the pipeline that supplies women at the entry level, but by the time, the some pipeline is filling leadership position; it is overwhelmingly stuck by men. Women lag behind men in their ambitions at workplace". Konrad *et al.* (2009) found that when jobs are described as powerful, challenging and involving high levels of responsibility, they appeal to more men than women. Men are praised for being ambitions and successful, while women are not. Heilman and Tyler (2007) have found that men are continuously praised for their ambitions and success, while women pay a social penalty for displaying those traits. So, the workplace does not offer equal opportunities to men and women employees.

Joan Williams (2014), the director of the Centre for Work Life Law at the University of California, has extensively researched over women at work. She has identified four biases that working women generally face. The first bias is that women have to prove themselves over and over again. Men are evaluated on the basis of their 'Potential', while women are evaluated on their performance. Women remain in constant pressure of performing well. Women's failure is easily noticed. Men's success is attributed to skill and women's success is attributed to luck. Second bias is the double standard expectation from women. On one hand, they are expected to behave in traditional way, while leadership traits are many 'masculine' labelled traits. Women who are traditional are judged as less competent as leaders at workplace. And if they exhibit masculine traits, they are blamed for not behaving like a woman. Third bias is associated with motherhood and low competence. Motherhood is generally associated with lack of competence and commitment. Women having smaller kids are not offered promotions or challenging assignments. The fourth challenge was the conflict among women. Within an organization, women adopt different strategies to combine the work and family roles. Women sometimes criticize each other and try to prove their own viewpoint. Thus, women start criticizing others in spite of supporting each other.

Discrimination in wage gap of men and women is also an important barrier to women's well-being. ILO's report shows that women are underpassed and discriminated in payment biases in large organization. ILO, *Global Employment Trends* (2003), Somander Tany (2014) have found that women in United States are paid only 78 cents for every dollar that men are paid. In India wage gap exists in many private and non-organized sectors. Women are forced to accept this disparity. This wage gap negatively influences women's self-esteem and self-worth and decreases their well-being.

Enhancing Well-being of the Working Women

Women well-being is consistently threatened by the gender stereotype perception and discrimination. Since working women constitute a significant population of total workforce, their well-being is very important. Well-being is earlier found positively correlated with better production, higher customer satisfaction, higher profitability, lower employee turnover and decreased absence level. Well-being is also positively correlated with personal achievements such as greater success in life, better health, greater success in career and better relationship with others. So, women's well-being must be increased. It can be increased by regular practice of techniques of mindfulness, hopefulness, increasing resilience and maintaining strong social relationship. These techniques would certainly help in managing the stress of life and increasing well-being.

First and foremost important way to increase well-being is to develop positive approach towards life in all circumstances. Women should try to have positive approach and remain calm and relaxed. Positive people have better mental health. Lyubomirsky *et al.* (2005) have found that positive people have better mental health and lesser anxiety and depression. Positiveness helps in becoming more resilient. Since positive people have effective coping styles, they use active and approach of coping style where confronted with stressful life conditions. Isen (1991) has found positively related with lower hypertension, diabetes and stroke. Positive people slept better, have fewer cold, and less pain than negative people.

Strong social relationship can also contribute to well-being. Working women should try to develop strong social relationship at workplace and at family both. Earlier research suggests that social relationship enhance our happiness level and psychological well-being. It makes one happier and adds meaning to life. Social relationship has the most significant impact on human flourishing people having more friends are happier. Friends advice and support one to cope with difficult life situation. Having close and strong relationship enhances physical well-being and longevity too. George Vaillant (2012) has extensively researched on secrets to a fulfilling life and found that "the warmth of people's relationship has the most significant impact on human flourishing. The only thing that really matters in life is your relationship to other people".

Martin Seligman and Diener (2002) have found that the single factor that distinguished the very happiest students from everyone else was they all had close meaning connections worth others. Relationships make to feel safe at time of difficulty. Friends' advice supports our self-confidence. Having close and strong social relationship also enhances our physical well-being and longevity. Baumeister (1999) has found that individuals who had high levels of social support had lower levels for stress and anxiety, they stayed healthier and had longer life too. Janice K. *et al.* (2009) have reported role of relationship in recovery from hurts. Barbara Fredrickson (2013) in her book "Love 2.0: Finding Happiness and Health in Moments of Connection" discusses how positive social connections raise our oxytocin levels. We experience significant health benefits as a result of increased levels of oxytocin in our bodies that occur when we connect to others.

Thus, it is suggested that women should develop healthy relationship with people around them at workplace and at home. Having good friend at home will give them more access to knowledge and information helping them to do their job better. Working with friends will lead to greater collaboration and lesser effort and stress. Friends can also help in coping with difficulties and bounce back quicker when we really need them. Working with close one gives a feeling of security. So, one is more able to take risk and tough decisions too. Supporting relationship encourages going beyond our comfort zone, leading to more career growth working with people we like energies and brings out our best ideas too.

Mindfulness is also helpful in enhancing well-being. It is the practice of focusing on present and not thinking about the past or future. We are unhappy when we think about past negative experiences and worry about future that is uncertain. Future worries and negative past makes one less happier. So, being mindful keeps one away from useless anxiety about the past and future. By being mindful keeps one away from useless anxiety about the past and future. By focusing on present one becomes able to notice the emotions that he is experiencing at that moment. When one is mindful, he not only better understands his own emotions, but he also better understands other's emotions too. By understanding other's emotions, social relationships are strengthened. Mindfulness is important in disengaging individual from automatic thoughts, habits and unhealthy behaviour patterns and thus plays important role in fostering informed and self-endorsed behavioural regulation which has been associated with well-being enhancement (Ryan and Deci, 2000). Mindfulness contributes to well-being by adding clarity and vividness to experience. Many theorists (Brazier, 1995; Mortin, 1997) have emphasized the positive relation of different attributes of mindfulness and well-being.

Hopefulness also facilitates to well-being. Hope works as a great motivator. Hopeful people are much happier and satisfied with their life. Hope about future give one encouragement to work hard to achieve it. Having a clear picture of one's future plans is an important element of hope. Women should have a clear ten or fifteen years future plan ready in their minds. Visualizing the future plans makes one energized and active. There is a difference between being hopeful and being optimistic. Optimism is a belief that good things will happen to them while hopefulness is a belief that one himself has to work hard to make his plans executed successfully. Hopeful person realize that they are responsible for moving towards their vision.

To conclude, it can be stated that women face many complexities at workplace in form of gender stereotypes, discrimination, gender pay gap, sexual harassment, glass ceiling. Their well-being undoubtedly threatened. But, women themselves can overcome this situation by practicing mindfulness, hopefulness, developing strong social relationships and being more resilient.

REFERENCES

Auletta , K. (2012). "A Women's Place: Can Shreyle Sandberg Upend Silicon Valley's Male Dominated Culture?" *The New Yorker*.

Baumeister, R.F. & Leary, M.R. (1995). "The Need to Belong: Desire for Interpersonal Attachment as a Fundamental Human Motivation", *Psychological Bulletin*, 117: 3.

Bradburn, N. (1969). *The Structure of Psychological Well-being*, Chicago: Aldine.

Cabrera, B. (2015). *Beyond Happy, Women, Work and Well-being*, ATD Press, U.S.A.

Catalyst (2015). *Women CEO's of the S&P 500, http:/www.catalyst.org/ knowledge/ women-ceos-sp-500*.

Diener, E. & Seligman, M.E.P. (2002). "Very Happy People", *Psychological Science*, 13: 81-84.

Diener, E. & Suh, E. (1997). "Measuring Quality of Life: Economic, Social, and Subjective Indicators", *Social Indicators Research*, 40(1-2): 189-216.

Diener, E. (2009). "Subjective Well-being", in Diener (Eds.), *The Science of Well-being*, New York: Spring, 11-58.

Eagly, A.H. & Karau, S.J. (2002). "Role Congruity Theory of Prejudice Towards Female Leaders", *Psychological Review*, Vol. 109, No. 3: 573-598.

Fredrickson, B. (2013). *Love 2.0: Finding Happiness and Health in Moments of Connection*, New York: Hudson Street Press.

Harter, J.K.; Schmidt, F.L. & Keyes, C.L.M. (2003). "Well-being in the Workplace and Its Relationship to Business Outcomes: A Review of the Gallup Studies", in C.L.M. Keys & J. Haidt (Eds.), *Flourishing, Positive Psychology and Life Well-lived*, Washington, DC: American Psychological Society.

Heilman, M.E. & Okimoto, T.G. (2007). "Why Women are Penalized for Success at Male Tasks?: The Implied Communality Deficit", *Journal of Applied Psychology*, Vol. 92, No. 1: 81-92.

Janice, K. *et al.* (2005). "Hostila Marital Interactions, Proinflammatory Cystokine Production and Wound Healing", *Archives of General Psychiatry*, 62: 12, 1377-1384.

Keys, C. (2002). "The Mental Health Continuum: From Languishing to Flourishing in Life", *Journal of Health and Behaviour Research*, 433: 207-222.

Konrad, A.M. *et al.* (2000). "Sex Differences and Similarities in the Job Attribute Preferences: A Meta Analysis", *Psychological Bulletin*, Vol. 126, No. 4: 593-64.

Lu, Y. (2007). The Impact of Work-family Conflict on Working Women in Taiwan: The Effects of Organizational Support, Ph.D. Thesis, Queensland University of Technology, Brisbane, Australia.

Michaelson, J.; Abdullah, S.; Stever, N.; Thompson, S. & Marks, N. (2009). *National Accounts of Well-being: Bringing, Real Wealth onto Balance Sheet*, London: New Economics Foundation.

Pollard, E. & Lea, P. (2003). "Child Well-being: A Systematic Review of the Literature", *Social Indicators Research*, 61(I): 9-78.

Powel, G.N. & Butterfield, D.A. (2003). "Gender, Gender Identity and Aspirations to Top Management", *Women in Management Review*, Vol. 18, No. 1: 88-96.

Recs, G.; Goswami, H. & Brasshaw, J. (2010). *Developing an Index of Children's Subjective Well-being in England: Summary Report*, The Children's Society, London.

Robertson, I. & Cooper, C. (2011). *Well-being: Productivity and Happiness at Work*, New York: Palgrave Macmillan.

Rogers, C. (1961). *On Becoming a Person*, Boston: Houghton Mifflin.

Rudman, L.A. (1998). "Self-Promotion as a Risk Factor for Women: The Cost and Benefits of Counterstereotypical Impression Management", *Journal of Personality and Social Psychology*, Vol. 74, No. 3: 629-645.

Ryff, C. & Singer, B. (2008). "Know Thyself and Become What You Are: An Eudaimonic Approach to Psychological Well-being", *Journal of Happiness Studies*, 9: 13-39.

Ryff, C. (2014). "Psychological Well-being Revisited: Advances in the Science and Eudaimonia", *Psychotherapy of Psychosomatics*, 83(1): 10-28.

Ryff, C.D. (1989a). "Happiness is Everything, or is it? Explorations on the Meaning of Psychological Well-being", *Journal of Personality and Social Psychology*, 57: 1069-1081.

Sandberg, S. (2013). *Lean In: Women Work and the Will to Lead*, New York: Affred A. Knopf.

Schulte, B. (2014). *Overwhelmed: Work, Love and Play When No One has the Time*, New York: Sarah Crichton Books.

Seligman, M.E.P. (2011). *Flourish: A New Understanding of Happiness and Well-being and How to Achieve Them*, London: Nicholas Brealey Publishing.

Shah, H. & Marks, N. (2004). *A Well-being Manifesto for a Flourishing Society*, London: The New Economics Foundation.

Shin, D. & Johnson, D. (1978). "Avowed Happiness as an Overall Assessment of the Quality of Life", *Social Indicators Research*, 5(I): 475-492.

Shyamsunder, Aarti; Pollack, Alexendra & Travis, D. (2015). *India Inc: From Intention to Impact*, Catalyst Survey.

Stevenson, B. & Wolfers, J. (2009). *The Paradox of Declining Female Happiness*, Working Paper, *http://www.nbir.org/paper/W14969.pdf.*

Stiglitz, J.; Sen, A. & Fitoussi, J.P. (2009). Report by the Commission on the Measurement of Economic Performance and Social Progress.

Ugwu, L. (2010). "Employed "Sandwich" Generation Women: Coping with Work/ Family Conflicts", *Eu. J. Soc. Sci.*, 15: 396-410.

Valliant, G.E. (2012). *Triumphs of Experience: The Men of Harvard Grant Study*, Cambridge, N.A.: Belknap Press.

Wei, F.; Y. Feng & L. Wu (2009). "The Stressors in Professional Women's Work-family Conflicts: A Chinese Conflict", *Canadian Soc. Sci.*, 5: 62-68.

Williams, J.C. & Dempsey, R. (2014), *What Works for Women at Work: Four Patterns Working Women Need to Know*, New York: New York University Press.

Younkin, F.L. (2010). Work-Family Spillover Division of Labour and Relationship Satisfaction, M.Sc. Thesis, Ohio State University.

Zhang, L. (2010). "A Study on the Measurement of Job-related Stress among Women Academics in Research Universities of China", *Frontiers Educa. China*, 5: 158-176. *DOI: 10.1007/s11516-010-0011-4*

Zikmund, V. (2003). "Health, Well-Being, and Quality of Life: Somc Psychosomatic Reflections", *Neuroendocrinology Letters*, 2(6): 401-403.

PART I

Workplace Difficulties, Biases and Perception of Working Women

2

Coping and Buffer in the Work Stress-Health Relationship: A Study on Career Women

Sushma Pandey and *Nidhi Gupta*

Introduction

Women in India have come a long way after Independence. From just a skilled homemaker, women today have acquired skills and capabilities of not just being a homemaker but being at par with their male counterparts. This is the new generation of women, who want to pursue their dream career. Indian families are undergoing rapid changes due to the increased pace of urbanization and modernization. Indian women belonging to all classes have entered into paid occupations. At the present time, Indian women's exposure to educational opportunities is substantially higher than it was some decades ago, especially in the urban setting. This has opened new vistas, increased awareness and raised aspirations of personal growth. Traditionally, the major responsibility of women has been perceived to be the maintenance of the family including home and childcare and bread winning was the main responsibility of men. However, with more and more women entering the workforce and pursuing careers, these clearly defined gender roles were forced to change (Sevim, 2006). Most women do not have responsibility only in one domain anymore; they have to balance the competing demands of both work and family domains (Biçaksiz, 2009).

'Families' and 'employment' are inter-related and socially constructed. Thus, women have to deal with home and family issues as well as job stress on a daily basis. The heavy stress and strain they face while combining the outside work and domestic work, child care, care for elderly make her more tiresome and she gain less leisure. Working woman's total hours of work increase at the expense of her leisure time. Imbalance between work and family life arises due to a number of factors. Various factors appear to strengthen the brunt of pressure on women such as job loss and to chronic work stressors such as role overload, instability, job dissatisfaction, inadequate child care and shift work etc. Thus, career-oriented females are considered as having more work stress in comparison with their male counterparts (Cartwright & Cooper, 1994). Factors, contributing such type of discriminatory practices are largely rooted in the socio-cultural and economic values of society. Hence, the status of women at workforce and stress they bear on a routine basis are not likely to change dramatically, unless and until the social attitudes, underlying the discriminatory behaviour towards females are changed.

When the stress is excessive, it overtaxes individuals' resources and leads to a breakdown on integrated functioning. The ill consequences of stress on employees and organization have been identified (Cooper *et al.*, 1996). Such outcomes include emotional problems, mental illness, physical illness and social deviance.

Conceptualization of Stress

The word 'stress' is not unfamiliar to most people. Stress is an adaptive response to a situation that is perceived as challenging or threatening to a person's well-being. As we shall see, stress is the person's reaction to a situation, not the situation itself.

Moreover, individuals experience stress when something is perceived to interfere with their well-being, that is, with their innate drives and need fulfillment. Stress has both psychological and physiological dimensions. Psychologically, people perceive a situation and interpret it as challenging or threatening. This cognitive appraisal leads to a set of physiological responses, such as higher blood pressure, sweaty hands, and faster heartbeat.

In the psychological view, stress is generally used to describe a response to demands that is greater than an individual's ability to cope, which disrupts the individual's physical or mental equilibrium and poses a threat to the individual's general well-being (Lazarus & Folkman, 1984). The body's reaction to stress involves psychological and physical arousal has been described abundantly in literature on its contribution in physical and mental health impairments (Melchior *et al.*, 2007).

Stress is a personal experience caused by pressure or demands on an individual and impacts upon the individual's ability to cope or rather, his/her perception of that ability. Stress refers to the generalized, patterned, unconscious mobilization of the body's natural ability (Yahaya *et al.*, 2009). The causes of stress can be environmental, social, biological or psychological factors that challenge an individual to change or adapt (Bourne & Yaroush, 2003). For instance, environmental and social factors include the environment of a workplace status, emotional well-being and overall health levels of an individual (Gazzaniga, Heatherton & Halpern, 2010).

Stress at study is a growing problem for all workers, including women. Furthermore, in women levels of stress-related illnesses are nearly twice as high as for men (Abdullah *et al.*, 2008). Stress in the workplace poses a major problem for both the organization and employees as it negatively affects the employees' general well-being and work performance, and incurs costs on the organization [National Institute for Occupational Health and Safety (NIOSH), 1999; Spangler, Koesten, Fox & Radel, 2012].

Work stress can be defined as the negative effects on the worker's physical and emotional health as a result of the mismatch between the worker's capabilities, resources or needs and the requirements of the job (NIOSH, 1999). The changing and modernization of the current working environment have had employees work longer hours, adapt effectively to change, task complexity and demands for greater technical skills (Snow *et al.*, 2003). In other words, the world is moving faster than it used to be. As employees engage more time in their work, work stressors are also increasing the risk and adversely affecting the employees' psychological and physical well-being (Snow *et al.*, 2003). Work stress refers to the interaction of work condition with worker characteristics which changes normal psychological or physiological functions (Beehr & Newman, 1978; Cooper, 1983). Sources of work stress such as work overload, job insecurity, interpersonal relationships, role conflict, commuting stress etc. have been identified to play a primary role in employee's health and are somewhat similar for both males and females (Days & Livingstone, 2001). Frequent absenteeism, mood disorders, tardiness and intentions to quit are usually predictors of stressful working conditions (Sandmark & Renstig, 2010).

Six major sources of work stress are presented by Cooper, Cooper and Ealler (1998), displayed in Figure 2.1.

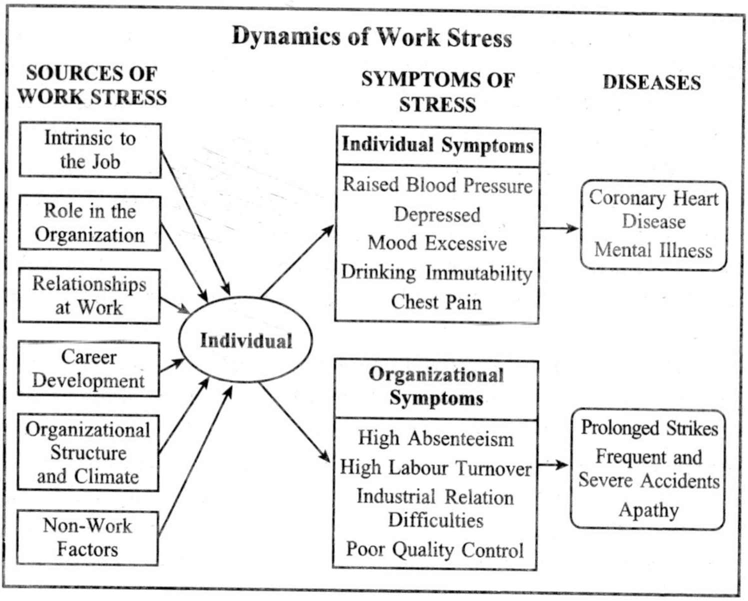

FIGURE 2.1: Source and Consequence of Work Stress

(i) *Job Specific Stress:* It includes poor work conditions, shift work, long hours travel, risk and danger, new technology, work overload and underload.

(ii) *Role Stress:* This includes role ambiguity, role conflict and responsibility.

(iii) *Interpersonal Stress:* The relationship at work place includes relationship with boss, relationship with subordinates and also with colleagues.

(iv) *Career Development:* Several issues can act as potential stressors throughout one's working life, i.e. lack of job security, fear of job loss, (obsolescence) or retirement and various performance appraisals can also create pressure and strain.

(v) *Organizational Structure and Climate:* Organization can present threats to a person's sense of freedom and autonomy. Inadequate opportunities for participation as lacking sense of belongingness led to predictor of strain and job related stress.

(vi) *Non-work Factors Like Home-work Interface:* Career-oriented females or young (male/female) managers face the inevitable conflict between organizational and family demands during the early development of their career. The adverse consequences of such conflicts are reported in interpersonal relations, health and performance (Carwright & Cooper, 1997; Cooper & Lewis, 1998). Based on the transactional model of stress and coping (Lazarus & Folkman, 1984), how employees cope and adapt to these demands may serve to lower or increase the risk for negative health outcomes.

Coping with Work Stress

Coping with work stress is a key concept in understanding people's adaptation to their work roles. In their jobs employees are confronted with various kinds of demands, which may become 'stressors' when they tax or exceed the employee's adaptive capabilities. Examples of common job stressors include work overload, role problems, poor job control, and lack of support from supervisors and co-workers, and interpersonal conflicts. These stressors may lead to negative psychological (e.g., depression, irritability, burnout), physical (e.g., headaches, heart palpitations, hyperventilation) and behavioural (e.g., absenteeism, turnover, violence) symptoms or 'strains'. More specifically, coping with work stress refers to the things employees do to handle the stressors they encounter in their work roles.

Coping Process

The psychological process that is involved in dealing with these work stressors in order to reduce strain is called 'coping'. Coping refers to the person's cognitive and behavioural efforts to manage (minimize/reduce, master or tolerate) the internal or external demands of the person-environment transaction that is appraised taxing or exceeding the person's resources. Lazarus and Folkman (1984) have identified two major forms of coping, i.e. problem-focused coping and emotion-focused coping:

(i) *Problem-focused Coping:* Strategies are similar to problem-solving tactics, these strategies encompass efforts to define the problem, generate alternative solutions, weigh the costs and benefits of various actions, take actions to change what is changeable, and, if necessary, learn new skills; and

(ii) *Emotion-focused Coping:* Strategies are directed toward decreasing emotional distress. These tactics include such efforts as distancing, avoiding, selective attention, and blaming, minimizing, wishful thinking, venting emotions, seeking social support, exercising, and meditating. Coping style and strategies, persons apply to confront stressful situations are viewed important to mitigating stress-illness relations.

Coping has been classified in many ways. Moos and Billing (1982) have grouped it into three domains, i.e. appraisal-focused, problem-focused and emotion-focused coping whereas Maddi and Kobasa (1984) have talked about two forms of coping: (a) Transformational, and (b) Regressive. Lazarus (1974) classified coping into direct action and palliative modes. Further, Prateek (1983) developed Role PICS (projective instrument for assessing coping styles) and has broadly grouped it as 'Approach' and Avoidance modes of coping. However, Carver *et al.*, (1989) argue that in assessing coping, dimensional approach is more accurate than categorical approach. They developed "Cope Scale" which includes fifteen coping strategies, broadly classified into active, adaptive and maladaptive styles.

Coping as Moderator

Stress-illness connection is moderated by several factors and coping is one of them. Srivastava and Singh (1987) examined the moderating effects of two coping strategies, i.e. approach and avoidance in relation between role stress and mental health in case of supervisors. Both coping strategies were found to modify stress-illness association, though in opposite direction. The approach coping exercised buffering effect whereas the avoidance coping had the intensifying effect on stress-illness relationship. Thus, moderating role of coping in role/occupation/ work stress-health connection has been investigated by a number of researchers (Caplan, 1979; Pandey & Srivastava, 2004; Srivastava, 2002).

Stress-Health Connection

A sizable number of researches evinced that excessive pressure at work place cause the most acute problems, which frequently damage the health and well-being of employees and organization too. Numerous studies showed the close association between stress and health (Friedman & Rosenman, 1974; Lazarus & Launier, 1978; Lazarus & Folkman, 1984; Ickovics & Park, 1988; Pestonjee, 1999; Pandey & Srivastava, 2004; Selye, 1956). The adverse consequences of work stress on health of employees have been identified by researchers (Beeher & Newman, 1978; Srivastava, 1999).

The concept of health has changed with the passage of time. Now, health is viewed not only as the total absence of disease, but also it includes social and behavioural well-being. It has more comprehensive meaning which is reflected in the definition of health given by World Health Organization (WHO). It provides a vivid conceptualization on health such as (i) something which goes beyond the more absence of disease, and (ii) that health has social and psychological characteristics.

Antonovsky (1979) argued that health cannot be understood using a pathologically oriented perspective. Since health is a relatively higher process rather than a state or static condition, influenced by the availability of genetic and major psychosocial resistance resources which include types of coping strategies, social matter, and degree of commitment and level of ego identity. He has also conceptualized health process as influenced by the specific social and cultural contexts. Stress may have effects on, at least four physiological systems of body: the sympathetic-adrenome-dullary system, the pituitary-adrenocortical system, the neuropeptide system and the immune system. To the extent that stress affects these pathways illness may result, and stress can produce physiological as well as psychological changes conducive to the development of illness, precursors of illness such as fatigue and achiness then develop, which, if untreated can lead to illness and illness is found to be an important factor in the origin of several diseases.

The reason for this stress-health connection lies in the way, in which the brain interprets what is going on, how it responds to perceived threat, and how it translates those perceptions into body responses. However, it is important to note here that the brain works in a literal way. When threat is present, the brain will sound the alert, and the body will respond by mobilizing its defensive systems. Several classical representative studies on stress-illness relationship, have proved that stressful events lead to several health problems (Mishra & Sinha, 1999; Selye, 1956). Studies reveal that moderate level of stress lead to adaptive responses, but stress above a threshold point would have adverse consequences on health and outcomes (Taylor & Schneider, 1991). Studies indicated that health is related to stress, but the impact of any stressful event is subsequently influenced by how a person appraises it. According to Lazarus's view of stress, any new event or change in the environment prompts the individual to make primary appraisals of the significance of the event. An event may be judged to positive, neutral, on negative in the implications for the self.

A close perusal of literature evinced that the extent of work stress is influenced by several factors such as, personality traits (Wallace, 1970), control (Rotters, 1966), coping strategies (Carver, 1989), social support (Caplan, 1979), lifestyle (Lam, 1988), job category (Yogrecha & Mishra, 1990), type of family (Thackray *et al.*, 1971) and job tenure (Pandey & Srivastava, 2000). Though findings seem equivocal however, it is not enough to explain which aspects of job (work) cause greater and lesser stress. Therefore, work stress should be still studied in relation to certain mediating and moderating variable such as coping strategies etc.

The nature and place of job have also significant impact on stress and health. In Indian context, joint family system may provide a large supportive social network to minimize stress-illness relation (Pandey & Srivastava, 2004). Similarly, job tenure is also found to be another moderating factor in health-illness relation (Pandey & Srivastava, 2000). Females, specially, young female employees face large amount of organizational and family demands during their early development of career. Since new set of demands and challenges are being gradually placed on females in their roles as career women, they experience certain level of stress related to work. In this connection, the experience of stress will be influenced by their coping styles and strategies. Apart from this, the current family structure, job tenure as well as job category of career women may play interactive role with work stress and coping for determining the health status of career women.

Objective and Hypotheses

Present study is planned to examine the relationship between work stress-coping and health. Furthermore, the contributing role of coping in work stress-illness connection is also examined.

Following research questions were raised and hypotheses were formulated:

1. How are work stress, coping and health associated and what would be the pattern of relationships among them across the groups?

   (a) It was hypothesized that work stress would be found positively linked with physical and psychological illness.

   (b) It was further expected that work stress and various coping strategies would be related, though in diverse ways. More specifically, active and adaptive related coping would be inversely related with work stress whereas a positive link between maladaptive coping and stress would be found. The extent of relationship would also vary across the groups.

(c) It was also assumed that coping responses would be differently related with physical and psychological illness. Active and adaptive related coping would be inversely related, whereas, maladaptive coping would be positively related with physical and psychological illness.

2. What would be the role of various coping styles and strategies in mitigating work stress-illness relationship?

   (a) It was hypothesized that coping would moderate work stress-illness relations. Specifically, Active and Adaptive coping strategies would exercise 'buffering' role in stress-illness connection.

   (b) Further, coping strategies related to maladaptive style would play "intensifying" role in Work Stress-Health relationship.

Method

Respondents

A total of 240 working women, 20 in each cell participated in the study. A 3 × 2 × 2 factorial design with three levels of job category (Teachers, Railway and Bank employees) × two types of family (Joint and Nuclear) × 2 (Job Tenure: Short Tenure, i.e. 0-5 years and long job tenure, i.e. above 6 years) was used and stratified random sampling techniques was applied in sample selection.

Measures

1. *Work Stress Profile:* Work stress was assessed by applying work stress profile (Carry Cooper, 1983). It includes 57 items to measure three levels of Work stress, i.e. interpersonal, physical conditions and job interest. Items pertaining to these areas were rated on five point scale. Items favourable to work stress were scored in 5, 4, 3, 2, 1 order and unfavourable items were scored in reverse order.
2. *Cope Scale:* Cope scale, developed by Carver, Scheiver and Weintraub (1989) was used to assess coping style and strategies

exercised by female personnel to cope with work stress. This scale includes 15 domains related to active, adaptive and maladaptive styles. Since "Alcohol and drug use domain" was not applicable on this sample hence, was omitted, and only 14 domains of cope scale were used in present study. Items pertaining to these areas were rated on four point scale.

3. *Health Questionnaire:* Cornell Medical Index (CMI) questionnaire, translated into Hindi by Wig, Prasad and Verma (1983) was used to assess health status of career women. This questionnaire contains 195 questions related to physical distress and psychological distress. Each "Yes" answered items were counted and considered as a score.

Procedure

Respondents were contacted at their workplace, and were introduced about the problem of the study. If they volunteered to participate in the study, then they were given a booklet containing background information, Work Stress Profile, Cope Scale and C.M.I. Health Questionnaire. They were requested to complete background information containing nature and hours of work, distance of workplace from the house, conveyance facility to reach the workplace and support in household work. Then, they were asked to respond on work stress profile. Afterwards, they were requested to answer on cope scale. Lastly, they were told to respond on C.M.I. health questionnaire. As they completed responses on above mentioned measures, data were collected and they were thanked for participation.

Results

Obtained scores were treated statistically in terms of both bivariate and multivariate analysis. First section deals to determine the association between work stress, coping and illness, correlation were computed to ascertain the relation of coping with work stress and illness (Tables 2.1, 2.2, 2.3, 2.4, 2.5 and 2.6).

Bivariate Analysis

(I) ***Relationship between Work Stress and Illness:*** In order to determine the relationship between work stress and illness, coefficients of correlation were computed. As correlational results (Table 2.1) indicate, objective work stress was found to be positively related with physical ($r = 0.13$, $P < 0.05$) and psychological illness ($r = 0.24$, $P < 0.01$). Feeling of work stress caused by physical condition was positively related with physical illness ($r = 0.17$, $P < 0.01$) and psychological illness ($r = 0.16$, $P < 0.01$). Similarly work stress caused by job interest was also found to be positively related with physical illness ($r = 0.16$, $P < 0.01$) and psychological illness ($r = 0.13$, $P < 0.05$).

TABLE 2.1: Correlation between Work Stress and Illness

	Physical Illness	*Psychological Illness*
Objective Work Stress	0.13	0.24
Feeling of Work Stress		
Interpersonal	0.04	0.03
Physical Condition	0.17	0.16
Job Interest	0.16	0.13

(II) ***Relationship between Work Stress and Coping:*** Further correlational analysis was done to determine the relationship of work stress with coping responses related to Active, Adaptive and Maladaptive strategies.

TABLE 2.2: Correlation between Work Stress and Coping

Dimensions of Coping	*Objective Work Stress*	*Feeling of Work Stress*		
		Inter-personal	*Physical Condition*	*Job Interest*
Active Coping				
Active Coping	0.5	– 0.37	– 0.24	– 0.25
Planning	0.12	– 0.33	– 0.20	– 0.32
Suppression of Competing Activities	0.06	– 0.13	– 0.01	– 0.20
Positive Refraining	0.03	– 0.34	– 0.30	– 0.29
Restraint Coping	0.07	– 0.23	– 0.14	– 0.23
Adaptive Coping				
Use of Instrumental Support	0.14	– 0.19	– 0.08	– 0.22
Use of Emotional Support	0.03	– 0.23	– 0.09	– 0.09
Religion	0.07	– 0.18	– 0.05	– 0.13
Maladaptive Coping				
Acceptance	0.09	– 0.24	– 0.08	– 0.21
Focus on & Venting Emotion	0.20	– 0.12	– 0.06	– 0.01
Denial	0.17	– 0.01	0.10	0.02
Mental Disengagement	0.16	– 0.01	0.12	0.14
Behavioural Disengagement	0.02	– 0.12	0.14	0.15
Humour	– 0.02	– 0.01	0.06	0.02

Results (Table 2.2), that objective work stress was found positively related with active coping style related planning ($r = 0.12, P < 0.05$) and adaptive related use of instrumental support ($r = 0.14, P < 0.05$).

Correlation results further showed that objective work stress was positively related with maladaptive related focus on and venting of emotion ($r = 0.20, P < 0.01$), denial ($r = 0.17, P < 0.01$) and mental disengagement ($r = 0.16, P < 0.01$).

Feeling of work stress was found to be inversely related with active and adaptive related coping responses however positive relations were found with maladaptive coping responses. More specifically, interpersonal work stress was found to be negatively related with active coping ($r = 0.37, P < 0.001$), planning ($r = 0.33, P < 0.001$) and restraint coping ($r = 0.23, P < 0.001$). Similarly, stress caused by physical condition and job interest was also negatively related with active coping ($r = 0.20, P < 0.001$ *vs.* $r = -0.32, P < 0.001$), positive reframing ($r = 0.30, P < 0.001$ *vs.* $r = -0.29, P < 0.001$) and restraint coping ($r = 0.14, P < 0.05$ *vs.* $r = -0.23, P < 0.01$). Interpersonal and job interest were negatively related with suppression of competing activities ($r = -0.13, P < 0.05$ *vs.* $r = -0.20, P < 0.001$).

Similarly, linkage between work stress and adaptive related coping responses were also found to be negative. Interpersonal work stress was inversely related with use of instrumental support ($r = 0.19, P < 0.01$), and religion ($r = 0.18, P < 0.01$). Job interest related stress was also negatively related with the use of instrumental support ($r = -0.22, P < 0.01$) and religion ($r = 0.13, P < 0.05$).

However, pattern of relationship between work stress and various domains of maladaptive coping was different. Interpersonal work stress was positively related with behavioural disengagement ($r = 0.12, P < 0.05$) but negatively related with acceptance ($r = 0.24, P < 0.01$) and focus on and venting of emotions ($r = 0.12, P < 0.05$). Whereas physical condition was positively related with denial ($r = 0.010, P < 0.05$), mental disengagement ($r = 0.12, P < 0.05$) and behavioural disengagement ($r = 0.14, P < 0.05$). Stress caused by job interest was also positively related with mental disengagement ($r = 0.14, P < 0.05$) and behavioural disengagement ($r = 0.15, P < 0.01$) but negatively related with acceptance ($r = 0.21, P < 0.001$).

Results indicate negative association between work stress and active and adaptive dimensions of coping whereas, positive linkage between work stress and maladaptive dimensions of coping.

(III) *Relationship between Coping and Illness:* To check the relationship of various coping responses with physical and psychological illness, coefficients of correlation were computed for overall groups. As Table 2.3 indicates several coping responses were found to be negatively related with illness, yet only a few domains were found to be significant. The relationship between adaptive coping, i.e. use of instrumental support ($r = 0.10$, $P < 0.05$) was found to be negatively related with physical illness, whereas, maladaptive coping, i.e. denial ($r = 0.16$, $P < 0.01$) and mental disengagement ($r = 0.19$, $P < 0.01$) were found to be positively related with physical illness. Maladaptive coping, i.e. Focus on and venting of emotion ($r = 0.12$, $P < 0.05$) and mental disengagement ($r = 0.21$, $P < 0.001$) were also found to be positively related with psychological illness.

TABLE 2.3: Correlation between Coping and Illness

Dimensions of Coping	*Physical Illness*	*Psychological Illness*
Active Coping		
Active Coping	– 0.01	0.03
Planning	– 0.06	– 0.01
Suppression of competing Activities	0.02	0.04
Positive Refraining	0.01	0.06
Restraint Coping	0.01	0.06
Adaptive Coping		
Use of Instrumental Support	– 0.10	0.02
Use of Emotional Support	– 0.02	0.05
Religion	0.08	0.08
Maladaptive Coping		
Acceptance	– 0.01	0.06
Focus on and Venting Emotion	0.02	0.12
Denial	0.16	0.09
Mental Disengagement	0.19	0.21
Behavioural Disengagement	– 0.01	0.01
Humour	– 0.02	– 0.08

It is clear from the results that active and adaptive coping were negatively related with physical and psychological illness. Whereas, various strategics of maladaptive coping were found positively correlated with physical and psychological illness.

Step-wise Multiple Regression Analysis

Based on the perusal of correlations reported in earlier section, it was considered appropriate to go for Step-wise Multiple Analysis in order to examine the relative contributions of work stress and coping on illness. The predicting role of coping in work stress-health connection was also ascertained on the basis of regression analysis.

(I) *Prediction of Illness by Work Stress:* Results (Table 2.4) revealed that physical illness was significantly predicted by the feeling of work stress related to physical condition (β = 0.17, R^2 = 0.03), which positively contributed 3 per cent variance independently.

TABLE 2.4: Step-wise Multiple Regression Analysis for Illness on to the Objective Work Stress and Feeling of Work Stress

Predictor Variables	*Criterion (Physical Illness)*			
	R^2	R^2 *Change*	*Beta β*	*T*
Feeling of Work Stress				
Physical Condition	0.03	0.03	0.17	2.78
Objective Work Stress	0.05	0.05	0.21	3.37
Feeling of Work				
Stress Physical Condition	0.07	0.02	0.12	2.04

Further, regression results (Table 2.4 and Figure 2.2) indicated that psychological illness was positively explained by the both factors as well; objective work stress was found strongest positive predictor of psychological illness, which contributed maximum (β = 0.21, R^2 = 0.05), followed by another positive predictor feeling of work stress related to physical condition (β = 0.12, R^2 = 0.02). Though, independently objective work stress contributed 5 per cent of variance and physical condition explained 2 per cent of variance but the composite contribution of objective work stress and physical condition was found 7 per cent variance in criterion variable.

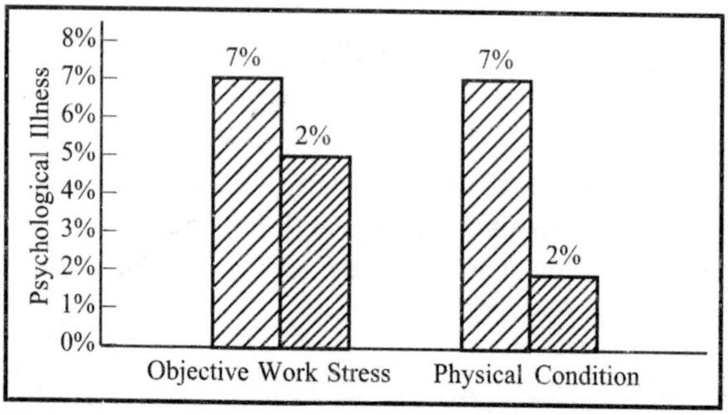

FIGURE 2.2: Prediction of Psychological Illness by Work Stress

(II) *Prediction of Work Stress by Coping Strategies:* A close perusal of regression results (Table 2.5) denote that objective work stress was predicted by maladaptive related focus on and venting of emotion.

TABLE 2.5: Step-wise Multiple Regression Analysis for Objective Work Stress, Feeling of Work Stress on to the Active, Adaptive and Maladaptive Coping Responses

Predictor Variables	*Criterion (Objective Work Stress)*			
	R^2	R^2 *Change*	β	*T*
Focus on and Venting of Emotion	0.03	0.03	0.19	3.13
Criterion (Feeling of Work Stress-Interpersonal)				
Active Coping	0.13	0.13	– 0.27	– 4.11
Positive Reframing	0.18	0.05	– 0.22	– 3.42
Criterion (Physical Condition)				
Positive Reframing	0.09	0.09	– 0.26	– 3.94
Denial 0.11	0.02	0.13	2.14	
Active Coping	0.13	0.02	– 0.15	– 2.30
Mental Disengagement	0.15	0.02	0.12	2.01
Criterion (Job Interest)				
Planning	0.10	0.10	– 0.18	– 2.40
Mental Disengagement	0.12	0.02	0.20	3.32
Use of Instrumental Support	0.15	0.03	– 0.15	– 2.34
Positive Reframing	0.16	0.01	– 0.18	– 2.40

Regression results (Table 2.5) shows that objective work stress was positively predicted by focus on and venting of emotion (β = 0.19, R^2 = 0.03). The contribution of focus on and venting of emotion was found 3 per cent variance in criterion variable (objective work stress).

Furthermore, it is clear from the regression results (Table 2.5) that interpersonal stress, domain of feeling of work stress was negatively predicted by active coping (β = – 0.27, R^2 = 0.13) followed by positive reframing (β = – 0.22, R^2 = 0.05).

Though, independently active coping (Figure 2.3) contributed 13 per cent of variance and positive reframing explained 2 per cent of variance but the composite contribution of active coping and positive reframing was found 18 per cent variance in criterion variable (interpersonal stress).

As regression results (Table 2.5) indicated that work stress caused by physical condition, was negatively predicted by positive reframing (β = – 0.26, R^2 = 0.09) and active coping (β = – 0.15, R^2 = 0.02). More specifically, work stress caused by physical condition was positively predicted by maladaptive coping, i.e. denial (β = 0.13, R^2 = 0.02) and mental disengagement (β = 0.12, R^2 = 0.02).

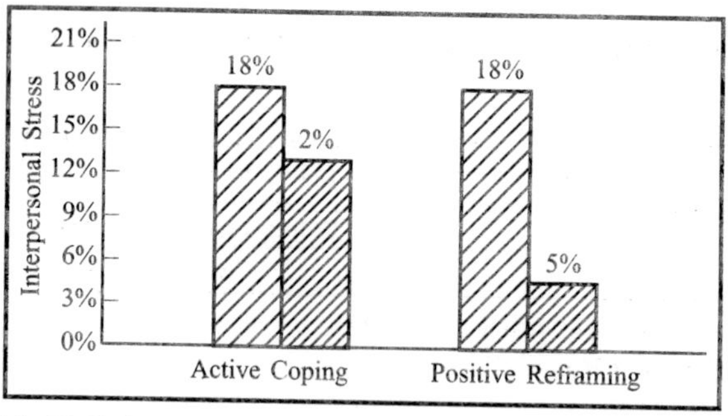

FIGURE 2.3: Prediction of Interpersonal Stress by Active Coping and Positive Reframing

Where contribution of positive reframing (Figure 2.4) was found maximum 9 per cent followed by denial 2 per cent, active coping 2 per cent and mental disengagement 2 per cent variance in criterion variable (Physical Condition). But, the composite contribution of positive reframing, active coping, denial and mental disengagement was 15 per cent variance in work stress caused by physical condition.

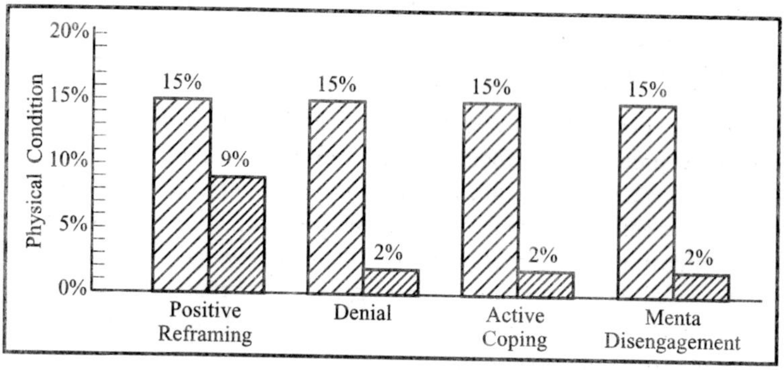

FIGURE 2.4: Prediction of Physical Condition by Coping

Furthermore, stress caused by job interest was negatively predicted (Table 2.5) by planning (β = – 0.18, R^2 = 0.10) where, mental disengagement explained positively (β = 0.20, R^2 = 0.02). Similarly, job interest explained negatively by use of instrumental support (β = – 0.15, R^2 = 0.03) and positive reframing (β = – 0.15, R^2 = 0.01). Though, independently (Figure 2.5) planning explained 10 per cent, mental disengagement 2 per cent, use of instrumental 3 per cent and positive reframing 1 per cent, but the composite of these factors was 16 per cent variance in criterion variable.

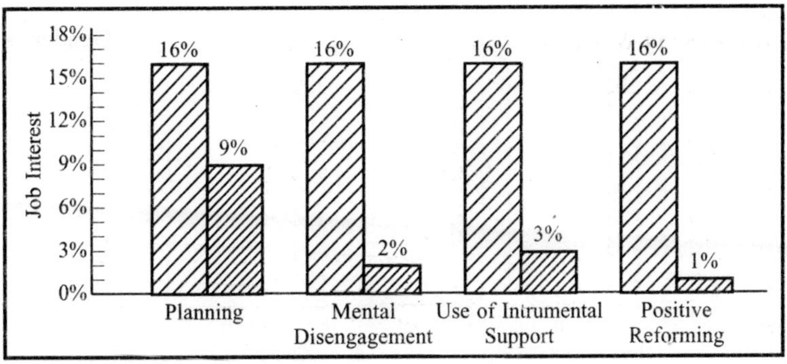

FIGURE 2.5: Prediction of Job Interest by Coping

(III) ***Prediction of Illness by Coping Responses:*** A close perusal of regression results (Table 2.6) denote that physical illness was predicted by three factors which are mental disengagement, denial, use of instrumental support and humour.

TABLE 2.6: Step-wise Multiple Regression Analysis for Physical and Psychological Illness on to the Active, Adaptive and Maladaptive Coping Responses

Predictor Variables	*Criterion (Physical Illness)*			
	R^2	R^2 *Change*	β	*T*
Mental Disengagement	0.03	0.03	0.24	3.53
Denial	0.06	0.03	0.18	– 2.80
Use of Instrumental Support	0.08	0.02	0.18	2.72
Humour	0.10	0.02	– 0.14	– 2.05
Criterion (Psychological Illness)				
Mental Disengagement	0.04	0.04	0.28	4.27
Humour	0.07	0.03	– 0.19	– 2.91

Results indicated (Table 2.6) that physical illness was positively explained by mental disengagement ($\beta = 0.24$, $R^2 = 0.03$), denial ($\beta = 0.18$, $R^2 = 0.03$), use of instrumental support ($\beta = 0.18$, $R^2 = 0.02$) where physical illness was inversely predicted by humour ($\beta = -0.14$, $R^2 = 0.02$).

Though independently (Figure 2.6) mental disengagement 3 per cent, denial 3 per cent, use of instrumental support 2 per cent and humour 2 per cent, but the composite of these factors was 10 per cent variance in criterion variable.

Similarly, (Table 2.6) psychological illness was explained positively by mental disengagement ($\beta = 0.28$, $R^2 = 0.04$) but inversely predicted by humour ($\beta = -0.19$, $R^2 = 0.03$).

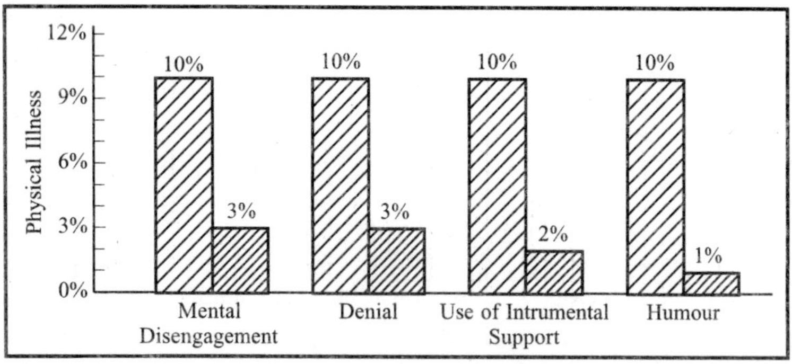

FIGURE 2.6: Prediction of Physical Illness by Coping

Though, (Figure 2.7) mental disengagement contributed 4 per cent followed by humour 3 per cent and the composite of these factors was 7 per cent variance in criterion variable.

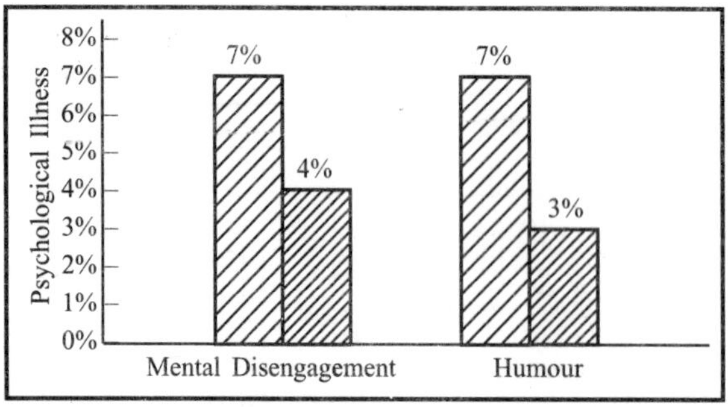

FIGURE 2.7: Prediction of Psychological Illness by Coping

Present findings have strongly proved that active and adaptive coping exerted pervasive role in minimizing work stress and its outcomes on health status of career women.

Discussion

Findings have been discussed and interpreted under two major sections. First part interprets the linkage between work stress, coping and illness and in the second section; contributing roles of coping in stress and illness have been discussed in the light of appropriate empirical and theoretical evidences.

Correlation results revealed close relationship between work stress and illness. Objective work stress was positively related with physical and psychological illness. Similarly, feeling of work stress caused by physical condition and job interest were positively associated with physical and psychological illness. Contrary to this active and adaptive related coping responses were found to be inversely related with work stress and illness, whereas, maladaptive related coping strategies were positively related with work stress and illness. Thus, results indicated that work stress-illness relationship is not linear but also moderated by coping strategies. Apart from this, regression results denote differential roles of coping on work stress and illness. Active and Adaptive coping have exerted pervasive role in mitigating high feeling of stress related to work place and its consequences on physical and psychological illness. In other words, work stress-health relationship was significantly modified by active and adaptive coping strategies but maladaptive coping strategies exerted "intensifying" impact on work stress and illness. Results thus, indicate that work stress-health relationship is not linear but is also moderated by different strategies of active and adaptive. Findings have been discussed in relation to a number of other empirical evidences.

Work Stress and Health Connection

It is apparent from present results, work stress was found positively linked with physical and psychological illness. This result has ample empirical supports. The effects of work stress on physical health status are well established. The major physical symptoms by work stress are: increased heart rate and blood pressure, cardiovascular disease, increased secretion of adrenaline and non-adrenaline, gastrointestinal disorders such as ulcer, respiratory problems increased sweating, skin disorders, headaches, cancer, bodily injuries, physical fatigue, muscular tension, sleep disturbance and death.

Some employees bring some physical health to the job like, high risk behaviour in the social environment. Work conditions may intensify the health problem, though making it more visible. But the job is attributed for the health problem.

Previous studies have proved the adverse consequences of stress related to work on heath (Cartwright & Cooper, 1994; Pandey & Srivastava, 2004; Pandey & Pandey, 2014; 2015). When the stress is excessive, it overtaxes individual's resources and leads to breakdown on integrated functioning. Such outcomes include emotional problems, mental illness, physical illness and social deviance (Rice, 1987). According to Rose (2003), employees have tendency towards high level of stress regarding time, working for longer hours which reduces employees urge for performing better. Other studies have also proved adverse consequences of stress on health, which include — increased heart rate and blood pressure, cardiovascular disease, gastrointestinal disturbance, headaches, hypertension, fatigue and sleep disturbance etc. (Maslach, Schaufeli & Leiter, 2001).

Stress may affect not only the individual, but also his/her family life, marriage and social life (McManus, Winder & Gordan, 2002). Earlier, Pandey and Srivastava (2004) reported a positive relationship between stress (work) and illness in career women. They also found that job category, joint/nuclear family structure and job tenure exercised influence on extent of work stress, coping and illness. In another study, Shukla (2010) evinced that work stress was found positively linked with physical and psychological illness in teachers. Pandey and Gupta (2016) found that stress related to time caused negative impact on health status of medical professionals.

Besides these outcomes work stress also cause some severe health problems, cognitive dysfunction, dementia, and excessive fatigue (Hasler, Buysse & Gamma *et al.*, 2005; Cho H.J., Bower J.E. & Kiefe, *et al.*, 2012).

Work Stress-Coping Relationship

Bivariate and multivariate results depicted that work stress caused by interpersonal was negatively linked with all dimensions of coping, i.e. active, adaptive and maladaptive. Whereas, work stress caused by physical condition and job interest were negatively related with active and adaptive coping but, positively related with maladaptive coping. Apart from this, active and adaptive coping exercised mediating role in lessening stress feeling and improving health status of career women. Findings of present study as well as other studies also confirm the buffering role of coping in work stress (Srivastava, 1997; Gaur & Dhawan, 2000; Pandey & Srivastava, 2004). Shane Schick (2007) stressed IT professional who use a balance problem-focused coping strategies and emotion-focused coping strategies are most successful in dealing with the stress of staying perceptually up-to-date. Findings of present study as well as other studies also confirm the buffering role of coping in work stress (Pandey & Srivastava, 2004; Srivastava, 2002; Pandey & Srivastava, 2000; Gaur & Dhawan, 2000; Srivastava, 1997).

Buffering Role of Coping in Work Stress-Health Connection

Results indicate that active coping and positive reframing contributed negatively whereas, maladaptive related denial and mental disengagement contributed positively to work stress. Similarly planning, use of instrumental support and positive reframing (all active styles) contributed negatively but mental disengagement contributed positively to feeling of work stress. It appears that active and adaptive related coping exercised buffering effect on work stress but maladaptive style exerted "intensifying" impact on work stress (Pandey & Srivastava, 2004; Srivastava, 1997).

Results revealed that active and adaptive coping exercised favorable impact on mitigating work stress-illness relation. The buffering role of such coping responses has also been identified in a number of studies (Pandey & Srivastava, 2004; Srivastava, 1997; Srivastava & Singh, 1987). Besides this, maladaptive coping have played negative role in mitigating stress-illness linkage. Other studies also support the intensifying roles of maladaptive coping in stress-illness connection (Srivastava, 2002; Srivastava, 1997).

Research that focused on interventions and stress management programmes for career women, especially working mothers (Harlin-Clifton, 2008; Kline & Snow, 1994) examined gender differences in work stress and coping (Shek, 1989), the well-being of working females (O'Neill & Zeichner, 1985; Noor, 1999; Raak & Wahren, 2005; Sandmark & Renstig, 2010) as well as psychological characteristics that influence the regulation of work stress in working females (Klainin, 2009; Snow, Swan, Raghavan, Connell & Klein, 2003).

In brief the findings of present study evince that active and adaptive related coping responses exert buffering role in minimizing the adverse effect of work stress on health status of career women whereas, maladaptive coping strategies exercise intensifying impact on work stress-illness connection. Results of present study as well as other representative studies confirm the moderating roles of coping in work stress and illness ((Srivastava, 2002; Pandey & Srivastava, 2000; Gaur & Dhawan, 2000; Srivastava, 1997; Cooper *et al.*, 1996; Caplan *et al.*, 1985).

Conclusion

Findings of this investigation evinced close linkage between work stress, coping and health. Results showed a positive link between work stress and illness. Obtained results can be interpreted in the light of workplace related model of stress and illness (Cooper *et al.*, 1996). According to this model various sources of stress related to workplace exercise negative feelings to individuals. As a result, they express various symptoms and consequently receive poor health status. Apart from this, certain contextual and personal factors (coping style) exercise influence on work stress and illness.

The findings of this research can also be linked with the transactional model of stress and coping (Carver *et al.*, 1989; Lazarus & Folkman, 1984). The interactions between situational and personal factors are implicit in transactional theory of stress and coping. Correlational as well as, regression analyses indicated the contributing roles of coping in work stress and illness. More specifically, active and adaptive related coping strategies exercised 'Buffering' role in stress-illness connection, whereas maladaptive coping exerted "intensifying" role in work stress-illness linkage. Thus, contributing roles of coping in mitigating work stress-illness relationship cannot be denied.

REFERENCES

Abdullah, R.; Jahan, S. & Saha, S. (2008). "Occupational Stress, Social and Family Difficulties and Job Contentment of Working Women: Bangladesh Perspective", *J. Bus. Econ.*, 3: 139-153.

Antonovski, A. (1979). *Health, Stress and Coping*, San Francisco: Jossey-Bass.

Beehr, T.A. & Newman, J.E. (1978). "Job-stress, Employee Health and Organizational Effectiveness: A Facet Analysis, Model and Literature Review", *Personnel Psychology*, 31: 665-669.

Biçaksiz, P. (2009). *The Effects of Gender Role Ideology,* Role Salience, Role Demands and Core Self-evaluations on Work-family Interface, M.Sc. Thesis. Middle East Technical University.

Bourne, L.E. Jr. & Yaroush, R.A. (2003). *Stress and Cognition: A Cognitive Psychological Perspective* (NASA Grant No. NAG2-1561), Boulder, Colorado: University of Colorado.

Caplan, R.D. (1979). "Social Support, Person-Environment Fit and Coping", in L.A. Ferman & J.P. Gordus (Eds.), *Mental Health and Economy*, Kalamazzoo. Mich: The W.E. Upjohn Institute of Employment Research.

Cartwright, S. & Cooper, C.L. (1994). *No Hassle: Taking the Stress Out of Workplace Situations*, London: Century Business.

Carver, C.S.; Scheiver, M.F. & Weintraub, J.G. (1989). "Assessing Coping Strategies: A Theoretically Based Approach", *Journal of Personality and Social Psychology*, 56: 267-283.

Cho, H.J.; Bower, J.E. & Kiefe, C.I. *et al.* (2012). "Early Life Stress and Inflammatory Mechanisms of Fatigue in the Coronary Artery Risk Development in Young Adults (CARDIA) Study", *Brain Behave Immun*, 26(6): 859-65.

Cooper, C.L. (1983). "Identifying Stressors at Work: Recent Research Developments", *Journal of Psychosomatic Research*, 27: 369-376.

Cooper, C.L. (1998). "A Multi-dimensional Approach to the Adoption of Innovation", *Management Decision*, Vol. 36, Issue 8: 493-502.

Cooper, C.L.; Liukkoen, P. & Cartwright, S. (1996). *Stress Prevention in the Workplace: Assessing the Caste and Benefits to Organization*, Luxemburg: European Foundation for the Improvement of Living and Working Conditions.

Day, A.L. & Livingstone, H.A. (2001). "Chronic and Acute Stressors among Military Personnel: Do Coping Styles Buffer their Negative Impact on Health?", *Journal of Occupational Health Psychology*, 6, 348-360.

Friedman, M. & Rosenman, R.H. (1974). *Type A Behaviour and Your Heart*, New York: Knopf.

Gaur, S. & Dhawan, N. (2000). "Work Related Stress and Adaptation Pattern among Women Professionals", *Psychological Studies*, Vol. 45: 58-64.

Gazzaniga, M.S.; Heatherton, T.F. & Halpern, D.F. (2010). *Psychological Science* (3rd ed.). New York: W.W. Norton & Company.

Harlin-Clifton, S. (2008). The Effects of Stress Management Training on Work-stress Coping Levels for Working Mothers (Doctoral thesis). Available from Pro Quest Dissertations and Theses database.

Hasler, G.; Buysse, D.J. & Gamma, A., *et al.* (2005). "Excessive Daytime Sleepiness in Young Adults: A 20-year Prospective Community Study", *J Clin Psychiatry*, 66(4): 521-9.

Iekovies, J.R. & Park, C.L. (Eds.) (1988). "Thriving: Broadening the Paradigm Beyond Illness to Health", *Journal of Social Issues* (special number), 57: 237-446.

Klainin, P. (2009). "Stress and Health Outcomes: The Mediating Role of Negative Affectivity in Female Health Care Workers", *International Journal of Stress Management*, 16(1): 45-64.

Kline, M. & Snow, D. (1994). "Effects of a Worksite Coping Skills Intervention on the Stress, Social Support, and Health Outcomes of Working Mothers", *Journal of Primary Prevention*, 15(2): 105-121.

Lam, Y.L.J. (1988). "External Environmental Constraints and Job-related Stress on School Administrators", *Journal of Educational Administration*, 26: 250-265.

Lazarus, R.S. & Folkman, S. (1984). *Stress, Appraisal and Coping*, New York: Springer Publishing Company.

Lazarus, R.C. & Launier, R. (1978). "Stress Related Transactions between People and Environment", in L.A. Pervin & M. Lewis (Eds), *Perspectives in Interactional Psychology*, New York, Plenum, pp. 287-327.

Maddi, S.R. & Khoshaba, D.M. (2005). *Resilience at Work: How to Succeed No Matter What Life Throws at You*, New York: AMACOM.

Maslach, C.; Schaufeli, W.B. & Leiter, M.P. (2001). "Job Burnout", *Annual Rev. Psychology*, 52: 397-422.

McManus, I.C.; Winder, B.C. & Gordon, D. (2002). "The Causal Links between Stress and Burnout in a Longitudinal Study of UK Doctors", *The Lancet*, 359: 2089-2090.

Melchior, M.; Caspi, A.; Milne, B.J.; Danese, A.; Poulton, R. & Moffitt, T.E. (2007). "Work Stress Precipitates Depression and Anxiety in Young, Working Women and Men", *Psychological Medicine*, 37(8): 1119-1129.

Mishra, G. & Sinha, D. (1999). *Coping Strategies of Underprivileged Disadvantaged University Entrants*, Unpublished Results University of Allahabad.

Moos, R.H. & Billing, A.G. (1982). "Conceptualizing and Measuring Coping Resources and Processes", in L. Goldberger & S. Breznitz (Eds.), *Handbook of Stress: Theoretical and Clinical Aspects*, New York: Free Press, pp. 212-230.

NIOSH (1999). *Stress . . . at Work*, Cincinnati OH: U.S. Department of Health and Human Services, Public Health Service, Center for Disease Control and Prevention, National Institute for Occupational Safety and Health, DHHS (NIOSH) Publication No. 99-101.

Noor, N. (1999). "Roles and Women's Well-being: Some Preliminary Findings from Malaysia", *Sex Roles*, 41(3-4): 123-145.

O'Neill, C.P. & Zeichner, A. (1985). "Working Women: A Study of Relationships between Stress, Coping and Health", *Journal of Psychosomatic Obstetrics & Gynecology*, 4(2): 105-116.

Pandey, S. (2012). "Future Orientation and Health Education in Promoting Reproductive Health in Rural Community", in S. Ojha & Pandey (Eds.), *Positive Psychology: Emerging Issues*, New Delhi: Shree Publishing Company.

Pandey, S. & Gupta, N. (2016). "Future Orientation and Time Management as Mediators in Time Stress-health Relationship", *Journal of Indian Health Psychology*, Vol. 11(01): 1-20.

Pandey, S. & Pandey, V.R. (2015). "Managing Time Stress in Medical Professionals: The Role of Future Orientation", *Asian Academic Research Journal of Social Sciences and Humanities*, Vol. 1(32): 314-336.

Pandey, S. & Pandey, V.R. (2014). "Time Management as Buffer in Time Stress-health Relationship: A Study on Medical Professionals", *Indian Journal of Psychological Issues*, 22, 1 & 2: 44-58.

Pandey, S. & Srivastava, S. (2000). "Coping with Work Stress: The Role of Job Category, Family Type and Job Tenure", *Journal of Research and Applications in Clinical Psychology*, 3: 1-10.

Pandey, S. & Srivastava, S. (2004). "Role of Coping in Work Stress-health Relationship: A Study on Career Woman", Akbar Husain & Tabassum Rashid (Eds.), *Stress Behaviour: The Coping Strategies*, Vol. 2, *Psychology of Education*, 6(2): 159-170.

Pestonjee, D.M. (1999). *Stress and Coping the Indian Experience* (2nd Ed.), New Delhi: Sage Publication.

Raak, R. & Wahren, L.K. (2005). "Headache and Coping in a Female Working Population", *Scandinavian Journal of Caring Sciences*, 19(4): 325-329.

Rice, P.L. (1987). *Stress and Health: Principles and Practices for Coping and Wellness*, California, U.S.A.: Brooks/Cole Publishing Company.

Rose M. (2003). "Good Deal, Bad Deal? Job Satisfaction in Occupations", *Work Employment Society*, 17: 503.

Rotter, J.B. (1996). "Generalized Expectancies for Internalized *versus* Externalized Reinforcement", *Psychological Monographs*, 80(1): 609.

Sandmark, H. & Renstig, M. (2010). "Understanding Long-term Sick Leave in Female White-collar Workers with Burnout and Stress-related Diagnoses: A Qualitative Study", *BMC Public Health*, 10(1): 1-12.

Selye, H.J. (1956). *The Stress of Life*, New York: McGraw Hill.

Sevim, S.A. (2006). "Religious Tendency and Gender Roles: Predictors of the Attitudes Towards Work Roles", *Soc. Behav. Personal Intl. J.*, 34: 77-86.

Shek, D.T.L. (1989). "Reliance on Self or Seeking Help from Others: Gender Differences in the Locus of Coping in Chinese Working Parents", *The Journal of Psychology*, 126(6): 671-678.

Shukla, A.K. (2010). "Coping, Time Management and Future Orientation as Moderators of Work Stress-Health Relationship", Unpublished Doctoral Dissertation in Psychology, D.D.U. Gorakhpur University, Gorakhpur.

Snow, D.L.; Swan, S.C.; Raghavan, C.; Connell, C.M. & Klein, I. (2003). "The Relationship of Work Stressors, Coping and Social Support to Psychological Symptoms among Female Secretarial Employees", *Work & Stress*, 17(3): 241-263.

Spangler, N.W.; Koesten, J.; Fox, M.H. & Radel, J. (2012). "Employer Perceptions of Stress and Resilience Intervention", *Journal of Occupational & Environmental Medicine*, 54(11): 1421-1429.

Srivastava, A.K. (1999). *Management of Occupational Stress: Theories and Practice*, New Delhi: Gyan Publication House.

Srivastava, A.K. & Singh, A.P. (1981) *Manual of the Occupational Stress Index*, Department of Psychology, Banaras Hindu University, Varanasi.

Srivastava, S. (2002). Work Stress, Coping and Health Status among Career Oriented Females, Unpublished Doctoral Dissertation, Department of Psychology, D.D.U. Gorakhpur University, Gorakhpur.

Taylor, S.E. & Schneider, S.K. (1991). "Coping and the Simulation of Events", *Social Cognition*, 7: 174-194.

Thackrey, R.I. (1981). "The Stress of Boredom and Monotony: A Consideration of the Evidence", *Psychosomatic Medicine*, 43: 165-176.

Wallace, R.K. (1970). "Physiological Effects of Transcendental Meditation", *Science*, 167(3926): 1751-1754.

Yahaya, A.; Yahaya, N.; Arshad, K.; Ismail, J. & Jaalam, S. *et al.* (2009). "Occupational Stress and Its Effects towards the Organization Management", *J. Soc. Sci.*, 5: 390-397.

Yogrecha, Y.S. & Misra, S.P.A. (1990). "Comparative Study of Organizational Role Stress between Clerical and Teaching Female Personnel", *Personality Study and Group Behaviour*, 10: 59-65.

Wig, N.N.; Prasad, D. & Verma, S.K. (1983). *Abridged Manual for C.M.I. Health Questionnaire (Hindi)*, National Psychological Corporation, Agra, India.

3

Gender Leadership Gap: Why does it Matter and How to Intervene?

Anubhuti Dubey

India is one of the youngest countries in the world. Presently, a substantial section of its population which is around 1.2 billion is in the age group of 20-35. India's economy is growing at an annual rate of 7 per cent. If this "demographic dividend", be mobilized effectively in such a pacing economy, this could transform the country and hasten its developmental dreams. As we know that this growth produces more jobs in stirring different sectors. And women's talent would be a big asset in "Making India" biggest and brightest economy, but why then are women in India being mostly sidestepped in this expansion process?

The ratio of female work force has significantly increased in last two decades in India, but the negative attitude towards working women and particularly the female leaders still persists and the same picture can be seen worldwide (Carlson, Kacmar & Whitten, 2006; Heilman, 2001). A study on the attitude towards women's employment on a sample of 260 men and women employees and 100 students conducted by Kuruvilla and Usha (1999) in University of Calicut revealed the positive attitudes of women students and employees and the negative attitudes of men students and employees towards women's employment.

In spite of the statements that female literacy and enrolment rates in schools and at higher educational institute have been showing an uprising trend, but the participation of its women's workforce is lower than even many countries in Sub-Saharan Africa and the Middle East. On the Gender Inequality Index India is ranked 125 of 159 countries and 108 of 144 countries in Global Gender Gap Index in year 2017. The reasons for lower ranking for India was mainly due to two indicators (i) Health and survival (India's poor sex-ratio at birth, which still points to a strong preference for sons); (ii) Economic participation and opportunities where on an average, an Indian woman is estimated to earn less than quarter of annual income earned by a man. She is paid only 60 per cent of what her male counterpart receives for similar work. Furthermore, women account for over third of labour force participation, but their share of daily unpaid work (household chores, childcare etc.) is 65 per cent while it is only 11 per cent for men. In addition, across sectors, only 13 per cent of senior officials, managers and legislators are women (UNDP, 2017). This gender gap is prevalent not only in terms of employment in labour force, but also in the kinds of work women are engaged in. As our country is still an agrarian economy a considerable section of women in India remain to exert them in rural agricultural work, however, it is usually thought that with growing economy, urbanization and industrial development more women should join the workforce and engage in productive sectors such as manufacturing and services. But, it is not happening with the proportion to such development, so the big question is *why*?

The increasing rates in enrolment of girls in every kind of educational institutions in recent years clearly suggest that parents of daughters of both rural and urban India are now not reluctant to invest in educating them but the idea of women working outside the home is yet to become acceptable and popular. In many parts of India it is still culturally difficult to digest the notion of working women. Hence, the conventional wisdom and societal barriers prevent women to fit into labour force. In the patriarchal system, common in most parts of India, have values like 'family honour', intensely ingrained notions about gender roles and also the apprehensions around the social implications of economic empowerment of women all these solidify the standpoint that home is safest place for female gender. Hence, for those bold women who are competent enough to triumph over the societal barriers, the structural restraints pose difficulties to them to break and enter into better paying and more stable jobs. The Indian data intimates that here women are mostly employed in informal, semi-skilled and unskilled sectors, like domestic work, where incomes are low, benefits are limited and job security is almost nil. India has pitiable data of female participation in the workforce. Relationship between women and professions could be supposed to be as — women in full fledged professions, medicine, law, academics etc. and another in the semi-professions — like nursing, teaching, clerks etc.

It is observed that in urban vicinity, where education and income levels are higher, many married women leave their job for motherhood and for raising children. Rising trepidations regarding the security and safety of women is also an obvious deterrent to women's employment. Some of the brutal incidents, like December 2012 gang rape case commonly named "Nirbhaya case" or "Shakti Mills gang rape" in July, 2013 or "Uber rape case" in December 2014 or May 2017 "Rohtak rape case"; all these and many more reported cases clearly suggest the increasing reports of sexual assault and violence in urban areas. Such incidents reinforced the existing gender stereotypes and added to the public perception that working women in cities are vulnerable to sexual assault. However, at the same time, it is true that gender inequality in the workplace has a negative impact on women, and it also considerably affect how economies and countries strengthen and grow. In a report brought out by the McKinsey Global Institute that approximates that India country can add as much as $ 2.9 trillion to its annual GDP by 2025 if it improves gender parity and engages the full potential of its women workforce (Woetzel *et al.*, 2015). Together with increasing the education levels of females, bringing more women into the workforce is one of the useful methods to deal with patriarchal norms and attend to matters of gender discrimination and violence that are widespread in Indian social settings.

Confrontation with Patriarchal Mindset

Participation of women in prominent decision-making positions is limited by severe cultural and social constraints because men think that women are not capable enough to take a good decision. Women face challenges all over the world and sometimes these challenges are context specific. The literature on the challenges and problems women face at the workplace is not only limited to women in the unorganized sectors, but also in formal organizations too, as women continue trying to contribute to their quality of life and that of their families and thereby to the economies of various countries through work. Wentling (2003) showed that the twin roles of women cause tension and conflict due to her social structure which is still more dominant. In her study on working women in Delhi, she has shown that "traditional authoritarian setup of Hindu social structure continues to be the same basically and hence women face problem of role conflict change in attitudes of men and women according to the situation can help to overcome their problem". A growing body of research suggests that women experience a "motherhood penalty" or "child penalty" when they attempt to combine earning and caring. In the study on motherhood, employment and the child penalty, Baker found that employment "choices" vary among women and are shaped by domestic arrangements, perceptions of support, occupational requirements and ideas about "good mothering". Marriage and parenthood encourage fathers to take their earning obligations more seriously while new mothers often reduce their employment commitments (Beaujot, 2000). Combining motherhood and paid work is particularly challenging in jobs that require high qualifications, entrepreneurial activities and continued productivity, such as university teaching and research (Bassett, 2005; Bracken, Allen & Dean, 2006). Since the mid-1980s, at regular intervals, British Social Attitudes surveys have incorporated attitudinal questions asking about the roles of men and women within the family, focusing on providing an income from work versus playing a caring role in the home and tracking the responses to these questions over the past three decades. In the mid-1980s, approximately half of the public have the opinion that 'a man's job is to earn money and a woman's job is to look after the home and family', however in 2012 only 13 per cent have this view. The authors of the article 'gender roles' in the 30th British Attitude Survey Report Scott and Clery (2013) stated that this decline is primarily a result of generational replacement, with consecutive generations being less supportive of traditional gender roles. In response to another question in 2012, 33 per cent think a mother should stay at home when there is a child under school age, compared with 64 per cent in 1989. The most popular choice now is for the mother to work part time (26% in 1989, 43% in 2012).

Trounce the Blame of Crossing the Traditional Role Boundaries

The participation of women in paid employment has been significantly increased in last two-three decades; however, men folk have not augmented their participation in household work in the matching amount (Evertsson & Nermo, 2004). Most of the women in workforce still do greater part of the care giving functions and juggling of work in the family. However, in very few pockets of social orders, husbands have taken on more domestic work than they did in earlier generations, this gain for women has been offset by "escalating pressures for intensive parenting and the increasing time demands of most high-level careers" (Eagly & Carli, 2007).

Gender is observed as a noteworthy factor of negative job brim-over. Making a work-life balance, the working women are likely to perform the responsibilities for family and still be able to efficiently deal with their work roles and pressures (Delgado & Canabal, 2006). Another phenomenon generally experienced by working women is better known as '*guilt*', a common sentiment of responsibility markedly concerning to their own offspring. It produces a sense of failure of responsibility which appears when they not have perceived control over the demands and challenges made on them from diverse walks of life. As a matter of fact women and particularly the working women have to face problems just by virtue of their being women. Here, by working women I meant to say those who are in paid employment.

Social attitudes to the roles of women consider that women suit for specific jobs and not for the other impact those who are engaged in the recruitment of female employees.

Yet, as in the early 1990s, women still undertake a disproportionate amount of unpaid labour within the home and are much more likely to view their contribution as being unfair. While the male breadwinner family system has been in decline for at least half a century, concerns about "work-family conflict" have only been voiced more recently. With the rise in mothers' labour market participation, there is a role for policy measures that seek to reduce family work conflicts. From the mid-1990s, full-time employment for both women and men continued to grow steadily and the gap between men and women's employment is narrowing. In 2010, a higher proportion of mothers still worked part-time (37%) rather than full-time (29%), sharing their time between work and looking after the family. In the mid-1980s, close to half (43% in 1984 and 48% in 1987) of people supported a gendered separation of roles. There is considerable support for both men and women contributing to the household income. In 1987, a third (36%) of the public thought that most women would prioritise their caring role over having a job. That proportion has dropped to a quarter (26%) in 2012. There has been very little change (from 41% in 1989 to 45% in 2012) in the proportion of people believing that the role of the housewife is just as fulfilling as the role of worker (Scott & Clery, 2013 in British Social Attitudes 30th Report). Attitudes have changed, but have behaviours? Scott and Clery (2013) have shown how, during the past three decades, the public has become less traditional in its views about mothers working *per se*, but that the majority view is that mothers, with young children at least, should still retain the primary care role (be that by staying at home or by combining part-time work with the care giving role) (Scott & Clery, 2013).

Donnelly and associates (2016) examined time period and generational differences in attitudes toward women's work and family roles in two large, nationally representative U.S. samples, the Monitoring the Future survey of 12th graders (1976-2013) and the General Social Survey of adults (1977-2012). Twelfth graders became more accepting of working mothers and equal roles for women in the workplace between the 1970s and the 2010s, with most change occurring between the 1970s and the late 1990s. Acceptance of dual-income families and fathers working half-time or not at all (stay-at-home dads) also increased. Thus, for the most part, Millennials (born 1980s-1990s) have continued trends toward more egalitarian gender roles. However, slightly more 12th graders in the 2010s (*vs.* the late 1990s) favoured the husband as the achiever and decision-maker in the family. Adults' attitudes toward working mothers became more egalitarian between the 1970s and the early 1990s, showed a small "backlash" in the late 1990s, and then continued the trend toward increased egalitarianism in the 2000s and 2010s. In hierarchical linear modeling analyses separating the effects of time period, generation/cohort, and age, trends were primarily due to time period with a generational peak in egalitarianism among White women Boomers (born 1946-1964). Policy-makers should recognize that support for working mothers is now a solid majority position in the United States and design programmes for working families accordingly.

However, as more and more women are starting participating in paid labour force, it has its own difficulties and tolls. As stated earlier that the traditional view of child caring is associated with women; women working in some industries, factories, banks, hospitals etc. complain that they do not get time to look after and give care to their babies. It has been acknowledged that in many organizations the long-hour work culture does not reinforcement apposite parenting (Wood & Newton, 2006). Women can either do something as supposed to superwomen so as to deal with the competing demands or challenges or unearth other modes of managing the overload at work or at home (Gordon & Whelan-Berry, 2005).

Work-Family Life Balance

Women, who felt overburdened by all of the pressures they must shoulder, run the risk of burnout and a possible end to their corporate aspirations.

MacDonald, Phipps and Lethbridge (2005), using original data on adult Canadian women and men revealed that women's larger hours of unpaid work at home contributed to their encounter with stress more than men. Success in the workplace as super mom in terms of balancing work and family may come at a high cost in the form of stress (Phipps, Lethbridge & Burton, 2006) and if not tackled cautiously such stress could have awful consequences on their careers and even their roles and obligations to their families. According to Elvin-Nowak and Thomsson (2001) a woman that worked was "exposed to the constant risk of her position as a mother and woman being questioned particularly where she has chosen employment for her own well-being rather than being forced to by external circumstances". Hakim (2000) makes use of 'preference theory', a new theory for "explaining and predicting women's choices between market-work and family work". According to Hakim, adaptive women prefer to combine employment and family work and these women are prepared to prioritize their jobs in the same way as men with family life fitted around their work and many of these women remain childless, even when married. Ahmad (2007) examined the work-family conflict experienced by 239 married female production operators in dual-career families, the social support they received and the coping strategies used to manage the conflict. The women experienced more work interference with family than family interference with work. The intensity of work interference with family was significantly higher in the earlier life-cycle stage than in the later stage. About two thirds of the women indicated that they intended to leave their job upon having another child, mainly due to the rising cost of child-care services. They received the least social support from their supervisors compared to other sources, and tended to cope with conflict using reactive role behaviour and personal role redefinition strategies. In a study among married women employees of BPO companies Gunavathy (2007) traced the causes, consequences of work-life imbalance and interventions for work-life balance. More than two-third of the respondents stated the experienced work-life imbalance primarily on account of work interference with personal life. The causes for work-life imbalance were classified as organizational and personal factors. The organizational factors included work related factors, time-related factors and relationship-related factors. The personal factors included lack of family support, marital conflicts and frequent change in sleeping patterns. According to the study, "the three main consequences of work-life imbalance were stress and burnout, ill-health and poor work performance. The respondents also experienced guilt of not being able to spend time with family, anxiety about poor performance, displacement of negative emotions on family members and on co-workers.

Overcome Prejudice and Discrimination

At all times, the competence of a working woman is suspected and questioned by most people, especially by their male equivalents. In the upper segments of organizations or companies, it is usually observed that remaining all testimonials analogous but men are typically has a preference over women. Many a times the authorities are unconvinced whether women would be able to supervise male subordinates, take independent decisions, cope with crisis and manage their duties properly (Narayana, 2002) albeit women substantiate they are competent, authorities ponder twice before promoting them. And even if women are handed over a task or given a chance, almost always they have to face a comment that they got this position by virtue of being a woman and not by competence.

Sexual harassment is one more crucial snag confronted by working women in all sectors of work life; whether in the organized or unorganized sector, whether illiterate, low paid workers or highly educated and highly paid executives. A considerable number of working women face sexual harassment at the workplace at one time or another and predominantly this is from other male employees or their superiors. Sometimes women are susceptible to hold lower-level positions than men even when they have sufficient skills to perform higher-level jobs. The reasons observed so for are — some are contented with their jobs or job environment; some are frustrated because of both mental and physical harassment; some are highly depressed because of issues with their male or female colleagues; some have family issues as taking a higher position may lead to resettlement in another city/area or region. One attention-grabbing fact was revealed by working women themselves that those women who are fine-looking or having attractive personality and can carry themselves in an appealing way; people instantaneously derive a fastidious conclusion about their character and that is highly negative. Many of the male members or employees generally think and assume that those women having a friendly nature inside workplace are kind of objects for them and they can take advantage of it (Kumari, 2014).

Career Development Plan

Ali (2011) investigated the challenges faced by women in career development. She found that most of the women employees were dissatisfied with their career development programmes and were discriminated in career development opportunities. The study recommended that organizations should strive to ensure that career development programmes were set to enhance career development amongst women employees. Top management should also be committed to the career development of women, and organizations should also introduce affirmative action to urgently address career development of women. The report, *Ambition and Gender at Work* (2011), suggests women's managerial career aspirations lag behind men's at every stage of their working lives, and that they have less clarity over traditional career direction than men. At the start of their careers, 52 per cent of male managers had a fair or clear idea that they wanted to work in a particular role, compared with 45 per cent of women managers. Only half of women said they expected to become managers, versus two-thirds of men. Even among the under-30s, gender aspirations remained entrenched, with 45 per cent of men and 30 per cent of women expecting to become managers or leaders. The findings, which came from an even sample of men and women with an average age of 43, also revealed that 24 per cent of women under 30 expected to start their own businesses within 10 years, compared with 20 per cent of men. Penny de Valk, the institute's chief executive Institute of Leadership and Management, said the pressure on many women to combine childcare with career aspirations was "part of the cocktail". If large organizations wanted to nurture the talent of their best female employees, they needed to start challenging some of the unwritten rules of what senior management roles looked like. "It is not that women are risk-averse; younger women in particular are incredibly ambitious around entrepreneurial activity. Yet, we can see that a promotion path within a large organization is almost seen as riskier for them, on a personal basis, than going out and setting up their own venture", she said.

Gender Leadership

Harvard's global online research study included over 2,00,000 participants, showed that 76 per cent of people (men and women) are gender-biased and tend to think of men as better suited for careers and women as better suited as homemakers. Although acceptance of female managers has increased in the last half-century, negative attitudes toward female leaders still persist (Carlson *et al.*, 2006; Heilman, 2001; Heilman *et al.*, 1995). For example, some research suggests that female leaders are evaluated less favourably than their male counterparts, are liked less than their male counterparts, and are penalized for adopting masculine leadership styles (e.g. Eagly *et al.*, 1992; Heilman *et al.*, 2004; Johnson *et al.*, 2008). Most women aspiring to senior management positions believe the glass ceiling to career progression still exists, according to a report by a leading UK management organization. The survey of 3,000 members of the Institute of Leadership and Management (ILM) found 73 per cent of female respondents felt barriers still existed for women seeking senior management and board-level positions in the UK. In contrast, just 38 per cent of men believed there is a glass ceiling.

The Guardian International edition published an article entitled "Women Still Face a Glass Ceiling" on February 20, 2011 issue. In this article there mentioned a report by the London School of Economics for cosmetics company Avon predicted a doubling in young female entrepreneurs over the next decade, with 72 per cent of the 2,000 16-24-year-old women questioned saying the idea of being their own boss appealed to them.

Sexism, including women being passed over for top jobs, serves to further reinforce the glass ceiling. All this can limit women's expectations for their career and acts as a brake on ambition. Some successful women entrepreneurs emphasizing that many years of beating away at the glass ceiling have left it stubbornly intact; now, it is time for women to put aside our drip-drip tactics and took bold actions to achieve real change.

Role congruity theory provides an explanation for the persistence of gender bias against female leaders. There is a discrepancy between the traditional female gender role and the leadership role (Eagly & Karau, 2002; Schein, 1975). In our society stereotypical female gender roles have included communal roles, which include nurturing, caring, and sensitivity. Male roles are more agentic, with men often being considered more aggressive, ambitious, assertive and direct. Individuals who act in ways that are incongruent with their sex role tend to be evaluated negatively (Eagly & Karau, 2002). This incongruity can create problems for female managers because characteristics necessary to be a successful leader are more frequently associated with the male gender role (Schein, 1975).

Stemming from this conflict between the feminine social role and the leadership role, role congruity theory predicts female leaders suffer two types of prejudice: descriptive and prescriptive (Eagly & Karau, 2002; Johnson *et al.*, 2008). *Descriptive bias* occurs when female leaders are stereotyped as possessing less potential for leadership than men. *Prescriptive bias* occurs when actual female leaders are evaluated less favourably because leadership is seen as more desirable for men than for women. Both sources of bias leave women in a double bind. If they conform to their traditional gender role, women are not seen as having potential for leadership; if they adopt the agentic characteristics associated with successful leaders, then they are evaluated negatively for behaving in an unfeminine manner. Empirical evidence of bias against female leaders is mixed, and is often dependent on whether the study methodology involves actual bosses in a workplace. Studies using actual bosses typically reveal little or no bias, while those that use hypothetical managers or laboratory-created leaders reveal more bias against female leaders. For example, one meta-analysis of studies that used vignettes of hypothetical leaders and laboratory confederates found male leaders were evaluated more favourably than female leaders (Eagly, Makhijani & Klonsky, 1992). By contrast, another meta-analysis of studies of actual leaders in organizations found no gender differences in ratings of leader effectiveness (Eagly, Karau & Makhijani, 1995). More recently, one study of ratings of actual managers found no gender differences in subordinate ratings of satisfaction with their manager, ratings of manager persuasiveness or ratings of manager supportiveness (Byron, 2007), and another found female leaders received higher ratings than male leaders in emotional and social competence (Taylor & Hood, 2011).

The most prevalent rationale for preferring female bosses was their compassion and understanding. Participants indicated female managers were more 'supportive', 'nurturing', 'personable', 'understanding', 'empathetic' and 'better listeners' than men. Female bosses were also preferred to men because of their competence. These respondents thought females were better managers, better organizers, and had better communication skills than male managers. Female bosses were viewed as more 'intelligent', better 'decision-makers', and 'more hardworking' than their male counterparts, and they were also credited with creating more collaborative work teams and environments. Some men favoured female managers because they are 'sexier', 'prettier', and more 'attractive' than male bosses. Female managers were described as "easier to look at than a male boss", and several men also mentioned the potential for a sexual relationship with a female boss as an additional benefit. Other men mentioned liking females because they are more gullible and easier to manipulate. Many participants indicated their preference for male leaders stemmed from a dislike of the personality of female managers.

In particular, they claimed female managers tended to be too 'emotional', 'moody', 'catty', 'gossipy', 'bitchy', 'backstabbing', 'dramatic', 'jealous', and 'petty'. Although these were the most popular adjectives used to describe disdain for female leaders, it is interesting to note that none of these adjectives appeared in the narratives disparaging the male leaders (Taylor & Hood, 2011).

In another meta-analysis Elsesser and Lever (2011) examined 60,470 women and men evaluations of their current managers as well as their preferences for male and female managers, in general. A cross-sex bias emerged in the ratings of one's current boss, where men judged their female bosses more favourably and women judged male bosses more favourably. The quality of relationships between subordinates and managers were the same for competent male and female managers. A small majority (54%) of participants claimed to have no preference for the gender of their boss, but the remaining participants reported preferring male over female bosses by more than a 2:1 ratio.

Women in Public Spheres: Political System

Although, the Lok Sabha speaker (Sumitra Mahajan), Finance Minister (Nirmala Sitaraman), Foreign Minister (Sushma Swaraj), a number of Chief Ministers of states (Mamata Banarjee, Vasundhara Raje, Mahbooba Mufti) and many other female politicians were at key positions still the gender gap, disparity and stereotypes towards female leaders prevails. As per (UNICEF, 2007) report in July 2006, only 17 per cent of parliamentarians world-wide were women, and a woman headed the government was only in seven countries and this scenario has not been changed much even after a decade. However, as far as legal aspects and legislations are concerned there is no restriction to women. They can vote, support candidates, run for office in almost every country. Rather, many suggest that in both rich and poor countries, women's access to public office is restricted by voter and party bias in favour of male politicians.

Intervention Strategies

Burke, Koyuncu and Fiksenbaum (2010) examined the relationship of the perceived presence of organizational practices designed to support women's career advancement and their work attitudes and satisfaction and their psychological well-being. Data were collected from 286 women in managerial and professional jobs working in a large Turkish bank.

Five organizational experiences were considered: negative attitudes towards women, equal treatment, support, career barriers and male standards. Women reporting more supportive organizational experiences and practices were more engaged in their work, more job and career satisfied, and indicated greater levels of psychological well-being.

Greater policy focus is necessitated to warrant women to advantage from the noteworthy growth that has occurred over the last decade in India. This denotes policy-makers will need to take more effective measures to support women's constructive engagement in the workforce through greater investments in secondary and tertiary education, vocational and skills training, and developing and strengthening laws and policies to support working women.

If India is to become the world's third largest economy in 2030, it can not afford to continue bypassing its over 600 million women from equal opportunity in the workforce. Singhal (1995) is of the opinion that, "Participation of women in workforce is essential for economic development and population planning".

At every single level of the corporate ladder, women are rated as better overall leaders than men by peers, bosses, direct reports and colleagues. What is even more interesting is that when such findings are shared with women, they believe what makes them great leaders is that they are not complacent and continuously try to out do themselves and prove themselves and are, therefore, more keen to take feedback to heart. In one such survey a participant stated, "We need to work harder than men to prove ourselves", while another delineated, "We feel the constant pressure to never make a mistake, and to continually prove our value to the organization".

Karren Brady, Vice-chairman of West Ham United and an Avon mentor, said she believed young women would "define the next generation of entrepreneurship and rewrite the rules in this perceived male-dominated world".

Liz Gardiner, head of policy at Working Families, a charity which campaigns for parents and carers, said the trend towards more women entrepreneurs sent out a message about the need for change to the overall design of work. "One of the reasons women want to set up businesses is because they have more control over the hours they work", she said. She said there was plenty of evidence that in many UK workplaces there was discrimination, "particularly against those who choose to be mothers, and also against those who choose non-traditional patterns of work".

Cranfield's "100 Women to Watch 2015" report shows the extraordinary field of strong female candidates poised for FTSE board positions, with many others reaching senior levels just below the boardroom. The FTSE 250 has also made great progress, more than doubling the percentage of women on their boards since 2011, from 7.8 to 18 per cent. The number of all-male boards in the FTSE 250 has also dropped from 151 in 2011 to 23 in 2015 (Vinnicombe, Doldor, Sealy, Pryce & Turner, 2015).

Rather than waiting for external legislation, at this point employers have to set voluntary targets for female representation at board and senior management level, and hold people accountable for meeting them. Business leaders must take responsibility for building an effective talent pipeline, and make it a commercial priority to proactively identify, develop and promote potential leaders of both sexes. Mandatory quotas (set through hard law usually with sanctions for non-compliance) may achieve early and significant results in terms of female board representation. However, voluntary targets for women's participation on boards and in executive ranks (proposed in soft regulation such as corporate governance codes and set as part of corporate strategy) may promote more effective cultural and practical change in support of greater representation of women in leadership (Klettner, Clarke & Boersma, 2016).

The lack of high profile women role models can make it hard for both women and men to imagine women running the show. The world of work has not caught up with the needs of modern families where both parents work, with few senior positions offering flexibility around working hours - and it is still on the whole women who require flexibility in order to manage childcare commitments, thus restricting their career.

Underpinning people's competence to determine their own priorities and to operate on them is the core of gender-equity based development. International and national policy interest about the key role women play in development has not essentially been translated into practice (Singhal, 2003).

Conclusion

Backing for a traditional division of gender roles within the home and the workplace has turned down considerably over the last three decades, a change that goes hand in hand with the noticeable escalation in the labour force participation of women and mothers (Baker, 2010). Changes in attitudes have been driven in part by generational replacement. Nevertheless, though dual-earner households are now the norm, it is erroneous to assume that the gender role revolution is wherever close to end. Gender equality in terms of who does the bulk of the chores and who is primarily responsible for looking after the children has made very little progress in terms of what happens in people's homes.

Men's uptake of unpaid domestic work is slow, and women continue to feel that they are doing more than their fair share. Whether women's 'double shift' — both doing a paid job and the bulk of family care and housework chores — is sustainable is an important question for the future. Gender inequalities in the home undoubtedly make it difficult to achieve gender equality in the workplace. This is a cause for public concern. The state has an important role to play in reducing work-family conflict for both men and women. However, the public is likely to be cautious about specific policy changes because opinions are shaped by existing practices and constraints. The literature depicts two extremes when discussing trends in gender equality. On the one hand there is a 'rising tide' of support for gender equality (Ingelhart & Norris, 2003); on the other hand there has been an 'incomplete revolution' (Esping-Andersen, 2009). Is the gender role revolution mired? Or are we seeing what can be called a 'structural lag' — whereby men and societal institutions (parental leave, childcare, employment, and so on) have to pull alongside with the realities of changing families and women's new roles? Only time will tell.

REFERENCES

Ahmad, A. (2007). "Work-family Conflict, Life-cycle Stage, Social Support, and Coping Strategies among Women Employees", *The Journal of Human Resource and Adult Learning*, 3(1): 70-79.

Ali, S.J. (2011). "Challenges Facing Women Employees in Career Development: A Focus on Kapsabet Municipality, Kenya", *International Journal of Current Research*, 3(8): 196-203.

Ambition and Gender at Work Report (2011), Institute of Leadership & Management. *https://www.institutelm.com*

Baker, M. (2010). "Motherhood, Employment and the "Child Penalty", in *Women's Studies International Forum* (Vol. 33, No. 3: 215-224). Pergamon.

Bassett, R.H. (2005). *Parenting and Professoring*, Vanderbilt: University Press.

Beaujot, R. (2000). *Earning and Caring in Canadian Families*, Peterborough, Ontario: The Broadview Press.

Bracken, J.K.; Allen & Dean, D.K. (Eds.) (2006). *The Balancing Act: Gendered Perspectives in Faculty Roles and Work Lives*, Sterling, Virginia: Stylus Publishing.

Burke, R.J.; Koyuncu, M. & Fiksenbaum, L. (2010). "Burnout, Work Satisfactions and Psychological Well-being among Nurses in Turkish Hospitals", *Europe's Journal of Psychology*, 6(1): 63-81.

Byron, K. (2007). "Male and Female Managers' Ability to Read Emotions: Relationships with Supervisor's Performance Ratings and Subordinates' Satisfaction Ratings", *Journal of Occupational and Organizational Psychology*, 80(4): 713-733.

Carlson, D.; Kacmar, M. & Whitten, D. (2006). "What Men Think about Executive Women", *Harvard Business Review*, 84(9): 28-29.

Delgado, E.A. & Canabal, M.E. (2006). "Factors Associated with Negative Spillover from Job to Home among Latinos in the United States", *Journal of Family and Economic Issues*, 27(1): 92-112.

Donnelly, K.; Twenge, J.M.; Clark, M.A.; Shaikh, S.K.; Beiler-May, A. & Carter, N.T. (2016). "Attitudes toward Women's Work and Family Roles in the United States, 1976-2013", *Psychology of Women Quarterly*, 40(1): 41-54.

Eagly, A.H. & Carli, L.L. (2007). "Women and the Labyrinth of Leadership", *Harvard Business Review*, 85(9).

Eagly, A.H. & Karau, S.J. (2002). "Role Congruity Theory of Prejudice toward Female Leaders", *Psychological Review*, 109(3): 573.

Eagly, A.H.; Karau, S.J. & Makhijani, M.G. (1995). "Gender and the Effectiveness of Leaders: A Meta-Analysis", *Psychological Bulletin*, 117(1): 125.

Eagly, A.H.; Makhijani, M.G. & Klonsky, B.G. (1992). "Gender and the Evaluation of Leaders: A Meta-Analysis", *Psychological Bulletin*, 111(1): 3-22.

Elsesser, K.M. & Lever, J. (2011). "Does Gender Bias against Female Leaders Persist? Quantitative and Qualitative Data from a Large-scale Survey", *Human Relations*, 64(12): 1555-1578.

Elvin-Nowak, Y. & Thomsson, H. (2001). "Motherhood as Idea and Practice: A Discursive Understanding of Employed Mothers in Sweden", *Gender & Society*, 15(3): 407-428.

Esping-Andersen, G. (2009). *Incomplete Revolution: Adapting Welfare States to Women's New Roles*, Polity.

Evertsson, M. & Nermo, M. (2004). "Dependence within Families and the Division of Labour: Comparing Sweden and the United States", *Journal of Marriage and Family*, 66(5): 1272-1286.

"Global Gender Gap Index 2017: India Ranks 108th", *Current Affairs Today, https://currentaffairs.gktoday.in.*

Gordon, J.R. & Whelan-Berry, K.S. (2005). "Contributions to Family and Household Activities by the Husbands of Midlife Professional Women", *Journal of Family Issues*, 26(7): 899-923.

Gunavathy (2007). *A Study of Work Life Balance in BPO Sector*, University of Madras, Chennai.

Hakim, C. (2000). *Work-lifestyle Choices in the 21st Century: Preference Theory*, Oxford: Oxford University Press.

Heilman, M.E. (2001). "Description and Prescription: How Gender Stereotypes Prevent Women's Ascent up the Organizational Ladder", *Journal of Social Issues*, 57(4): 657-674.

Heilman, M.E.; Block, C.J. & Martell, R. (1995). "Sex Stereotypes: Do they Influence Perceptions of Managers?", *Journal of Social Behaviour and Personality*, 10(6): 237-252.

Inglehart, R. & Norris, P. (2003). *Rising Tide: Gender Equality and Cultural Change around the World*, Cambridge University Press.

Johnson, S.K.; Murphy, S.E.; Zewdie, S. & Reichard, R.J. (2008). "The Strong Sensitive Type: Effects of Gender Stereotypes and Leadership Prototypes on the Evaluation of Male and Female Leaders", *Organizational Behaviour and Human Decision Processes*, 106(1): 39-60.

Klettner, A.; Clarke, T. & Boersma, M. (2016). "Strategic and Regulatory Approaches to Increasing Women in Leadership: Multilevel Targets and Mandatory Quotas as Levers for Cultural Change", *Journal of Business Ethics*, 133(3): 395-419.

Kumari, V. (2014). Problems and Challenges Faced by Urban Working Women in India (Doctoral dissertation), Department of Humanities and Social Sciences, National Institute of Technology, Rourkela.

Kuruvilla, M. & Usha, P. (1999). "Attitude towards Women Employment: Study on a University Sample", *Journal of Psychological Researches*, Vol. 43 (2): 61-65.

MacDonald, M.; Phipps, S. & Lethbridge, L. (2005). "Taking Its Toll: The Influence of Paid and Unpaid Work on Women's Well-being", *Feminist Economics*, 11(1): 63-94.

Narayana, A. (2002). *Women and Indian Society: Options and Constraints*, Rawat Publications.

Phipps, S.A.; Lethbridge, L. & Burton, P. (2006). "Long-run Consequences of Parental Paid Work Hours for Child Overweight Status in Canada", *Social Science & Medicine*, 62(4): 977-986.

Schein, V.E. (1975). "Relationships between Sex Role Stereotypes and Requisite Management Characteristics among Female Managers", *Journal of Applied Psychology*, 60(3): 340.

Scott, J. & Clery, E. (2013). "Gender Roles", in Park, A.; Bryson, C.; Clery, E.; Curtice, J. & Phillips, M. (eds.), *British Social Attitudes: The 30th Report*, London: NatCen Social Research, available online at: *www.bsa-30.natcen.ac.uk*

Singhal, R. (2003). "Women, Gender and Development: The Evolution of Theories and Practice", *Psychology and Developing Societies*, 15(2): 165-185.

Singhal, S. (1995). *Development of Education, Occupation, and Employment of Women in India*, New Delhi: Mittal Publications.

Taylor, S.N. & Hood, J.N. (2011). "It may not be What You Think: Gender Differences in Predicting Emotional and Social Competence", *Human Relations*, 64(5): 627-652.

UNDP (2017). *Human Development Reports*, United Nations Development. *www.hdr.undp.org*

Vinnicombe, S.; Doldor, E.; Sealy, R.; Pryce, P. & Turner, C. (2015). *The Female FTSE Board Report 2015.*

Wentling, M.R. (2003). "The Career Development and Aspirations of Women in Middle Management-revisitcd", *Women in Management Review*, 18(6): 311-324.

Woetzel, J.; Madgavkar, A.; Ellingrud, K.; Labaye, E.; Devillard, S.; Kutcher, E.; Manyika, J.; Dobbs, R. & Krishnan, M. (2015). *The Power of Parity: How Advancing Women's Equality Can Add $12 Trillion to Global Growth*, McKinsey Global Institute.

Women Still Face a Glass Ceiling, Money, *The Guardian*. *https://www.theguardian.com/society/2011/.../women-glass-ceiling-still-exists-top-jobs February 20, 2011.*

Wood, G.J. & Newton, J. (2006). "Childlessness and Women Managers: 'Choice', Context and Discourses", *Gender, Work and Organization*, 13(4): 338-358.

4

Glass Ceiling: A Form of Gender Discrimination

Sakshi Seth

People usually use the terms 'gender' and 'sex' interchangeably, but there exist a difference between these two terms. Sex is our biological identification that is known it the time of birth because of a child's genitals and gender is the social identification that a person has. This origin of gender in a person basically comes because of the roles and responsibilities that are given to a particular person. The process of gendering starts from the childhood itself, when boys are asked to play with balls and girls with dolls. Both the genders are discriminated everywhere and every time in society. The basic discrimination between males and females start from home when they are taught their basic roles and responsibilities. Women are always taught to be in limits and are expected to take care of the house and family whereas make are believed to be stronger and are expected to be bread-maker of the family. Gender has been studied by number of disciplines to know its origin reason and impact. Many gender researchers like Agars (2004) has states that gender stereotype has been under examined and they do play a role in the origin of gender discrimination at places like organization leading to glass ceiling.

Women have always tried to move out of the boundaries and have tried to prove that they are no less than males. No matter how hard women try but they fall because of the discrimination they face at every level. This discrimination on the basis of gender in organization is termed as Glass ceiling. This term which is used by different researchers and philosophers to explain the condition of women in organization, where they face discrimination on the basis of gender. Glass ceiling is usually regarded as the transparent barrier which prevents women to climb the success ladder in organizations. Pai and Vaidya (2009) has said that glass ceiling is a barrier that prevents women and minorities to reach the heights of organizational hierarchy. Also, Appelbaum *et al.* (2011) define this phenomenon as the barrier which hinders the qualified women in advancing upward in an organization's hierarchy.

Glass ceiling has always prevented females from reaching to the higher positions and even if they are successful in reaching to the higher position, they fail to reach a position where they do not face gender discrimination.

> The 'glass ceiling' (the subtle and invisible barrier that prevents women and minorities from moving beyond a certain levels in the corporate hierarchy) which restricts women from entering the upper echelons in organization, the differential treatment that women receive in organization as compared to the men, the discrimination in performance evaluation of women in organization and other such issues exist across the world to a lesser or greater extent and have been researched well in the Western literature.
>
> Even the women who do make it past the glass ceiling top top executive positions apparently do not reach a place where gender equality is the norm (Sujoya Basu, 2008).

Many researchers have seen that glass ceiling is measured and exist majorly in two forms that are discrimination on basis of salary and promotional opportunities. Sampson and Moore (2008) noticed that there exist wage dissimilarity amongst men and ladies in the formative field, even Farroq and Sulaiman (2000) found the same. Alongside 'glass ceiling' there are a few different terms like 'glass wall' and 'glass elevators'. 'Glass wall' is where ladies are not allowed to take part in different activities or roles. These ideas of 'glass wall' and 'glass elevators', essentially keep away women from the roles that need higher official capacities. These phenomenon keep women to the post where they already are. However, another term that is utilized nearby is 'glass cliff'. This exhibit a situation where the ladies at the higher positions are subjected to tricky occupation as contrast with their men partners. Unsafe employments include more hazard as contrast with different occupations. Taking ladies to such difficult and tricky roles make them inclined to more disappointment and feedback. These disappointments do make women feel that they are incapable of these roles, and this could lead to the rise of internal hurdle that would not make them successful or let them climb the organizational ladder. Along these lines, we can state that breaking 'glass ceiling' can bring about 'glass cliff'.

Though there has been a number of researchers who support that glass ceiling do exist and prevent females to reach to the higher level, there also exist group of researchers who believe that glass ceiling is just a myth for example, Rai and Srivastava (2008), according to them, glass ceiling is just a myth and does not exist in the organizations. According to them there is no phenomenon called as glass ceiling that stops women to reach the higher levels in the organization. According to them if there is a discrepancy in the salary paid, then it is because women mostly quit the job in midway because of the household responsibilities. But in the recent times Bell (2013) claimed that no doubt women have progresses in the past but glass ceiling effect do exist in the present times.

The problem and the challenges which women face in organizations in form of glass ceiling can be regarded as the form of discrimination which women face in this scenario. They are been discriminated from getting better job opportunities, promotions and equal level of pay in organizations.

Glass Ceiling: A Global Phenomenon

It is not the case that glass ceiling exists only certain parts of world and not in other. Many of researchers have claimed that glass ceiling is a global phenomenon. Women all over the world do face discrimination on the basis of gender in organization. Researches have shown that there are less number of women that are working on the higher position in different countries for example in Australia (Davidson, 2009; Maginn, 2010), China (Tan, 2008), France (Barnet-Verzat & Wolff, 2008), South Africa (Booysen & Nkomo, 2010), United Kingdom (Davidson, 2009; Thomson *et al.*, 2008) and United States (Fassinger, 2008). It is not restricted to a continent or a country but can be found all over the globe. The percentages of women at the higher level management can be summarized in this way. Mainland China (51%), Poland (48%), Latvia (43%), Estonia (43%), Baltics and Lithuania (40% each) leads in the terms of business, having females as a senior manager. Those with the lowest number of women are Japan (7%), UAB (11%), Switzerland (14%) and Argentina (18%). If we talk globally women make up 35 per cent of the total workforce. Leaders are Latvia (46%), Hong Kong (45%), Botswana (44%), Mainland of China and Estonia (42% each).

While the countries like UAB (14%), India (15%), Argentina (24%) and Chile and Turkey (25%) have the lowest business women.

But, the question remains the same that why women representatives in the higher posts are too less? Its just the responsibilities and the changes in the life that they face or conditioning and other cognitive factors like stereotype to plays a major role. This chapter has been written with the aim to study the causes of the glass ceiling and how it can be overcome.

Picture of Glass Ceiling in India

Like in other parts of world India do face the problem of gender discrimination, and like other areas this problem is also there in organizations or in the corporate world. Though, women in India are highly educated but still they are not seen in the higher levels (Mukherji, 2010). As per the Statistical Survey women account of 40 per cent of the total working force in our nation but only 7 per cent are seen when it comes to the level of board directors. According to a recent study, only 26.1 per cent of the listed companies have women in their boards. Out of the 278 directors on the BSE Sensex companies, there are only 10 women directors. Also, women executives in India earn 40 per cent less than what men earn in their entire career. Only 36 per cent of the Indian companies have women holding senior management positions as compared to the 91 per cent companies in China. According to the study by McKinsey and company, India is among the bottom three Asian countries in female representation on boards of direction (Sarika, 2015). Only 5 per cent women are found on executive boards. As per the Global Gender Gap report in 2015 issued by World Economic Forum, India rank 108 out of 145 countries in the world with the overall score of 0.664. The labour force participation gap index is 0.35, wage equality for similar work gap index is 0.51 and estimated earned income gap index is 0.25 though literacy gap index is 0.75. These figures predominantly show the gender inequality in India (Global Gender Gap Report, 2015).

According to the article in *'The Indian Express'*, 68.5 per cent of women of India Inc. feels that gender parity is still a concern and it's the time that organizations should talk about it. Still there has been number of steps that has been taken 62.4 per cent of women feel that males get more promotional opportunities as compared to female, they feel that gender do play a major role in deciding upon the promotional opportunities.

Females also added that it's not just the glass ceiling that impacts the growth of women in organization, but also 'glass floors', 'glass doors' and 'glass walls'.

There are many researchers who stated that many women in India have been able to reach the higher positions (Malhotra, 2010). This has also been supported by women like Chanda Kochar, Head of ICICI bank, and Shikha Sharma, Head of Axis Bank and many others in banking sector. But if we talk about the gender discrimination index of India, India still rank 113 out of 157 countries. This trend of breaking glass ceiling effect is evident mainly in the **banking sector**, but not has been seen in the other sectors. Sachdeva (2014) attempted to throw light on reasons why women are more successful in banking sector as compared to other sectors. According to her one of the reason for this is that banking sector prevents female from facing the gender stereotypes as in other sectors like manufacturing sectors. The other reason is that banking sector has started developing in diversity which other sectors has failed to develop. No doubt there has been number of researches that states that in banking sector women have been able to reach the higher level, but there still exist a wage gap. According to the latest article in *Mint* "addressing the gender wage gap in India" there exists a wage gap of 21.5 per cent in banking, financial and insurance sector, therefore, we can say that women might have been able to crack glass ceiling by reaching to the higher positions, but still have not broken it, as they are still facing discrimination on the basis of salary.

If we see the picture of women working in IT sector, according to Ganesh Natarajan, CEO of Zensar Technologies and chairman of NASSCOM, gender discrimination has made glass ceiling in Indian IT industry. He further added that out of 23 per cent of women working in IT sector only 7 per cent hold the higher levels in management hierarchy. It has been noted that male-female ratio in Indian IT companies is 4:1. Even in the article titled "addressing the gender wage gap in India" states that women do face the wage gap of 25.8 per cent in technology sector. Similarly for the education and research sector article quotes that there exist a wage gap of 14.7 per cent in education and research sector. Also Sharma *et al.* (2011) studied glass ceiling effect in educational sector. He concluded that both the genders are paid equally in government aided institutes, though discrimination do exist in self-financed institution, also promotional opportunities were also different for both the genders. Also, Sharma and Chaturvedi (2017) also noted that females are only restricted to the roles and responsibilities of teacher.

Forms in which Glass Ceiling Exist

Many authors claim that glass ceiling majorly exists in two forms where females are discriminated because of their gender, these two forms are *promotion opportunities* and the *salaries* given to the person. Along with these two factors that form of *roles and responsibilities* and the *level at which* they are selected are also forms in which women face discrimination in organizations. There has been number of research papers which claim that women are discriminated on the basis of salary which they are getting, number of researchers have claimed that male and females are discriminated on the basis of *promotional opportunities*. If a male manager gets an opportunity to choose between a male and a female with same capabilities, a male will prefer a male candidate rather than female. There could be number of reasons for doing it might be their existing cognitions that females are not capable enough, or they would finally leave the job for their families or their conditioning to dominate females rather that working under a female. Researchers like Pai and Vaidya (2009); Sharma *et al.* (2011) have supported the notion that women are given less promotional opportunities as compared to males. But, the major question that arises is why women are not promoted to higher level? The answer lies in the cognitive structure of that man hold. Again in this the reasons that are explained further in the chapter do answer this question. But, if I try to explain in simple words, less faith of men or men at the higher positions on the ability of women could be one reason. Also one major issue that arises is of attribution, the success of females is mainly attributed to the external factors like luck rather than to the internal factors like their ability. An example of lacking promotional opportunities can be taken from book gender stereotypes in corporate India which states the following:

> One consequence of inaccurate gender stereotyping is that women are less likely to be chosen or recruited for traditionally male positions, such as those in senior management. This occurs because the perceived lack of congruence between the job requirement and the stereotypic attributes ascribed to women leads to expectations that they will fail (Heilman, 1983, as quoted by Sujoya Basu in the book).
>
> Women, therefore, receive fewer developmental opportunities than men. Research has indicated that managerial development results from job characteristics associated with higher level positions (Sujoya Basu, 2008).

Another bunch of researchers claim that women are also being discriminated on the basis of the *salaries* they are given. For example, Sharma *et al.* (2011) showed that females are usually paid less in self-financed and private educational sector as compared to the government financed institutes. Yet, another example is given by Srivastava and Bajpai (2015), they stated that women are paid half of the three quarters as compared to their counterparts for the same job. They do not directly become prey of this form of discrimination. When a woman enters an organization they are appointed for a lower post as compared to their counterpart with same qualification and experience thus they are paid less. The recent article in *Mint* titled "Addressing the Gender Wage Gap in India" states the recent survey which shows that there exists a gap between the wages on the basis of gender. According to the Global Wage report 2016-17 released by the International Labour Organization (ILO), India has the worst level of gender wage disparity that is 30 per cent. According to the National Sample Survey Office's 68th round conducted in 2011-12 shows that gender wage gap declined by 10 percentage points from 29.2 per cent in 2004-05, this shows that even in recent times there exist a large gap between wage on the basis of gender. Also, according to the Monster Salary Index on gender for 2016, the gender pay gap in educational and research sector is 14.7 per cent, in banking, financial and insurance sector the gap is 21.5 per cent, 25.8 per cent in technology sector, 29.9 per cent in manufacturing, 39.9 per cent in healthcare, caring services and social work, 18.1 per cent in construction and technical consultancy, 42.4 per cent in legal and market consultancy and business activities and 5.2 per cent in transport, logistics and communication sector. Also according to 2012 "gender pay gap in the formal sector" reported that the gap in wage increases with the increase in age and experience. Also according to Monster India Report Indian women earn less 25 per cent less than males, according to which median for men's earning is of ₹ 345.80 while for the female it is ₹ 259.8.

Also, an article in *'The Indian Express'* women do feel that gender do play role in decisions regarding promotional opportunities and promotion, they also feel that men do get more promotional opportunities as compared to females. According to Sanjay Modi, Managing Director, APAC and middle east monster.com, states the following:

> In India, the gender pay gap holds true and the overall gap across India Inc. is at 25 per cent. This primarily is a manifestation of the

> underlying diversity challenges that organizations face . . . there is a dire need for tangible initiatives to bridge this pay gap with removing structural impediments to women's growth providing access to skill trainings, jobs and decision-making.

Sharma *et al.* (2011) showed in their research that females are appointed at a *lower position* as compared to their counterparts. Yet, another way in which women do face discrimination is the types of *roles and responsibilities* they get in organization. It has been seen that women are usually given role or responsibility which they think are easy or suit their character. For example Sharma and Chaturvedi (2017) noted that women in educational institutes are usually restricted to teaching jobs. Females have also faced discrimination on the basis of the responsibilities they have been given to be completed. Though, there has been number of evidences that glass ceiling do exist in the organization that do not allow females to climb the higher ladder in the organizations (Bell, 2013), but, there are also number of evidences that there is no such phenomenon called as glass ceiling in organization (Rai & Srivastava, 2008).

Yet, another form that take the face of glass ceiling is the biased evaluation that women face. The book gender stereotypes in Indian Corporates states the following:

> Another cause of concern is that women's achievement tends to be devalued or attributed to the luck or effort rather than to the ability or skill (Deaux, 1976; Nieva & Guteck, 1980), which may reduce the organizational rewards that they receive.

This shows that the stereotype that exist in the mind of managers do impact the evaluation that they do. Even though females are doing their delegated roles responsibly, just because they are females, they are devalued or face the biasness during evaluation.

Reasons for Glass Ceiling

Everything that exist, exists because of some reasons. As we have earlier discussed that glass ceiling is just not the cause of many things, but also an effect of several things in organization. There has been number of researchers to find out why women are discriminated in organization and one common reason that emerge was the gender stereotypes that exists in the mind of men and sometimes even in mind of women. There has been number of researches and explanations describing the causes of glass ceiling effect (Barreto *et al.*, 2010). Some of the theories that make the ground for glass ceiling are explained in this section.

Explaining all the theories and the explanations for the phenomenon would be far difficult, though some of the influential theories and explanation are discussed. Some of the *evolutionary psychologists* believe that glass ceiling effect is the result of the process of natural selection (Browne, 2006). According to Weyer (2007), Okimoto and Brescoll (2010), Catalyst (2011) and many other researchers the less number of female leaders is linked to the ongoing prejudice and discrimination that is there against women in organizations. Some theorist also point gender discrimination as an explanation for glass ceiling effect. For example, Hakim (2006), proposed her *preference theory* citing the gender differences, which can be responsible for the competitiveness and thus responsible for the glass ceiling effect. Glass ceiling effect can also be explained by the cognitive theory of prejudice toward female employees. This theory is based on the some of the *communal characteristics* that are associated with female workers and male workers. It is assumed that female leaders are nurturing, helpful, kind and sympathetic while male leaders are assertive, ambitious, independent and self-confident (Embry *et al.*, 2008; Phelan *et al.*, 2008). These characteristics of male leaders are considered as *agentic* and are associated with more success (Eagly & Carli, 2007). Other than these characteristics effective leadership is also linked with behaviours like brazenness, fierceness and sovereignty, which are labelled as "masculine" personality. Women are projected by society as cheerful, reliant and nurturing. Researchers have noted that people who are successful as leaders usually have the masculine traits and if women are observed behaving in such characteristics they are behaving outside the societal norms (Burton & Parker, 2010). If women behave according to the agentic traits which are expected to be good leader, it gives rise to 'blashlash effect', according to which if women behave in the manner which are against the stereotypical behaviour then they are negatively evaluated. This stereotypical and societal pattern of thought discriminates between men and women even when they are behaving in same way. Men behaving with these characteristics are labelled as "direct", but females with these characteristics are called as "punitive" (Galloway, 2012). One of the concepts that relates to the communal characteristic find the traits that are associated with successful leadership and then checking whether females have those traits or not.

Even in context for these traits there lie managerial gender stereotypes, a managerial gender stereotypes is a managerial characteristic on which a significant perceived difference is found, coupled with significant association with managerial success. An example for the communal characteristics can be taken from the book "gender stereotypes in corporate India" which is as below:

> ". . . to illustrate further, let us consider a managerial trait like 'analytical ability'. For example ability to be considered a managerial gender stereotype, respondents would have to first associate analytical ability with managerial success and then again would have to make a significant difference while rating men and women on the trait of analytical ability. So, on the same scale pertaining to the analytical ability, if they rate successful managers and men managers high while rating women managers low, analytical ability would be considered managerial gender stereotype.

The above-mentioned characteristics according to the norms were also supported by the *social role* theory, proposed by Eagly in 1987, as a reason for glass ceiling effect. According to this theory the behaviour of each gender is dictated by the stereotype associated with their respective gender. Communal characteristics are those characteristics itself which are associated by each gender thus, supporting the social role theory as a reason for glass ceiling effect. It has been found that women are expected to be more empathetic, emotional and soft and these characteristic behaviours are not in line to the corporate board room. Contrary to this Daily *et al.* (2003) said that though these characteristics are not expected in the corporate board room that does not mean that they are not beneficial for the organization, having a presence of female director can enhance the decision-making. This theory explains that there are certain responsibilities that are given to each gender and if we feel that a particular gender is moving out of the expected role one is not able to accept it. In the case of glass ceiling as women move out of the stereotypical role of theirs or the role assigned by the society, it become difficult for them to accept it and women in the organizations and higher roles. There is preconceived picture in every person's mind of everyone which related to the characteristic of each gender. For example, male are perceived to be physically strong and dominating which is not expected in a female. When a woman comes to the leadership role they behave and work according the role expectation. These are incongruent to the cognitions that are been there. Thus, indirectly become reason for not promoting women to the leadership role as they are not 'expected' to be dominating, thus, promoting glass ceiling effect on organization. One of the major theories underlying both the reason could be the theory of *conditioning*. Reason of the behaviour of not promoting woman to the leadership roles and other higher post could be the conditioning that takes place in the homes and societies. This conditioning is responsible for giving rise to such cognitions and behaviour. Conditioning not only promotes glass ceiling effect on the part of males, but also females. There are certain cognitional dispositions in the mind of females that their primary role is to be home-maker and take care of the family and children. This preconceived cognition do become hurdle for their success and their motivation to fight for the equal opportunities to climb the higher levels in organization. Other than this theory of *similarity attraction* theory can also explain the reason of less number of women in organization. The corporate world is already dominated by men. As they are dominating the companies, they try to get more similar people into the organization. Thus, they are more inclined towards choosing more men in the organizations. Yet, another *cognitive theory* is based on two form of stereotypes that are descriptive stereotypes, i.e. expectations about what members of a group are like and the prescriptive stereotype, i.e. what they should ideally be like. The interplay of these two result in women being less suitable for the higher posts in the organization. According to Eagle and Carli (2007) and Weyer (2007), these two forms of prejudices are responsible for glass ceiling effect. If leaders truly wants to reduce or get rid of 'glass ceiling' they should understand that a successful leader is the one who possess competency and characteristics of a good leader. It is never dependent on the gender of the person whether he or she can be a good leader or not (Northouse, 2012).

Many authors have focused on *theory of similarity* while stating the reason for glass ceiling. But as per author this cannot be regarded as the major cause of glass ceiling. According to this theory, managers promote those whose are similar to them. That mean women would promote women and male would promote male. But the concept of "*queen bee syndrome*" contradicts the notion. According to this syndrome women at the higher position are more critical to the subordinates who are females. Thus, we can say preferences towards males to promote them can become the reason for glass ceiling effect. Though, it has been seen that males are preferred for the promotion, but the reasons are still not clear for such behaviours. Also, queen bee syndrome do prevent women to climb up.

Yet, another reason for glass ceiling according to author is family support. It becomes very important that females should get family support to be successful. According to Sarika (2015) that women face complexities and obstacles in their career due to the multiple roles they have to play at organization and house. As females are playing major role of care giver in families, it might interfere with the role they play at organizations, which impact their performance. Therefore, it becomes important to get the family support, so, that they can responsibly complete their organizational roles. Also, Williams and Coopers (2004) acknowledges that family obligation do impact women's performance in organization, in addition Clancy and Tata (2005) argues that husband's support plays a crucial role for the success of women in organization.

It is not that only theories are the major reason for the existence of glass ceiling, author believe that to a great extent women too are responsible for glass ceiling. Women can prevent the impact of glass ceiling on them, which further prevents the glass ceiling to get strengthen. Women's own perception that their major task is to take care of family and they have to kill their dreams in order to take care of family is the major disbelief that they are holding. Women should understand that there are many helps available in the society which can help them to fulfil their dreams. They must understand that if they need help in order to have work life balance they must take it. If they are able to maintain the work life balance they might not able to break glass ceiling, but yes at least they can reduce the impact of glass ceiling.

Do Glass Ceiling Impact Women?

One of the major questions that arises is, that whether the gender discrimination that is prevailing in organization impacts women or not. Channar *et al.* (2011) found that gender discrimination faced by women impact the satisfaction, motivation, enthusiasm and commitment. It has been observed that women who face gender discrimination are less motivated and enthusiastic as compared to females who do not face any form of gender discrimination. The enthusiasm or the motivation of a person would be better if he or she feels that the efforts of that person are respected and are receiving the reward according to the efforts. When females feel that they are discriminated despite of the efforts they are facing their motivation would decrease. This discrimination could also impact the commitment women would show toward the organization.

The relationship between motivation and gender discrimination can also be studied with the help of Herzberg theory. The main assumption of this theory is that satisfied employees are motivated and dissatisfied employees are not self-motivated. According to this theory there are two sets of factors that impact the motivation level of the employees. The first set is called as the 'satisfiers' or the 'motivators' that are responsible for the intrinsic motivation of the employees and the second set of factors are called as the 'hygiene factors' or the 'maintenance factors'. Factors like promotion, salary would work as the motivators, but when females are discriminated on the basis of pay and promotion that they should get but are not getting, would decrease the motivation level of women facing discrimination.

In several researches gender discrimination has been seen as an important factor for the attributes like satisfaction, organizational commitment etc. (Sattar & Nawaz, 2011). Irfan, Hussain and Yousaf (2009) has observed that women working in organization are more committed and show better performance in an indiscriminative workplace environment as compared to the discriminative environment.

According to Ehsan, Ghafoor and Salman (2011), the performance of the employees and the achievement of organizations' goal depend on the factors like job satisfaction of employees, commitment of employees, the promotional opportunities they get etc. as the women who are discriminated would not be satisfied with the job they are doing which will impact their performance. Also, as they are facing glass ceiling, they are discriminated for promotions and are not getting equal opportunities as males, which again impact their performance and would decrease their performance in organization. Therefore, we can say that indirectly the gender discrimination faced by women impact their overall performance, impacting the organizational goal.

According to author, glass ceiling not only impacts the organizational attributes of females, but it also impacts the personality and other psychological factors in females. When females are discriminated and they do not get equal opportunities for growth as compared to their counterparts despite the equal amount of efforts they put in, it will definitely impact the self-esteem and the worth of women. The impact of gender discrimination undoubtly depends on the individual coping mechanism of women, thus, it could be the case that some females get more impacted as compared to others.

Overcoming Glass Ceiling

After understanding these factors, it becomes important to understand ways to overcome the problem of glass ceiling effect. These methods

were analysed and conversation were done to understand the experiences of newcomers.

4. *Flexible Working Policy:* Bank started with flexible working hours which were proved to be beneficial for the women working in the organization. This step helped women to maintain their work-life balance.

Source: Sarika, G. (2015).

(b) *Case of IBM India*

IBM's major focus area was in diversity management as to make women progress in the organization. It ensures the increase in representation of women in leadership and executive roles to ensure that the brand image of company is the best employer for women (Karine Schomer, 2010). IBM took the following initiatives to break glass ceiling in the organization:

1. Gender sensitivity workshops to the managers.
2. Quotas for women candidates in searches for senior positions.
3. Special recruitment drive for women.
4. Welcoming women back after period of leave.
5. Formal monitoring programme.
6. Paring high potential women with senior executives.
7. Flexible transfer policies.
8. Home connectivity were tried to be provided.
9. A streamline transport system with radio networks to address safety concerns.

Source: Sarika, G. (2015).

(c) *Case of Deloitte*

Deloitte has successfully integrated development of women into the blood of company. The aim and the vision of the drive was marketplace growth and create a source where the best employee was selected irrespective of gender. The following were the vision of the drive:

1. Organization believes in gender equity and optimum utilization of employee talents irrespective of gender has been realized.
2. Company adopted flexible work arrangements through virtual connectivity so that employees do have tools to work when they are away from office.

3. Web communities were built so that both males and females could share their views and perspective about career life balance.
4. Pick up and drop facilities were provided to female executives.
5. Apprentice programme which aligns young women with senior leadership.
6. Tracking hiring and promotion number to focus on equity.
7. External support of India women forums.

Source: Sarika, G. (2015).

TABLE 4.2: Glass Ceilling Summary Table

Forms	*Reasons*	*Solution*
Salaries	Social role theory	Break the conditioning
Promotional opportunities	Communal characteristic theory	Family support
Hired at lower levels	Conditioning	Overcome own obstacles
Roles and responsibilities	Biased evaluation	Women themselves
Organizational efforts		

REFERENCES

Agar, M.D. (2004). "Reconsidering the Impact of Gender Stereotypes on the Advancement of Women in Organizations", *Psychology of Women Quarterly*, 28(2): 103-11.

Applebaum, S.H.; Asham, N. & Argheyd, K. (2011). "Is the Glass Ceiling Cracked in Information Technology? A Qualitative Analysis", Part 1, *Industrial and Commercial Training*, 43(6): 354-361.

Barnet-Verzat, C. & Wolff, F.C. (2008). "Gender Wage Gap and the Glass Ceiling Effect: A Firm Level Investigation", *International Journal of Manpower*, Vol. 29, No. 6.

Barreto, M.; Ryan, M.K. & Schmitt, M.T. (2009). *The Glass Ceiling in the 21st Century: Understanding Barriers to Gender Equality*, American Psychological Association, Washington DC.

Bell, G. (2013). "Cary Cooper on Engagement, Well-being, and the Persistence of Glass Ceiling", *Human Resource Management*, 33(4): 549-560.

Booysen, L.A.E. & Nkomo, S.M. (2010). "Gender Role Stereotypes and Requisite Management Characteristics: The Case of South Africa", *Gender in Management: An International Journal*, Vol. 25, No. 4.

Channar, Zahid Ali; Zareen Abbasi & Imran Anwar Ujan (2011). "Gender Discrimination in Workforce and Its Impact on Employees", *Pakistan Journal of Commerce, Social Science*, 177-191.

Clancy, M. & Tata, J. (2005). "A Global Perspective on Balancing Work and Family", *International Journal of Management*, 2(2): 234-242.

Davidson, M. (2009). *The Glass Ceiling — Australian and British Women in Management, Myth or Reality?*, Paper Presented at the 44th Australian Psychological Annual Conference, September 30-October 4, Darwin Australia.

Eagly, A.H. & Carli, L.L. (2007). *Through the Labyrinth: The Truth About How Women Become Leader*, Boston, M.A.: Harvard Business School.

Economicstimes.indiatimes.com, 25 May, 2012, 12.43 AM IST, ET Bureau.

Embry, A.; Padgett, M.Y. & Caldwell, C.B. (2008). "Can Leaders Step Outside of the Gender Box? An Examination of Leadership and Gender Role Stereotypes", *Journal of Leadership and Organizational Studies*, Vol. 15, No. 1.

Fassinger, R.E. (2008). "Workplace Diversity and Public Policy: Challenges and Opportunities for Psychology", *American Psychologist*, Vol. 63, No. 4.

Hakim, C. (2006). "Women, Careera and Work Life Preferences", *British Journal Of Guidance and Counselling*, Vol. 34, No. 3.

Irfan, S.M.; Hussain, T. & Yousaf, I. (2009). "Organizational Culture: Impact on Female Employees' Job Performance", *Journal of Quality and Technology Management*, 11(5): 1-16.

Jani, N. & Mukherji, S. (2010). "The Perception of Glass Ceiling in Indian Organization: An Exploratory Study", *South Asian Journal of Management*, 23-42.

Maginn, P.J. (2010). "Breaking through the Glass Ceiling of Local Government? The Gender Profile of Australian Mayors in Metropolitan Australia 1985-2010", *Fact Base Bulletin 11*, The University of Western Australia and Committee for Perth, Perth.

Malhotra, S. (2010). *The Equality Illusion Financial Express*, March 2007. Available at *http://www.financialexpress.com/news/the-equality-illusion/587681/0.*

Mukherji, N.J. (2010). "The Perception of 'Glass Ceiling' in Indian Industry: An Exploratory Study", *South Asian Journal of Management*, 28-38.

Okimoto, T.G. & Brescoll, V.L. (2010). "The Price of Power: Power Seeking and Clacklash against Female Politician", *Personality and Social Psychology Bulletin*, Vol. 36.

Pai, K. & Vaidya, S. (2009). "Glass Ceiling Role of Women in the Corporate World: Competitiveness Review", *An International Business Journal*, Vol. 19, No. 2.

Rai, U.K. & Srivastava, M. (2008). "Women Executives and the Glass Ceiling: Myths and Mysteries from Razia Sultana to Hillary Clinton", *BHU Management Review*, 1(2): 79.

Sachdeva, G. (2014). *Glass Ceiling Converted into Glass Transparency: A Study on the Factors Making Women Executives Successful in the Indian Banking Sectors.*

Sampson, D.S. & Moore, L.L. (2008). "Is there a Glass Ceiling for Women in Development", *Non-profit Management and Leadership*, 18(3): 321-339.

Sarika, G. (2015). "Breaking the Glass ceiling: Initiatives of Indian Industry (A Study with Special Reference to Exemplary Organization)", *The International Journal of Business Management*, 3(3): 255-260.

Sattar, A. & Nawaz, A. (2011). "Investigating the Demographical Impacts of the Job Satisfaction of District Officers in the Province of KPK, Pakistan", *International Journal of Management and Business Studies*, 1(3): 68-75.

Sharma, A.; Sharma, S. & Kaushik, N. (2011). "An Exploratory Study of Glass Ceiling in Indian Education Sector", *International Journal of Multidisciplinary Research*, Vol. 1, Issue 8.

Sharma, S. & Sehrawat, P. "Glass Ceiling for Women: Does It Exist in Modern India?", *Journal of Organization and Human Behaviour*, 3(2): 9-15.

Sharma, R.K. & Chaturvedi, S.K. (2017). "Glass Ceiling Effect in Professional Institutions in India", *International Journal of Advanced Research and Development.*

Srivastava, S.K. & Bajpai, S. (2015). *Organizational Studies and Innovation Review*, Vol. 1, No. 1.

Tan, J. (2008). "Breaking the Bamboo Curtain and the Glass Ceiling: The Experience of Women Entrepreneurs in High Tech Industries in an Emerging Markets", *Journal of Business Ethics*, Vol. 80.

Thomson, P.; Graham, J. & Lloyd, T. (2008). *A Woman's Place is in the Bedroom: The Roadmap*, Palgrave MacMillian, Houndmills, Basingstoke, Hampshire.

Weyer, B. (2007). "Twenty Years Later: Explaining the Persistence of the Glass Ceiling for Women Leaders", *Women in Management Review*, Vol. 16, No. 4.

Williams, J.C. & Cooper, H.C. (2004). "The Public of Motherhood", *Journal of Social Issues*, 60(4): 849-865.

"Women Earn Less Salary than Men: Gender Key in Promotion", *The Indian Express*, March 6, 2017, 6.56 pm.

"Women in India Earn 25 per cent Less than Men: Survey", *The Outlook*, March 6, 2017.

5

Sexual Harassment at Workplace: A Cross-Cultural Perspective

Tulika Anand

Introduction

Women's experiences of public places and their understanding of the speciality of work environment deffer from that of man. From the time women venture out from their home, they negotiate with the various situations differently and also perceive the circumstances that they undergo in another way from that of men as they have a different mental map of a workplace (Polly Vauquline, 2014). Violence against women surrounds all of us, whether or not we are aware of it and appears clearly a fundamental aspect of culture. It is so common that some experts consider it as a normal aspect of women's experiences. Among different types of violence against women, sexual harassment is the commonest form of violence which women encounter in society. Sexual harassment is a profoundly negative and traumatic life event with widespread psychological and sociological effects on the victim irrespective of their gender. It often gives rise to a wide range of negative emotions, embarrassment, and existential questions such as "Why me?" It increases feelings of helplessness and powerlessness in the victim affecting their self-esteem and producing feelings which suggest that they may be vulnerable to further violence.

Globalization continues to fuel multiculturalism and diversity in the workplace, and few employers can afford to ignore the culturally-based experiences that their employees bring to their work lives (Timmerman & Bajema, 1999). In this context, sexual harassment must be understood in terms of cross-cultural perspectives. Even within a single culture, the definition of sexual harassment is often misunderstood and is the subject of considerable debate in legal, psychological, and human resource management literature, both domestically and abroad (Li & Song Mei Lee-Wong, 2005). Defining the concept of sexual harassment becomes even "more complex and controversial in multicultural environments where culturally-derived values and beliefs serve as norms that determine when certain behaviours and feelings are appropriate and when they are not". Cultural perceptions vary because people differ in how they encode and decode messages (Hofstede, 2001; Soares, Farhangmehr & Shoham, 2007). Whether employees perceive workplace conduct, particularly ambiguous conduct, to be sexually harassing will be influenced by their respective cultural backgrounds. Similarly, an employer's response to such conduct and the manner in which it deals with the resultant issues will be influenced by cultural determinants.

What is Sexual Harassment?

Although, the concept of sexual harassment is an old one (Thornton, 2002), it was acknowledged as a socio-legal phenomenon in recent times, coming to the limelight partly due to the rise of radical feminist movements sprouting in the US (MacKinnon, 1979).

The term "sexual harassment" first came into use in the United States in the late 1970s. The origin of the term trace back to a course on "work and women" which was taught by Lin Farley at Cornell University. It was Catherine MacKinnon, a legal scholar from the United States who made the first argument in 1979 "that sexual harassment is a form of sexual discrimination prohibited by the constitutional laws of the United States". Since, then many international bodies and national organizations have made various efforts to prohibit and define sexual harassment.

Empirical researches in Europe also exhibited that majority of women experience sexual harassment at their workplace, thus, bringing the issue to the knowledge of general public (MacKinnon, 1979; Rubinstein, 1987) where it soon became focus of attention for women's activist movements and equality of employment opportunity discourse, and shortly afterwards transformed into laws and practices in distinctive social, political and legal contexts worldwide (Zippel, 2006). Sexual harassment has been recognized and addressed at international level by various organizations including the International Confederation of Free Trade Unions, International Labour Organization, the United Nations Committee on the Elimination of Discrimination against Women, and the European Union. To confront the challenge, associations and organizations have formulated policies and introduced mutually agreed clauses, provided direction to abide by the laws, organized trainings, and introduced procedures with regards to filing sexual harassment complaints (McCann, 2005).

Sexual harassment in the workplace is usually associated with a heterosexual employee making unwelcome sexual advances to another heterosexual employee of the opposite gender. And from a traditional perspective, sexual harassment is a demand that subordinates, usually women, and grant sexual favour to retain a job benefit (Lindemann & Kadue, 1992). A more encompassing definition defines sexual harassment as the imposition of any unwanted and discarded condition of any person's sex, which in most cases puts women in the receiving end. Under this definition, harassment includes jokes, direct taunting, disruption of work, vandalism or destruction of property, and physical attack (Tangari, Burt & Johnson, 1982).

The World Health Organization (WHO) defines sexual harassment as "any sexual act or an attempt to obtain a sexual act, unwanted sexual comments, or advances, acts to traffic or otherwise directed, against a person's sexuality using coercion, by any person regardless of their relationship to the victim in any setting, including but not limited to home and work" (2002). Sexual harassment happens in all cultures (Rozee, 1993; El-bushra & PizaLopez, 1993) with varying definitions of what constitutes sexual harassment (Heise *et al.*, 1996).

Types of Sexual Harassment

Sexual harassment can occur in a wide variety of forms including rape, pressure for sexual favours, sexual touching, suggestive looks or gestures, sexual joking or teasing, and the display of unwanted sexual material. MacKinnon conceptualized two forms of workplace sexual harassment: *quid pro quo* harassment and the creation of a hostile environment.

Quid pro quo comes from a Latin terminology, which literally means "this for that". When a person submits to or refuses the immoral requests of the harasser and such requests are made for the employment decisions affecting the harassed individual, this is termed as *quid pro quo* harassment (Notice of Policy Guidance, 1990). It involves the exchange of sexual favours for special employment treatment. Those who refuse risk punishment, such as demotion, dismissal, or denial of basic necessities for doing their jobs. It is usually perpetrated by a person with the power to hire, promote, or assign benefits.

Hostile environments are a kind of sexual harassment that gives rise to an intimidating, hostile, or offensive work environment (Equal Rights Advocates, Inc., 2013).They are created in workplaces where sexualized talk and behaviour are experienced by some as demeaning and humiliating, affecting their work. The behaviour may or may not target an individual, but it differs from *quid pro quo* sexual harassment because there is no exchange of favours, reward for participation, or punishment for refusing. Studies have shown that hostile climates are created in organizations with values supporting or allowing gender inequality and hostility against women.

However, it should be noted that both categories of sexual harassment can occur simultaneously. Therefore, an explicit distinction between the two has remained an ambiguous phenomenon. Both categories can share similarities in situations where the supervisor abuses his authority over employment decisions to force the victim to endure or participate in the sexual conduct (Notice of Policy Guidance, 1990). Furthermore, retaliation may also occur if the supervisor terminates his employee due to the latter's denunciation of repeated abuse.

Sexual Harassment and Contextual Factors

Gutek (1985) suggested that sexual harassment might be viewed as a subset of social-sexual behaviours that occur in organizational settings. Studies suggest that subjective interpretations play a role in determining what is considered sexually harassing (Burns, 1992, 1994-95). What is harassing to one person may not necessarily be so far for another. There are several popular cultures which provide examples that illustrate how contextual factors like social status, gender, and halo effect influence bystander responses to harassment. If the harasser is believed to have a high social status, such as that of a popular actor or athlete, society may interpret the harassment as being more welcomed or complimentary than the victim felt that it was. Our society believes that those with high social status possess some quality that makes them less culpable of behaving unlawfully. It is also possible that other contextual factors, such as where the harassment occurred or the nature of the harassment (verbal or physical and verbal), also dictate public perception.

Halo Effect

A popular theory developed by Thorndike (1920), known as the halo effect, might explain why harassment by people with desirable characteristics might be perceived as welcomed and not harassment by bystanders. The halo effect is a cognitive bias by which possession of one desirable trait is said to influence other traits about a person in positive ways. Dion, Berscheid, and Walster (1972) studied how physically attractive people benefit from the halo effect. Through survey research, they were able to conclude that attractive people were rated higher than unattractive people on each of twenty-seven desirability traits, including being more altruistic, kind, sophisticated, and sincere. Those considered to be more attractive were also rated as more likely to have successful marriages and careers than their unattractive counterparts (Dion, Berschied & Walster, 1972). More recent research has found that attractive people are more likely to be viewed as good, smart, cheerful, likeable, and socially skilled than those who are less attractive (Rhode, 2010).

Power

Because sexual harassment is ultimately about **power** (MacKinnon, 1979), it is importantly to consider how power, and not just the attractiveness that might come from status, influences the way that a harassing situation is interpreted. Research has found that when a power imbalance is evident between the harasser and the victim, bystanders are more likely to label the act as harassment (Dougherty *et al.*, 1996). Thompson (2001) argues that in all cases of sexual harassment, the harasser necessarily acts on power gained from some combination of three sources. These sources are: (1) a legitimate position of power, such as a boss over a subordinate; (2) an organization that is permissive toward sexual harassment and sexist attitudes; and (3) a peer relationship in which social norms dictate power differences. This third source of power explains why men most often perpetuate harassment over women. Harassment by men against women both creates and relies upon the imbalance of power between the two genders. Men use sexual harassment as a way to achieve a higher status as an individual while also elevating the greater social condition of male dominance (Langelan, 1993). Although power derived from gender may seem less threatening than legitimate power (boss/subordinate), it is no less influential than the other sources of power.

Location of Harassment

Sexual harassment may be interpreted in different ways depending on the **location** of the harassment. It has to be noted that sexual harassment not only exist in the workplace, but also in the educational institutions. Incidences of sexual harassment in the educational institutions occur in subtle manner. Some professor, teachers and mostly the head of the institution have used their position of power to obtain sexual favour from the students and also the junior or part timer other female faculties. Colleges, in particular, have established organizational norms that discourage harassment (Bursik & Gefter, 2011) which may influence how harassment on campus is perceived. In reference to Lukes's (1986) second source of power, organizations act as a power source by creating a culture in which behaviour, including sexual harassment, is seen by members as either acceptable or unacceptable based on both formal and informal rules and policies (Wilson & Thompson, 2001).

Gender

The way in which an individual comes to define and understand harassment is also influenced by their gender. It has been postulated that gender equality may increase sexual harassment in the form of male backlash (Martin *et al.*, 2006) with men being more commonly known to commit sexual harassment across different cultures (Koss *et al.*, 1987). The Indian society is at present witnessing a shift from being male-dominating to being gender equal; it is thus possible that the recent increase in the number of sexual harassment cases in India is a result of the male backlash for the growing gender equality. It is also entirely possible that increased media attention may attract some individuals to perform these acts so that they gain a degree of infamy. Women label a wider range of behaviours as harassment (Rotundo, Nguyen &Sackett, 2001). Men rate hypothetical situations (Gutek, Morasch & Cohen, 1983) and social-sexual behaviours (Gutek *et al.*, 1980) as less harassing than women do, even when a man is the target of the harassment. Compared to women, men are also more likely to agree that the amount of sexual harassment in the workplace is exaggerated (Collins & Blodgett, 1981), and support more lenient policies for dealing with those found guilty of harassment in a work setting (Benavides-Espinoza &Cunningam, 2010). Although, the overall report rate of sexual harassment is quite low (Knapp, *et al.*, 1997), men are less likely than women to file a report (U.S. Merit Systems of Protection Board, 1981). These differences between the attitudes of men and women toward sexual harassment are a result of the disproportionate rate of men who harass women in the workplace, academic contexts, and in public spaces (Wilson &

Thompson, 2001). Since, men are more often the harassers, they may sympathize more with the accused or believe that the woman welcomed the behaviour.

With several alternative standards already in existence, there still exists the need for incorporation into at least one of the standards for "the study of other variables such as attitudes to women, to homosexuals, to sex-role stereotyping, and to personal experiences of harassment". Cultural beliefs and values comprise key foundational elements underlying what will or will not be perceived as sexual harassment. Much of what an individual is today is shaped by the culture that he or she is born in and lives through, acquiring cultural values, attitudes, and behaviours. Culture determines definitions and descriptions of normality and psychopathology. Culture plays an important role in how certain populations and societies view, perceive, and process sexual acts as well as sexual violence.

Sexual Harassment and Culture: An Intersection

Oncale (1998) recognized that the cultural context of the workplace in which the purported harassment occurred is a critical factor when making evaluations of sexual harassment. Cultural context is also stressed in the Equal Treatment Directive of the EU, with the belief that "'cultural relativism' exerts considerable influence over definitions, tolerance levels, and legislative solutions to workplace harassment". Cultural factors would clearly influence the degree of welcome response with which a recipient would view or respond to a sexually-tinged comment or action. Differential understandings and interpretations of the language (as studied in international graduate students and faculty) spoken in a particular work setting contribute to misunderstandings and misperceptions (both over-perceiving and underperceiving) of sexual harassment (Andrea Tyler & Diana Boxer, 1996). Cultural differences will influence not only what kinds and intensities of conduct will be found unwelcome, but also the distinct means by which alleged victims of such conduct will demonstrate its unwelcomeness.

Even when sexual harassment is perceived as such, it may not be reported or may not be reported promptly; the tendency to report varies, as well, with culture (Duncan & Hively). Higher rates of sexual violence are expected to be more prevalent in cultures that encourage objectification of women, thus making them appear inferior to men (Daley & Noland, 2001). Not all cases are reported to the respective authorities and as high as 67-84 per cent of cases of sexual violence may go unreported (Greenfield, 1997) due to the sensitivity of the issue (Watts & Zimmerman, 2002). In studies conducted in both the United States and Israel, women who experienced many of the behaviours examined by the Sexual Experiences Questionnaire still failed to label or report their experiences as sexual harassment (Michelle, J. *et al.*, 1995). Some groups of women (for example, Turkish and Hindi women in Europe) hardly ever file sexual harassment complaints for fear that their families would be humiliated and blame them for any approaches, claiming that the women had invited the harassment by behaving or dressing in appropriately (Timmerman & Bajema, *supra* note 1, at 433). In many South American and Asian nations, rates of reporting sexually harassing acts is low as compared to the rest of the world (Anne M. Fiedler & R. Ivan Blanco, 2006). It has been postulated that the rates of unreported sexual offences are higher in some Asian cultures where virginity is highly valued and a woman's modesty is of utmost importance that gives her family the much required respect (Ward & Inserto, 1990).

International organizations cannot ignore the potential for conflicts between employees or between managers and employees from cultural backgrounds with differing views on sexuality, sexual approaches, and reporting of such activities in varying contexts. All individuals strongly internalize their cultures of origin. Employees from different cultures, even those who have lived in a country like the United States for some period of time, may define what constitutes a hostile environment (in relation to sexual harassment) differently than their peers; they may well possess varying motivations and thresholds that would allow or prevent their reporting of sexual harassment, even after acknowledging its existence (*Ibid.* at 275-77, 282-83; Timmerman & Bajema, *supra* note 1, at 424). The studies that *do* exist in this area often report or compare responses to written accounts of sexual harassment allegations (Timmerman & Bajema, *supra* note 1, at 435). While studies of individuals from different cultures within one country like the United States would be invaluable in understanding cultural determinants of perceiving harassment, such studies are not readily available. Nevertheless, the existing (and more available) studies comparing different cultures *within* their countries of origin may shed light on the cultural influences in defining sexual harassment issues (*Ibid.* at 422-23, 430-31).

Many difficulties exist in comparing data from different countries and settings. Studies of university students may not be readily comparable with those of actual employees, even within the same culture. While many nations outside the United States claim they have fewer reported sexual harassment cases as compared to the U.S., this statistics may be based upon differences in the law, "accepted differences in the power structures between men and women in the workplace" (Fiedler & Blanco, *supra* note 58, at 275). Cultural views of male-female relationships, and cultural views in relation to reporting indiscretions. In patriarchal countries, far fewer women work in male-dominated occupations; research into sexual harassment is not welcomed and can jeopardize participants' careers (Eros R. DeSouza *et al.*, 2004). The lack of standardized research instruments across studies of cross-cultural sexual harassment has made generalization even more difficult (Azy Barak, 1999). The studies performed have employed "different definitions, different terminology, different survey methods and instruments, and different time frames" (Timmerman & Bajema, *supra* note 1, at 421) over which incidents occurred, making comparison complicated. Some have included men, while others have been restricted to women only (*Ibid.*, at 428). While some very limited research examines differences among different cultural groups within one nation, other studies compare nations or simply focus on one cultural group in a single nation (Madhabika B. Nayak, 2003). Moreover, as researchers acknowledge, many of the studies have emerged from wealthy, industrialized, individualistic cultures, ignoring the poorer populations from non-industrialized, collectivist cultures (Harry C. Triandis *et al.*, 1993). A range of studies have reported statistical differences and qualitative depictions of work environments in different cultures, but definitive conclusions about the nature and etiologies of differences in the perception of sexual harassment in the workplace have been limited. Keeping in mind the problems associated with drawing conclusions from such reports, the rough comparisons can still provide some insight in the range of approaches to sexual harassment worldwide. A diverse sampling of studies from different areas of the world has been presented to demonstrate the broad range of cultural biases that affect perception and reporting of the hostile environment.

The study revealed that North American, Australian, and German students were much more likely to perceive the scenarios in terms of power abuse, gender discrimination, and harm — factors which, in their minds, lead to sexual harassment. By contrast, Brazilian students were more likely to perceive the scenarios in terms of innocuous sexual behaviour aimed at procuring a romance or even sexual intimacy, but not constituting the abuse of power or gender discrimination harmfulness required to constitute sexual harassment (John B. Pryor *et al.*, 1997). Researchers depicted Brazilian society as patriarchal and hierarchical, in which women are subordinate to men and males are entitled to make sexual advances (DeSouza, Pryor & Hutz, *supra* note 60, at 913-14, 921-23; DeSouza *et al.*, *supra* note 68, at 34-35). As a result, women in Brazil may perceive Brazilian men's sexual advances to be entirely normal (DeSouza *et al.*, *supra* note 68, at 34-35). Moreover, penal codes in Brazil have a far higher threshold for what actions constitute rape or sexual assault (Sigal *et al.*, *supra* note 59, at 209-10).

In one study of Hong Kong working women, researcher found Hong Kong working women's coping strategies, in relation to sexual harassment, tended to be less assertive and more indirect than those of U.S. counterparts. While sharing of experiences of harassment with friends and co-workers to gain support, was common, formal reporting of sexual harassment was very low. This failure to report has proven to be a complex phenomenon. Women in Hong Kong are often unaware of their basic rights to protection from harassment in their jobs and academic institutions, but there are also concerns with the possibilities for retaliation and loss of privacy (Chan, Tang & Chan, *supra* note 97, at 669-70). Yet, it is likely that cultural values related to "interdependence, harmony, and cooperation" also result in the avoidance of acknowledging or complaining to an authority about sexual harassment.

Less-developed countries demonstrate more widespread sexual harassment than developed countries. Factors that contribute to non-reporting include a lack of awareness of what constitutes sexual harassment, the absence of women's advocacy organizations, and the inconsistency of legislative enforcement (if the legislation exists at all). Fears of humiliation, retaliation, and blacklisting for *all* jobs can prevent women from being open about incidents of harassment (Fiedler & Blanco, *supra* note 58, at 280-81). Those who do come forward often find themselves with an onerous burden of proof and nearly impossible criteria in order to meet this burden; as a result, sexual harassment is nearly impossible to establish in court. Laws in such cultures are clearly interpreted through the lenses of societal norms that individuals have internalized.

Russia presents a unique European example in which laws regarding sexual harassment — even the *quid pro quo* form, which is defined as a criminal offense — are rarely enforced and often completely ignored. Russian women are routinely referred to in sexually-categorizing terms

(Michele V. Gee & Sue M. Norton, 1999). Even in those countries in which there is *overall* similarity in *response* to sexual harassment situations as compared to that of Americans, Europeans appear to apply different shades of meaning in *conceptualizing* of sexual harassment. While the United States seems to focus on rules and their associated sanctions, Europeans seem to refer to ethical traditions to a greater degree (Fiedler & Blanco, *supra* note 58, at 278).

It is possible that in cultures where man and his manly role are prized better, additional perceived or real power may encourage them to think of their "rights" (Daley & Noland, 2001). If a woman resists sexual intercourse, it may be perceived as a direct threat by men to their masculinity, triggering a crisis of male identity and contributing to sexual control and violence as it is seen as a way of resolving this crisis. It has been reported that victims who attempt resistance or escape from the situation are more likely to be brutalized by the offender (Levine & Koenig, 1983) thereby giving an inflated sense of power to the abuser as was seen in the New Delhi gang rape case of *Nirbhaya* in December 2012. It is likely that in patriarchal cultures, any resistance from the woman victim is perceived by the offender as an insult to his "manhood" further provoking him to resort to more violent means to control the victim.

Although, India does not have any specific law to protect individuals from sexual harassment at workplace, but the Constitution of India has several provisions for positive discrimination for women. For example, individuals enjoy certain Fundamental Rights under Part-III of Indian Constitution, which negate sexual harassment at workplace. Sexual harassment infringes the Fundamental Right of a woman to gender equality under Article 14 (Right to Equality) and her Right to Life and live with dignity under Article-21 (Right to Protection of Life and Personal Liberty). It also violates her Freedom of Speech and Expression under Article-19 of the Indian Constitution.

Based on important factors such as gender power equations, moral values, attitudes toward violence, Sanday (1981) divided cultures into two types: Rape-free and rape-prone cultures which are moulded by socio-cultural values; the former are more balanced in gender equality and have low rates of rape, whereas the latter have high rates where women are excluded from positions of power while restricting their freedom and objectifying them. Sanday (1981) pointed out the widespread existence of rape-prone societies, but absence of rape-free societies. On similar lines, Otterbein (1994) examined 17 cultures and reported that cultures with rigid sex-role systems showed higher sexual violence. The socio-cultural theory, thus, explains sexual violence in terms of social expression of male power or patriarchy. If one agrees with this hypothesis, it would mean that patriarchal societies will witness more sexual violence compared to the gender-equal societies. Thornhill and Palmer (2001) collate these two hypotheses, arguing that the socially learned behaviours known as culture are largely biological and hence an overlap of biological and cultural factors occurs in sexual violence.

Consequences of Sexual Harassment

Sexual harassment can have widespread consequences not only violating its immediate victims, but also the wider meaning of freedom and basic human rights (Herbert, 2002). The perceived consequences of sexual harassment vary across cultures. In socio-centric societies where shame is a more prevalent emotion, the victims of sexual violence may not open up about their trauma and hence may not report it. This not only affects the victim negatively but also affects an understanding of the true nature of trauma and rates of these acts, thereby influencing policy-making. In socio-centric cultures, relations between people are at the core and individual identity is subsumed in the family or kinship. Comparatively in ego-centric cultures, relations with the "self" are at the core with "independence" being given more importance than "interdependence". Socio- and ego-centric cultures are said to have different emotional expressions and experiences in terms of shame and guilt, respectively (Zimmerling, 2003). These different emotional experiences are due to the very basic tenet of these cultures: Socio-centric cultures being more socialized tend to give rise to a more social feeling of shame which cannot be felt in the absence of social relations. In contrast, ego-centric cultures are more individualistic and give rise to a more private feeling of guilt (Zimmerling, 2003). Thus, the emotions in a victim of sexual violence are shaped by the culture of the victim. In socio-centric cultures, where the dignity of the family comes before that of the individual member, the notion about harm resulting from sexual violence is shared more by the family members. On the contrary, in ego-centric cultures, this harm from sexual violence is much concentrated around the dignity and identity of the individual member. Thus, concepts of self also vary. Hofstede (2001) has also divided a cultural dimension on masculinity and femininity of cultures where gender roles are different.

Victims of sexual violence face the danger of suffering negative reactions upon disclosing their trauma, the most traumatizing of which includes being blamed for the assault (Campbell *et al.*, 2001). Studies have indicated a relationship between high levels of gender prejudice and stereotyping and high levels of victim blame (Lonsway & Fitzgerald, 1994; Pedersen & Strömwall, 2013). The social stigma resulting from sexual abuse is higher in Asian cultures where anything with sexual connotations is highly stigmatized (Ward & Inserto, 1990).

Conclusion

Hopefully, these examples reinforce the view that "cultural relativism (the conceptualization that values, ethics, beliefs, and behaviours are a function of culture) exerts a powerful influence on the perception, definition, tolerance, and legislative remedies surrounding sexual harassment in the workplace", with "considerable divergence" found around the world in terms of what constitutes a hostile environment. A disproportionate number of sexual harassment complaints in companies with cross-cultural employment pools involve alleged perpetrators and victims from different cultural backgrounds as "what's acceptable in one culture may be disrespectful and confusing in another" (Wendy Hardman & Jacqueline Heidelberg, 1996). More women will continue to enter the workforce, many in positions traditionally limited to men. Further, understanding of the specific factors underlying cross-cultural differences in perception and reporting of sexual harassment will be invaluable in preventing a range of problems, including uncomfortable misunderstanding, diminished ability of workers to fulfil their responsibilities, and costly litigation. It is an important research question as to what causes variation in the incidence of sexual violence in different cultures. Cross-cultural aspect of sexual harassment is a highly under-investigated and under-researched area. An important step toward understanding sexual harassment and its victims would be to re-phrase and re-understand various models of patriarchy/matriarchy and various gender roles and gender expectations. It is high time we start understanding barriers and cultural strengths that are responsible for higher or lower rates of sexual harassment cases in different cultures.

REFERENCES

Andrea Tyler & Diana Boxer (1996). "Sexual Harassment? Cross-Cultural/Cross-Linguistic Perspectives", *Discourse & Soc'Y,* 107.

Anne M. Fiedler & R. Ivan Blanco (2006). "The Challenge of Varying Perceptions of Sexual Harassment: An International Study", *J. Behav. & Applied Mgmt.*, 274, 279.

Azy Barak (1999). "Cross-Cultural Perspectives on Sexual Harassment", in *Sexual Harassment: Theory, Research, and Treatment* 263 (William O'Donohue, ed., 1997); Janet Sigal & Heidi Jacobsen, "A Cross Cultural Exploration of Factors Affecting Reactions to Sexual Harassment: Attitudes and Policies", *Psychol. Pub. Pol'y & L.*, 760: 764-66.

Campbell, R.; Ahrens, C.E.; Sefl, T.; Wasco, S.M. & Barnes, H.E. (2001). "Social Reactions to Rape Victims: Healing and Hurtful Effects on Psychological and Physical Health Outcomes", *Violence Vict.*, 16: 287-302. [PubMed]

Daley, E.M. & Noland, V. (2001). "Intimate Partner Violence in College Students: A Cross-cultural Comparison", *Int. Electron J. Health Educ.*, 4: 35-40.

El-bushra, J. & Piza Lopez, E. (1993). "Gender-related Violence: Its Scope and Relevance", *Focus Gend.*, 1: 1-9. [PubMed]

Eros R. DeSouza *et al.* (2004). "Female Nurses and Educators' Reactions to Sexual Harassment Charges: A Cross-Cultural Perspective", *Inter American J. Psychol.*, 33, 34, 38.

Geneva: World Health Organization (2002). *World Health Organization: World Report on Violence and Health.*

Greetje Timmerman & Cristien Bajema (1999). "Sexual Harassment in North-West Europe", *Eur. J. Women's Stud.*, 419, 435.

Harry C. Triandis *et al.* (1993). "An Etic-Emic Analysis of Individualism and Collectivism", *J. Crosscultural Psychol.*, 366.

Heise, L.; Moore, K. & Toubia, N. (1996). "Defining "Coercion" and "Consent" Cross-culturally", *Siecu Rep.*, 24: 12-4. [PubMed]

Herbert, T.W. (2002). *Sexual Violence and American Manhood*, Cambridge: Harvard University Press, Illustrated ed.

Hofstede, G. (2001). *Culture's Consequences: Comparing Values, Behaviours, Institutions, and Organizations Across Nations*, Thousand Oaks, CA: Sage Publications.

John B. Pryor *et al.* (1997). "Gender Differences in the Interpretation of Social-Sexual Behaviour: A Cross-Cultural Perspective on Sexual Harassment", *J. Cross-Cultural Psychol.*, 509.

Koss, M.P.; Gidycz, C.A. & Wisniewski, N. (1987). "The Scope of Rape: Incidence and Prevalence of Sexual Aggression and Victimization in a National Sample of Higher Education Students", *J. Consult Clin Psychol.*, 55: 162-72. [PubMed]

Levine, S. & Koenig, J. (1983). *Why Men Rape: Interviews with Convicted Rapists*, London: W.H. Allen.

Lindmann, B. & Kadue, D.D. (1992). *Sexual Harassment in Employment Law*, Bureau of National Affairs; ISBN0871797046, 9780871797049.

Lonsway, K.A. & Fitzgerald, L.F. (1994). "Rape Myths: In Review", *Psychol Women Q.*, 18: 133-64.

MacKinnon, C. (1979). *The Sexual Harassment of Working Women*, New Haven, CT: Yale University Press.

Madhabika B. Nayak (2003). "Attitudes Toward Violence against Women: A Cross-Nation Study", *49 SEX Roles*, 333.

Martin, K.; Vieraitis, L.M. & Britto, S. (2006). "Gender Equality and Women's Absolute Status: A Test of the Feminist Models of Rape", *Violence Against Women*, 12: 321-39. [PubMed]

McCann, D. (2005). *Sexual Harassment at Work: National and International Responses*, Geneva: International Labour Office.

Michelle J. Gelfand; Louise F. Fitzgerald & Drasgow Fritz (1995). The Structure of Sexual Harassment: A Confirmatory Factor Analysis "Across Cultures and Settings", *47. J. Vocational Behav.*, 164, 167-68.

Notice of Policy Guidance (19 March 1990), EEOC. Number N-915-050. Retrieved from: *http://www.eeoc.gov/policy/docs/currentissues*

Oncale V. Sundowner Offshore Servs., Inc., 523 U.S. 75 (1998).

Otterbein, K. (1994). "A Cross-cultural Study of Rape", in Otterbein K., editor, *Feuding and Warfare*, Amsterdam: Gordon and Beach Science Publishers, pp. 119-32.

Pedersen, S.H. & Strömwall, L.A. (2013). "Victim Blame, Sexism and Just-World Beliefs: A Cross-Cultural Comparison", *Psychiatry Psychol Law* [Last accessed date on 2013 June 5]. Available from: *http://dx.doi.org/10.1080/13218719.2013.770715.*

Rozee, P.D. (1993). "Forbidden or Forgiven? Rape in Cross-cultural Perspective", *Psychol Women Q.*, 17: 499-514.

Rubinstein, M. (1987). *The Dignity of Women at Work: A Report on the Problems of Sexual Harassment in the Member States of the European Community*, COMV/412/87.

Sanday, P.R. (1981). "The Socio-cultural Context of Rape: A Cross-cultural Study", *J. Soc. Sci.*, 37: 5-27.

Soares, A.M.; Farhangmehr, Minoo & Shoham, A. (2007). "Hofstede's Dimensions of Culture in International Marketing Studies", *Journal of Business Research*, 60: 277-284. *doi:10.1016/j.jbusres.2006.10.018*

Tangri, S.S.; Burt, M.R. & Johnson, L.B. (1982). "Sexual Harassment at Work: Three Explanatory Models", *Journal of Social Issues*, Vol. 38, Issue 4: 33-54.

Thornhill, R. & Palmer, C.T. (2001). *A Natural History of Rape: Biological Bases of Sexual Coercion*, Massachusetts: Massachusetts Institute of Technology Press.

Thornton, M. (2002). "Sexual Harassment Losing Sight of Sex Discrimination", *Melbourne University Law Review*, 26(2): 422-444.

Ward, C.A. & Inserto F. (1990). *Victims of Sexual Violence: A Handbook for Helpers*, Illustrated ed., Singapore: Singapore University Press.

Watts, C. & Zimmerman, C. (2002). "Violence against Women: Global Scope and Magnitude", *Lancet*, 359: 1232-7. [PubMed]

Wendy Hardman & Jacqueline Heidelberg (1996). "When Sexual Harassment is a Foreign Affair", *Personnel J.*, 91, 94.

Zimmerling, R. (2003). International University Bremen: AK Interkultureller Demokratievergleich; 2003. *Jun, 'Guilt Cultures'* vs *'Shame Cultures': Political Implications?* Paper given at the International Conference on Reassessing Democracy: New Approaches to Governance, Citizenship and Multiple Identities in Comparative Research; pp. 20-21.

Zippel, C. (2006). *The Politics of Sexual Harassment: A Comparative Study of the US, the European Union and Germany*, New York: Cambridge University Press.

6

Work Pressure and Women's Well-being

Shilpi Singh

In the fast changing world of today, no individual is free from stress and no profession is stress free. Work stress is still a major rising concern in most countries. Work stress is defined as the occurrence of negative emotions that are evoked by demanding situation in the workplace. Work stress and strain affect mental and physical health. Whether people perceive condition as stressful or whether these perceptions of stress lead to psychological, physiological or behavioural and situational factors conditioning variable (House & Wells, 1978; House, 1981; La Racco, House & French, Jr., 1980).

Stress is a state of tension experience by individual facing extra-ordinary demand, constraints or opportunities. According to health and safety executive (HES) Stress is defined as "the adverse reaction people have to excessive pressure personality to cope". Stress is an unavoidable part of life. Stress can help compel us to action; it can result in a new awareness and an exciting new perspective. It is only when stress becomes too great, affecting our physical or mental functioning, then it becomes a problem. It can become destructive and can turn into distress. Stress affects individuals not only psychologically but also physically. Robbins (2001) defines stress as a dynamic condition in which the individual is confronted with an opportunity, constraint, or demand related to what he or she desires and for which the outcome is perceived to be both uncertain and important. Stress also interacts negatively with job satisfaction.

It is estimated that five of the ten leading causes of disability around the world are due to mental health disorder on women productivity has long been underestimated, even though the workplace is where one spends most of their professional life. We live in a world where appraisals, feedback, competition, meeting deadline and constant. The working space, context of work, and interpersonal relationship are also unavoidable factors that impact the well-being of women.

Good health and well-being is one of the most prevalent issues in the present scenario and it is commonly observable whether it is though the presence malnourishment or female infanticide in India. Women experience lots of stress at place of their work as well as their home. Both employed and unemployed women play significant role in household activates of their families. Their life is more family-centred that of man. Working women are often loosed between home and job. The double work pressure affects their life satisfaction, adjustment, happiness and mental health.

India is leading nation when it comes to stress for women. About 87 per cent of women were stressed most of their time and 82 per cent claimed that they did not find to relax. The reason behind is that Indian women have to play deterrent role daily life for example work and home related activities. Career opportunities for Indian women are increasing, but social norms and family expectations are the root cause of the stress. Women face most stress and hard struggle to balance their home and social activities or job.

Traditional family structure is effect on the lives of Indian women. It is also affect women from urban areas those highly educated and probably the first one in their family to go for professional career. Most of researches showed that the women wake up as early in the morning preparing breakfast for in-laws, children and husband than going to their work. After returning home, they have to prepare dinner for family and other activities such clean up their clothes, home etc. It is common perception that women work until they are married and considered as she is no longer source of income. Balancing work and family task produce more stress on women (Binachi & Milkil, 2010).

Women, have a lot of balancing between social and personal requirements. Moreover, the conflict of women will be all the more intense if her employer, as well as her family member holds unreasonable expectation from her. Women's involvement in multiple role had a deleterious effect on their mental as well as their physical health. Due to this a woman is constantly under stress either at home or at workplace. Ansuman, Adithya and Modhulita (2014) determined that maximum number of women is suffering from poor mental health. According to them home and workplace atmosphere played a major in deciding mental health status of women.

Additionally, this study is a comparison in the degree of occupational stress experienced by married and unmarried women, and the stress is explained in terms of traditional trends, demand of society and more roles and responsibilities assigned to them as a mother, wife and homemaker.

Well-being is defined as a person's cognitive and affective event as well as cognitive judgement of satisfaction and fulfillment. Thus, well-being is a broad concept that includes experiencing pleasant emotion, low levels of negative moods high life satisfaction. More specifically, well-being involves our experiences of pleasure and our appreciation of life's rewards. "*Subjective well-being as a combination of positive affect (in the absence of negative affect) and general life satisfaction*" (Diener *et al.*, 1984). Life satisfaction and quality of life are two important aspects of well-being.

Well-being is a complex, multi-dimensional and multiphase construct. This construct has been variously defined by different perspectives. Well-being is defined as a person's cognitive and affective event as well as cognitive judgement of satisfaction and fulfillment. Thus, well-being is a broad concept that includes experiencing pleasant emotion, low levels of negative moods and high life satisfaction. More specifically, well-being involves our experiences of pleasure and our appreciation of life's rewards. "*Subjective well-being as a combination of positive affect (in the absence of negative affect) and general life satisfaction*" (Diener, 1984, 2000; Diener, Lucas, & Oishi, 2002).

The concept of well-being has its roots in philosophy (Cantril, 1965). In twentieth century social scientists tried to examine well-being, empirically. Sumner (1996) had classified the various well-being definitions as subjective and objective definition of well-being. Objective definition assumes that the criteria can be defined without preferences, interests, ideals, values and attitude matter. Subjective definition requires that individual's own preferences, interests, ideals, values and attentions. Diener and Suh (1997) stated that health and well-being include people's evaluations (both affective and cognitive) of their lives.

Biological, socio-cultural, psychological, economic and spiritual factors play a significant role in health and well-being. Argyle (2001) calls for attending to a large number of the notion of health and emphasizes on the need to bring to our psychological inquiry something of the sanctity, insights and cumulative wisdom of the people with whom we live. It is clear that well-being is closer to the concept of mental health and happiness, life satisfaction and actualization of one's full potential.

General well-being is the subjective feeling of contentment, happiness, satisfaction with life's experiences and of one's role in the world of work, sense of achievement, utility, belongingness and no distress, satisfaction or worry. The concept of well-being is too much inspired by Diener and group (Diener 1984, 2000; Diener *et al.*, 2003). Health and well-being are both personal as well as social. The desire for the well-being of everyone (*Kamaye duhktanam praninamartinshanam*) has been a core Indian concern that has par-human relevance. Undoubtedly, such a conceptualization of health and well-being is significant in its own right (Sharma & Mishra, 2010).

Life satisfaction is one of the three components of the global judgement of subjective well-being (SWB) (Diener, 2000). People assess their lives as satisfied based on their evaluation of different, but significant domains of lives, as marriage, work, health, and general life. Due to differencing experiences, values and belief, and life expectations people evaluate their lives differently. These subjective variables in people's lives are of great importance as they are reflecting a person's thought connected to his/ her life. It indicates that researchers are looking at the appraisal made by people in order to trap the subjective ideas of people about their. In contrast to the affective appraisal there is another kind of appraisal related to life circumstance, which is a global judgement related to the quality of someone's life.

The global judgement is a cognitive judgement related to circumstances in one's life and it also called life satisfaction. It is a cognitive judgement since people are using cognitive processing when appraising their lives. According to Demerouti *et al.* (2000) life satisfaction can be described as the extent to how much a person's life is satisfying her/his physical and psychological desires and wishes.

A research related to life satisfactions in seventeen different countries by Deiner (2000) reported that life satisfaction was the one factor which was thought of as important in all the seventeen countries and with money not being mentioned as important for life satisfaction. Thus, it can be seen that people are thinking of happiness as something important, even in those countries which are labelled as quite unhappy societies. Hence, the life satisfaction concept has emerged as a universal concept.

The concept of quality of life (QOL) takes a multidimensional view of well-being and includes physical, mental, spiritual and social aspects. However, QOL has not been well defined or consistently utilized in the literature. The evaluation of quality in life is increasingly dependent upon the quality and emotional judgement to various domains of life.

WHO (1997) has defined quality of life as, "*individual's perception of their positive in life in the context of the culture and value system in which they live and in relation to their goals, expectations, standards and concerns*". This definition also indicated that quality of life is self-reported from the individual, which is not directly related to reports or judgement of others. Growing body of the researchers established that quality of life is an important health outcome and must be taken into consideration in assessing the functioning of individuals under stress. Hornquist (1993) define quality of life as recognized need and functional satisfaction within number of fundamental life domains with special emphasis on well-being. According to Hornquist, the quality of life concept has been operationalized to evaluate the following domains:

(i) Physical domain, which covers, overall bodily health and specific sickness impact.
(ii) Psychological domain which covers satisfaction with life well-being in general and intellectual functioning.
(iii) Social domain, which covers capacity for self-care, work and mobility.
(iv) Structural domain which covers religious faith.
(v) Material domain which cover the individual's personal economic status.

Well-being is a state in which a person thinks about the positive aspect of herself and about society. Well-being is based on the perception of happiness regarding oneself and others. Some of the studies in conducted in this area have been discussed in the following paragraphs.

Praveen N. (2009) investigated occupational stress experience by working and non-working women of Hyderabad city. A sample of 180 working women was taken out of which 90 were married and 90 were unmarried. These two graphs were analysed by organizational stress scale. Five point Likert scale was used and it was found that unmarried working women experience low stress as compared to married women. It was concluded that household responsibilities, marital adjustment, child caring issue and family relationship are the sources of stress for married working women.

Nezhad *et al.* (2010) examined the occupational stress and family difficulties among working female. A sample 250 married working women with two or more children was taken. Sources of work stress inventory consisting of sources of stress scale and general work scale were used. Five point Likert scale was used. SPSS was used and data analysed using multivariate and correlation analysis. Family and difficulty and can make negative influence on individual mentality and health.

Balaji (2014) studied various factors which could lead to work-family conflict and stress undergone by women employee. He concluded that married employed experience work family conflict due to the number of hours working hours, size of the family and number of dependent of the family. These factors have severe consequences for the psychological distress and well-being of working women. Balaji studied various factors which could lead to work life balance and stress undergoing working women. He found that the number of hours worked per week, the amount and frequency of overtime, inflexible work schedule, supportive supervisor are the factors that lead to stress among the women employees.

Kristina and Stephen (2005) stated that working women are facing higher level of stress than compared to men. The stressors are multiple role, discrimination and stereotyping.

Research has demonstrated that many women feel cultural and social pressure to meet idolized image of being a "Supermom" (Halrynjo, 2009). The role aspiration focuses on excelling of balance. This may be particularly trace for women working full-time. While they still may struggle with work-life balance issues. It should be noted that women who are working part-time and maintaining responsibility for the care of home and children report more satisfaction and happiness than those working full-time or not working at all (Buehler & O'Brien, 2011).

Workplace mental health is an important aspect of working women's life and overall well-being. With time large number of companies are getting open to the idea of accommodating to address mental health within workplace. Although, it is difficult to quantify the impact of work on personal, social and psychological well-being. It is agreed workplace can offer several measures to promote psychological well-being and positive mental health. Majority of companies have stepped out to help stressed women and Infosys in this regard is worth to mention. They engaged women to work in a friendly environment and pursue the stress point that forces women to leave the organization.

On the basis of above discussion it can be concluded that stress is growing problem in the workplace and a particular magnitude for working women. The problem due to high level of stress can be exhibited physically, psychologically and behaviourally by an individual. The most serious effects of stress relate to performance. Women employees report more non-fatal, but long term and disabling health problem. This chapter described that working women generally involved simultaneously in many tasks, juggling between family and work responsibilities which leads towards stress among them.

REFERENCES

Anuman, P.; Adithya, P.P. & Madhulita, P. (2014). *Mental Health Status among Married Working Residing in Bhubaneswar City: A Psychological Survey*, BioMed Researcher International.

Argyle, M. (2001). *The Psychology of Happiness* (2nd ed), London: Routledge.

Balaji, R. (2014). "Work Life Balance of Women Employee", *International Journal of Innovation Research in Science*, 13(10): 2319-8753.

Binachi, S.M. & Milkie, M.A. (2010). "Work and Family Researcher in the First Decades of the 21 Century", *Journal of Marriage & Family*, 72(3): 705-725.

Bueheler, C. & O' Brien, M. (2011). "Mother's Part-time Employment: Association with Mother and Family Well-being", *Journal of Family Psychology*, 25(6): 895-906.

Cantril, H. (1965). *The Pattern of Human Concern*, New Brunswick.

Demerouti, E.; Bakker, A.B.; Nachreiner, F. & Schaufeli, W.B. (2000). "A Model of Burnout and Life Satisfaction amongst Nurses", *Journal of Advanced Nursing*, 32(2): 454-464.

Diener, E. (1984). "Subjective Well-being", *Psychological Bulletin*, 95: 542-575.

Diener, E. (2000). "Subjective Well-being: The Science of Happiness and a Proposal for a National Index", *American Psychologist*, 55: 34-43.

Diener, E.; Emmons, R.; Larsen, R. & Griffin, S. (1985). "The Satisfaction with Life Scale", *Journal of Personality Assessment*, 49: 71-75.

Diener, E.; Lucas, R. & Oishi, S. (2002). "Subjective Well-being", in C.R. Snyder & S. Lopez (Eds.), *Handbook of Positive Psychology* (pp.63-73), New York: Oxford University Press.

Diener, E.; Suh, E.; Lucas, R. & Smith, H. (1999). "Subjective Well-being: Three Decades of Progress", *Psychological Bulletin*, 125: 273-302.

Diener, E.; Suh, E. & Oishi, S. (1997). "Recent Findings on Subjective Well-being", *Indian Journal of Clinical Psychology*, 24: 25-41.

Diener, E.S.; Oishi, S. & Lucas, R.E. (2003). "Personality, Culture, and Subjective Well-being: Emotional and Cognitive Evaluation of Life", *Annual Review of Psychology*, 54: 403-25.

Halrynjo, S. (2009). "Men's Work-life Conflict: Career, Care and Self-realization: Patterns of Privileges and Dilemmas", *Gender, Work, and Organization*, 16(1): 98-125.

Hörnquist, J.O.; Wikby, A.; Hansson, B. & Andersson, P.O. (1993). "Quality of Life: Status and Change (QLSC) Reliability, Validity and Sensitivity of a Generic Assessment Approach Tailored for Diabetes", *Quality of Life Research*, 2(4): 263-279.

House, James S.; & James A. Well S. (1978). *Occupational Stress and Social Support*, Reading MA: Addision-Wesley.

House, James S.; & James A. Well S. (1978). *Occupational Stress, Social Support and Health in Reducing Occupational Stress*, Proceeding of a Conference, edited by Alan Michal Colligan. Wahingtion, D.C.: U.S. Department of Health, Education and Welfare.

Kristina, G. & Stephen, P. (2005). "The Role of Gender in Workplace Stress: A Critical Literature Review", *Health Education Journal*, 64(3): 271-288.

Nezhad, M.Z.; Goodarzi, A.M.; Hasannejad, L. & Roushani, K. (2010). "Occupational Stress and Family Difficulties of Working Women", *Current Research in Psychology*, 1(2): 75-81.

Parveen, N. (2009). "Investigating Occupational Stress among Married and Unmarried Working Women in Hyderabad City", *Bahria Journal of Professional Psychology*, 5: 21-37.

Robbins, S.P. (2001). *Organizational Behaviour*, 9th ed. New Jersey: Prentice-Hall.

Sharma, S. & Mishra, G. (2010). "Health Psychology: Progress and Challenges", in Mishra, G. (Ed.), *Psychology in India*, Vol. 3: 265-316. *Clinical and Health Psychology*, New Delhi: Pearson Education.

Sumner, L.W. (1996). *Welfare, Happiness, and Ethics*, Oxford University Press.

World Health Organization (1999). *WHOQOL Measuring Quality of Life*, Geneva: WHO.

7

Psychological Well-being of Working Women

Preeti Tamta and *Manoj Rao*

Introduction

In India 27 per cent of working-age women were working in paid jobs in 2015-16. A decade ago, in 2004-05, this share was 43 per cent, the same as in 1993-94. In rural India, the slide has been much worse as agriculture fails to absorb them. India was ranked 136 among 144 countries on the economic participation and opportunities index in the Global Gender Report 2015. Clearly, something is wrong somewhere in our society that prevents women from working. Indian women have been gradually coming out of traditional roles and entering into the male dominated areas. In recent years the role and status of the women have been changed tremendously. With increasing female education and more liberty for their rights and privileges, women's attitude towards their stereotyped role has been changing. Their participation in education and work place has also led to their increased socio-familial roles. Women who work outside the home are required to make many socio-familial adjustments that may contribute more stress and anxiety. The problem of stress in women, particularly working women is an important aspect on the process of social and emotional changes.

Conceptualization of Well-being

Health is regarded as a state of complete physical, mental and social well-being and not just the absence of disease (World Health Organization, 1948). To advance health, one route is construed as the presence of wellness. It is recognized that the experience of well-being contributes to the effective functioning of multiple biological systems,

FIGURE 7.1: Women Entering into the Male Dominated Areas

which may help keep the individual from succumbing to diseases, or when illness or harsh conditions occurs may help promote rapid recovery. A subjective feeling of well-being is one of the hallmarks of the health. The term 'well-being' has no universally accepted definition. General well-being has been defined and measured in a variety of ways such as —

- as a sense of well-being measured by three aspects; satisfaction of life, general effect, negative effect and perceived stress as a reflection of the one's level of happiness for a human being (Campbell *et al.*, 1976).
- as global well-being including three components positive effect, negative effect and cognitive evaluation (Andrew & Withey, 1976).
- as a subjective well-being having four conceptualizations: happiness, positive effect, negative effect and life satisfaction (DeNeve & Copper, 1998).
- as a subjective trait that measures the general feelings people hold regarding their overall satisfaction with life and that these individuals are well aware of their own sense of well-being (White, 2007).

The definitions of well-being can be grouped into three categories. First well-being has been defined by external criteria such as virtue or holiness. The criterion for well-being is not the actor's subjective judgement, but the value framework of the observer. Second, social scientists have focused on the question of what leads the people to evaluate their lives in positive terms. This definition of well-being has come to be labelled life satisfaction and relies on the standards of the respondent to determine what the good life is. A third meaning of well-being comes closest to the way the terms is used in every day discourse—a denoting a preponderance of positive effect over negative effect (Bradburn, 1969).

Empirical research on well-being was launched in the 1960 *via* an interest in depicting the quality of life in America (Campbell *et al.*, 1976). Since that time, the scientific study of well-being has proliferated (Diener *et al.*, 1999) with distinctions increasingly drawn between eudemonic and hedonic aspect of of well-being (Kahneman *et al.*, 1999) suggest well-being has, in recent publications, has been viewed in two main ways. The First is Eudaimonic well-being: the realization of personal potential. According to this view, each individual comes into life with unique capacities, known as one's 'daimon'. The eudaimonic approach considers well-being in terms of recognizing and realizing these talents and the extent to which the individual is functioning at their full capacity. Waterman (1993) argued that well-being or eudaimonia, occurs when individual engage in activities which hold true with their core values, which may offer a sense of 'completeness' or worthiness, providing 'personal expressiveness'. The second is Hedonic well-being: experiences of happiness and satisfaction. The hedonic approach defines well-being in terms of *what brings us happiness, satisfaction and pleasure, as well as sadness, dissatisfaction and pain*. This is the definition *that is most* relevant to the topic of well-being. This approach seems more occupied with subjective well-being. Most of earlier empirical research in this realm falls under the umbrella of 'subjective well-being'.

Subjective Well-being

Subjective well-being refers to all the various types of evaluations, both positive and negative, that people make of their lives. According to Diener and Lacas (1999), subjective well-being includes two components, (a) reflective cognitive evaluations, such as life satisfaction and satisfaction with life domains such as marriage, work, income, housing and leisure; and (b) affective domain, such as feeling positive effect (pleasant, emotions and moods) most of the time and experiencing infrequent feelings of negative effect (such as depression, stress and anger). Overall subjective well-being refers to judging one's life to be fulfilling and meaningful and dominance of pleasure over pain in his or her life.

Subjective well-being is an umbrella term for the different evaluations people make regarding their lives, the events happening to them, their body and mind and the circumstances in which they live. There are three hallmarks of Subjective well-being (Diener, 1984). First, it is subjective. According to Campbell *et al.* (1976), it resides within the experience of the individual, with subjective well-being, people comes to conclusion about their own lives using their own set of criteria. In the field of subjective well-being, a person's beliefs about his or her own well-being are of paramount importance. Second, subjective well-being covers the entire range of well-being from agony (negative factors) to ecstasy (positive factors). Finally, subjective well-being measures a global assessment of all aspects of a person's life. The field of subjective well-being focuses on longer terms states, not just momentary moods. Researchers in Subjective well-being field are interested in relatively enduring feelings of well-being, not just fleeting emotions.

Psychological Well-being

Psychological well-being has been described as the cornerstone of mental health. According to the World Health Organization (2011) mental health is, "a state of well-being in which every individual realizes his or her own potential, can cope with the normal stresses of life, can work productively and fruitfully and is able to make a contribution to her or his contribution to her or his community". While traditionally, psychological well-being has been defined by a lack of symptoms distress (i.e. lack of depression, anxiety and other symptoms of mental disorder), over time, the term has taken on a more positive definition (Keyes & Magyar-Moe, 2003). That is, psychological well-being has become increasingly recognized as more than just an absence of distressful symptoms, but now includes positive qualities individuals possess that can lead to mental health.

The positive psychology, as a modern approach, emphasizes on perception and interpretation of happiness and well-being and prediction of the factors related to them as well. Psychological well-being is a multi-dimensional concept; optimism, self-control, happiness, sense of interest, free of failure, anxiety and loneliness has been considered as the special aspects of well-being (Sinha & Verma, 1992). The term "psychological well-being" can be explained through two perspectives — the Hedonic and Eudiamonic perspective of well-being, the former indicating emotional well-being and the latter indication well-being (Deci & Ryan, 2008). Research has taken place in the both perspectives, making psychological well-being, a much research topic.

Psychological well-being is about lives going well. It is a combination of feeling good and functioning effectively. By definition, therefore, people with high psychological well-being report feeling happy, capable, well supported, satisfied with life and so on; Huppert's (2009) review also claims the consequences of psychological well-being to include better physical health, mediated possibly by brain activation patterns, neurochemical effects and genetic factors. At the most basic level, psychological well-being is quite similar to other terms that refer to positive metal states, such as happiness, satisfaction and in a many ways it is not necessary, or helpful to worry about fine distinctions between such terms. If I say I am happy, or very satisfied with my life you can be pretty sure that my psychological well-being is quite high.

Psychological well-being refers to how people evaluate their lives cognitively and effectively, in terms of satisfaction (Diener, Emmons, Larsons & Griffin, 1985). Therefore, psychological well-being is a subjective construct based on a range of psychological needs that are being met or not. It is also regarded as a construct that has many facets involving the self-introspectively as well as the self-pertaining to interpersonal relationships (Wissing & Van Eeden, 2002).

According to Kitchener and Jorm (2002) Psychological well-being can be described as a state of mind with an absence of a mental disorder, from the perspective of positive psychology, it may include an individual's ability to enjoy life, and create a balance between life activities and efforts to achieve psychological resilience. Ryff and Singer (2008), Ryan and Deci (2001); Waterman (1993) conceptualized positive well-being as subjective (hedonic) well-being, which emphasizes happiness and pleasure; and psychological (eudaimonic) well-being, which focuses on the fulfillment of human potential. Snyder and Lopez (2007) correctly proposed the formula: Happiness + Meaning + Well-being. In words of Ryan and Deci (2001), it refers to subjective well-being by which an individual subjectively assess one's life. Psychological well-being is about lives going well. It is the combination of feeling good and functioning effectively.

The majority of research on sexual harassment and gender discrimination has focused on experiences of majority women (Cortina, 2001; Mecca and Rubin, 1999) and the study of race-based discrimination has predominately analysed the experiences of minority men (Hull *et al.*, 1982).

Consequently, our understanding of discrimination experiences of minority women and consequences of that discrimination is limited. Therefore, we thought, it instructive to establish a context by providing summaries of a few brief anecdotal examples from minority women (across several races) of their work experiences related to discrimination and workplace well-being. We used a panel of minority women with extensive experience in both the public and private sectors. All of our panelists have held leadership roles in their respective fields at either middle or executive levels. In addition, four of our panelists have experience in consulting, three panelists work in higher education, and one has extensive entrepreneurial experience across different industries. With this panel, a wide range of experiences are represented. These summaries are in no way represented here as scientific analysis, but merely for the purpose of illustration.

A relevant, yet insufficiently explored, issue is whether psychological and occupational consequences of experiencing multiple forms of harassment are qualitatively different for minority women, leaving an important opportunity for future research (Buchanan & Fitzgerald, 2008). The research imperative is illustrated in a comment from one minority woman: I take pride in being a Black woman. Sadly others do not always understand or accept all that I bring to the workplace. I think that the lens from my view is one by which I can offer much. Unfortunately, I am treated sometimes in a manner that is inappropriate, but I am not able to pinpoint it to my gender or race. I think it is because of both.

The aim of the present chapter to develop a comprehensive understanding of the well-being of working women. Women in India today have more opportunities to pursue their higher education and more and more women have started taking up the jobs outside their homes. Women are existing under cultural norms and values, so, the working women are expected to make adjustments with the family. So this in turn leads to a number of stress and strain among working women.

REFERENCES

Akram, M. (2017). "Self-esteem and Psychological Well-being among Working and Non-working Women", *International Journal of Indian Psychology*, 5(1).

Andrews, F.M. & Withey, S.B. (1976). *Social Indicators of Well-being: Americans' Perception of Life Quality*, New York: Plenum Press.

Bradburn, N.M. (1969). *The Structure of Psychological Well-being*, Chicago: Aldine.

Campbell, A.; Converse, P.E. & Rodgers, W.L. (1976). *The Quality of American Life*, New York: Russell Sage Foundations.

Deci, E.L. & Ryan, R.M. (2008). "Hedonia, Eudaimonia and Well-being: An Introduction", *Journal of Happiness Studies*, 9: 1-11.

DeNeve, K.M. & Cooper, H. (1998). "The Happy Personality: A Meta-analysis of 137 Personality Traits and Subjective Well-being", *Psychological Science*, 8: 141-144.

Diener, E.; Emmons, R.; Larson, R. & Griffin, S. (1985). "Satisfaction with Life Scale", *Journal of Personality Assessment*, 49(1): 70-75.

Diener, E. & Larsen, R.J. (1984). "Temporal Stability and Cross-situational Consistency of Affective, Behavioural and Cognitive Responses", *Journal of Personality and Social Psychology*, 47: 580-592.

Diener, E. & Lucas, R.E. (1999). "Personality and Subjective Well-being", in D. Kahneman; D. Diener & N. Schwarz (Eds.), *Well-being: The Foundations of Hedonic Psychology* (pp. 213-229), New York: Russell Sage Foundations.

Huppert, F.A. (2009). "Psychological Well-being: Evidence Regarding Its Causes and Consequences", *Applied Psychology: Health and Well-Being*, 1: 137-164.

Keyes, C.L.M. & Magyar-Moe, J.L. (2003). "The Measurement and Utility of Adult Subjective Well-being", in S.J. Lopez & C.R. Synder (Eds.), *Positive Psychological Assessment: A Hand Book of Models and Measures* (pp. 411-425), Washington, DC: American Psychological Association.

Kitchener, B.A. & Jorm, A.F. (2002). *Mental Health First Aid Manual*, Canberra: Center for Mental Health Research.

Ryan, R.M. & Deci, E.L. (2001). "On Happiness and Human Potentials: A Review of Research on Hedonic and Eudaimonic Well-being", *Annual Review of Psychology*, 52(1): 141-166.

Ryff, C.D. & Singer, B.H. (2008). "Know Thyself and Become What You Are: A Eudaimonic Approach to Psychological Well-being", *Journal of Happiness Studies*, 9: 13-39.

Sinha, J.N.P. & Verma, J. (1992). "Social Support as Moderator of the Relationship between Alcoholism and Psychological Well-being", *Social and Applied Issues*.

Snyder, C.R. & Lopez, S.J. (2007). *Positive Psychology: The Scientific and Practical Explorations of Human Strengths*, Thousand Oaks, CA: Sage Publications.

Waterman, A.S. (1993). "Two Conceptions of Happiness: Contrast of Personal Expressiveness (Eudaimonia) and the Hedonic Enjoyment", *Journal of Personality and Social Psychology*, 64: 678-691.

Wissing, M.P. & Van Eeden, C. (2002). "Empirical Clarification of the of Psychological Well-being", *South African Journal of Psychology*, 2: 32-44.

World Health Organization (1948). *World Health Organization Constitution: In Basic Documents*, Geneva: Author.

8

Work-life Balance: The Secret of Life

Laxmi Vajpeyi

Work-life balance has come to the forefront of policy discourse in developed countries in recent years, against a backdrop of globalization and rapid technological change, an ageing population and concerns over labour market participation rates, particularly those of mothers at a time when fertility rates are falling [Organization for Economic Co-operation and Development (OECD), 2004]. Within the European Union the reconciliation of work and family has become a core concern for policy and encouraged debate and policy intervention at national levels. From as far back as the 1960s studies have proliferated (Lewis & Cooper, 2005: 9) on the linkages between work and family roles, originally concerned mainly with women and work-family stress. New concepts emerged, such as work-family conflict or interference, work-family accommodation, work-family compensation, work-family segmentation, work-family enrichment, work-family expansion and, of course, work-family balance (for full definitions, *see* Greenhaus & Singh, 2003; *see* also Burke, 2004). This last concept preceded that of work-life balance and implies "the extent to which individuals are equally involved in- and equally satisfied with — their work role and family role" (Greenhaus & Singh, 2003: 2), thus suggesting that by giving equal priority to both roles, work-family conflict — mutually incompatible pressures from the two domains — could be rapidly resolved. By focusing on employees with family responsibilities, however, the notion of work-family balance was considered in practice as triggering off a backlash in the workplace among non-parents (Haar & Spell, 2003). The term "work-life balance" gained widespread use in English language research and policy arenas, enabling a wider understanding of non-work concerns to be encompassed in employment research. As Alan Felstead and his colleagues note

(Felstead *et al.*, 2002:56), work-life balance can be defined as "the relationship between the institutional and cultural times and spaces of work and non-work in societies where income is predominantly generated and distributed through labour markets". Work-life balance practices in the workplace are therefore, those that, intentionally or otherwise, increase the flexibility and autonomy of the worker in negotiating their Gender, Work and Organization, attention (time) and presence in the workplace, while work-life balance policies exist where those practices are intentionally designed and implemented. "Work-life balance" is, however, a contested term. For some, the term 'balance' suggests that work is not integral to life, and implies a simple trade-off between the two spheres. It encourages quick-fix solutions that do not address fundamental inequalities, and that therefore, shift responsibility for balancing work and home life on to individuals (Burke, 2004; Lewis *et al.*, 2007). Other terms that suggest the mutual reinforcement of the two spheres, such as work-personal life integration, work-life articulation, or work-personal life harmonization, are therefore preferred (Crompton & Brockmann, 2007; Lewis & Cooper, 2005; Rapoport *et al.*, 2002). However, this terminology too remains contentious: 'integration', while creating the image of more positive organizational change, nevertheless implies the two spheres must be merged, leading to fears of a contamination or the domination of personal life by the demands of paid employment (Lewis & Cooper, 2005). "Work-life harmonization" and "work-life articulation", while promising, came to prominence after our call for papers and have not to date been widely used in the English language literature. For this reason we have retained the original, long-standing, and easily-understood term, 'work-life balance' throughout this special issue. The popularity of work-life balance research was confirmed at the 2005 conference of Gender, Work and Organization, when we received more than double the expected number of paper submissions for a stream under that title, and a similar response met our subsequent call for papers for this special issue. The presentations and discussions in the 2005 conference stream demonstrated the vitality of research in this area, as well as the breadth of methodological approaches (qualitative and quantitative, comparative and single-country case studies, sectoral and organizational studies, individual and organizational perspectives). In formulating our call for papers for the special issue we decided to focus particularly on issues of choice and constraint. Work-life balance policies are predicated on perceived or recorded employee preferences for certain types of work arrangement, relating to their time and presence, and in policy discourse today it is often taken for granted that the work-life balance should be formulated in terms of a win-win situation, where employees' preferences coincide with their employers' desire for greater flexibility of working practices, particularly working time. However, many of the papers presented in 2005 raised questions about such assumptions; whether in relation to entrenched gender attitudes in organizations [notably, the choice between male career patterns or the 'mommy track': see also Smithson and Stokoe, (2005)], gendered sectoral cultures, the advantages and disadvantages of particular work-life balance measures, or cultural attitudes and the negotiation of gender roles in the household and at work. A further concern in our selection of papers for the special issue was to examine how far the work-life balance, traditionally seen through the lens of female employment, has broadened to include men's as well as women's negotiation of the demands of paid employment and personal and domestic life. This concern, reflected in the terminological shift noted above from the work-family to the work-life interface, corresponds to research findings that suggest that a holistic approach is more likely to mobilize workplace support (thus avoiding the risk of backlash) and effect wider organizational change than policies aimed solely at women or those with childcare responsibilities. However, researchers need to be alert to differences in the way that men and women take up such measures. Finally, in selecting papers for this special issue, we attempted to cover as many countries as possible. We were particularly interested in the potential for policy learning, notably in the context of EU policy recommendations. Country case studies offer valuable lessons about the relationship between policy and organizational practice, as well as the cultural attitudes that underpin both.

Work-life Balance in Organizational Practice: Gendered Choices, or Gendered Organizations?

Existing literature casts the work-life interface in terms of three issues: time management; inter-role conflict (role overload and interference) and care arrangements for dependents. Preferences are shaped not only by individual values and predispositions, but also by current reality and objective factors within each individual's life (such as the public provision of childcare and the labour market situation). Thus, preferences take account of perceived constraints: they are "usually compromises between what is desirable and what is feasible" (Bielenski *et al.*, 2002:16). Employees' work-life balance priorities are considered to fall within three general categories: working time arrangements (total working hours and flexibility); and, for those with parenting or other care responsibilities, parental leave entitlements (maternity, paternity, parental and careers); and childcare (subsidies or direct provision) (McDonald *et al.*, 2005; Thornthwaite, 2004). Where these needs are met through organizational work-life programmes, employees are found to have increased organizational commitment and job satisfaction. A greater sense of control over their own work schedules leads to improved mental health (McDonald *et al.*, 2005).

Further, work-life programmes that allow employees to have a greater involvement at home appear to be linked to employee well-being (Greenhaus *et al.*, 2003) for men as well as women (Burke, 2000). Organizations can benefit in a number of ways, including reduced absenteeism and better integration of women returnees after maternity (McDonald *et al.*, 2005). Work-life balance measures can present opportunities for organizations to learn new ways of working (Lee *et al.*, 2000; Lewis & Cooper, 2005). Where employees' needs are not met, employees are expected to experience work-life stress, although, it may be that, particularly for those without caring responsibilities, time stress is partially or wholly offset by other factors, such as material rewards or job enjoyment. European surveys suggest that unmet demand for work-life balance (especially a mismatch between desired and actual hours) is increasing (Gallie, 2005; Green & Tsitsianis 2005), with possible adverse consequences for employees' well-being and performance at work. It is widely recognized that even where work-life balance measures are extensively available in organizations, such measures are not necessarily extensively utilized (Pocock, 2005). Take-up has been linked to the factors that make up the organizational work-life culture, such as the extent of manager and co-worker support, the career consequences of taking a work-life balance measure, organizational time expectations and gendered perceptions of policy use (McDonald *et al.*, 2005). The degree of use is also variable across groups of staff in an organization. These measures are often targeted at highly skilled people in an effort to recruit and retain key staff (Gray & Tudball, 2003). However, those with managerial responsibilities can find it difficult to take up work-life measures, whether because of explicit exclusions or because in practice they have to do whatever it takes to get the job done (Gregory & Milner, 2006; McDonald *et al.*, 2005). More broadly, changing organizational structures, flexible work organization (lean production and supply chain management in manufacturing and retailing, and new service requirements in both public and private sector services) and work intensification throw up new challenges to work-life balance in the new economy (Brannen *et al.*, 2001; Perrons *et al.*, 2007). In the UK, although 'high-performance' management is found to be associated with the formal presence of work-life balance policies (Dex & Smith, 2002), there has been concern about the negative impact of such practices on the work-life balance of individuals, particularly men (White *et al.*, 2003). In his overview of organizational work-life balance policies, Steven Fleetwood (2007:394) argues that the discourse "no longer reflects the practice"; rather, a discourse of employee-friendly work practices disguises employer-friendly practices that enhance individual work-life balance only indirectly, if at all. Organizational structures and cultures can therefore undermine formal work-life balance policies, leaving those who take them up undervalued and marginalized (Gambles *et al.*, 2006). Piecemeal measures that do not tackle organizational cultures may also reinforce gender segregation in the workplace, since the take-up of work-life balance measures is strongly gendered (Houston, 2005). Women with dependent children are most likely to take up measures such as part-time working and other reduced working-hour arrangements, and school term-time working (where it is available, mostly it is almost exclusively female). A number of barriers appear to limit men's take-up of such measures: the organization of the workplace (including perceptions of their entitlement, that is, perceptions that men's claims to family responsibilities are valid), the business environment and the domestic organization of labour in employees' homes (including the centrality of career for the father and mother and their degree of commitment to gendered parenting, both closely class-related) (Bittman *et al.*, 2004; Bygren & Duvander, 2006; Crompton & Lyonette, 2007; Duncan, 2007; Singley & Hynes, 2005). "Organizational career cultures" prevent men from overtly choosing a work-life balance over their career. Consequently, men are often found using informal flexibility, or taking advantage of gender-neutral flexibility such as flexi time systems, to improve their work-life balance at the margins (Gregory & Milner, 2006, 2008). Organizational cultures thus tend to reinforce the traditional separation of gender roles, leading to a polarization between the working experiences of men and women. Such organizational practices are established within and influenced by gendered societal norms about the 'ideal career' and capitalism's norm of the 'ideal worker', usually defined in terms of presence and commitment (Cooper, 2000; Gambles *et al.*, 2006). Gendered societal norms have, of themselves, been conceived as being the product of institutions such as the family, the labour market and the welfare state, along with power structures, gender role norms (and the value attached to them) and the division of labour in the family (Crompton, 2006; Pfau Effinger, 2004). The terms in which the work-life balance agenda is cast at a national level through government policy and discourse, are shaped by welfare state regimes (Esping-Andersen, 1990, 1999). In the liberal welfare states, for example, work-life balance has to be examined in the context of both a traditional reluctance to intervene in the private sphere, and at the same time relatively high employment rates. As a result, public childcare provision is relatively weak and the work-life balance agenda tends to be framed in terms of flexible working hours and the growth of part-time working. Scandinavian and continental welfare states, on the other hand, tackle work-life balance by focusing on reduced working time for all (Björnberg, 2000). In Scandinavian welfare states, the explicit objective of gender equality means that family-friendly measures target men as well as women. The liberal and continental welfare states are more likely to cast work-life balance in gendered terms.

Work-life Balance and Woman

This issue looks through a gender lens at the ways in which both men and women negotiate the relationship between work and home life, particularly when they have caring responsibilities at home. It explores the relationship between formal policies and their impact on men and women's ability to affect a choice in shaping their careers and their day-to-day commitments. Cécile Guillaume and Sophie Pochic examine the career and life choices of top managers in a French company with a specific, paternalistic culture. Their article demonstrates the structural constraints of an organizational culture which emphasizes employee availability, particularly through geographical mobility, and which is disruptive to family formation. The term "work/life balance" could be defined as a state of equilibrium in which the demands of both a person's job and personal life are equal. This term was coined in 1986, although its usage in everyday language was sporadic for a number of years. Work/life balance initiatives are a global phenomenon. Abraham (2002) stated that women, who work, carry a double load as an employee and housewife. They are super moms playing varied roles and reconcilling between tradition and modernity. Employees in global communities also want flexibility and control over their work and personal lives. Van

Fleet and Sourage (1984) in their research findings stated that although "women can assume the role of a scientist or a technocrat, they do experience difficulty in having a similar role as housewife or mother". Women in India have struggled to establish an identity and create a life space in social as well as work organizations. Considerable research has highlighted the importance of Work-Life Balance for organizational performance (e.g. Druskat & Wheeler, 2003; Durham, Knight & Locke 1997). Work-life balance, in its broadest sense, is defined as a 'fit' between the multiple roles in a person's life (Hudson, 2005). These practices include flexible work hours (e.g. flex time, which permits workers to vary their start and finish times provided a certain number of hours is worked; small work week, in which employees. Hence, work a full week's worth of hours in four days and take the fifth off), working from home (tele-work), sharing a full-time job between two employees (job sharing), family leave programmes (e.g. parental leave, adoption leave, onsite childcare, and financial and/or informational assistance with childcare and eldercare services. There are changes in large part due to a significant cultural shift in parental perspective that is, an increased acceptance of giving education to girls that allows for the possibility of women working outside the home, contributing economically to the family and even pursuing a career. With more Indian women in the workforce, a number of rates of female workers in rural areas are 31 per cent and 11.6 per cent in urban areas. Employment numbers for women, further detailed in women workers in the twenty first' century-Unemployment and Underemployment, indicate that of India's 397 million workers, 123.9 million are women: 106 million women are in the rural areas and 18 million in the urban areas. However, only 7 per cent of India's labour force is in the organized sector workers on regular salaries in registered companies), with the remaining workers (93%) in the unorganized or informal sectors. (Including as a brief comparison, in the United States in 2008, of the 121 million women ages 16 years and older, 72 million (59.5%) were labour force participants. Women comprised 46.5 per cent of the total U.S. labour force (68 million women were employed in the United States — 75 per cent of employed women worked in full-time jobs and 25 per cent worked on a part-time basis). Women are projected to account for 49 per cent of the increase in total labour force between 2006 and 2010. In 2008, the largest percentage of employed women (39%) worked in management, professional and related occupations and women accounted for 51 per cent of all workers in the high-paying management, professional and occupation. Globally, the number of women senior managers in large corporations is low. The March 2009 report, women CEOs of the fortune 1000, related published by Catalyst (the U.S. firm working to expand opportunities for women and business), identifies the women CEOs of the forte 500 companies. It was found that 15 CEOs are women, including Indian, Indra K. Nooyi, Pepsi Co. Inc. The statistics at the CEO level of these large companies clearly show that there is much progress to be made for women worldwide at this level of management. Women in India have held important roles in politics, social organizations and administration. There is a need for educated women to reach very high level in the government and the number of women in the corporate sector is gradually growing. Gulhati (1990) compared the attitudes of male and female managers in India. A study on women managers in public sector organizations by Buddhapriya (1999) provided an insight into their attitude at their workplace. Raman Kumar (1993) had done a study on women executives in banks. A few studies by Preeti Singh [7-9] focused on women employment in the hotel industry in Delhi and on the status of women in the hospitality industry. These studies are relevant from the point of view of understanding women at work. The objective of the present study is to understand the problems that are common to the women employed in different types of industries. Freedman and Greenhaus reveal that women in workforce have increased considerably, however, women face a lot of issues and challenges. They are still seen as the primary caretakers of the home and family, even if they work just as much as men. Work role is often seen as secondary to family roles. Not just men but women also hold themselves and other women to the homemaker standard. Women spend more time on housework, child care and family responsibilities. Women used to spend almost 24 per cent of their time on housework in 1966 to 30 per cent of housework in 2005. However, women miss more work for child care. Twenty per cent of women take care of both children and elders. Greenhaus and Beutell defined work-family conflict as "a form of inter-role conflict in which the role pressures from the two domains, that is, work and family, are mutually non-compatible so that meeting demands in one domain makes it difficult to meet demands in the other". That is, participation in the work role is made more difficult by virtue of participation in the family and *vice versa*. The major concern in this most widely used definition of work-family conflict is that role conflicts cause due to problems of role participation and emotional intelligence. Hence, difference in values, social relationships and requirements between work and family do not constitute conflict *per se*. Waite and Gallagher documented the tensions within and between dual career couples brought about by the transformation of marriage and family life. At the personal level, marriage and family functioning have become fundamentally personal choices and responsibilities, making the maintenance of both more vulnerable. At the cultural level, while traditional values such as gender role ideologies are constantly being challenged, balance related to the importance of work life and personal life still persists to role efficacy and emotional intelligence. Landsman disclosed the employer provided resources can help women a great deal in balancing work-life balance issues. It employers provide facilities like onsite child care or referral, it would help in decreasing absenteeism and turnover from work. It would further help in increasing women employee's willingness to work overtime, from work and take-home dinner, family-friendly benefits packages and exercise equipments can help in removing the stress of working women in a big way. A 2005 study of senior women in public and private sector firms, titled women in management in the new economic environment: the case of India, found that women look for work from economic necessity and for personal goals. Women in lower to middle socio-economic status seek income opportunities and those in the upper middle class pursue a career for professional ambitions. Women with higher education have more interest in independence, are career-oriented and interested in quickly moving up the organizational ladder. The key challenge for career women is managing both their traditional roles as housewives and their career. Women experience great pressure to work hard to prove them in the workplace. Career women frequently express a concern of being inadequately prepared to lead such interventions and feel challenge to take on such a role. In most of the available literature, the problems faced by Indian women are mainly restricted to technical problems hindering business efforts (Nayyar *et al.*, 2007) or motivation-stress-related issues (Das, 2001; Lilian, 2009). Meanwhile, the WLB issues of women in India have not been highlighted much in any previous empirical research papers. Even in the international arena, studies on this topic are scarce, especially with regard to developing and underdeveloped countries. The available reports (CIBC, 2004; Godwyn, 2009) mainly discuss developed nations where the prevailing situations are quite different than those of developing and underdeveloped nations (UNIDO, 2001, 2003). The issue of WLB for women in such nations thus needs to be recognized as vitally important to society and as requiring intensive research. Work-Life Balance is an important consequence of the professional world for both men and women. However, in the present chapter we are examining the nuances of the construct from the perspective of the women professional. It has been suggested that in examining the relationship between work and personal lives, gender is a significant moderating variable. Whitehouse *et al.* (2008) state that, even though women participation in the work force is widely accepted, majority of the caring responsibilities of the family lie with the fairer sex. Though the phenomenon has global relevance, the issue is more significant for a developing country like India. As a country surges towards development and enlightenment, its social structure becomes more open and progressive in providing equal opportunities to all members of the society. In India, this development has resulted in better opportunities for the Indian women in terms of education and employment opportunities. Present study deals with not only pressures of being women and being a part of the family in contemporary India, but also with the pressure on organizations to attract and retain women in the workforce. The present study is an attempt to gain insight in to the role of a sample population of women employed in different occupations, in balancing work and life. The emphasis is primarily on professionalism and was carried out by conducting a survey among respondents who were first generation women earners. The respondents were also surveyed on the awareness of various WLB initiatives taken by different organizations. The data collected was studied in order to explore and portray the sensitivity of women and their perceptions of the society as well as to highlight the values, and primary family system. The demands and pressures of work and family may give rise to work-life balance issues to an individual. The changing socio-cultural balances in India and the increase in the number of working women, make the issue more relevant for the study. Work-Life Balance has been studied from two perspectives. The first focuses on work related factors and their impact on family life, while the second perspective focuses on family focused factors and their effect on the work life. This study builds on integration of these two perspectives in investigating both work and family pressure in their influence on the performance of working women. Thus, the intention was to cover the vast arena of professions that are most popular with Indian women professional organizations.

As a result, it forces managers, especially women, to make choices about work and family. On the other hand, they find evidence of women developing strategies that enable them either to conform to or bypass organizational norms. Their research, based on access to company personnel data covering all employees as well as interviews with 60 managers (men and women), raises valuable questions about structure and agency and highlights the relationship between formal and informal routes to power. No specific work-life balance policies are in evidence in the organization under study, although, it has attempted to address the gender imbalance at higher levels through targeted recruitment policies. Guillaume and Pochic show that such policies are inadequate for tackling both the highly formal recruitment and promotion procedures, based on educational attainment through competition, and the informal processes that favour 'unencumbered' workers, or those with the kinds of relational resources making it possible for their spouse to follow them. Part-time work is devalued in career terms. Thus, the typical career pattern implicitly assumes that managers are male. Moreover, organizational practices are based on an underlying set of traditional gender values regarding the household division of labour which appear to be unchallenged in human resources practice. The authors identify three types of strategy employed by women in response to this organizational culture. Some single women, and women in dual-career households, decide to pursue a typical male career pattern. They do not relinquish their careers because they earn enough to employ domestic careers, in a country where public provision of childcare is also relatively plentiful. Others choose an alternative career model, resisting forced mobility at the risk of an implicit "withdrawal from the competition for power", or constructing joint mobility strategies with their spouse. Such individual strategies appear to be limited to those with exceptional leverage (extremely highly qualified individuals or couples) and to have little or no impact on organizational culture. Like Guillaume and Pochic, Jacqueline Watts looks at strategies employed by women in a male-dominated profession in an engineering culture (although in the case of Guillaume and Pochic's French organization, the engineering culture has given way in recent years to a more commercial focus). Watts' interview-based research was carried out in the UK, but the strong sectoral culture is likely to predominate across national cultural variations. It is nevertheless exacerbated by the UK's 'long hours' culture. Again, the profession is dominated by values of availability and presenteeism — and increasingly, of geographical mobility — which implicitly assume an unencumbered male worker. Female interviewees pointed to deadline-dependent project work and 'fire-fighting' rather than strategic management as factors. As a result, those with childcare commitments experience work-life stress.

In line with existing research on work-life adaptation of women in male dominated professions (following Cockburn, 1991), Watts shows that traditional strategies adopted by women civil engineers — such as, on one hand, adopting male career strategies and outsourcing domestic work, or on the other hand, juggling through part-time working, self-employment and flexible work schedules — have brought mixed blessings. Adaptive strategies have no impact on men's employment behaviour and may reinforce segmentation, excluding these women from career advancement or from decision-making roles. Some women interviewees felt able to resist at the margins (for example, by not fulfilling their colleagues' expectations about socializing outside work) but, as in Guillaume and Pochic's study, such strategies have limited impact. Elin Kvande's innovative study also examines the experience of working in 'greedy' organizations (Coser, 1974) whose claim on male workers' presence and commitment is intensified by the demands of a globalized marketplace. As in Watts' study, project-based work is identified as a feature of work in the new knowledge economy, which tends to reduce the amount of time available to employees for their life outside work. But she places this experience in the Norwegian and wider Nordic context, which, she argues is different from other western European contexts. In the Norwegian context the family friendly welfare state, and specifically a father-friendly welfare state, gives parents unparalleled opportunities to combine work and family life. In investigating fathers' time practices, Kvande discusses two specific cases drawn from different research projects. Both cases highlight the way in which organizational flexibility is internalized by employees, so, that the work-life balance is felt to be a matter of individual organization and boundless work is seen as a problem that individuals must resolve. These experiences help to explain why, although the relatively generous provision of paternity leave in these countries allows men to spend more time with their children and to reflect on their working practices as a result, male employees are nevertheless not in a position to effect long-term change on their return to full-time employment. Parental leave therefore, needs to be maintained and reinforced as a collective right if it is to have a boundary-setting function, rather than being a matter of individual choice. In several countries flexible working arrangements are advocated as a means of balancing work and other commitments, and thus reducing work-life conflict and work pressure. Based on an analysis of the first national survey of employees in Ireland, Helen Russell, Philip J. O'Connell and Frances McGinnity examine the impact of three main types of flexible work arrangements on employees' perception of work-life stress and their ability to carry out their caring responsibilities. Their basic hypothesis is that flexible work arrangements — flexi time, or flexible working hours, part-time work and working from home — will reduce work-life conflict because they give employees greater choice. In reality, part-time work and flexible working hours are the most common forms of flexible working, with the take-up of home-working being limited to a small percentage of employees (8%). The authors observe that the take-up of flexibility is gendered, and that women are considerably more likely than men to work part-time or to experience other forms of flexibility that reduce their earnings, and men are more likely than women to work from home. The availability of flexi time also depends strongly on the sector, with public-sector employees having greater access than others to flexible working hours. In this study a reduction in working hours appears to lessen work-life conflict for both men and women. Part-time work is also associated with reduced work pressure, but it does so significantly only for women. The relationship between flexi time, reduced work pressure and reduced work-life conflict is significant only in the public sector, indicating that the effectiveness of flexible work practices depends on the institutional context. However, those working from home report significantly higher levels of work-life conflict. The authors suggest that this negative relationship between working from home and work-home conflict is partly due to long working hours, but also to other factors, such as intrusion into family space. As Russell, O'Connell and McGinnity observe the availability and take-up of flexible working arrangements have important consequences for the division of domestic labour. Their findings corroborate other studies that suggest that flexibility for men may mean increased working hours and reduce their availability to their family. This, in turn, has consequences for women's employment options, making their recourse to part-time work more likely. More optimistically, the authors also note that men working in organizations with a greater range of flexible work arrangements reported lower levels of work-life stress, suggesting that such measures may have beneficial effects for all employees, regardless of take-up. Drawing on a strategic sample of structured interviews with 102 men from six countries (Austria, Bulgaria, Germany, Israel, Norway and Spain) working in either technical or financial organizations or social and health-related organizations, Sigtona Halrynjo analyses men's experience of work-life balance and the strategies they develop. Her analysis puts into a broader context

Guillaume and Pochic's and Kvande's findings about organizational assumptions on employee availability (particularly on male availability), following Acker (1998). She finds that encumbrance is not necessarily a feminine hallmark. Within the all-male sample, segments of encumbered men struggling with varying degrees of 'competing devotions' are identified. Halrynjo uses multiple correspondence analyses to map her sample of men according to their volume of work and volume of care. Her findings corroborate earlier findings on men and women's relational resources as a determinant of volume of work and care. Referring to Mary Blair-Loy's "work devotion schema" (Blair-Loy, 2001), the author identifies four ideal types in order to illustrate the various combinations of volume of work and care, and strategies for dealing with them. Men in the 'career' category find their work absorbing and fulfilling and are unencumbered by family duties, usually because their wife takes full-time care of the children or because the couple outsource childcare, while at the opposite pole men in the 'caring' category more closely resemble a traditional female working pattern: they work part-time and experience satisfactory work-life balance by spending more time with their family, but at the cost of lower wages, poor career opportunities and reduced job security. A third group of men attempt to combine care and career by working full-time, but caring for their children as much as possible outside work, and experience a 'time squeeze' and work-life strain as a result. Halrynjo's research is particularly innovative in identifying what she terms "patchwork career men", who find their job stimulating but "put work in its place", reject traditional career norms and combine part-time or temporary work with home responsibilities and with other leisure or artistic pursuits. These men are in a minority. Thus, men are shown to adapt to the different demands of work and family life in different, albeit gendered ways, which also presumably depend on negotiations in the couple. Tracey Warren, Elizabeth Fox and Gillian Pascal, using data from the British Household Panel Survey, examine the ways in which the gendered nature of employment shapes the choices of low-waged women in England in relation to their caring and employed lives. Low-waged women represent a sizeable proportion of the female workforce and their employment is characterized by low hourly wages and a high preponderance of part-time work. Familiar work-life balance measures, such as flexitime or job sharing are not available to them. Since their partners are most often also in low-wage employment or not employed, these women also have limited access to private childcare. Warren *et al.*, interviewed a smaller sample of (35) male-female couples in order to investigate their childcare strategies and found a variety of strategies based largely on informal care arrangements and shifting patterns of shared childcare in the couple, reinforcing traditional gender roles. Informal care and recourse to part-time work represent expressed preferences, but the authors argue that they also reflect financial and labour market constraints, in the relative absence of affordable formal childcare. In particular, long male working hours create strains on family life as well as on women's ability to access better-paid employment. Rather than greater provision of formal childcare, the authors identify a strong demand for working-time reduction and for parental leave policies in order to give both men and women a better balance between work and family, particularly for low-waged couples. Exploring similar issues relating to the ways that men and women negotiate the relationship between paid work and other areas of life, Carol Emslie and Kate Hunt look more closely at caring responsibilities of Scottish men and women in mid-life, using a life course approach. They focus on the mutual interactions and spillovers between paid employment and home life which, they argue, are often interpreted in a gender-neutral way. Emslie and Hunt take another approach, seeking to integrate gender more fully into such interpretations, in particular Sue Campbell Clark's 'work-family border' theory, which aims to explain how people "manage and negotiate the work and family spheres and the borders between them in order to attain balance" (Clark, 2000:750). Their qualitative, small-scale research (based on a small, representative sub-sample of a larger longitudinal database) reveals how work-life strains were experienced by interviewees over the life course in a gendered way, with women using images of 'juggling' to describe their coping strategies and middle-class women, in particular, expressing their sense of sacrifice. The male interviewees, on the other hand, were found to accept work-life conflict as natural. Emslie and Hunt's article, like that of Warren, *et al.*, also highlights the impact of social class position on work-life choices. The manual workers in their sample tended to display pragmatic attitudes towards paid employment and had a stronger sense than middle-class women of boundaries between work and home life. Thus, work-life boundaries are not only gendered but are also mediated by people's socioeconomic position, and in addition, as Emslie and Hunt show, they may shift over the life course as gender identities are reconfigured.

Work-life Balance: A Matter of Choice?

In this article I have sought to address the question whether work-life balance is freely determined by individuals or whether it is constrained by a wide range of factors operating at a micro (individual), meso (organizational) and macro (national) level. The articles presented here draw us into the wider debate over the role of structure and agency in determining women's labour-force behaviour (Hakim, 2000). They demonstrate that individual choice is constrained by organizational culture, which in turn is strongly related to sector-specific cultures (as in engineering or knowledge work, for example). Individual choice is also circumscribed by prevailing national gender cultures and expectations and labour market opportunities. In addition to gender, the articles bring to our attention the variation in preferences and constraints available to individuals according to their socio-economic group, and the stage in their individual life course. They also substantiate earlier research (das Dores Guerreiro & Pereira, 2007; Gambles *et al.*, 2007) finding that organizations play a crucial mediating role in this complex and dynamic set of relationships. The articles highlight the work-life balance challenges posed by new organizational practices and strongly gendered organizational and national cultures. At the same time they give us some pointers for improving employees' work-life balance. Most importantly perhaps, they demonstrate the limitations of adaptive strategies for achieving work-life balance and the need for collective rights to back up individual choice, as in the case of parental leave in the Nordic context. Giving fathers specific leave entitlements and framing rights to, for example, working-time reduction in a gender-neutral way can both represent a way forward for men and for women and help to rebalance the gender division of labour.

Steps to a Work-Life Balance

The coupling of increased workloads with technology that keeps us constantly connected to our jobs finds an increasing number of workers feeling overwhelmed, discouraged and depleted. In 2006, 53 per cent of employees felt they had a good work-life balance, according to a Corporate Executive Board (CEB) report. That number fell to 30 per cent in the first quarter of 2009, the CEB reported. Many employees today are so busy making a living that they have no time to make a life. In contrast, numerous studies have shown the most productive employees are well-rounded professionals with full and well-balanced lives — both in and out of the workplace. Likewise, the most successful companies are those that foster employee health and well-being while enhancing organizational performance and productivity.

Today work-life balance ranks as one of the most important workplace attributes — second only to compensation, and workers who feel they have a better work-life balance tend to work 21 per cent harder than employees who feel overworked.

Achieving a healthy work-life balance requires managing our professional and personal life in sustainable ways that keep our energy flowing, our minds and bodies healthy and our whole selves happy and content. It means giving due attention to all of the things that enrich and fulfil us including work and career, health and fitness, family and relationships, spirituality, community service, hobbies and passions, intellectual stimulation, rest and recreation.

To get there:

1. **Track Your Time:** Analysing your present situation is the beginning step in achieving a balanced life. Keep a time log of everything you do for one week, including work-related and personal activities. This data will serve as an eye-opener, helping you understand how you are using — and where you are losing — your time.
2. **Determine Your Priorities:** Spend some time seriously reflecting on what is most important to you, and make a list of your top priorities at work and at home. Then analyse your time audit by asking yourself these key questions: What do I need to Start doing? Stop doing? Continue doing? Do more of? Do less of? Do differently?
3. **Set Specific Goals:** Take your list of priorities and turn them into concrete and measurable goals. Block time into your schedule for activities just like you would for an important meeting or a doctor's appointment.
4. **Schedule Scrupulously:** Successful people plan their work and then work their plan. You have one life, so have one date planner. Whether paper or electronic, this is the vehicle by which you turn your priorities and goals into reality. Set aside 10 to 20 minutes at the beginning of each day (or the night before) to plan your tasks and activities for the day and evening ahead.
5. **Establish Boundaries:** Set fair and realistic limits on what you will and will not do both at work and at home. Clearly

communicate these boundaries to your supervisor, coworkers, partner and family. For instance, you might commit to not working late on certain days unless there is a crisis. Additionally, set aside a time at home during which you will not check or respond to work-related emails or voice mails.

6. **Take Care of Your Health:** Your health should always be your No. 1 priority. If you are not in good shape physically, mentally, and emotionally, both your work life and your personal life will suffer. Take care of yourself by eating healthy meals (especially breakfast), exercise at least three times per week and sleep a minimum of seven hours per night. While you may not think you have time to add exercise and extra sleep to your jam-packed schedule, these practices relieve stress, raise your energy level, increase your stamina, improve your mental clarity, boost your immune system, and make you a happier, more engaged, and more productive person. Additionally, refrain from the excessive use of alcohol, tobacco, or drugs to relieve stress. These substances only tend to keep the body in a stressed state and cause even more problems.
7. **Nurture Your Family/Relationships:** Relationships with family, friends, and loved ones are, by far, the greatest source of inner satisfaction. If your job or career is damaging your personal relationships, both areas will ultimately suffer. Sure there will be days when you will need to work overtime. The issue becomes problematic when these days become the rule, not the exception. By making your personal relationships a priority, your productivity and effectiveness on the job will actually increase.
8. **Make Time for You:** As much as work, health, and relationships take priority in your life, it is also important to schedule time for your own renewal. Indulge in some small pleasure daily. Take at least 30 minutes of uninterrupted "you time". It will do wonders for your well-being, and your relationships and your career will benefit too. Connect with your spiritual source. Belief in God, or a higher power, can be a deep well from which to draw inspiration, guidance, and strength. Setting aside a weekly day of rest can be helpful, as well.
9. **Leave Work at Work:** Develop a mental on-off switch between work and home. It helps to establish a transitional activity between the two realms. This might consist of listening to music or recorded books during your evening commute,

exercising at the fitness center, running errands, or keeping personal appointments. Scheduling such activities immediately following your normal work hours also prevents you from spending that extra twenty minutes at the office which then turns into several hours.

10. **Exercise Your Options:** Many forward-thinking companies today are creating policies and programmes that facilitate work-life balance. Find out what options your business offers in terms of flex hours, telecommuting, a compressed work week, job-sharing, or part-time employment. You may find an arrangement that allows you to work more productively, while at the same time cutting stress and freeing-up valuable personal/family time. If your company does not yet have a flexible scheduling programme, consider proposing one.
11. **Work Smarter Not Harder:** Using time more efficiently is an important skill that everyone from the receptionist to the CEO can learn. Adopting the right combination of time-management practices can cut stress and save you up to an hour a day. This can include the use of technology to become more organized, grouping emails and voice messages, avoiding procrastination and learning to say "no".
12. **Know When to Ask for Help:** If you are overwhelmed at work, and it is causing undue stress do not suffer in silence. Shed the Superwoman/Superman image and explain your situation to your boss or supervisor. Untenable work situations can usually be alleviated, but it will take some assertiveness on your part. Similarly, if a balanced life continues to elude you, or you are experiencing chronic stress, talk with a professional — a counsellor, mental health worker, or clergy person. Take advantage of the services offered by your employee assistance programme. Try as we all may, work-life balance is not an exact science. Each person must find his or her own way of combining career, relationships, and personal care into an integrated whole. What is right for you now will likely change as new circumstances arise, so periodically review your situation and adjust accordingly. Do not get overwhelmed by assuming that you need to make big changes all at once. Even if you implement only a few of the above strategies, they will have a positive and measurable impact in your life. Start with one clear goal — then add another, and another. The process of achieving a healthy work-life balance is like becoming a

Clark, S.C. (2000). "Work/family Border Theory: A New Theory of Work/family Balance", *Human Relations*, 53(6): 747-70.

Cockburn, C. (1991). *In the Way of Women: Men's Resistance to Sex Equality in Organizations*, London: MacMillan & Co.

Cooper, M. (2000). "Being the 'Go-to Guy': Fatherhood, Masculinity and the Organization of Work in Silicon Valley", *Qualitative Sociology*, 23(4): 379-405.

Coser, L.A. (1974). *Greedy Institutions: Patterns of Undivided Commitment*, New York: Free Press.

Crompton, R. (2006). *Employment and the Family: The Reconfiguration of Work and Family Life in Contemporary Societies*, Cambridge: Cambridge University Press.

Crompton, R. & Brockmann, M. (2007). "Class, Gender and Work-life Articulation", in Perrons, D.; Fagan, C.; McDowell, L.; Ray, K. & Ward, K. (eds.), *Gender Divisions and Working Time in the New Economy: Changing Patterns of Work, Care and Public Policy in Europe and North America*, pp. 103-122, Cheltenham: Edward Elgar.

Crompton, R. & Lyonette, C. (2007). "Occupational Class, Country and the Domestic Division of Labour", in Crompton, R.; Lewis, S. & Lyonette, C. (eds.), *Women, Men, Work and Family in Europe*, pp. 116-32, London: Palgrave.

Das Dores Guerreiro, M. & Pereira, I. (2007). "Women's Occupational Patterns and Work-family Arrangements: Do National and Organizational Policies Matter?", in Crompton, R.; Lewis, S. & Lyonette, C. (eds.), *Women, Men, Work and Family in Europe*, pp. 171-89, London: Palgrave.

Dex, S. & Smith, C. (2002). *The Nature and Pattern of Family-Friendly Employment in Britain*, Bristol: Policy Press and Joseph Rowntree Foundation.

Duncan, S. (2007). "Mothers' Work-life Balance: Individualized Preferences or Cultural Construction?", in Perrons, D.; Fagan, C.; McDowell, L.; Ray, K. & Ward, K. (eds.), *Gender Divisions and Working Time in the New Economy: Changing Patterns of Work, Care and Public Policy in Europe and North America*, pp. 127-47.

Esping-Andersen, G. (1999). *Social Foundations of Post-industrial Economies*, Oxford: Oxford University Press.

Felstead, A.; Jewson, N.; Phizacklea, A. & Walters, S. (2002). "Opportunities to Work at Home in the Context of Work-life Balance", *Human Resource Management Journal*, 12(1): 54-76.

Fleetwood, S. (2007). "Why Work-life Balance Now?", *International Journal of Human Resource Management*, 18(3): 387-400.

Gallie, D. (2005). "Work Pressure in Europe 1996-2001: Trends and Determinants", *British Journal of Industrial Relations*, 43(3): 351-75.

Gambles, R.; Lewis, S. & Rapoport, R. (2006). *Work-personal Life Harmonization*, Chichester: Wiley.

Gambles, R.; Lewis, S. & Rapoport, R. (2007). "Evolutions and Approaches to Equitable Divisions of Paid Work and Care in three European Countries: A Multi-level Challenge", in Crompton, R.; Lewis, S. & Lyonette, C. (eds.), *Women, Men, Work and Family in Europe*, pp. 17-34, London: Polity Press.

Gray, M. & Tudball, J. (2003). "Family-friendly Work Practices: Differences within and between Workplaces", *Journal of Industrial Relations*, 45(3): 269-91.

Green, F. & Tsitsianis, N. (2005). "An Investigation of National Trends in Job Satisfaction in Britain and Germany", *British Journal of Industrial Relations*, 43(3): 401-29.

Greenhaus, J.H.; Collins, K.M. & Shaw, J.D. (2003). "The Relation between Work-family Balance and Quality of Life", *Journal of Vocational Behaviour*, 63(3): 510-31.

Greenhaus, J.H. & Singh, R. (2003). *Work-family Linkages: A Sloan Work and Family Encyclopedia Entry*. Available online at *http://wfnetwork.bc.edu/encyclopaedia_entry.php?id=263&area=All Last consulted 1 October 2008.*

Gregory, A. & Milner, S. (2006). "Les entreprises et la conciliation de la vie professionnelle et familiale: vers le mod le du 'p re au travail'?", *Recherches et Prévisions*, 85, June, 5-16.

Gregory, A. & Milner, S. (2008). *Fathers and Work-life Balance in French and British Organizations*, Paper presented to the European Work and Employment Research Centre, Manchester Business School, 27 February.

Haar, J. & Spell, C.S. (2003). "Where is the Justice? Examining Work-family Backlash in New Zealand: The Potential for Employee Resentment", *New Zealand Journal of Industrial Relations*, 28(1): 59-75.

Hakim, C. (2000). *Work-lifestyle Choices in the Twenty-First Century*, Oxford: Oxford University Press.

Houston, D. (ed.) (2005). *Work-life Balance in the Twenty-First Century*, Basingstoke/ New York: Palgrave.

Lee, M.D.; MacDermid, S.M. & Buck, M.L. (2000). "Organizational Paradigms of Reduced-load Work: Accommodation, Elaboration and Transformation", *Academy of Management Journal*, 43(6): 1211-26.

Lewis, S. & Cooper, C. (2005). *Work-life Integration: Case Studies of Organizational Change*, Chichester: Wiley.

Lewis, S.; Gambles, R. & Rapoport, R. (2007). "The Constraints of a Work-life Balance Approach: An International Perspective", *International Journal of Human Resource Management*, 18(3): 360-73.

McDonald, P.; Brown, K. & Bradley, L. (2005). "Explanations for the Provision Utilization Gap in Work-life Policy", *Women in Management Review*, 20(1): 37-55.

Organization for Economic Co-operation and Development (OECD) (2004). *Babies and Bosses — Reconciling Work and Family Life*, Vol. 4: Canada, Finland, Sweden, UK, Paris: OECD.

Perrons, D.; Fagan, C.; McDowell, L.; Ray, K. & Ward, K. (2007). *Gender Divisions and Working Time in the New Economy: Changing Patterns of Work, Care and Public Policy in Europe and North America.*

Pocock, B. (2005). "Work-life 'Balance' in Australia: Limited Progress, Dim Prospects", *Asia Pacific Journal of Human Resources*, 43(2): 198-209.

Rapoport, R.; Bailyn, L.; Fletcher, J.K. & Pruitte, B. (2002). *Beyond Work-family Balance: Advancing Gender Equity and Workplace Performance*, San Francisco, CA: Jossey Bass.

Singley, S. & Hynes, K. (2005). "Transitions to Parenthood: Work-family Policies, Gender and the Couple Context", *Gender & Society*, 19(3): 376-97.

Smithson, J. & Stokoe, E.H. (2005). "Discourses of Work-life Balance: Negotiating 'Genderblind' Terms in Organizations", *Gender, Work & Organization*, 12(2): 147-68.

Thornthwaite, L. (2004). "Working Time and Work-family Balance: A Review of Employees' Preferences", *Asia Pacific Journal of Human Resources*, 42(2): 166-84.

White, M.; Hill, S.; McGovern, P.; Mills, C. & Smeaton, D. (2003). "'High-performance' Management Practices, Working Hours and Work-life Balance", *British Journal of Industrial Relations*, 41(2): 175-95.

9

Gender Equality: A Far Cry

Issue of Feminine Freedom in Literary and Real Life Contexts

Shreosi Biswas

Feminism is a serious attempt to formulate issues and find solutions to gender problems. It was started by Simone de Beauvoir in *The Second Sex* (1949) and gained momentum in the 1960s. The core belief of feminist theory and criticism asserts that all people—women and men — are politically, socially and economically equal. Although diverse in its social theories, values, and politics, feminist criticism chiefly advocates for the rights of women. The feminist critics believe that the women must define their roles, their values, their aspirations, and their places in the society. And to do so women must analyse and challenge the established literary canon that has shaped the ideas and images of female inferiority and subordination. Women must also challenge the patriarchal assumptions about their sex and gender. Through a re-examination of the established literature in all disciplines, by defining and validating what it means to be a woman, and by establishing and creating feminist literary theories and criticism, women can secure autonomy and power.

Kate Millet's *Sexual Politics* (1970) makes a distinction between 'sex' and 'gender'. 'Sex' is determined biologically, whereas 'gender' is culturally, socially and psychologically constructed through sex-role stereotyping and historical conditioning. Millet argues that women as much as men are responsible in perpetuating the existing sex-role images. The proponents of the feminist literary theories assert that in this patriarchal world woman has become the 'other', the 'not-male'. Man is the subject, the one who defines meaning. Woman is the object, having her existence defined and determined by the male. The feminist theorists and critics endeavour to correct such erroneous ways of thinking. Women, they assert, are individuals and are people in their own right. They are, by no means, incomplete or inferior to men. But quite frequently literature and society have marginalized and stereotyped females as angels, barmaids, brainless housewives, whores etc.

Virginia Woolf, though not a feminist in the modern sense, was an important writer who in her book *A Room of One's Own* examined certain problems which women usually have to face. She advocated a balance between a 'male' self-realization and 'female' self-annihilation. She rejected the notion of a separate feminist consciousness and hoped to achieve a femininity of the unconscious, so, that there is no conflict between male and female sexuality, an "escape from the confrontation with femaleness and maleness". Very meaningfully, Woolf contrasts the actual condition of women in society with that depicted in literature from time to time:

> Imaginatively she is of the highest importance; practically she is completely insignificant. She pervades poetry from cover to cover; she is all but absent from history. She dominates the lives of kings and conquerors in fiction; in fact she was the slave of any boy whose parents forced a ring upon her finger. Some of the most inspired words, some of the most profound thoughts in literature fall from her lips; in real life she could hardly read, could scarcely spell, and was the property of her husband. It was certainly an odd monster that one made up by reading the historians first and the poets afterwards — a worm winged like an eagle; the spirit of life and beauty in a kitchen chopping up suet. But these monsters, however, amusing to the imagination, have no existence in fact (36-37).

Woolf gives the example of Shakespeare's sister to describe the difficulties of working women. Shakespeare's sister, supposedly named Judith, may have taken birth with the same imaginative quality and genius of Shakespeare, but she had to face innumerable adversaries throughout her life, which her brother Shakespeare, because he is a male, never suffered — not educated, pressure of household works, betrothed before age, emotional blackmail from family, ridiculed by patriarchal society, used and ditched for carnality, ultimately raped or committed suicide. Woolf questions, "who shall measure the heat and violence of the poet's heart when caught and tangled in a woman's body?" (40) Women were not allowed to culture and attain the genius of Shakespeare: ". . . it was impossible for any women, past, present, or to come, to have the genius of Shakespeare" (39).

Though Woolf mainly talks of the Elizabethan women, still the problems faced by women can explicitly be related to contemporary society. It is true that most of the women are educated today, except in some Muslim countries like Iraq and Afghanistan. Still, women hardly have sitting-rooms to themselves. They have to look after their children and household from early morning to late night, and though a large section of women today are working, the general pay scale for women is far less and unjustified compared to that for men in the same job status. All heads get turned on the big question of how much Bollywood actresses are paid ever since Kangana Ranaut came out strongly against the disparity in the pay checks compared to their male counterparts in the industry. For instance, the highest paid actor earns at least four times the highest paid actress does! While the fee of the Indian actors keeps on increasing with each film, indicating that there is no recession in our industry, it has remained static for the actresses. With a surge in female-centric films and their successful outing at the box office, our female leads have begun questioning the long-standing disparity and sought equality. Apart from Kangana, Vidya Balan and Katrina Kaif have also been vocal about it:

> Remuneration has changed but if you compare it with what the men get it is still very different. But I would say let's not compare it because just five per cent of these films are being made. I think we will get our due. We are slowly moving towards that. – *Vidya Balan*

In Katrina Kaif's words:

> Indian cinema has come a long way. But one thing which has not changed is the remuneration for women. There is still a huge disparity. Let's see what happens with that.

(https://amp.indiatimes.com/entertainment/bollywood/11-bollywood-actresses-pay-packages-revealed-but-it-s-the-men-who-are-raking-in-the-moolah-247365.html)

Priyanka Chopra has taken over international television with her hit show 'Quantico'. The actress, who has made her presence felt on all media platforms, has time and again spoken up for the cause of women. After talking about the importance of gender equality in the film industry, the actress has now spoken about the disparity in pay between male and female actors.

This pay gap is equally huge in many other job sectors. In information and communication technology services, the average gender pay gap is 38.2 per cent. Women earn ₹ 142.5 less per hour than men. The gender pay gap in the financial services, banking and insurance sector amounts to 21.5 per cent. This is slightly under the general gender pay gap in India (25%). On average, men earn an hourly median wage of ₹ 346.4 and women ₹ 272. In 2016, however, wages rose by ₹ 144.3 (+45.4%) for male employees and by ₹ 79.5 (+29.8%) for female employees. Therefore, while the gender pay gap shrank slightly from 2014 to 2015, it grew again in 2016 to 25 per cent. In the education and research sector, the gender pay gap amounts to 14.7 per cent on an average. It is nearly 10 percentage points below the overall level of 25 per cent. Hourly median wages for men have risen by 7 per cent from ₹ 190.5 to ₹ 203.8 between 2014 and 2016. Women also gained more in 2016 than 2014 as much as ₹ 50.5 (32.8%). The gender pay gap increased again from 19.2 per cent and 13.1 per cent in 2014 and 2015, respectively, to – 3.4 per cent in 2016. On an average, a 22.6 per cent gender gap exists in the healthcare, caring services, and social work sector. Male employees earned ₹ 242.4, female employees ₹ 187.6 per hour (– ₹ 54.8). The gender pay gap was smallest in 2015 with only ₹ 8.3 (3.6%) making wages nearly equal. In 2016, however, the gap increased significantly to ₹ 103.3 (39.9%). In construction and technical consultancy, on an average, men earned ₹ 52.2 more than women. Thus there is a gender pay gap of 18.1 per cent. Men witnessed a minor wage increase of ₹ 6.4 (2014-2015) and a major increase of ₹ 18.3 (2015-2016). On an average, the gender pay gap in the legal and market consultancy and business activities sector is 27.5 per cent (₹ 73.9) per hour. Women earn ₹ 195, men ₹ 268.9. Wages for male employees seem to stabilize at ₹ 259.8 after a drop of ₹ 6.4 in 2015. Women's wages in the sector decreased in 2015. The gender pay gap seems to be growing as in 2015 it was 27.9 per cent, but rose significantly to 42.4 in 2016. Finally, in the transport, logistics and communications sector, women remain underpaid by 5.2 per cent. Wages of men went up after a drop in 2015 to reach ₹ 264.4 in 2016. Those for female employees increased in 2015, but then decreased more than 8 per cent to stay at ₹ 244.1. The gender pay gap in 2016 is around ₹ 20 (7.7%).

(www.livemint.com/Industry/n6vXUU0TRB44SFg6uXSRel/Indian-men-earn-25-more-than-women-Monster-Salary-Index.html)

Not only in pay scale, the patriarchal bias is evident everywhere. Women are harassed in day to day work life-public ridicule by boss, stagnation and hurdles in promotion, illicit offers by colleagues, undue advantages taken by 'friends' and so called well-wishers, and even jealousy of other women. This whole scenario is perfectly presented by Vijay Tendulkar in his 1963 Marathi play Shantata! Court Chalu Aahe (*Silence! The Court is in Session*). Kumud Mehta in his 'Introduction' to Tendulkar's play observes that in the play "What began as a game has evolved into a hunt". (Tendulkar Introduction vi) A reader, as he or she proceeds through the play, realizes the truth of Mehta's observation. In course of the mock trial of Miss Benare on the charge of infanticide, all the co-actors heap charges on her. She is cornered and maliciously attacked by all her companions. Her personal life is publicly scandalized. Her love-life, which is purely personal, is exposed with the open intention of deriving sadistic pleasure. The mock trial which started merely as a game soon becomes a very serious affair. Miss Benare, who started paying her role as the accused in a playful, facetious manner, becomes grim, stunned and silent by the severity of the charges on her. She is shocked and almost frozen in anguish at this unexpected turn of the situation. Her voice is choked and she is full of tears. The spirited, lively and frank-hearted Miss Benare is forcibly silenced.

Rokde's witness first changes the playful game-like atmosphere maintained in the beginning. He reveals the bit of information that he saw Miss Benare in Prof. Damle's room late in the evening, suggesting clearly that she has an illegitimate love relationship with Prof. Damle. If Rokde consciously damages Miss Benare's honour to take revenge on her, Samant quite unconsciously leads her to further troubles. For Samant, the whole mock trial is a fun, absolutely untrue. So, he reads from a cheap novel in his witness, but coincidentally what he says from the book perfectly matches Miss Benare's present state of life. She loved Prof. Damle and has been made pregnant by him. But the man has denied his responsibility. Miss Benare finds herself trapped and made the target of a severe psychological torture by others. Her condition worsens as Ponkshe in his witness further reveals how Miss Benare met him secretly in the Udipi restaurant with a request of marriage. Her early heart-breaking affair with her maternal uncle and her unsuccessful attempt to commit suicide out of frustration — all are revealed. She becomes extremely agonized and speechless in the end. She stands cornered, thrashed, humiliated and hunted by her companions and co-actors.

Towards the end of the play the atmosphere becomes really serious. Kashikar and Sukhatme, the self-styled guardians of the society, talk in a grave voice the corruptions in the society due to the moral depravity of women like Miss Benare. The hypocrisy and cruelty of the male associates of Miss Benare make the atmosphere quite heavy. And silence deepens in the court room when Miss Benare delivers her moving monologue. Silence also deepens in the minds of the audience and readers at the exposure of male chauvinism and hypocrisy in the so called progressive society of the urban middle class. Her monologue at the fag end of the play expresses her pent up, long suppressed feelings, and at the same time it becomes a fitting reply to the accusations made against her in the mock-trial.

As Miss Benare stands up to speak, the whole court 'freezes'. She starts in the form of self-meditation:

> For many years, I have not said a word. Chances came and chances went. Storms raged one after another about my throat. And there was a wail like death in my heart. But each time I shut my lips tight. (72)

Her agonized inner self is gradually explored. She admits painfully that 'life was a burden' to her. However, this negative attitude to life is only a passing thought. For, a contrary feeling soon comes to her and she thinks that, "There's great joy in a suicide that's failed". (73) In her long speech Miss Benare shifts quickly from one state and situation to another — from classroom to courtroom, from meditative reflections to painful confessions. In a classroom manner she talks of the pains and deceits of her life: "Life is a betrayal. Life is a fraud. Life is a drug". (73) But in the next moment she takes up a courtroom attitude and seems to appeal to the Judge: "Milord, life is a very dreadful thing. Life must be hanged". (73) Sometimes, again, Miss Benare becomes furious to think how her employers have punished her, not because of any lapse in her profession as a teacher, but because of something that is exclusively personal to her. She demands, "My private life is my own business. I'll decide what to do with myself". (73) She accuses all men as 'hypocrites'. Commenting on her co-actors she observes, "These are the mortal remains of some cultured men of the twentieth century. See their faces-how ferocious they look!" (74) She is frightened by those who are all around her.

In the second half of the monologue Miss Benare becomes more confessional and remembers how she fell in love with her mother's brother. The man was not a lover, but rather a pervert who had his eyes only on her new blossomed beauty. So, when it comes to marriage this "brave man turned tail and ran". (74) She made an attempt to commit suicide by jumping off the parapet of their house, but survived. Again, as a grown up woman she loves Professor Damle for his intellect, and offered herself. He too cared for her body alone. He too ignores and abandons her when she is in trouble. So, she screams in utter frustration: "This body is a traitor!" (75) However, she soon asserts that she now must have her body for the baby in her womb. Miss Benare's monologue is a powerful defence of herself against the ruthless attacks of the so called upholders of social norms, who can hardly tolerate a successful and economically independent woman like her. She contrasts sharply all the emotionally starved and unsuccessful men who vindictively prosecute her. The long monologue artistically elevates the play from the farcical plain which it occupied during the mock-trial to the level of serious consideration about the double standard of the male dominated Indian society.

Having talked of the oppression of women in various professions, we once more may look back to Virginia Woolf's *A Room of One's Own* to get a clear idea of the treatment of the society in general towards, and as a result the fatal condition of, women who were writers or those who wanted to be one:

> When, however, one reads of a witch being ducked, of a woman possessed by devils, of a wise woman selling herbs, or even of a very remarkable man who had a mother, then I think we are on the track of a lost novelist, a suppressed poet, of some mute and inglorious Jane Austen, some Emily Brontë who dashed her brains out on the moor or mopped and mowed about the highways crazed with the torture that her gift had put her to (41) . . . It was the relic of the sense of chastity that dictated anonymity to women even so late as the nineteenth century. Currer Bell, George Eliot, George Sand, all the victims of inner strife as their writings prove, sought ineffectively to veil themselves by using the name of a man (42). . . . Mr. Oscar Browning was wont to declare "that the impression left on his mind, after looking over any set of examination papers, was that, irrespective of the marks he might give, the best woman was intellectually the inferior of the worst man" (45). . . . The history of men's opposition to women's emancipation is more interesting perhaps than the story of that emancipation itself (46).

The struggle for freedom and identity of women, it is needless to say, is a long process. So many historical, social, political and economic considerations are closely associated with this. Starting from sixteenth century Italian society, the cultural and political power was held mostly by men. There was a growing concern for female chastity, legitimacy and purity of blood. But curiously and unjustifiably, such a concern was only exclusively directed towards women. Men were not considered responsible for maintaining fidelity in relationships and purity of blood. The noblewomen were universally dependent on the husband and family. The renaissance love theory of Italian courts was indifferent to the interests of women. The lady was bound to merely procreative sex of political marriage. Women were denied the right and power to love. Women were transformed into passive 'others' who were only meant to serve. Observations of Kelly are quite relevant in this connection. Kelly writes: "Renaissance ideals on love and manners, more classical than medieval, and almost exclusively a male product, expressed this new subordination of women to the interests of husbands and male-dominated kin groups and served to justify the removal of women from an 'unladylike' position of power and erotic independence. All the advances of Renaissance Italy, its protocapitalist economy, its states, and its humanistic culture, worked to mold the noblewoman into an aesthetic object: decorous, chaste, and doubly dependent on her husband as well as the prince" (Kelly, 197).

The male-oriented and partial ideals of the Renaissance Italy were strictly followed by eighteenth and nineteenth century bourgeoisie England. The eighteenth century was an age of literary prolificacy. It was also the age of proper formation of the new genre in literature, namely the novel. Besides being titled as the Age of Reason, Neoclassical Age, Augustan Age etc., the eighteenth century was also called the age of experimentation (from French 'experimenter', meaning 'to experience'). While authors like Richardson, Fielding, Smollett *et al.*, were bringing out their first-hand experiences on novel writing, the women were certainly not far behind. I would like to draw attention on one such female author whose works in her lifetime were a super hit, starting from her very first novel, but is not usually read today. She is none other than Frances (Fanny) Burney, the just predecessor of Jane Austen.

The body of woman is seen as a repository of honour and propriety which is the chief cause behind their loss of job and economic power in the society. The patriarchal society wanted their women to be confined within the domestic spheres as an ornament or a show-piece. Not only that, they were constantly kept under strict vigilance. Having no work, therefore, it became almost a necessity for women to read and write to pass their time. This may also be a reason why many of the novels in this period had women protagonists. The novelists were aware of the fact that the primary readers of their works were the women. Men could not stop women from reading. Hence, they became more concerned about what type of books should reach the women. The reason behind the excessive concern over the question of morality and immorality in eighteenth century novels may fruitfully be traced in the condition of the women, specially the educated upper class women, of the contemporary society.

The eighteenth century, again, was the age of industrialization and urbanization. London society was bursting with many new libidinous people with different professions. People, especially women, had to rub shoulders with many unknown people, men in particular. That was why the 'conduct-book' for women was very necessary — how a woman should behave in society, whether or not she is supposed to accept a ball-dance offer, how to say 'no' to a man, and how to stand, sit, walk, talk etc. in public. Governesses were kept for young girls to train them how to enter the public world. The governesses also read and decided which books should or should not be offered to the young girls. The common dress for women was 'crinoline' (a Victorian gown having a wooden frame). Crinoline is also the name for a stiff coarse fabric used to stiffen clothing. The gowns were made of this fabric. It restrained the free movement of women. Their legs were tightly bound. They could not walk, sit, work, or stretch or do anything freely and properly. Every possible measure was taken by the patriarchal society, so, that the young girls or women do not get detached from acquaintances and find themselves lost in a rowdy crowd which approaches them in inappropriate manners.

Women who tried to write or publish their writings were called, rather derogatively, quill drivers or scribblers. This was because writing, specially a novel, meant expressing their feelings which were likely to be read by the whole world. Thus, the women were exposing their souls to the public. Such an exposure of feminine selves to the world was nothing better than prostitution and women writers were sometimes called whores. For a woman, expression of feelings to the public was treated almost as disgraceful as the exposure of her body to others. The people in general thus could know about her, and get an access into her life. The world would try to find her out and be ready to pounce upon her since she allowed herself to be a public property through her writings. Writing novels was paralleled with trading an intimate part of one's own self.

Fanny Burney, we should keep in mind, wrote her novels in such a discouraging social atmosphere. She was the third among the six siblings, and she lost her mother at the age of ten. She was neither sent to school, nor had any governess to teach her at home. But the spirit of writing was in her blood. Literary aspiration, combined with an open access to her father's library, instilled in her the desire to carve out a career for herself. But during her time, the process of writing, especially for a woman, was a continuous frustration. In order to write, a woman had to manage or manipulate various conditions in her favour. To be seen writing was considered a sin. She had to steal time for writing. One had to get secret opportunities to be able to write. The publication of her writings was, quite understandably, was almost impossible for a woman. Due to such constant and continuous frustrations (also perhaps due to the dominant presence of step-mother in her life), Fanny burnt down all her writings on her fifteenth birthday. But her passion did not die. Fanny was acutely aware of the position of women writers during her time. When *Evelina* was complete, the question arose for its publication. Her father was a musicologist, and she used to scribe for her father's works. So, before sending the manuscript of the novel to the publisher for publication, she feigned her handwriting, so, that it could not be traced. The manuscript was taken to the publisher by her brother who was disguised in a long overcoat and a large hat, so, that he could not be traced either. Thus, Fanny wanted badly to publish her novel amidst such obstacles. She badly wanted Evelina, the protagonist of her first novel *Evelina, Or the History of a Young Lady's Entrance into the World* to enter the world.

This struggle of women to make their own space in the patriarchal society and live according to their rules and views has been a continuing process. If there had been a Frances Burney, an Evelina in the eighteenth century who could go to any extreme to give success to her economic independence, there is a Rosie in the twentieth century who would do anything for dance which is her life-long vocation. She even leaves her husband in such a time and place (i.e. India) when/where marriage is considered sacred and of greatest significance in the life of a woman. Rosie in R.K. Narayan's novel *The Guide* is, in fact, as multi-faceted a personality as Raju, the protagonist of the novel. She was destined to be a '*devdasi*', but she raises herself much above the expected height. She becomes an M.A. in Economics, marries a very scholarly person, and acquires a social identity for herself. Though, she is later rejected by her husband for infidelity, she becomes a very successful professional dancer. Rosie is self-assertive. She is child like in following her desires without giving thought to consequences, and a woman of the world in the way she manages her career after her separation from Raju after his forgery of her signature. She is not only utterly sincere and totally committed to her art, but also has considerable knowledge of its classical traditions. She partly challenges the orthodox Hindu conception of what a woman should be.

Rosie's non-traditional name is a marker of her social hybridity. She is unable to give her father's name, and thereby locate her social identity. She belongs to a caste and a class outside the organized patriarchal Hindu society. She hails from a family of '*devdasis*', and she is under no illusion as to how '*devdasis*' are regarded: "We are viewed as public women...We are not considered respectable; we are not considered civilized" (Narayan, 84). And the incident of Rosie's marriage to Marco from a newspaper matrimonial advertisement may be the result of Rosie's desperate endeavour to erase the stigma of belonging to a '*devdasi*' family. The result is a loveless, stifling marriage where Rosie is definitely the loser because she gains neither any emotional-physical compatibility, nor any artistic independence. Marco refuses to even recognize that dancing can be as important a mode of self-expression as archaeology, his own vocation. He literally insults her:

> This (Archaeology) is a branch of learning, not street-acrobatics. . . . An acrobat on a trapeze goes on doing the same thing all his life; well, your dance is like that. What is there intelligent or creative in it? You repeat your tricks all your life. We watch a monkey perform, not because it is artistic but because it is a monkey that is doing it (Narayan, 147-148).

Marco's words recall Dr. Samuel Johnson's views about women writers, as quoted by Virginia Woolf in her *A Room of One's Own:* "Sir, a woman's composing is like a dog's walking on his hind legs. It is not done well, but you are surprised to find it done at all" (46). It proves that for centuries women are being persecuted by the so called educated scholarly men, not only in India but around the world. This negligence from her husband indirectly inspires Rosie — an educated, self-conscious woman — to be attracted to Raju from whom she gets that emotional support as well as continuous encouragement for dancing. Thus, if she is morally fallen, her husband is no less responsible for it.

In the Rosie-Marco relationship it is usually Rosie who always enjoys the sympathy of the readers. Marco is strictly against her dancing, and punishes her by deserting her in the Malgudy station. Marco is obsessively engaged in his studies of ancient cave art. He dislikes being disturbed by anyone, even by his wife, in his studies and professional activities. Rather, he longs for appreciation from his wife which he himself can never give to Rosie. Marco never wanted a wife, but a servant in his life who would just give him food in time. That was the position of Rosie in his life. But Rosie too, on the other hand, had intellectual pursuit like Marco. She tells him that she has many ideas like him which in fact hurts the male ego of Marco and he takes it to be a competition: "Oh, you want to rival me, is that it?" (147). But truly, Rosie's interests are no less serious than his. She starts her dancing practice at five in the morning and continues for full three hours. In the afternoon, she spends her one or two hours by studying *Natya Shastra* of Bharat Muni in order to keep the purity of classical forms. She looks for the ideas in the *Ramayana* and the *Mahabharata*. But Marco finds nothing intellectual in her, which shows that Marco's approach to Rosie's aspiration is unimaginative and deliberately callous. This approach of Marco is incompatible with Rosie.

The women, it is quite evident, have still a long way to tread before they really may acquire gender equality with their male counterpart. One Sunita William or Kalpana Chawla may go to the outer space, a few Saina Nehawals or Serena Williams may achieve their dreams in the world of sports, or certain Priyanka Chopras may prove their talents in their respective fields. Even they may thus enjoy enviable freedom in their individual lives. But they are also not free from the angsts of gender discrimination both in private and in professional fields. And when such celebrities are occasional victims of gender inequalities, the numberless ordinary women who have almost no identities of their own can hardly even dream of gender equality in near future. Literature which is, in fact, a reflection of real life also confirms this truth.

REFERENCES

Beauvoir, Simone de (2010). *The Second Sex*, New York: Vintage Books.

"Bollywood Actresses Pay Packages". https://amp.indiatimes.com/entertainment/bollywood/11-bollywood-actresses-pay-packages-revealed-but-it-s-the-men-who-are-raking-in-the-moolah-247365.html.

Burney, Fanny (!994). *Evelina: Or the History of a Young Lady's Entrance into the World*, London: Penguin Books Ltd.

Gender Pay Gap. www.livemint.com/Industry/n6vXUU0 TRB44SFg6uXSRel/Indian-men-earn-25-more-than-women-Monster-Salary-Index.html.

Kate Millet (1970). *Sexual Politics*, New York: Columbia University Press.

Kelly, Joan (1984). *Women, History and Theory: The Essays of Joan Kelly*, Chicago: The University of Chicago Press.

Narayan, R.K. (2003). *The Guide*, Chennai: India Thought Publication.

Tendulkar, Vijay (2002). *Silence! The Court is is Session* (Translated by Priya Adarkar), New Delhi: Oxford University Press.

Woolf, Virginia (2002). *A Room of One's Own*, UK: Penguin Books Ltd.

10

Corporate Social Responsibility and Women Empowerment

Aastha Dhingra and *Amit Shekhar*

Introduction

Using sweatshops to manufacture designer clothes, pumping hazardous waste into water supplies, racial profiling within the workplace, wage discrimination based on sex, violations of labour laws, inhuman treatment in un-organized sector — the list goes on and on. Many of the common problems are found within nearly every major corporation across the world. In the heyday of *laissez faire* capitalism in Europe, the basic saying was to maximize profits. Social responsibility or charity while doing business had no place in this mass production scheme. The business of business is business. Business began merely as an institution for the purpose of making money. People felt no obligation and acknowledged no responsibility to the community or society amidst which they are operating or drawing productive resources. During the early years of Globalization decade, the corporate leveraged the opportunity to establish production units and use local resources without concern for future. But such an attitude does not hold well in the present situation. Globalization also created opportunities for human breed through scientific discoveries and innovations, which made the information dissemination and news propagation simpler and within reach of almost all sections of societies through telecommunication and media. This technological revolution has made societies aware and alert for larger interest and sustainable development processes, which also get reflected in change of related policy and approach of corporate governance for "responsible business". The recognition of social responsibility by the Corporate has been termed as emergence of "corporate conscience" which says that business is not an end in itself; rather it's only a means to an end. Society acts as fertilizer for business to grow, right from providing a ground till flourishing it successfully. Therefore, business has to contribute to human's happiness, his freedom, his material, moral and spiritual growth.

According to Keith Davis (1966) Social Responsibility begins where the law ends. A firm is not being socially responsible if it merely complies with the minimum requirements of the law because this is what any good citizen would do. Social responsibility goes one step further. It is a firm's acceptance of a social obligation beyond the requirements of law and envisions a larger change in society which is positive and sustainable.

After the Amendment of the Companies Act in 2013, the Corporate Social Responsibility (CSR) is not a fad or a passing trend, it has become a business imperative that many Indian Companies are essentially going to take up or are already engaging within one way or another. However, it remains as a concept whereby organizations consider the interests of society by taking responsibility for the impact of their activities on customers, suppliers, employees, shareholders, communities and the environment in all aspects of their operations.

The general principle of corporate social responsibility is that a company integrates "social values" into its decision-making, "so as to achieve positive and sustainable outcomes towards the business, environment and community at large". The concept of corporate social responsibilities originated in the year 1950 in USA. It came into prominence after public debate during 1960s and 1970s to meet the problem of poverty, unemployment, population growth, corruption, and women empowerment etc.

The sole objective of this chapter is to talk about the significant role of corporate to build society and to establish the fact that the society and corporate are interdependent, growth of both highly effect each other and also to focus light on women's significant but underrated role in the society as well as in national economy and corporate world.

Status of Women in India

Indian society is unique in terms of socio-demographic characteristics *vis-à-vis* because of the rich and ancient history of the land. The religious belief and cultural practices of India although recognizes women as important part of the society and consider them as deity or saint but on the other hand, the patriarchal mindset does not permit women to enjoy same socio-economic status as men do. Although, women represent 48 per cent of the total population in the country, but they face disparities in access to the control over services and resources. India's child sex ratio is 919/1000 males as per Census 2011. Over 40 per cent girls are married before age of 18 and 55 per cent pregnant women are anaemic. Gross enrolment for girls in schools is 34 per cent in secondary and dropout rate is 65 per cent. In 2015, overall literacy rate among women in India is 62.58 per cent only, much lower than male counterpart.

As growth-oriented and rapidly changing society in global platform, Indian society has to accept and recognize contribution of women in socio-cultural and economic spheres. As working mothers women give their blood and sweat to their family from managing it emotionally till providing financial support to their family needless to say women are backbones of family as well as society. Women are majority the ones who are more connected to natural resources whether it be agricultural field, water, forest etc. and hence, they are best preserver for natural resources also by default.

In corporate world, women are often kept away from key leadership roles such as CEO and out of the boardroom arguably because they are thought of as weak and non-competitive. Carol Gilligan's research is widely used to display the role forced upon women, making it difficult to break the glass ceiling and achieve the power-positions in the corporate world. Women are thought of as care givers who "will devote their lives to the needs of others and expend less energy on their own desires". We have formed our own stereotypes of women shaped from the traditional roles of women — such as mothers, daughters, and wives etc. being translated to the workplace, making it difficult for women to form relationships with businessmen.

The women who succeed despite such obstacles can be seen as a positive influence in the executive suite. They often focus on shaping the policies within their corporations in a socially responsible manner, thereby taking into account the role their companies and their practices have on society at a global level. Perhaps this is because they pay more attention to the future, long-term impact rather than a short-term, purely profit-based perspective. Social responsibility should be very important to women. Not only do women have a tendency to be more altruistic than men, but women tend to be the most affected by discriminatory practices within the workplace such as sexual harassment, failure to be promoted or hired based on sex, and receiving lower pay than men, making it personal.

Despite significant progress, gender equality remains one of the most pervasive bases for inequality worldwide. Carroll (1999: 269) notes the invisibility of women in the corporate field with the consequent assumption that businesswomen did not exist: "there apparently were no businesswomen during this period, or at least they were not being acknowledged in formal writing". This raises questions about the visibility of women in the corporate and of gender issues in the field of CSR today. To say that an organization, is gendered means that advantage and disadvantage, exploitation and control, action and emotion, meaning and identity and in terms of a distinction between male and female, masculine and feminine are patterned. Gender is not an addition to ongoing processes; rather, it is an integral part of those processes, which cannot be properly understood without an analysis of gender. McKinsey and Company (2007) found that gender diversity in senior management correlates with "organizational excellence" as measured by a set of criteria including: leadership, direction, accountability, coordination and control, innovation, external orientation, capability, motivation, work environment and values. The study found that companies with more than three women in senior management functions score more highly, on average, for each organizational criterion of "excellence" than companies with no women at the top.

Discourse on gender equality and rights of women has taken momentum during 1990s and with emergence of women rights organizations, feminist movement, introduction of rights to education as fundamental rights for all and prioritization of gender agenda in corporate social responsibility domain, changes are happening. We are now witnessing a steady improvement in the enrollment of girls in schools, colleges and even in profession institutes. Their health is better as compared to earlier decades as many health programmes are targeting development of girl child. In twenty first century, women are entering into the job market in increasing numbers and also holding responsible positions. They are showing their skills and taking up leadership positions even in non-traditional sectors like police, defense, administration, media and research fields. Women icons like Kalpana Chawla, Pratibha Patil etc. have made India proud across globe but still the status of women is poor when it comes to our society mindset. Many initiatives are being undertaken by Government in terms of campaigns and schemes like *Beti Bachao Beti Padhao Abhiyan* etc. Corporate and various NGO's have prioritized gender equality and women empowerment under policy and organizational mandate to improve the status of women.

God has gifted women with compassion, tender-heartedness, caring nature, concern for others, adaptability and empathy, attitude for developing others, influencing without power, open mindedness and integrity. These are the basic skills set required by an individual to be socially responsible, which a woman already owns. These are very positive signs which imply that women can be leaders. Though some women have shown their courage yet a large number of them have to sharpen their leadership qualities in various ways. In order to help women to be in limelight, they need to be empowered.

Corporates and Glass Ceiling

Glass ceiling is the kind of unofficial barrier for women and minority section to advance at the workplace. It is the term coined by the *Wall Street Journal* which describes the barriers that prevent women from reaching the top of the corporate hierarchy. It starts to form itself very early on. From the moment a woman enters the workforce after college, she may come across with much discrimination and unjust belief that she will not be able to do as well of a job than a man. A man and a woman, who both have the same education and training for a job, might have a considerable gap in their yearly income. Different types of glass ceiling barriers are —

- Different wages for the same or comparable work.
- Discrimination against people due to their race, ethnicity, religion, or age.
- Lack of family-friendly work environments.
- Gender stereo-typing or preconceptions of women's work and abilities.

Following are some of the efforts being taken to empower women in the society thereby empowering her in the corporate:

- To provide promising platform to women in corporate sector.
- To undertake campaigns for weaker section of women (poor, illiterate, handicap etc.).
- To provide employment at different levels in corporate.
- To stress on overall development of women.
- To provide financial assistance to needy women.
- To motivate deserving women in sports, defense, education, politics and so on.
- To protect the right and interest of women.

- To battle against gender discrimination.
- To provide promising platform to women in corporate sector.
- To undertake campaigns for weaker section of women (poor, illiterate, handicap etc.).

Empowerment of Women and Role of CSR

For general meaning, the word 'empowerment' is derived from the word 'power' the prefix 'em' is attached to it forms verb meaning to 'make into' or 'to cause power'. Thus, 'to empower' is to 'make or cause power'. Women empowerment generally has the following components: firstly, women's sense of self worth; secondly, their right to have the power of control their own lives, both within and outside home; and lastly, their ability to influence the direction of social change to create a just social and economic order nationally, internationally and universally. Women empowerment in context of CSR mean they should have equal opportunity in the socio-economic-political spheres of our society. Ironically, women in the Indian society still look towards the society to grant them power or empower them in various ways. Women empowerment talks much about enabling women in various ways on multifarious fronts like financial, social, cultural, legal and political. Therefore, women empowerment is not about sending girls to school or allowing them to go out for work but it is about change in societal mindset where we treat women equally and recognizes her contribution in growth and social development. Since, the corporate plays yet another role in boosting the economy by making available employment to every section of society. Therefore, role of corporate specially under the CSR initiatives around empowerment of women is the redefined prerequisite to transform a developing country into a developed country.

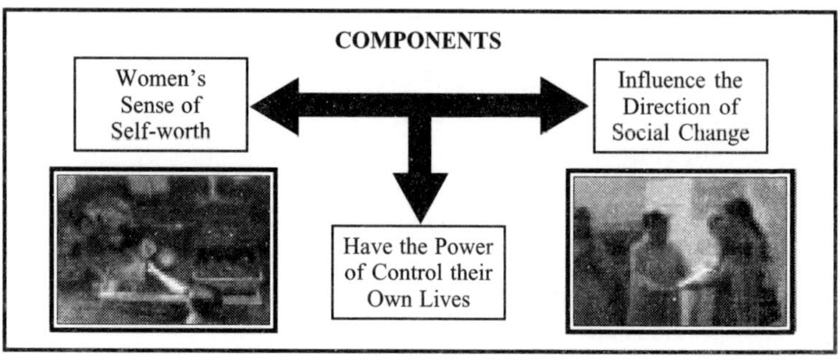

FIGURE 10.1: Women Empowerment

CSR is an opportunity to empower the world's one half population so that civilization and global society develop to the imaginable extent. Empowering women is all about encouraging Self-Empowerment, Self-Esteem, Personal Growth, Spiritual Growth, Reclaiming Authentic Power and the power Goddess within. The organizational aim to ignite women empowerment should be through inspiring women with the courage to break free from the chains of limiting belief patterns and societal or religious conditioning that have traditionally kept women suppressed and unable to see their true inner power. This objective can be achieved through CSR in a systematic manner. The Department of Public Enterprises (DPE) in India has come up with its latest comprehensive guidelines on Corporate Social Responsibility in March, 2010 with respect to the concept, planning, research, documentation, advocacy, promotion, funding aspects, documentation and monitoring the CSR activities. The concept of CSR as per the latest guidelines emphasizes on Sustainable development and clearly states that CSR is a company's commitment to operate in an economically, socially and environmentally sustainable manner, while recognizing the interests of its stakeholders. This commitment is beyond statutory requirements. Corporate social responsibility is, therefore, closely linked with the practice of Sustainable Development.

The World Business Council for Sustainable Development has described CSR as the business contribution to sustainable economic development. Building on a base of compliance with legislation and regulations, CSR typically includes 'beyond law' commitments and activities pertaining to:

- Women empowerment.
- Health and safety.
- Environmental stewardship.
- Human rights (including core labour rights).
- Sustainable development.
- Community involvement, development and investment.
- Involvement of and respect for diverse cultures and disadvantaged peoples.
- Corporate philanthropy and employee volunteering.
- Customer satisfaction and adherence to principles of fair competition.
- Anti-bribery and anti-corruption measures.
- Accountability, transparency and performance reporting.

- Supplier relations, for both domestic and international supply chains.
- Industrial relations.

Empowerment of women is one of the crucial concerns of the Sustainable Development Goals (SDGs). Women in the Indian society still look towards the society to grant them power or empower them in various ways. Women empowerment talks much about empowering women in various ways (financial, social, cultural, legal and political). Twenty first century women are now have become vital part and parcel of society.

Women made up more than half the world's population, produced 80 per cent of its food, laboured for two-thirds of its working hours, were paid 10 per cent of its income and owned one per of its property. These figures manifold forms of the disadvantaging and discrimination of women. Such as Unjust division of burdens of families, the economic exploitation of women, the loss of their control over resources and the unequal rating of paid and unpaid work.

CSR deals with corporate responsibility towards society, talking about women workforce. Corporate world now recognizes women in every possible area in which it functions. Society's development without development of women is unimaginable and hence, women's role must be recognized in all spheres as mentioned below:

- Growing role of women in corporate
- Women as employees
- Women in management
- Women as owners/shareholders
- Women as professionals
- Women as suppliers

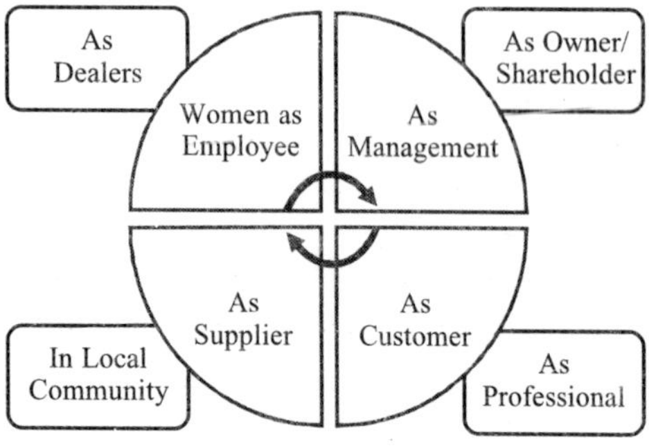

FIGURE 10.2: Women's Role Recognized in All Spheres

- Women as customers
- Women as dealers
- Women in local communities.

Need for Focus on Women Empowerment through CSR in India

Amendment in Companies Act, 2013 has provided an entire gamut to cover dimensions of Women Empowerment. The activities defined under Schedule VIII as indicated in box below highlights the activities related to women empowerment and their entitlements.

MINISTRY OF CORPORATE AFFAIRS
NOTIFICATION
New Delhi, the 27th February, 2014

G.S.R. 130(E) — In exercise of the powers conferred by sub-section (I) of Section 467 of the Companies Act, 2013 (18 of 2013), the Central Government hereby makes the following amendments to Schedule VII of the said Act, namely: —

(I) In Schedule VII, for items (i) to (x) and the entities relating thereto, the following items and entries shall be substituted, namely: —

(i) Eradicating hunger, poverty and malnutrition, promoting preventive health care and sanitation and making available safe drinking water;

(ii) Promoting education, including special education and employment enhancing vocation skills especially among children, women, elderly, and the differently abled and livelihood enhancement projects;

(iii) Promoting gender equality, empowering women, setting up homes and hostels for women and orphans; setting up old age homes, day care centres and such other facilities for senior citizens and measures for reducing inequalities faced by socially and economically backward groups.

CSR initiatives can address issues at the ground level and one such area at the base level is empowering women. Companies are initiating numerous CSR activities focused to encourage women empowerment. Yet, it has been observed that the companies do not reflect the activities with proper gender related information like education, health, and women rights etc. Companies should not only encourage women empowerment as a part of CSR in rural area but also should initiate empowerment of women at organizational level too. They must ensure that they have the following practices as a part of the organizations:

- The companies are required to have distinct and well-defined women empowerment policy.
- Gender-based reporting needs to be incorporated in corporate report. Hence, the engendering policies are clear and understandable.
- The reporting system should reflect the gender employment ratio.
- Reporting practices have failed to reflect the unethical practices against women within the workplaces of the companies. Same has to be reflected in CSR reports and provision of Audit by Government Empanelled Experts for CSR can change the scenario.

Corporates Setting Examples in Women Empowerment

1. *Jindal Stainless Foundation*

Jindal Stainless Ltd. (JSL) CSR Initiative has focused its activities on two basic entities, i.e. the internal environment as also the community. Both these target groups have been addressed through various supportive programmes toward sustainable development. The CSR Initiatives include women empowerment through vocational education and training programmes, reproductive child health care programmes, medical health camps, environment conservation programmes, promotion of sports and a host of extracurricular activities at local levels.

2. *ITC*

ITC believes that economic empowerment of women transforms them into powerful agents of social change. ITC has forged an empowering partnership with rural women — the most effective development workers. ITC's intervention leverages micro-credit and skills training to generate alternate employment opportunities. Increased income in the hands of rural women means better nutrition, health care and education for their children. Working with NGOs, ITC has organized village women into micro-credit groups.

3. *SAIL*

SAIL has initiated Mahila Samaj Performance of community welfare programmes which includes manufacture of products and services for SAIL employees. The Mahila Samiti in SAIL plants has 4000 members and 15 affiliated to national level organization for community development.

4. *TATA*

More than 60 per cent of the women members of Tata Parivar have launched income generation programmes with an objective of making their families economically sustainable. At the moment there are 22 all-women Tata Parivar SHGs. In order to achieve better levels of income, the rehabilitation and resettlement team of Tata Steel is continuously imparting Capacity Building Training in the sectors Soura Painting, Stitching, Poultry & Goat Rearing and Computer based literacy programmes.

5. *HUL's Shakti*

SHAKTI means 'Strength'. Project SHAKTI is HUL's initiative to upliftment of standard of living in rural India by creating income-generating capabilities for underprivileged rural women by providing a small-scale enterprise opportunity, and to improving rural lives through health and hygiene awareness. Project SHAKTI is taken up in rural areas only whereby women are the Distributors for HUL products and are called "Shakti Ammas". This identity is ushering prosperity in their lives and most importantly self-respect.

6. *Avon*

Avon Cosmetics' commitment to women runs deeper than the boundaries of business. Women are the heart of Avon's success and Avon continues to support and understand their needs through Avon's Breast Cancer Crusade. The goal of the Avon Foundation Breast Cancer Crusade is to improve access to quality breast health care for underserved, uninsured and low income populations, and to support biomedical research focused on prevention and improved methods of Diagnosis and treatment to cure and prevent breast cancer.

7. *Infosys*

Infosys is an Indian IT company that puts a focus on gender diversity. The company has established the Infosys Women Inclusivity Network to encourage a gender sensitive work environment and the Family Matters Network to offer help to employees on parenting matters. As a result of, today women make up above 32 per cent of the Infosys workforce.

8. *Titan*

Titan Industries Ltd. ("Titan") is an Indian company that is part of the Tata Group and that manufactures watches, jewellery and glasses. Through its programme, MEADOW, i.e. (Management of Enterprise and Development of Women), the company has created opportunities for poor women from rural Indian communities to become wage earners and supported women's entrepreneurship through business education.

9. *Johnson & Johnson*

Johnson & Johnson, headquartered in New Jersey, is one of the world's leading providers of health care products and services. The company includes diversity as a significant process not only in recruiting, but also in its supply chain, product development, sales, marketing and advertising. The company is also promoting women to senior management positions, which signifies gender diversity.

10. *Ericsson*

Ericsson, a Swedish provider of technology and services to telecom operators, has started a programme to bring high speed internet connectivity to rural Tamil Nadu, India. The programme aims to provide the region with a wide variety of internet-based resources which will help the region's women to access to regular medical checkups *via* telemedicine and to register newborn children online, ensuring eligibility for essential health and education services.

Various Challenges to CSR Initiatives in India

Corporate social responsibility is more than a topic to discuss. As it is changing fate and face of society, it should be adopted by all the business houses voluntarily. Country like India should specially advocate for corporate social responsibility as it can bring possible remedies for many issues like illiteracy, poverty, child labour, unemployment and rural development. Women related issues need important attention from government, society and especially from corporate sector. Corporate can definitely empower women right from encouraging them to get education till getting respectable livelihood to become productive citizens.

Economic empowerment programme for women should be encouraged to bring confidence in them to challenge the societal mindset and become economically independent. Women related issues at work like sexual harassment, unequal pay, indifferent behaviour though comes under legal framework but it can be stopped by corporate if internal control within organization gives due importance to women related rules. Development of corporate and society is unattainable without an active support of women. The government, media, NGOs should collectively join hands with corporate in common interest of upliftment of women.

Though the concept of Corporate Social Responsibility (CSR) has been working efficiently in various organizations and has brought up many outstanding changes in education, economic development, environment etc. yet, it has faced a lot of challenges. Following are a few of the challenges being faced in the implementation of various methods and ideas regarding women empowerment under CSR:

- No knowledge of the social factors and approach to deal with it.
- Inward looking approach and less/no participation from local community.
- Lack of Role of Media and lesser understanding of Behaviour Change aspects.
- Issues of Transparency and Accountability.
- Narrow perception, overlooking root causes of social barriers.
- No guidelines for Law and Activities hence, interpretation as per convenience.
- Lack of consent in implementing the policies.
- Lack of effective resources, financial as well as human resources.
- External changes such as cultural diversity and understanding of local law.

Recommendations

It is clear from the findings in general that many actions are necessary and critical if gender equality is to be achieved and if CSR is to play a part in affecting gender equality in the workplace.

1. Success of CSR must be defined and measured appropriately. Success cannot be reduced to the types of metrics now familiar in Western corporate suites, such as how many women are in senior management positions or how many women groups

formed under income generation activities but it should measure the qualitative change in the socio-economic-political status of women in society.

2. Bring change in perception, behaviour, organizational cultures and practices that are biased against women.
3. Objective delegation of roles and responsibility overcoming stereotype perception of men and women related jobs segmentation.
4. Encourage more women related projects under CSR where they are in lead role, challenging the stereotype socio-economic structures and expectations.
5. Encourage more women at internal workplace and provision for trainings, easier shifts, work from home, flexi-hours etc. for women.
6. Training of women employees on handling conflict, sexual harassment and making complaints etc.
7. Actively advocate and encourage female applicants to non-traditional posts by supporting them and enabling them to work in groups so as to overcome the traditional mindset.
8. Conducive environment for women should be created like one woman in a male-dominated department can be recruited to avoid isolation.

Conclusion

Historically, women in Indian society have been considered as supportive family member who is responsible to take care of secondary work in household. Her contribution in economic terms like working in agricultural fields, care giver role in family, upbringing of children etc. has always been neglected due to dominance of patriarchal mindset. Women rights movement during last two decades has highlighted discrimination in the global leaders and national policy-makers, but most of legislations and policies are ineffective because of prevalence of deeply rooted stereotype mindset, social barriers and customary practices. As an integral part of nation and society, corporate has an important role to play in social transformation and in women's advancement. Hence, it is right opportunity for corporate to strive for strengthening existing CSR instruments to promote women's equality. Empowerment means to inspire women with the courage to break free from the chains of limiting beliefs, patterns and societal or religious conditions that have traditionally kept women suppressed and enable them to realize their true beauty and power.

Although many such initiatives have been taken by the Government, Civil Society and Corporate, but a lot of work has to be to made 50 per cent of our population socially, economically and politically empowered. India is still have growing concern on issues like female foeticide, discrimination with girl child, dowry system, isolation during menstrual period, social boycott of widows etc. Though women today have become very independent and, equally competent to men in all sectors, still there is a strong need for the society to accept and accommodate women with equal respect and honor and give her a status at par with the men. She is still a victim of gender discrimination, sexual harassment, and sarcastic behaviour of co-employees thereby blocking their path to flourish and reach at the top. India has witnessed remarkable campaigns to ensure gender equality, reservation and inclusive work environment for women, however, we as a progressive society have miles to go.

Corporate social responsibility towards women empowerment can become ray of hope in many ways right from changing attitude towards women in the society to making women independent financially, physically and socially and enabling them to be self-reliant. The motive behind joining CSR with women empowerment is to provide solutions to women related issues as highlighted above. Corporate can make conscious and strategic efforts in gender mainstreaming towards rural or urban development activities, income generation and skill building programmes, leadership development initiatives in panchayats or local self-governance *vis-à-vis* in developing conducive environment for women employee internally. Initiatives should not be limited in showcasing International Women's Day or celebrating womanhood on specific day but it has to be integrated to organizational cultural, system and practices as well. In context of CSR activities defined under Schedule VII of Companies Act, 2013, the corporate have immense potential to become prime mover of women empowerment movement in India and paving way for other countries for social transformation.

REFERENCES

Barrientos, A. (2012). *Social Transfers and Growth: A Review*, BWPI, University of Manchester, UK. Available at: *www.chronicpoverty.org [Accessed on 5th, March, 2012]*

Bhavini Arora & Dr. Jagdeep Singh (2012). "Women Rights in Corporate Sector", *Review of Research*, June.

Organization, unpublished working document, WHO/GHW). Therefore, it is important to address mental health issues of women because at present mental health problems among women constitute a wide spectrum ranging from sub-clinical states to very severe forms of disorders. Further, there also lies a significant difference in disease pathology among men and women and thus gender specific diseases are reported, like men are more vulnerable to life-threatening chronic diseases, including coronary heart disease, cancer, cerebrovascular disease, emphysema, cirrhosis of the liver, kidney disease and atherosclerosis whereas women are more susceptible to chronic disorders such as anaemia, thyroid conditions, gall bladder conditions, migraine, arthritis, colitis, eczema, upper respiratory infections, gastroenteritis and short-term infectious diseases (Verbrugge & Wingard, 1987). Further, a study done by Orfila *et al.* (2006) found poor mental and physical health status among women in comparison to men and women were reported to live 6 to 8 years longer than men. Moreover, mental health problem among women has always been less concerned issues and has remained unexplored and unaddressed. Further, it is very disappointing for communities that only clinically evidenced mental disorders are thought to be significant and are attended otherwise the common mental restlessness is largely ignored and has been less attended.

Why it is Important to Address Mental Health Issue of Women in India?

- Mental disorders affect large numbers of women, residing in urban, rural and slums of India.
- Women with mental illness are often stigmatized and excluded by family and society. They also tend to under-perform in education and work, thereby remain increasingly deprived of economic and social opportunities, with a decreased their quality of life.
- Mental illness and suicide are closely interlinked. At its worst, mental illness can lead to suicide and recognizing the mental disorders at an early stage is critical for reducing suicidal deaths and deliberate self-harm across the spectrum.
- Often it is seen that in India mental health problems are largely ignored and labelled as taboo and people escape from it and is regarded as a matter of shame if a woman suffers from it and creates problem in her marriage and other social issues.

- In India when a woman is suspected of some mental health issues it is not noticed and goes undetected which creates more problem and makes vulnerable to other psychiatric problems which further aggravates the problem.
- Women with mental disorders do not get adequate care due to various reasons, ranging from non-availability of services to prevailing stigma and discrimination.
- Mental illness among women is a major public health problem in India, contributing to significant morbidity, disability as well as mortality, along with significant socio-economic losses.
- Causes of mental illness among womens are varied which, include biological, social, economic and cultural factors, which are triggered by environmental factors.
- The economic impact of mental disorders is huge and unmeasured and vitiates the cycle of poverty and poor health. Lower and middle class women are affected the most.
- Several evidence-based and cost-effective pharmacological and non-pharmacological interventions are available for managing mental disorders. These can be delivered in different settings by different groups of health and non-health professionals and related service providers.
- Strengthening of women health system through appropriate staff training, uninterrupted supply of drugs, availability of psychotherapy, counselling services, good referral systems and continuity of care is essential.

Psychological Disorders among Women

In Indian society changing social structure, family structure, belief system, rules, regulation, law, customs, rituals, tradition have significantly affected the women health. And epidemiological evidences shows that 9.5 to 370/1000 of Indian population (Math & Srinivasaraju, 2010), suffer from psychiatric disorders and 20 per cent of adult Indian population suffers with one or more psychiatry disorders. Mental health problem have affected both male and female and there do not appear sex difference in overall prevalence of mental disorders. But some researches has evidenced that psychiatric disorders like depression, anxiety, schizophrenia, psychogenic non-epileptic seizures (PNES) and conversion to be more prevalent among women as compared to males (Lewinsohn, Gotlib, Lewinshon, Seeley & Allen, 1998; Christiansen, pp. 18-48). Further, it can be argued that the difference observed among women vulnerability to these disorders can be attributed to the biological differences between male and female behavioural and functional anatomy.

Moreover, disorders like depression, anxiety, PTSD and PNES are more frequently reported among women population whereas substance abuse and anti-social behaviour are reported more among men. There are varied number of reason, which causes mental unrest among women. Explaining those can be categorized broadly among three factors, i.e. societal factors, personal factors and organizational factors. The most prevalent and common disorders which are frequently reported among women are discussed below.

Anxiety Disorders among Women

Anxiety disorder can is a normal phenomenon which is characterized by a state of apprehension or unease arising out of anticipation of danger (Ahuja, 2002). In anxiety the danger is largely unknown. It is the most frequently reported psychiatric disorder (McLean, Asnaani, Litz & Hofmann, 2011) where its prevalence among women is 1.5 to 2 times higher as compared to males. Anxiety disorder is reported more among females and some studies have even reported it from the age of 4 (Howell, Brawman-Mintzer, Monnier & Yonkers, 2001). This can be explained that in India from the beginning girls are socialized with specific roles and are instructed to behave according to their gender norms. Therefore, pressure to conform with societal norms creates dissonance and conflict among them and experience greater proportion of anxiety (Yonkers & Gurguis, 1995). In addition, females also diagnosed frequently agoraphobia (AG), panic disorder (PD), separation anxiety (SA), specific phobia (SP), social anxiety disorder (SAD), generalize anxiety disorder (GAD), obsessive compulsive disorder (OCD), acute and post-traumatic stress disorder (ASD-PTSD) comparing to males (Bekker & van Mens-Verhulst, 2007; Shear, Jin, Ruscio, Walters & Kessler, 2006). Cause of female preponderance to anxiety can be explained by genetically or biologically defined mechanism. Substantial amount of research has shown that their lies a difference in brain region associated with cognition, memory and affect and Lochner *et al.* (2004) have found structural and functional difference among both sexes in specific brain regions associated with anxiety.

Neurobiology of Anxiety

Further, neuro-chemical bases has also been studied, which explains why women are more prone to anxiety and suffer from emotional stability. Female hormones like oesterogen and progesterone plays important role in regulating the neurotransmitter responsible for anxiety and thus reducing the response towards stress and suppressing the activity of hypothalamic pituitary adrenal axis (HPA) (McHenry, Carrier, Hull & Kabbaj 2014). Moreover, Altemus (2006) found that varying amount of oesterogen and progesterone which interact with HPA axis, glucocorticoid feedback mechanism and GABA neurotransmitter in brain to create imbalance in homeostatic conditions which causes emotional instability among females and males vulnerable to anxiety.

Depression among Women

Depression is the most commonly reported health issue among women and is a major comorbid condition with conversion, dissociation, psychogenic-seizures including many organic and multiple stress related problems. Depression is more common among females than men and is most commonly documented psychiatric disorder. The prevalence of depression among female is twice than men (Shors & Leuner, 2003) and it has been confirmed by World Health Organization's Global Burden of Disease (GBD) which estimate that depression to be the most prevalent disorder affecting women majorly with life time prevalence of 21.3 per cent as compared to men with only 12.7 per cent (Murray & Lopez, 1996; Kessler *et al.*, 1994). Women are most affected by depression than male can be explained by the presumption that women are more willing to admit their depression than men and are more open to discuss their problem freely whereas men do not disclose their problem freely and fixate their behaviour in the form of anti-social behaviour. That is why men are more reported to be anti-social than women.

Surveys of depression among children and adolescents show that the gender differences are there and first emerge in the age range 11-14 (Angold, Costello & Worthman, 1998) and is high among women. But Weissman, Bland, Joyce and Newman (1993) study has refuted this argument and in his study he found no difference in prevalence of depression among men and women. Moreover, study done by Gove (1972) among married and unmarried women concluded that married women are more depressed than unmarried or single ones. This stand can be argued that married women are more strongly exposed to traditional sex-roles experiences as compared to unmarried ones. Further, depression also affects the stability of men and women differently. For example financial pressure is depressogenic for men than women while family problems are more depressogenic for women than men (Kessler & McLeod, 1984).

Neurobiology of Depression

During 1960s it was discovered that depression can be treated with the drugs that enhances monoamines in the brain. It was observed that patient suffering from depression has decreased activity in serotonergic or noradrenergic systems and this hypothesis was called *monoamine hypothesis of depression*. The hypothesis was strengthened by the discovery of drugs that enhances both the serotonergic and noradrenergic systems, the so-called monoamine oxidase (MOA) inhibitors, were effective in the treatment of depression. Drugs which has been widely accepted to treat depression are selective serotonin reuptake inhibitors (SSRIs). The SSRIs increases the bio-availability of serotonin in the synapse without side effect like headache, nausea and drowsiness. In addition to serotonergic dysfunction, depression has also been associated with disturbances in the hypothalamic-pituitary-adrenal axis (HPA) in humans with enhanced level of adrenal hormones and corticotrophin releasing factor (CRF) in the blood (Banki, Arato, Connor & Nemeroff, 1987).

As discussed above depression is more among women than men and research have shown that ovarian hormones play a pivotal role in causing depression among female suggesting a potential role of estrogen and progesterone. These hormones interact with serotonin to modulate different aspects of serotonergic function and available researches indicate that estrogen may be pharmacologically be effective in ameliorating depressive symptoms. Further, findings by Epperson, Wisner and Yamamoto (1999) have revealed that estrogen treatment repeatedly improves the physical and psychological symptoms of depression among women.

Psychogenic Non-epileptic Seizures (PNES) among Women

PNES (a type of dissociative disorder ICD-10) are episodes of altered movement sensation or experiences similar to epilepsy, but caused by psychological process and not associated with abnormal discharges in the brain (Lesser, 1996). It consists of episodes of paroxysmal impairment of self-control associated with a range of motor, sensory and mental manifestation which represent an experiential or behavioural response to emotional or social distress (Reuber, House, Pukrop, Bauer & Elger, 2001). PNES can be defined as mental sufferings, usually in response to a psychological conflict or other kind of stressors (Reuber & Elger, 2003). Although PNES mimic epileptic seizures (ES) it is suspected to have non-organic base and majority of the neurologists agree that it has its psychogenic origin and is different from ES on the basis of semiological details and patient history. Moreover, patient referred to epilepsy care unit of which 5 to 33 per cent are PNES, 10 to 40 per cent (PNES) of refractory seizures, among which mostly are women (75%) with age range of 20 to 30 years. Usually, PNES is assumed as an unintentional manifestation of emotional distress which can be explained on the basis of neurophysiological, psychological and social base.

Neurobiology of PNES

A number of studies have investigated the organic pathology of PNES and concluded that PNES is caused due to organic brain pathology and dissociation between neural networks. PNES patient exhibits spells of altered movement, sensation and experience caused due to disruption in connection between thought, memories, feelings and sense of identity with loss in their ability to properly integrate and channelize their emotion. And all these are having a neurological base because each of these entity are governed by specific brain area like somatosensary area, insular area, orbito-frontal area, frontal area, parietal area and many other brain circuits, which works in integrated fashion and helps individuals to deal with the current demand of the situation. Therefore, any structural or functional changes or alteration/atrophy/degeneration detected through neuro-imaging techniques in these areas can be potential biomarker of PNES.

Post-traumatic Stress Disorders (PTSD)

PTSD is a psychiatric sequel to a stressful event or situation of an exceptionally threatening or catastrophic nature. PTSD was added to American psychiatric nomenclature in the year 1980 with the publication of third edition of official manual of American Psychiatric Association,

Diagnostic and Statistical Manual of Mental Disorders (DSM III) after Vietnam war. PTSD syndrome is a conglomeration of various cognitive, behavioural, and physiological disturbances characterized by three symptom clusters, i.e. intrusion, avoidance, and arousal (Kar, 2011). The persons who have been sexually abused, or were in combat situation, or have been victims of violent, or aggressive non-sexual assault or close road traffic accidents or disaster worker or a victim of terrorism and physical assault or even sometimes repetitive household violence are commonly reported vulnerable at the risk of developing symptoms of PTSD (Briere & Zaidi, 1989). Moreover, an individual suffering from PTSD can be identified clinically as he or she has history of distressing event that is outside the range of usual human experience; has complaints of re-experiencing traumas in nightmares, intrusive thoughts or flashbacks; shows numbing responsiveness or avoidance of acts related to the trauma; have symptoms of dysphoria and arousal. Apart from depression and anxiety, PTSD is commonly reported illness among women and is more twice likely to develop PTSD than men and four times more to get it chronically ill. The individual with PTSD shows significant decline in behavioural aspects such as hyper-alertness (exaggerated startle response), sleep disturbances, guilt, trouble in concentrating, avoidance of activities prompting the recall of original event, memory loss, lack of reasoning, and worsening of symptoms by exposing to the event resembling the original event (Helzer, Robins & McEvoy, 1987).

Extremely threatening situation and catastrophic are regarded the most obvious reason for developing PTSD, and PTSD is the most debilitating psychological disorder occurring after natural disaster. In India a study done after Asian tsumani which occurred in 2004 by Rajkumar, Premkumar and Tharyan (2008) found that people in various districts of Tamil Nadu valued their unique individual, social and spiritual coping strategies more than formal mental health services. With catastrophic, family dysfunction, family disharmony, house hold violence, intimate partner violence also plays significant factors responsible for developing PTSD among Indian population. In one study done by Chandra, Satyanarayana and Carey (2009) reported that out of 105 individuals who developed PTSD 56 per cent of the women were the victim of intimate partner violence. Also Woods (2005) has found a strong base of household violence responsible for developing PTSD among women.

Neurobiology of PTSD

The neurobiology of PTSD and depression are similar in some respect, but PTSD is different from depression in the way that PTSD is stress induced (specific threatening in nature) whereas depression has multiple explained etiology. Researchers have extensively evaluated the role two biological systems which plays an important role in causation of PTSD, i.e. hypothalamic-pituitary-adrenal (HPA) axis and catecholamine/ sympathetic nervous system. Patients suffering from PTSD show hyperactivity in HPA and catecholamine/sympathetic nervous system and is associated with hypocortisolaemia despite the hypersecretion of corticotropin-releasing factor (CRF). But among these two axis HPA is widely studied to elucidate the underlying pathophysiology that might explain the frequently reported hypocortisolemia in patients with PTSD (DeBellis *et al.*, 1999). Further, amygdala plays a key role in consolidating the emotional significance of events and plays crucial role in our understanding of conditioned fear processing, a process that is important in the pathophysiology of PTSD. Moreover, deficits in explicit memory function is often seen among PTSD.

Studies have also reported greater increase in orbito-frontal and anterior temporal cortical activation level whereas small increases in the area of anterior cingulate activation with decreases in left inferior-frontal region. In addition, the role of anterior cingulate gyrus which is responsible for the maintenance of social mores, fear-related behaviour, and selective attentional processing (as evidenced by the Strooptask) has also been studied. Therefore, anterior cingulate dysfunction may play a role in the re-experiencing phenomena reported in PTSD (Shin *et al.*, 1999). Besides this role certain neurotransmitters like of norepinephrine (NE), Dopamine (DA) and glutamate hyperactivity have also been postulated to play a role in the neurobiology of PTSD (Kagan, Leskin, Haas, Wilkins & Foy, 1999).

Cause of Mental Illness among Women

There is a significant difference between men and women in mental illness, with women being more prone than men to mental health issues. Although significant difference in men and women mental health are well documented, but the sources of these differences remain disputed. There are number of factors which influence and affect the mental health of women are following:

- Gender discrimination
- Social stereotype
- Lack of education
- Early socialization
- Difference in social position
- Gender specific role
- Family dysfunction
- Family disharmony
- Household violence
- Patriarchal type of family system
- Lack of self-awareness
- Lack of proper nutrition
- Dependency on male guardian
- Carelessness towards health
- Economical and financial position.

Our social and cultural background has tremendous effect on our lives and contributes a lot to our health and experience. Our accumulated societal experiences reflect in our psychological make-up and are one important predisposing factor towards individual's health. Our society is witnessed with varied number of social and cultural constraints which might be problematic and plays important role in mental illness. Further, in India changing socio-demographic and epidemiological transition has significantly affected the mental health of women. Moreover, there are a number social and cultural factors which predisposes an individual to mental illness.

Gender is recognized as one of the major social determinants of health. According to the American Psychological Association, gender norms refer to, "the socially constructed roles, behaviours, activities, and attributes that a given society considers appropriate for boys and men or girls and women" thus a person's behaviours are critical to their ability to fit into cultural gender norms. These gender norms can play a powerful role in a person's life since deviating from the norms associated with one's biological sex can be met with censure from peers, social exclusion, and sometimes even emotional or physical violence (van Wijk & Kolk, 1997). Therefore, it raises an issue that why disconfirming gender norms met with such vulnerability, probably the answer can be faulty early socialization where society deliberately declares specific activities, roles and behaviour suited for women. When the norms are not met with the part of women's social behaviour, which society consider appropriate, results in unethical behavioural pattern from the side of authority responsible for care giving. Women are left with two options either they have to conform or reject. In both cases women meet with negative impact. When she conform the pre-decided role then she has to suffer from mental dissonance which significantly affect the mental health. Second when she refuses to conform the specific role than she has to suffer from violence. Ultimately, these all results in family dysfunction and family disharmony, in turn affecting the mental health of the women.

Our society has already labelled and stratified specific position and activities related to men and women. But advancement in technology, information exchange and global exposure has wired pool of information, with change in gender stereotype. Now with women being more aware of their rights. This has significantly checked the deterioration of women's social position and prejudiced role related activities. But this is not encouraging since a large number of women population are still discriminated due to prevalence of patriarchal type of family system. A number of women are victim of household violence due to dependency on their male guardian, restricting them with their independence which creates mental dissonance among them. This significantly affects their mental health. Besides this in India maximum women are not financially independent and they have to be dependent on their male guardian if unmarried or husband if married. For each and every small things they have to depend upon them, sometimes their demand get restricted and they have no options other than to feel distressed. Even for small things they have to ask their help. In this way from the beginning this happens to her and slowly and slowly this distress piles up in them making them vulnerabie to stress. Thus, affecting their mental health. Therefore, financial dependency play a major role in mental illness of women. Although societal, cultural and economic issues predisposes women to suffer from mental health issues, besides this there are also some individual factors which affect mental health of women. Among those factors lack of self-awareness and carelessness towards self-health are important. In India often due to lack of education especially in rural areas women are less aware of the benefit of health. There is no culture that one should be conscious about his/her health and thus they neglect it. Also, lack of proper nutrition and less availability of medical health care facilities predisposes them to poor health.

Thus, we can conclude that various social, cultural, economic and individual factors interplay and predisposes individuals at the risk of developing mental illness among women.

REFERENCES

Ahuja, N. (2002). *A Short Textbook of Psychiatry*, 5th edition, Jaypee Brothers.

Altemus, M. (2006). "Sex Differences in Depression and Anxiety Disorders: Potential Biological Determinants", *Hormones and Behaviour*, 50(4): 534-538.

American Psychological Association (2011). *Answers to Your Questions about Transgender People, Gender Identity, and Gender Expression*. Available from: *http://www.apa.org/topics/lgbt/transgender*.

Angold, A.; Costello, E.J. & Worthman, C.W. (1998). "Puberty and Depression: The Roles of Age, Pubertal Status, and Pubertaltiming", *Psychological Medicine*, 28: 51-61.

Banki, C.M.; Arato, M.; O'Connor, L. & Nemeroff, C.B. (1987). "Cerebrospinal Fluid Corticotropin-releasing Factor-like Immuno-reactivity in Depression and Schizophrenia", *American Journal of Psychiatry*, 144: 873-877.

Bekker, M.H. & Van Mens-Verhulst, J. (1996). "Anxiety Disorders: Sex Differences in Prevalence, Degree, and Background, but Gender-neutral Treatment", *Gender Medicine*, 2007; 4(Suppl. B): S178-S193.

Briere, J.; Zaidi. & Lisa, Y. (1989). "Sexual Abuse Histories and Sequelae in Female Psychiatric Emergency Room Patients", *The American Journal of Psychiatry*, 146(12).

De Bellis, M.D.; Keshavan, M.S.; Clark, D.B.; Casey, B.J.; Giedd, J.; Boring, A.M.; Frustaci, K. and Ryan, N.D. (1999). AE Bennett Research Award, "Development Altraumatology, Part II: Brain Development", *Biological Psychiatry*, 45: 1271-1284.

Dorte M. Christiansen (2015). "Examining Sex and Gender Differences in Anxiety Disorders: A Fresh Look at Anxiety Disorders", Dr. Federico Durbano (Ed.), *InTech*, DOI: 10.5772/60662. Available from: *https://mts.intechopen.com/books/a-fresh-look-at-anxiety-disorders/examining-sex-and-gender-differences-in-anxiety-disorders*

Epperson, C.N.; Wisner, K.L. & Yamamoto, B. (1999). "Gonadal Steroids in the Treatment of Mood Disorders", *Psychosomatic Medicine*, 61: 676-697.

Gove, W.R. (1972). "The Relationship between Sex Roles, Marital Prevalence, Correlates and Course of Minor Depression and Status, and Mental Illness", *Social Forces*, 51: 34-44.

Helzer, J.E.; Robins, L.N. & McEvoy, L. (1987). "Post-Traumatic Stress Disorder in the General Population", *New England Medicine*, 317: 1630-1634.

Howell, H.B., Brawman-Mintzer O, Monnier, J. & Yonkers, K.A. (2001). "Generalized Anxiety Disorder in Women", *Psychiatric Clinics of North America*, 24(1): 165-178.

Kagan, B.L.; Leskin, G.; Haas, B.; Wilkins, J. & Foy, D. (1999). "Elevated Lipid Levelsin Vietnam Veterans with Chronic Posttraumatic Stress Disorder", *Biological Psychiatry*, 45: 374-377.

Kar, N. (2011). "Cognitive Behavioural Therapy for the Treatment of Post-traumatic Stress Disorder: A Review", *Neuropsychiatr Disease Treatment*, 7: 167-181.

Kessler, R.C. & McLeod, J.D. (1984). "Sex Differences in Vulnerability to Undesirable Life Events", *American Sociological Review*, 49: 620-631.

Kessler, R.C.; McGonagle, K.A.; Zhao, S.; Nelson, C.B.; Hughes, M.; Eshleman, S.; Wittchen, H. & Kendler, K.S. (1994). "Lifetime and 12-month Prevalence of DSM-III-R Psychiatric Disorders in the United States", *Archieve of General Psychiatry*, 51: 8-19.

Lesser, R.P. (1996). "Psychogenic Seizures", *Neurology*, 46: 499-507.

Lewinsohn, P.M.; Gotlib, I.H.; Lewinsohn, M.; Seeley, J.R. & Allen, N.B. (1998). "Gender Differences in Anxiety Disorders and Anxiety Symptoms in Adolescents", *Journal of Abnormal Psychology*, 107: 109-117.

Lochner C.; Hemmings, S.M.J.; Kinnear, C.J.; Moolman-Smook, J.C.; Corfield, V.A. & Knowles, J.A. *et al.* (2004). "Gender in Obsessive-compulsive Disorder Clinical and Genetic Findings", *European Neuropsychopharmacology*, 14(2): 105-113.

Math, S.B. & Srinivasaraju, R. (2010). "Indian Psychiatric Epidemiological Studies: Learning from the Past", *Indian Journal Psychiatry*, 52, (Suppl 1): S95-S103. doi: 10.4103/0019-5545.69220

McHenry, J.; Carrier, N.; Hull, E. & Kabbaj, M. (2014). "Gender Differences in Anxiety and Depression: Role of Testosterone", *Frontiers in Neuroendocrinology*, 35(1): 42-57.

McLean, C.P.; Asnaani, A.; Litz, B.T. & Hofmann, S.G. (2011). "Gender Differences in Anxiety Disorders: Prevalence, Course of Illness, Comorbidity and Burden of Illness", *Journal of Psychiatric Research*, 45(8): 1027-1035.

Murray, C.J.L. & Lopez, A.D. (1996). "Alternative Visions of the Future: Projecting Mortality and Disability 1990-2020", in Murray, C.J.L. & Lopez, A.D. (Eds.), *The Global Burden of Disease: A Comprehensive Assessment of Mortality and Disability from Diseases, Injuries, and Risk Factors in 1990 and Projected to 2020*, Boston: Harvard University Press, pp. 325-395.

Orfila. F.; Ferrer, M. & Lamarca, R. *et al.* (2006). "Gender Differences in Health-related Quality of Life among the Elderly: The Role of Objective Functional Capacity and Chronic Conditions", *Soc. Sci. Med.*, 63: 2367-2380.

Prabha, S.; Chandra Veena, A.; Satyanarayana & Carey, M.P. (2009). "Women Reporting Intimate Partner Violence in India: Associations with PTSD and Depressive Symptoms", *Archieve Womens Mental Health*, 12: 203-209. DOI 10.1007/s00737-009-0065-6.

Rajkumar, A.P.; Titus, S. & Tharyan, P.P. (2008). "Coping with the Asian Tsunami: Perspectives from Tamil Nadu, India on the Determinants of Resilience in the Face of Adversity", *Social Science & Medicine*, 65(5): 844-853.

Reuber, M. & Elger, C.E. (2003). "Psychogenic Non-epileptic Seizures: Review and Update", *Epilepsy & Behaviour*, 4: 205-216.

Reuber, M.; House, A.O.; Pukrop, R.; Bauer, J. & Elger, C.E. (2001). "Somatization, Dissociation and Psypathology in Patient with Psychogenic Non-epileptic Seizures", *Epilepsia*, 3: 122-128.

Shear, K.; Jin, R.; Ruscio, A.M.; Walters, E.E. & Kessler, R.C. (2006). "Prevalence and Correlates of Estimated DSM-IV Child and Adult Separation Anxiety Disorder in the National Comorbidity Survey Replication", *The American Journal of Psychiatry*, 163(6): 1074-1083.

Shin, L.M.; McNally, R.J.; Kosslyn, S.M.; Thompson, W.L.; Rauch, S.L.; Alpert, N.M.; Metzger, L.J.; Lasko, N.B.; Orr, S.P. & Pitman, R.K. (1999). "Regional Cerebral Blood Flow during Script-Driven Imagery in Childhood Sexual Abuserelated PTSD: A PET Investigation", *American Journal of Psychiatry*, 156: 575-584.

Shors, T.J. & Leuner, B. (2003). "Research Report Estrogen-mediated Effects on Depression and Memory Formation in Females", *Journal of Affective Disorders*, 74: 85-96.

Van Wijk, C.M. & Kolk, A.M. (1997). "Sex Differences in Physical Symptoms: The Contribution of Symptom Perception Theory", *Social Science Medecine*, 45: 231-246.

Verbrugge, L. & Wingard, D.L. (1987). "Sex Difference in Health and Mortality", *Women and Health*, 12(2): 103-145.

Weissman, M.M.; Bland, R.; Joyce, P.R. & Newman, S. (1993). "Sex Differences in Rates of Depression: Cross-national Perspectives Special Issue: Toward a New Psychobiology of Depression in Women", *J. Affect. Disord.*, 29(2-3): 77-84.

Woods, S.J.C. (2005). "Intimate Partner Violence and Post-traumatic Stress Disorder Symptoms in Women What We Know and Need to Know", *The University of Akron Journal of Interpersonal Violence*, 20: 394-402. DOI: 10.1177/0886260504267882c 2005, Sage Publications

Yonkers, K.A. & Gurguis, G. (1995). "Gender Differences in the Prevalence and Expression of Anxiety Disorders", in M.V. Seeman (Ed.), *Gender and Psychopathology* (pp. 113-130), Washington, DC: American Psychiatric Press.

12

Suicide Ideation Correlates of Depression and Hopelessness in Working Women

Sonam Begum, Puran Chandra and *C.P. Khokhar*

Introduction

Suicidal behaviour is complex. It is an irrational desire to die. Suicide effects are tragic and felt long after the individual has taken his own life. A person who dies by suicide leaves behind a tangled confusion of family members and friend who try to make sense of a senseless and a purposeless act. It is usually second or third cause of death among teenagers, and remains one of the top ten leading causes of death well into middle age. The rationale behind suicide, which is defined as intentional taking of one's own life, can be as simple or as complex as life itself. The primary motivation to suicide is depression which is characterized by mood disturbance, feelings of sadness, despair and discouragement, resulting from personal loss and tragedy.

The concept "suicidality" refers to thoughts and plans of suicide, suicide attempts and completed suicide, and thus comprises a wide range of phenomena. A concept synonymous to "suicidality" is "suicidal behaviour" (which thus not only refers to acts but also to thoughts). "Suicidal ideation" refers to suicidality without action, i.e. all types of suicidal thoughts and plans. Suicide ideation refers to the thoughts about taking one's own life with some degree of intent (Johnson, 2006). A "suicide attempt" not only refers to an unsuccessful suicide but also comprises deliberate acts of lower lethality and intention. Several definitions have been proposed over the years to define a suicide attempt. Suicidal ideation is a common medical term for thoughts about suicide, which may be as detailed as a formulated plan, without the suicidal act itself. Suicidal ideation have incorporated different thoughts as attitudes to suicidal behaviour, for example, considering the suicidal act as a potential coping option, and contemplated plans and preparations for self-harm.

As already stated, suicide is the third leading cause of death among 15- to 24-year olds (Anderson & Smith, 2005) and the second leading cause of death among college students (Schwartz, 2006). Worldwide, suicide is among the top five causes of mortality in the 15- to 19-year age group. In many countries it ranks first or second as a cause of death among both boys and girls in this age group. In the last three decades (1975 to 2005), the suicide rate increased by 43 per cent.

Suicide can be understood from many different perspectives, from religious, philosophical, and sociological to psychological and biological. Historically, the meaning of suicide has reflected the religious tradition of given culture (Stevenson, 1988). Depression and suicidality are deeply entangled. Suicidality is a diagnostic symptom for major depression, and depression is the most common mental disorder leading to suicide, although substance abuse and schizophrenia are also major contributors (WHO, 2001). Women who have experienced both sexual and physical assaults are at greater risk for depression (Bergen, 1999). A successful theory of depression must explain suicidality, and the bargaining model, building on the work of, Watson and Andrews (2002), Brown (1986), Giddens (1964) does.

According to the existing literature, married women are less prone to suicide than single, divorced and widowed women. Never married, divorced or widowed women conduct most suicides (64.4%) in the US.

International studies show that depression and anxiety symptoms are more prevalent among women (Almeida *et al.*, 2004; Andrade *et al.*, 2006 & Desjarlains *et al.*, 1999). Women, and people with low education and economically impaired have greater risk of presenting depression (Patel, 2001). According to World Health Organization, depression is currently one of the world's most under-treated disease, and is the leading cause of disability among women (Murray & Lopez, 1996). In an earlier article by Rothblum (1983), lack of paid employment was considered as causing factor for depression among females. On contrary, in general assumptions, working women may be prone to depression because they bear the double burden of housework and a job outside the home. Because they have to work in two environments, one is the office environment and the other is home environment. Both are vastly different from one to another. Stress arising from working conditions may be manifested in suicidal ideation and chronic disorders such as depression, insomnia and hypertension. Hopelessness is one of the major components of Beck's negative cognitive trait, i.e. negative cognitions about future. When confronted with a negative event, individuals with a negative thinking process are vulnerable to depression, because they will infer that negative consequences will follow from this negative event and that occurrence of that event means that the individuals themselves are worthless or flawed (McGinn, 2000). The expression of hopelessness in conjunction with a mental disorder such as depression represents a very dangerous warning sign and always needs to be taken very seriously. It is a feeling that conditions will never improve, that there is no solution to a problem, and, for many, a feeling that dying by suicide would be better than living. Most people who feel hopeless have depression, and untreated depression is the number one cause for suicide.

There is a high association with hopelessness in long-term suicide risk. Not specific to depression, hopelessness can accompany demoralization with a number of other syndromes: schizophrenia, anxiety disorder, and chronic conditions, including medical condition. According to Beck's formulation, hopelessness is a core characteristic of depression and serves as the link between depression and suicide. Furthermore, hopelessness associated with other psychiatric disorders also predisposes the patient to suicidal behaviour. The central role of hopelessness in the development of suicidal ideation has been supported by empirical research (Dyer & Kreitman, 1984; Nekanda-Trepka, Bishop & Blackburn, 1983; Bedrosian & Beck, 1979; Minkoff, Bergman & Beck *et al.*, 1973). Wetzel *et al.* (1980) reviewed studies addressing the relationships among depression, hopelessness, and suicidal ideation and concluded that the preponderant evidence supported the linkage of hopelessness and suicide intent.

The current study expands the existing literature by incorporating various improvements and refinements in the methodology. The relationship suicide ideation with depression and hopelessness has been examined separately for Unmarried and Married working women.

Objectives

1. To examine the relationship of suicide ideation with depression.
2. To examine the relationship of suicide ideation with hopelessness.
3. To examine the relationship of suicidal ideation with depression after partialling out the influence of hopelessness.
4. To examine the association between suicidal ideation with hopelessness after partialling out the influence of depression.

Hypotheses

1. Suicide ideation would be positively correlated with depression.
2. Suicide ideation would be positively correlated with hopelessness.
3. Suicide ideation would correlate positively with depression after partialling out the influence of hopelessness.
4. Suicidal ideation would correlate positively with hopelessness after partialling out the influence of depression.

Methodology

Sample

The sample consists of 100 unmarried women and 100 married women in the age range of 35-45 years working in Public and Private sectors in Uttar Pradesh and Delhi. The sample was selected by the technique of random sampling. The final samples selected consisted of middle class and upper middle class women as per their education, family background and their job status.

Tools

Scale for Suicide Ideation (Beck, Kovacs & Weissman, 1979): Beck's Scale for Suicide Ideation includes 21 items designed to evaluate the presence and severity of suicidal thoughts. The first 19 items measure the severity of suicidal wishes, attitudes, and plans. Patients rate each item on a scale of 0 to 2. The SSI has been found useful in quantifying the degree of suicidal ideation a person is experiencing and can serve as a key warning sign in identifying suicide risk. The SSI has demonstrated strong internal consistency with a coefficient alpha of 0.93 among psychiatric outpatients (Beck & Steer, 1988). Among psychiatric inpatients, the SSI has demonstrated coefficient alphas of 0.89 (Beck *et al.*, 1979) and 0.96 (Beck *et al.*, 1988). Studies on the psychometric properties of the SSI have shown evidence of inter-rater reliability (Beck *et al.*, 1979), convergent validity (Holden & DeLisle, 2005), concurrent, and construct validity (Beck *et al.*, 1988).

Beck Depression Inventory (Beck, Ward, Mendelson, Mock & Erbaugh, 1961): The Beck Depression Inventory (BDI) is a self-administered scale comprising of 21 items assessing cognitive, emotional, and physical symptoms of depression (Beck, Rush & Shaw *et al.*, 1979). In each item the respondent selects one of four statements that best describe how he/she has been feeling over the past few days. Each statement receives a score of 0 to 3, with 3 indicating the highest level of severity for each item. The scale score is computed as the sum of the 21 items. Scores range from 0 to 63, with zero indicating no depressive symptoms and 63 indicating the highest level of depressive symptoms possible. The BDI demonstrated high internal consistency (Cronbach's $\alpha = 0.882$) in a study by Arria *et al.* (2009).

The Beck Hopelessness Scale (Beck, Weissman, Lester & Trexler, 1974): Hopelessness Scale is a 20-item self-report measure assesses the feelings about the future, future expectations, loss of motivation and overall hopelessness in which participants are asked to read a statement and responds true or false based on how they currently feel. In scoring the measure, each item receives a 0 or 1. Nine items are keyed false and 11 items are keyed true, so, that the total hopelessness score is a sum of the scores on the individual items. The BHS score indicates severity of pessimism about the future, ranging from 0 to 20. Among psychiatric patients, the BHS has yielded a reliability coefficient of 0.93 (Beck, Weissman, Lester & Trexler, 1974), and more recent data has supported comparable findings (Dyce, 1996; Young, Halper, Clark, Scheftner & Fawcett, 1992).

Procedure

After clarifying the instructions of the concerned tests Beck's Suicide Ideation Scale, Beck Depression Inventory and Hopelessness scale were administered on selected sample in groups and tests were given one by one. The correlation values were calculated for suicide ideation with depression and hopelessness and with these correlation values, the partial correlations were calculated for Unmarried and Married working women respectively.

Analysis

Keeping in view the various hypotheses, the association between different variables was examined by computing correlations, separately for Unmarried and Married working women.

Results and Discussion

The current study was primarily concerned with examining the relationship of suicide ideation with depression and hopelessness. This was done by computing Pearson's product-moment correlation separately for Unmarried and Married working women. The correlations are shown in Table 12.1. Keeping in view, hypotheses 3 and 4, partial correlation between variables of interest were also computed. The partial correlations are shown in Tables 12.2 and 12.3.

TABLE 12.1: Correlation of Suicide Ideation with Depression and Hopelessness for Males and Females

Unmarried/Married	*Suicide Ideation*	*Depression*	*Hopelessness*
Suicide Ideation	—	0.54	0.65
Depression	0.48	—	0.48
Hopelessness	0.57	0.40	—

Note: Correlations above the diagonal values indicating correlations for Unmarried working women and correlations below the diagonal values indicating correlations for Married working women.

TABLE 12.2: Partial Correlation for Suicide Ideation and Depression

Partial Correlation	*Unmarried Working Women*	*Married Working Women*
R 12.3	0.34	0.33

TABLE 12.3: Partial Correlation for Suicide Ideation and Hopelessness

Partial Correlation	*Unmarried Working Women*	*Married Working Women*
R 13.2	0.53	0.30

An examination of Table 12.1 reveals that for Unmarried working women, the correlations of suicide ideation with depression and hopelessness were 0.54 and 0.65 respectively. For Married working women, the correlations of suicide ideation with depression and hopelessness were 0.48 and 0.57 respectively. All these correlations were found to be significant at 0.001 level of significance, suggesting thereby that suicide ideation is associated markedly with depression and hopelessness. The same trend operates even after partial correlations were computed which shows that Unmarried working women are higher on relevance of suicide ideation when we partialled out the role of depression it is signifies the tendency to be hopeless in future for Unmarried working women as comparison of Married working women.

The obtained results are in concordance with the earlier studies which have also found the role of depression and hopelessness in suicide ideation. Hopelessness is one of the major components of Beck's negative cognitive triad, i.e. negative cognitions about future. When confronted with a negative event, individuals with a negative thinking process are vulnerable to depression, because they will infer that negative consequences will follow from this negative event and that occurrence of that event means that the individuals themselves are worthless or flawed (McGinn, 2000). The expression of hopelessness in conjunction with a mental disorder such as depression represents a very dangerous warning sign and always needs to be taken very seriously.

Since hopelessness is positively related to suicidal ideation, it is important to cultivate the sense of hope in women. Khokhar, C.P. and Chatterjee, M. (2010) also found that women who have high level of stress, depression and personality disorders hence leading to a high level of suicidal ideation.

The results also support the differential activation model of suicidality (Lau *et al.*, 2004; Williams *et al.*, 2008). The model assumes that during a depressive episode an association is formed between sad moods and suicidal and hopelessness cognitions, so that in the future, a mild mood fluctuation acts as a prime to re-activate such cognitions, increasing the risk of relapse. The unique association of the past symptoms of guilt and suicidality with current Hopelessness and Suicidal reactivity was replicated (Williams *et al.*, 2008). This trend indicates there is a strong relationship of suicide ideation with depression and hopelessness. The results of the present study suggest that targeting hopelessness may be as important in adolescence women as in adults to reduce suicidal ideation and prevent suicidal attempts. Stress arising from working conditions may be manifested in suicidal ideation and chronic disorders such as depression, insomnia and hypertension. India being a democratic country with traditional society, women are expected to stay at home and do house work but on the other hand, women in India, have been contributing a lot in workforce. So, the health of women is being questioned, whether unmarried or married working women.

REFERENCES

Anderson, R. & Smith, B. (2005). "Deaths: Leading Cause for 2002. National Vital Statistics Report: From the Centre for Disease Control and Prevention", National Centre for Health Statistics, *National Vital Statistic System*, 53: 1-89.

Beck, A.; Kovacs, M. & Weissman, A. (1979). "Assessment of Suicidal Intention: The Scale for Suicide Ideation", *Journal of Consulting and Clinical Psychology*, 47: 343-352.

Beck, A.; Rush, A.; Shaw, B. & Emery, G. (1979). *Cognitive Therapy of Depression*, New York: Guilford.

Beck, A. & Steer, R. (1988). *Manual for the Beck Hopelessness Scale,*. San Antonio: Tex, Psychological Corporation.

Beck, A.; Steer, R. & Ranieri, W. (1988). "Scale for Suicide Ideation: Psychometric Properties of a Self-report Version", *Journal of Clinical Psychology*, 44: 499-505.

Beck, A.; Ward, C.; Mendelson, M.; Mock, J. & Erbaugh, J. (1961). "An Inventory for Measuring Depression", *Archives of General Psychiatry*, 4: 561-71.

Beck, A.; Weissman, A.; Lester, D. & Trexler, L. (1974). "The Measurement of Pessimism: The Hopelessness Scale", *Journal of Consulting and Clinical Psychology*, 42: 861-865.

Bedrosian, R. & Beck, A. (1979). "Cognitive Aspects of Suicidal Behaviour", *Suicide and Life Threat Behaviour*, 2: 87-96.

Brown, M. (1986). "Power, Gender, and the Social Meaning of Aguaruna Suicide", *Man: New Series*, 21: 311-328.

Dyce, J. (1996). "Factor Structure of the Beck Hopelessness Scale", *Journal of Clinical Psychology*, 52: 555-558.

Dyer, J. & Kreitman, N. (1984). "Hopelessness, Depression, and Suicide Intent in Parasuicide", *British Journal of Psychiatry*, 144: 127-133.

Giddens, A. (1964). "Suicide, Attempted Suicide, and the Suicide Threat", *Man*, 64: 115-116.

Holden, R. & DeLisle, M. (2005). "Factor Analysis of the Beck Scale for Suicide Ideation with Female Suicide Attempters", *Assessment*, 12: 231-238.

Ibadat, K. (2011). "Relationship of Suicidal Ideation with Depression and Hopelessness", *Indian Journal of Psychological Science*, December, Vol. 2(2): 126-133.

Johnson, C. (2006). "Familicide and Family Law: A Study of Filicide-suicide Following Separation", *Family Court Review*, 44: 448-463.

Khokhar, C.P. (2007). *Stress, Coping and Health*, Shalabh Publishing House, 259/5 Shastri Nagar, Meerut.

Khokhar, C.P. & Chatterjee, M. (2010). "Suicide in Relation to Role Stress, Work Schedule and the Personality of Working Women", *Indian Journal of Psychological Science*, Vol. 01(1): 57-68.

Lau, M.; Segal, Z. & Williams, J. (2004). "Teasdale's Differential Activation Hypothesis: Implications for Mechanisms of Depressive Relapse and Suicidal Behaviour", *Behaviour Research and Therapy*, 429: 1001-1017.

McGinn, L. (2000). "Cognitive Behavioural Therapy of Depression: Theory, Treatment and Empirical Status", *American Journal of Psychotherapy*, 54: 254-260.

Minkoff, K.; Bergman, E. & Beck A. *et al.* (1973). "Hopelessness, Depression, and Attempted Suicide", *American Journal of Psychiatry*, 130: 455-459.

Nekanda-Trepka, C.; Bishop, S. & Blackburn, M. (1983). "Hopelessness and Depression", *British Journal of Clinical Psychiatry*, 132: 954-956.

Schwartz, A.J. (2006). "College Student Suicide in the United States: 1990-91 through 2003-04", *Journal of American College Health*, 54: 327-337.

Shek, D. (2007). "Adolescent Developmental Issues in Hong Kong: Relevance to Positive Youth Development Programmes in Hong Kong", in Shek, D.T.L.; Ma, H.K. & Merrick, J., Eds. *Positive Youth Development: Development of a Pioneering Programme in a Chinese Context*, London: Freund Publishing House.

Stevenson, J. (1988). "Suicide", in *The American Psychiatric Press Text Book of Psychiatry*, Edited by Talbot, J.A.; Hales, R.E.; Yudofsky, S.C., Washington, DC: American Psychiatric Press, pp. 1021-1035.

Watson, P. & Andrews, P. (2002). "Toward a Revised Evolutionary Adaptation's Analysis of Depression: The Social Navigation Hypothesis", *Journal of Affective Disorder*, 72: 1-14.

Wetzel, K.; Margulies, T. & Davis, R. (1980). "Hopelessness, Depression, and Suicide Intent", *Journal of Clinical Psychiatry*, 41: 159-160.

WHO (2001). Cf. Hagen, E.H. (2003). *The Bargaining Model of Depression, Genetic and Cultural Evolution of Cooperation*, Humboldt University, Germany: The MIT Press.

Williams, J.; Van der Does, A.; Barnhofer, T.; Crane, C. & Segal, Z. (2008). "Cognitive Reactivity, Suicidal Ideation and Future Fluency: Preliminary Investigation of a Differential Activation Theory of Hopelessness/Suicidality", *Cognitive Therapy and Research*, 321: 83-104.

Young, M.; Halper, I.; Clark, D. & Scheftner, W. (1992). "An Item Response Theory Evaluation of the Beck Hopelessness Scale", *Cognitive Therapy and Research*, 16: 579-587.

13

Management of Occupational Stress among Working Women

Satarupa Datta

Introduction

Across the world, more and more women than ever before are completing higher levels of education. Better job opportunities have increased many women's independence and resulted in a new status and role in their families and society. In India, women are becoming educated and also doing different kinds of jobs in different fields. They are best recognized for organizing their role as professional as well as homemaker. However, this organizing may cost them more stress than they can actually manage. It is better known as dual role stress.

The new generation of women want to pursue their dream career. But this life is not a bed of roses for all. One has to fulfil the demands at work as well as various demands at home. Women have been found to suffer from physiological, psychological and behavioural symptoms of stress. Consistently increase in psychosomatic diseases and psychological problem among women indicate the high level of stress being experienced by them. In the present day both the husband and wife work towards creating a balance between their work life and home with their children. But it is still difficult for the woman as she has to play multiple roles of a cook, a family maid, a tutor, a nurse as well as cater to the demands of workplace. This can leave a working woman stressed and anxious; more so if the family is not supportive.

Literature Review

The widespread entry of females into the labour force is a characteristic of the past decades. Females are increasingly entering the workforce to contribute financially to the family survival (Lim, 2009). They are not only entering the workforce in greater numbers but also remaining in the workforce throughout their child-bearing and child-rearing years (Lim, 2009). Even with the changing societal trends and expectations, it is still 'expected' that working females should assume the traditional role of a homemaker (Noor, 1999; Nair, 2011). The added elements of motherhood in some working females increased the possibility of acute dual-role or multiple role stress as a mother, employee and spouse or partner (Kline & Snow, 1994). Noor's (1999) preliminary findings on Malaysian working women's roles and well-being showed that the juggle between work and family demands have contributed to the adverse psychological and emotional well-being for the working mothers resulting in feelings of guilt, anxiety or decreased role satisfaction at work and home. Killien and Brown (1987) summarized that when demands from work and family roles opposes each other, the mother is likely to suffer stress and negative health consequences. Canam (1986) further discovered that work deadlines were the most frequently mentioned stressor and interfered with the family environment. On the contrary, Ritchie's (1982) findings indicated that even though working mothers found it more stressful than full-time mothers in caring for their children, working mothers were rated warmer, more confident and less anxious than full-time mothers. The mother-child relationship among working mothers were likely to be positively evaluated as well when compared to full-time mothers (Ritchie, 1982). Sources of work stress such as work overload, job insecurity, work interpersonal relationships, role conflict, commuting stress etc. have been identified to play a primary role in employee's health and are somewhat similar for both males and females (Days & Livingstone, 2001). Frequent absenteeism, mood disorders, tardiness and intentions to quit are usually predictors of stressful working conditions (Sandmark & Renstig, 2010). Furthermore, work stressors unique to working females also include sexual harassment, lower chances of career advancement and sexual inequality, may negatively impact females (Street, Gradus, Stafford & Kelly, 2007). Street *et al.* (2007) highlighted that sexual harassment in the workforce is more likely to happen to single females in their twenties. Furthermore, a longitudinal study by Melchior *et al.* (2007) assessed 891 participants (45.6% female) at the age of 32 found that participants exposed to high job demands experienced a double risk of major depressive disorder (MDD) and generalized anxiety disorder (GAD). Similarly, Snow *et al.* (2003) also found work stress as a significant contribution factor to the increase of negative psychological symptoms in 239 females employed in secretarial positions in the USA. In the attempt to maintain their work performance and expected responsibilities as a wife, mother or partner, the working females had little time for themselves in terms of recuperation due to long working hours and commitment to work (Sandmark & Restig, 2010).

Objectives

The main objective of the current study is to ascertain:

(a) The causes of occupational stress among working women.
(b) Consequences of stress among working women.
(c) Coping strategies adopted by working women to mitigate stress.

Case Studies

Case Study 1

The aim of the review by Lian *et al.* (2014) was to evaluate research relating to the effects of coping strategies and resilience on the level of workplace stress. Much of the research focused on working mothers and working females in general. It was found that working females experienced more work stress as compared to men. And currently in Malaysia, social policies that support working females, especially working mothers, has not been adopted fully by most corporations. Furthermore, the evidence for effective problem-focused and emotion-focused coping was inconsistent. It was concluded that correlation between work stressors and the adopted coping strategies may vary depending on the type of problems being dealt with and the interplay between the employee and the demand.

Case Study 2

This chapter by Joshi *et al.* (2014) examines stress of working women due to her dual role in education field. The purpose of present study is to know the stress of women because of her dual role and attempt to provide a preventive and positive approach to women experiencing stress at work and at home. For the present study purposive random sampling has been chosen and the sample consists of married Assistant Professors of Bhilai Mahila Mahavidyalaya Hospital Sector, Bhilai. Self-designed questionnaire was distributed to 50 Assistant Professors of college. Questions comprised their views and attitude towards home and institute. For analysis of data percentage, mean score were computed with the help of bar diagram. The result showed that the major stressors for working women were excessive work. Sixty per cent suffer from stress-related diseases. Most of them have full support from family. Seventy per cent agreed that they have stress due to upgradation of education in the institute. Eighty five per cent managed their stress by watching television. Ten per cent strongly agreed that they have stress due to upgradation of education, whereas 70 per cent agreed for that and 20 per cent disagreed; 60 per cent agreed that they have good support from family members whereas 40 per cent do not have. Thirty per cent agreed that they miss out quality time with family and friends, 50 per cent disagreed. Sixty per cent professors suffer from stress-related disease such as diabetes, hypertension, obesity etc. Fifty per cent agreed that they experience excessive work load. Only 10 per cent agreed that they work for long hours. Negative attitude of heads, colleagues, juniors, spouse and children affect in balancing work and family commitments. Eighty per cent agreed that they suffer with excessive household work.

Causes of Occupational Stress among Working Women

Imbalance between work and family leads to occupational stress, which arises due to a number of factors. Various factors are as follows:

Mental Harassment

It is an age old convention that women are less capable and inefficient in working as compared to men. The strongest harassment in the modern workplace is against mothers. Mothers are assumed as less competent and less committed towards their jobs because they cannot be good mothers and good employees simultaneously.

Sexual Harassment

Even today, almost all working women are prone to sexual harassment irrespective of their status, personal characteristics and the types of their employment. They face sexual harassment on transports, at working places, educational institutions and hospitals, at home and even in police stations when they go to file complaints.

Discrimination at Workplace

True equality between men and women has not yet been achieved.

Gender discrimination lowers job satisfaction, motivation, commitment level and increases the level of occupational stress among the women employees. Gender discrimination transforms the emotionally brittle, simple and peace loving women employees into suspicious, anxious and angry individuals. They are often deprived of promotions and growth opportunities at work places but this does not apply to all working women. A majority of working women continue to be denied their right to equal pay, under the Equal Remuneration Act, 1976 and are underpaid in comparison to their male colleagues. This is usually the case in factories and labour-oriented industries.

Lack of Family Support

Family support is very much essential for working women. At times, the family does not support women to leave the household work and go to office. Especially, working mothers are forced to leave their jobs due to lack of adequate family support.

Insufficient Maternity Leaves

Insufficient maternity leave is a major issue that is faced by working mothers in private organizations. Very recently Central Government has enhanced maternity leave up to 9 months but still the State Government and private organizations do not extend this facility to the women employees. Women working in the private organization should also get child care leave like their government counterparts. This affects the performance of women employees at work, as well as it is detrimental to their personal lives.

Job Insecurity

During corporate reorganizations women employees are most vulnerable and thus suffer from severe stress. Increased workload, extremely long working hours and intense pressures to perform at peak levels all the time especially in the private organizations, can actually leave the women employees physically and psychologically exhausted. Excessive travel and too much time away from family also act as a major stressor.

Workplace Adjustment

Even today women face severe psychological stress to adjust themselves with the male-dominated working environment. Maladjustment to workplace cultures lead to subtle conflicts with colleagues or even with superiors. In many cases workplace politics or gossips can be major stress inducers.

Consequences of Stress among Working Women

Physical Symptoms of Stress

- Chronic Headaches
- Migraine
- Thyroid problems
- Spondylosis
- Chronic low back pain
- Stomach problems
- Eating disorders
- Sleep disturbances
- Fatigue
- Muscle aches and pains
- High Blood Pressure
- Heart disease.

Psychological and Behavioural Symptoms of Stress

- Serious depression
- Forgetfulness
- Inefficiency at work
- Suicidal behaviour
- Domestic violence
- Anxiety
- Irritability
- Low morale
- Worried about job security
- Alcohol and drug use
- Feeling powerless
- Temper outburst.

Coping Strategies Adopted by Working Women to Mitigate Stress

At Personal Level

This brings up some important issues regarding women and stress, that women need to be aware of:

- They must prioritize what's necessary and what can be avoided.
- They should alter or change their perspective.
- Fast stress relievers may be adopted by working women to avoid the monotony of stress. Such may include reading a book of jokes, listening to songs or discussion on general topics with colleagues.
- One can avoid stress from occurring in the first place by maintaining or practising regular stress relieving activities. It may include Exercises, Yoga, meditation etc.
- They should think positively.
- They can embrace spirituality.
- They can maintain a strong social network.

At Organizational Level

Coping strategies adopted at organizational level are:

- Employee Assistance Programmes like counselling should specially be designed to assist women employees in dealing with the basic causes of stress.
- Stress Management Training (SMT) is employed by many organizations today as a method to get employees to either work through regular stress or to control their stress levels.
- Establishment of Anti-sexual harassment cell comprising of women members where women employees can register their complaints.
- Several researches have been conducted that link certain interventions, such as narrative writing or topic-specific training to reduce physiological and psychological stress.
- In the organizational front, celebration of employees' birthdays, picnic, family get togethers, cultural programmes, outdoor tours help to restore friendly relationship among the male and female colleagues in the workplace.
- In India organizations should implement stress audits which will ascertain the causes of occupational stress, high rate of attrition and reasons of absenteeism among the employees.
- Social support is found to reduce stress among the employees. Today women are organizing themselves to meet the challenges of the workplace. Male colleagues should always provide a supportive working environment to the females.

Conclusion

Stress in the work front is a communality throughout the world. Management of stress enhances the job performance of the working women as well improves their relationship with colleagues and family members. Supportive work environment reduces work stress. Making the environment less competitive between employees decreases some amounts of stress.

Suggestions

The present scenario demands change in the traditional mind-set of the society that males are the bread earners and females are the house-keepers. So, there is a need to change the attitude of the employers, policy-makers, politicians and family members. They should provide a tension free environment to working women at place of work as well as at home.

Limitation of the Study

The chapter is based on secondary data. Original field based study has not been undertaken due to shortage of time and resources.

Scope of Further Research

(a) An empirical study can be conducted among working women of Kolkata.

(b) Comparisons can be made to measure work-related stress levels among working females of different occupations belonging to different states of India.

REFERENCES

Canam, C.J. (1986). "Perceived Stressors and Coping Responses of Employed and Non-employed Career Women with Preschool Children", *Canadian Journal of Community Mental Health*, 5(2): 49-59.

Garg, N. (2014). "Occupational Stress and Challenges Faced by Working Women in India", *Paripex-Indian Journal of Research*, 3(7).

Joshi, S.; Banerjee, S. & Mohan, S.M. (2014). "Stress Due to Dual Role of Working Women", *Indian Journal of Science and Research*, 9(1): 163-166.

Killien, M. & Brown, M.A. (1987). "Work and Family Roles of Women: Sources of Stress and Coping Strategies", *Health Care for Women International*, 8(2-3): 169-184. *http://dx.doi.org/10.1080/07399338709515780*

Kline, M. & Snow, D. (1994). "Effects of a Worksite Coping Skills Intervention on the Stress, Social Support, and Health Outcomes of Working Mothers", *Journal of Primary Prevention*, 15(2): 105-121. *http://dx.doi.org/10.1007/BF02197142*

Kok, H.L. (1982). "Age at First Marriage in Peninsular Malaysia", *Journal of Marriage and Family*, 44(3): 785-798. *http://dx.doi.org/10.2307/351600.*

Lian, S. & Tam, C.L. (2014). "Work Stress, Coping Strategies and Resilience: A Study among Working Females", *Asian Social Science*, 10(12): 41-52.

Lim, L.L. (2009). "Female Labour-force Participation", in United Nations (Eds.), *Completing the Fertility Transition* (pp. 203-221). United Nations Publication, Retrieved from *http://www.un.org/esa/population/publications/completingfertility/RevisedLIMpaper*

Lim, S.; Cortina, L.M. & Magley, V.J. (2008). "Personal and Workgroup Incivility: Impact on Work and Health Outcomes", *Journal of Applied Psychology*, 93(1): 95-107. *http://dx.doi.org/10.1037/0021-9010.93.1.95*

McLaughlin, M.; Cormier, L.S. & Cormier, W.H. (1988). "Relation between Coping Strategies and Distress, Stress, and Marital Adjustment of Multiple-role Women", *Journal of Counselling Psychology*, 35(2): 187-193. *http://dx.doi.org/10.1037/0022-0167.35.2.187*

Melchior, M.; Caspi, A.; Milne, B.J.; Danese, A.; Poulton, R. & Moffitt, T.E. (2007). "Work Stress Precipitates Depression and Anxiety in Young, Working Women and Men", *Psychological Medicine*, 37(8): 1119-1129. *http://dx.doi.org/10.1017/S0033291707000414*

Michie, S. (2002). "Causes and Management of Stress at Work", *Occupational and Environmental Medicine*, 59: 67-72. *http://dx.doi.org/10.1136/oem.59.1.67*

Nair, E. (2005, December). *Women in the Boardroom*, Invited paper presented at 8th GOPIO (Global Organization of Persons of Indian Origin) International Convention, 17-18 December, 2005, Furama City Centre, Singapore.

Nair, E. (2011). "Urban Career Women and Stress in South-East Asia", *Journal of Adult Development*, 18(2): 62-65. *http://dx.doi.org/10.1007/s10804-010-9115-6*

Noor, N. (1999). "Roles and Women's Well-being: Some Preliminary Findings from Malaysia", *Sex Roles*, 41(3-4): 123-145. *http://dx.doi.org/10.1023/A:1018846010541*

O'Bryan, A. (2008). *Perceived Stress, Coping Strategies, and Role Strain of Working Mothers Enrolled in a Master's Programme* (Doctoral thesis). Available from ProQuest Dissertations and Theses database (UMI No.: 3325345).

O'Neill, C.P. & Zeichner, A. (1985). "Working Women: A Study of Relationships between Stress, Coping and Health", *Journal of Psychosomatic Obstetrics and Gynecology*, 4(2): 105-116. *http://dx.doi.org/10.3109/01674828509085266*

Ritchie, J. (1982). "Child-rearing Practices and Attitudes of Working and Full-time Mothers", *Women's Studies International Forum*, 5(5): 419-425. *http://dx.doi.org/10.1016/0277-5395(82)90004-8*

Rutter, M. (2012). "Resilience as a Dynamic Concept", *Development and Psychopathology*, 24(2): 335-344. *http://dx.doi.org/10.1017/S0954579412000028*

Sandmark, H. & Renstig, M. (2010). "Understanding Long-term Sick Leave in Female White-collar Workers with Burnout and Stress-related Diagnoses: A Qualitative Study", *BMC Public Health*, 10(1): 1-12. *http://dx.doi.org/10.1186/1471-2458-10-210*

Shek, D.T.L. (1989). "Reliance on Self or Seeking Help from Others: Gender Differences in the Locus of Coping in Chinese Working Parents", *The Journal of Psychology*, 126(6): 671-678. *http://dx.doi.org/10.1080/00223980.1992.10543397*

Snow, D.L.; Swan, S.C.; Raghavan, C.; Connell, C.M. & Klein, I. (2003). "The Relationship of Work Stressors, Coping and Social Support to Psychological Symptoms among Female Secretarial Employees", *Work & Stress*, 17(3): 241-263. *http://dx.doi.org/10.1080/0267837031000162563O*

Street, A.E.; Gradus, A.L.; Stafford, J. & Kelly, K. (2007). "Gender Differences in Experiences of Sexual Harassment: Data from a Male-dominated Environment", *Journal of Consulting and Clinical Psychology*, 75(3): 464-474. *http://dx.doi.org/10.1037/0022-006X.75.3.464*

Tripathi, P. & Bhattacharjee, S. (2012). "A Study of Psychological Stress of Working Women", *ZENITH International Journal of Multidisciplinary Research*, 2(2): 434-445.

Wee, Y.G.; Ibrahim, M.D.B. & Poerwowidagdo, S.J. (n.d.). *Occupational Stress: A Survey of Women Managers in Malaysia*, 1-18. Retrieved from *http://www.wbiconpro.com/451-Wee.pdf*

14

Enhancing Women Challenges and Women Empowerment in India

G. Kumaravelu

Introduction

Empowerment of women put forwards to increase the social, educational, spiritual, political, gender strength of individuals and women community. Empowerment of women in India is largely relied on various factors that include rural and urban educational status, caste and class social status and age. Women's empowerment policies are made at the local, state and national levels in many dimensions that include education, health, gender-based violence, economic opportunities and political participation. Even though there are noteworthy gap between actual practice and policy advancements at the community level.

Women empowerment is fundamentally the course of lifting education, social, economic and political status of women, the conventionally disadvantaged ones of the society. It is the course of protecting women from various forms of violence. Empowerment of women involves the constructing up of a healthy society, a good political environment, where the women can breathe the air with no fear of domination, exploitation, apprehension, discrimination and the general sentiment of maltreatment in woman in this male dominated society.

Almost women comprise about 50 per cent of the world's population whereas India has shown unequal sex ratio making women's population comparatively lesser than males. With regard to their social status they were not treated equally to men in all walks of life. The women have got equal status and rights equal to men in every walks of life in the Western societies. But, in India even today gender discriminations and disabilities exist. The inconsistent situation where women were treated equal to Goddess and at the same time merely as slave.

Past Status of Women

Being equal in all aspects to male is still a unreachable stone for Indian women. Women are equally in figures as compared to their male counterparts managing all the works at home or outside. In 2012, in the union council of ministers women occupied only 8 out of 74 ministerial positions. Only there were 2 women judges in the Supreme Court out of 26 judges and there were only 54 women judges in the High Courts out of 634 judges.

Shocking Facts

According to UNDP report in 2013 on Human Development Indicators, South Asian Countries were ranked better for women except Afghanistan. It further forecasts that an Indian girl child aged between 1-5 years has got maximum chances to die than the boy child. Further it was reported that in every twenty minutes, a woman is raped and only 10 per cent of the crimes are reported. Women constitute 48 per cent of the India's population, 29 per cent of the National defense force, 26 per cent of women only are have access to formal credit.

Why Need of Women Empowerment?

Looking back to the *Vedas* of Indian culture, women are being worshipped as Lakshmi for wealth, Saraswati for knowledge, Durga for *shakti*. The position of women in India especially in rural areas has to suitably empower regarding the issue of empowering women. Major part of the of the female population remains unutilized in rural areas, these all exists due to the existing social customs. Women contribute nearly 85 per cent of the workforce with regard to agriculture and animal care. Women works nearly two third of the working hours, receiving one tenth of the world's income and own less than one hundredth the world property. Of the world's population, 900 million women were illiterate and 70 per cent of women are living in poverty. Women hold just 10 per cent of seats in World Parliament and 6 per cent of seats in National Cabinet.

Status of Women Empowerment

The position of empowerment of women cannot be pictured only with single element rather multidimensional evaluation has to be carried out in terms of different dimensions of women's life and their status will definitely convey a clear outset Therefore, this chapter tries to present a basic idea about the status and life condition of women in terms of education, health, employment and social status. If we look at overall status of women in terms of gender gap index prepared by World Economic Forum in 2012, India ranks next to Sri Lanka in every sub-indexes of gender equality. In political empowerment and educational attainments India gained eight places from 113 rank in 2011 to 105 rank in 2012. Apart from Political Empowerment, the other fields like education, health and social ranked above hundredth position. Due to the importance given in the 73rd and 74th Constitutional Amendments for Women, this political empowerment raised the status of women to greater heights.

Reasons for the Empowerment of Women

At present there are various schemes in India offered by the Central and State Governments in order to empower the women. In India women are marginalized and discriminated at various levels of the society irrespective of political participation, economic participation, social participation and access to education. Women are economically weaker and only few are engaged in services and other activities all over India. Therefore, they are in need of economic empowerment to stand on their own legs equal to men. Also, it is observed that women are less literate than men. The literacy rate among men if 76 per cent and among women is 54 per cent based on 2001 census. Thus, increasing the education status is of prime importance of women in empowering their lives. It is also observed that women are weak at their work because of the less food they consume but work more. Therefore, women folk who are to be made stronger from the point of health. Another firing problem is the sexual harassment of women in their workplace. At present there are many cases related to women like rape, dowry harassment and kidnapping of girl. In order to overcome all these problems they need empowerment in various aspects so as to safeguard themselves and to live a secure life through purity and dignity. In total, empowerment of women will not happen unless women come with and help to self-empower themselves. There is a dire need to prepare reducing feminized poverty, promoting women education and prevent violation against women.

Challenges

There are various limitations that ensure the development of empowerment of women in India. Family structure and social customs in growing countries like India are visible and enables the secondary status of women. One of the customs is the ongoing preference for a son over the birth of a girl child which we can see almost in all societies and communities. The society is highly partial towards male child with regard to nutrition, education and other opportunities. This is due to the attitude and belief that male child looks after the family with an exception of Meghalaya. Women frequently assess on them the traditional concept of their role as natural thus inflict an injustice upon them. Poverty is the certainty of life for many of the women in India and in fact it is the major factor that challenges the women in realizing their empowerment. There are several factors and challenges that affect the issues of women's right in India. Aiming on these issues will honestly profit the women empowerment in Indian education. As far as the education is concerned after Independence, we find an enormous gap between men and women. Men are 82.14 per cent educated while only 65.46 per cent of women are educated in India. Gender partiality is there in specialized professional trainings, higher education which wounds women in employment and to attain leadership in any field.

Suggestions

1. The primary and important, emphasis must be given to women's education which seems to be the grassroot problem. Therefore, women education must be paid particular attention.
2. Awareness programmes have to be conducted with the aim of creating awareness towards women especially for the women belonging to weaker sections in order to know about their rights.
3. Women must be encouraged to work and enough safety and support has to be provided at workplace. They must be given good wages and their work positions must be at par with men in the society.
4. Programmes and Acts must be strictly implemented in order to control the mal-practices prevalent in the society.

Conclusion

Thus, the achievement in the fields of education, health, employment, the situation of women empowerment is moderately poor. It is the need of the hour to recognize the hindrances which reduces the women empowerment and necessary initiative must be taken by the Central and State Government. We should also take oath that we need an democratic society where everybody are equal in their opportunity, well-being irrespective of their gender.

Women's empowerment is a greatest challenge across the globe, lot of struggles have been seen in challenging and shifting gender inequalities right from the commencement of the history. These challenges have also been supported by many men who have been outraged at injustice against women. Women are almost half of the globe's population and inequality of gender exists in every nation on the world. If women are not given the importance as it is given for men, the society will be intended to execute below their true potentials. Therefore, the need of the hour is to change the social attitude to women. "When women marches ahead, the family moves, the society ahead and the nation ahead". Empowerment of women will be effective only when they are endowed property and income so that they stand on their own step and can grow their individuality in the society. The women empowerment seems to be the important problems of twenty first century both at national level and international level. Government initiatives alone will not be adequate to reach the destination. Society also should take necessary measures to ensure a society where there is no gender bias and women should have freedom in self-decision and participating in education, social, health, political and economic life of the country with a sense of equality.

REFERENCES

Baruah, B. (2013). *Role of Electronic Media in Empowering Rural.*

Goswami, L. (2013). "Education for Women Empowerment", *Abhibyakti: Annual Journal*, 1: 17-18.

Kadam, R.N. (2012). "Empowerment of Women in India — An Attempt to Fill the Gender Gap", *International Journal of Scientific and Research Publications*, 2(6): 11-13.

Kishor, S. & Gupta, K. (2009). *Gender Equality and Women Empowerment in India*, National Family Health Survey (NFHS-3) India, 2005-06, International Institute for Population Sciences, Deonar, Mumbai.

Pankaj Kumar Barol & Rahul Sarania. "Employment and Educational Status: Challenges of Women Empowerment in India", *A Peer-Reviewed Indexed International Journal of Humanities and Social Science.*

Suguna, M. (2011). "Education and Women Empowerment in India", *Zenith: International Journal of Multidisciplinary Research*, 1(8): 19-21.

Vinze, Medha Dubashi (1987). *Women Empowerment of India: A Socio-Economic Study of Delhi*, Delhi: Mittal Publications.

PART II

Well-being of Women Across Profession

15

Bollywood as Workplace: Challenges Faced by Women

Chetana Pokhriyal and *Sonali Lakhera*

Introduction

Throughout 'History' and 'Her-Story', the second sex has been contemplating over interrogating the power structures of the society to have an understanding of the reasons as to why she stands, where she does. Patriarchal society predetermines the space for women — little away from his world and his domain, making woman as no-man. In the patriarchal universe, woman constitutes everything that she lacks as a man and thus woman becomes a 'no-man'. This construct, and structure is universal. The place of woman in this patriarchal structure cannot be explained any better as suggested by Tennyson (1897) in "Man for the field and woman for the hearth/Man for the sword and for needle she/ Man with the head and woman with the heart/Man to command and woman to obey;/All else confusion" (p. 110).

There is no reservation about the shifting positions of woman from hearth to fields but, every woman, trying to make her entry into the 'field' (workplace) is surrounded by centralization of power within a creamy gender group. She undergoes multiple attempts of breaking the glass ceilings inevitably revolving around difficulties of women trying to enter into a man's space and simultaneously comes across a new challenge. Working women, never considered serious workers other than in marriage, have to deal with prejudices at multiple levels. Hence, it takes a lot of courage and effort for women to break the norms and step out in men's world. Even after being equipped with all the knowledge and qualification, courage, and talent, women face various workplace challenges, such as harassment and gender-pay gaps. Women, seldom considered eligible candidates for authoritarian or power positions, succumb to pressures to the extent that they have to quit their jobs if at all they plan to start a family. These uncertainties are universal in every industry. This chapter focuses on the challenges faced by women in the Indian Film Industry. The glittery and jazzy world of showbiz is superficially illusionary, but, when it comes to the work conditions of women actors, challenges pertaining to gender-pay gap and comparative shorter job terms as compared to their male costars due to various reasons, which will be discussed at length in this study. Rather than reinventing cinema to represent feminine desire and their point of view, it is struggling with the prevailing monstrous problem of the casting couch.

Films certainly are the modern pieces of literature, a sociological tool and, a representation of the society. It is a two way process-taking from the society and giving back to it. Cinema represents every bit and segment of the society, every problem cropping in it, every custom and tradition; it talks about the gender and races; continents and oceans; people and animals; aliens and machines; and the parallel universe. It talks about the time travels and light-years and the discoveries and the inventions and politics and society and psychology of the society.

While contesting women, we aim to focus on the perspectives and secondly how it has been treated and conceptualized in Indian cinema. There has been a major paradigm shift in socio-cultural scenario in the twenty first century, or seemingly so.

The main highlight of this chapter is to focus on those historic landmarks in which gender intersects the cultural and political aspect. Starting with the concept of cinema, the chapter will move to the major discussion on how gender is read in Indian cinema. With its inception in the early years in twentieth century and its development as the major force in mass media, cinema has emerged as a powerful tool either to legitimize or challenge or for that matter reproduce in some case the values and imagination of culture.

When we talk about Indian cinema, we are usually referring to the popular culture in Indian cinema, which usually consists of both new and old elements. While constantly identifying with the new like new stars, technologies, plots and twists are adhered with unflinching loyalty towards old and time-tested images, old formulas and old values. Erroneously, this formula is visible in the portrayal of women characters-though modern but dominant and durable images of women deep rooted in the psyche of Indian cultural history whether in the elite or popular forms.

Both literature and electronic media have taken the liberty of portraying women in many ways like metaphorical images of Sita and Savitri and thirdly as and emerging independent woman. While, the first two images of women are virtuous but vulnerable characters and last but not the least protective only under the male patronage and support. Hence, they are often submissive and pure. While bizarre to the popular virtuous image is the image of a sexual temptress and an alluring women often tempting men into the pit of sin. In our conventional formula of virtue and vice, such women are often punished. The image of an independent woman is strong and has appeared in the Indian cultural history since the era of Indian independence movements. Independent women characters are often the combination of the virtuous image and the seductive temptress to independently overcome her challenges, fight her battles and survive in the hostile circumstances. These images of women have survived the emerging tides of change in the global as well as local market.

Every film like a good piece of literature is again made up of a good plot, good direction and interesting characters played by good actors. These actors are men and women who have proved themselves over sometime by showing their talent in various films. This article focuses on women actors and the industry of Bollywood as their workplace focusing on the important issues of role and representation of women in cinema, gender age gap, gender pay gap, comebacks and casting couch.

Background

Before delving into the feminist perspective of film industry, one has to understand that the film industry is a microcosm of society and everything that prevails in the larger society outside echoes in the film society as well. Film as a language shows signs of similar binary order as the one that pervades our phallocentric society. The year 1889 marks the birth of Indian cinema with the screen adaptations of religious epics like *Ramayana*, *Mahabharata*, *Sri Krishna* and *Harishchandra*. From then to now, Indian cinema has evolved to talk about the day-to-day social, political and psychological issues and with this has evolved the role and representation of women in Indian cinema from revered goddess-like figure and an idealized woman to self-dependent contemporary woman. With this evolution, feminist film theory has also found new directions.

Semiotics of Indian cinema best explains the stereotyping of women and their repeated representation on screen with weak images. Until1980s, women were shown as central female character in strong shades of either black or white. In Indian cinema, in particular, the negative woman characters were often those who were liberal in their ideology and usually clad in western costume most of the time even smoking a cigarette; while, the later was often a self-sacrificing motherly figure clad in typical Indian attire sacrificing herself at the altar of her family; overflowing with love for everyone. In brief, she was a stereotypical ideal woman desired by every Indian male. Hence, this cinema was usually melodramatic in tone and overstuffed with emotion, best described by Haskell (1973) as:

> At the lowest level, as soap opera, the "woman's film" fills a masturbatory need; it is soft-core emotional porn for the frustrated housewife. The weepies are founded on a mock Aristotelian and politically conservatory aesthetic whereby women spectators are moved, not by pity and fear but by self-pity and tears, to accept, rather than reject, their lot. That there should be a need and an audience for such an opiate suggests an unholy amount of real misery (p. 22).

Haskell's imagery of woman character is a quick reminder of *Kati Patang*, a 1971 film by Shakti Samanta and based on the novel written by Gulshan Nanda who had based his novel on the novel *I Married a Dead Man* written by Cornell Woolrich. Asha Parekh, the famous star of the yesteryears was acclaimed for her role of a pretentious but weeping widow and her ensuing trials and tribulations with same fervor as the miniscule but nonetheless very pertinent role of Shabnam or Shabbo, who is a negative character though but an object of male desire. In popular cinema, the representation of women is either as a mother or wife and is often placed in an over-determined space within the Indian context, whereas, in the broader analysis of gender or class or culture or race, popular cinema forges a definitive interpretation of women and their work and their sexuality. In an attempt to interpret their specific roles, it constructs an obtrusive relation between the two.

Over the years, the imaging and re-imaging of women have been often modified by discourses of feminine culture, which subtly operates within the stereotypical constructions of sexuality. Contextually, these prototypes of vamp and heroine were in their own way the objects of male desire, one of lust and the other of possession as wife and hence, were masochistic constructions for the pleasures of male characters.

Physically, the contours of women characters are subjected to desires traditionally within the cultures and conventions of Indian narrativity. Here comes in Althusser's theory of ideology as applied by the Claire Johnston who describes the ways by which conventional cinema constructs the "ideological image of woman".

In reality, too, women have been excluded from cultural participation and cinema has been taking liberty of exploiting and contaminating their image. Patriarchal notions and ideas, whether pertaining to the image of a woman as a wife or a mother or as a prostitute or a wicked woman, are buried within the layered sediments of metaphorical reality. Women and the Media captured the public glare at the UN's Fourth World Conference on Women in Beijing in 1995 and focused on its strategic objectives, such as:

> The continued projection of negative and degrading images of women in media communications — electronic, print, visual and audio must be changed. . . . Print and electronic media in most countries do not provide a balanced picture of women's diverse lives and contributions to society in a changing world (Rao, 2000: 403).

However, it is unpleasant and not far from being true that most of the times, women appear in the commercial films as the objects of male gaze, what Judith Roof describes as the politics of negotiation in contrast to the prototypical image "female characters who are married — tragically not, fallen, recovered, all in relation to men" (Roof, p. 51). Sleazy item numbers in an otherwise serious film made on some grave issue further explains this theory. One can see an out of context song and dance sequence often performed by the actresses with the potential for great talent for acting like Aishwarya Rai, Kareena Kapoor, Priyanka Chopra to name a few. On the other hand, in Indian film industry, there are actors like Mallaika Arora, cut out for performances like this. The issues of gender and power politics reveals the vision of the world with the chronic movements of camera, which constructs the traditional gender codes or signs conventionally associated with women and captures the voluptuous female body in an explicitly arouse carnal pleasures. The shots are usually taken either from a low angle or from a high angle to emphasize on the contours of the female body. Nevertheless, different genres of art like literature, painting and cinema have been instrumental in exploring and representing female sexuality. Broadly speaking, in various imaginative fields of art, whether it was for the sake of art or for mass construction, women have occupied sex-roles. The rising number of item numbers is directly proportional to the box office success of an average or below average film. However, the image of a woman in Indian cinema evolved in nineties with the emerging image of the working woman or the college going girl, but this hardly changed the stereotypical image of women but they remained consistently submissive. No matter how well-equipped with education, but was still denied the "voice and status as subjects" (Kaplan, p. 200). Indian cinema projects its central female character as the damsel in distress waiting for her Knight in shining armor to save her from the adverse situations. According to Johnston, cinema has thus shifted its mode from reflecting the reality to construction a specific ideological and illusory image of reality.

Role and Representation of Women on Indian Screen

A panoramic view of Hindi Cinema from 1960 to 2017 shows the progression of role of women characters in Indian Cinema. Films like *Maine Pyar Kiya* (1989), *Khoobsoorat* (1980), *Ram Teri Ganga Maili* (1985), *Baaghi* (1990), *Lamhe* (1991), *Pardesh* (1997), *Koyla* (1997), *Kuch Kuch Hota Hai* (1998), *Hum Dil De Chuke Sanam* (1999), *Dhadkan* (2000), *Kabhi Khushi Kabhi Gham* (2001), *Chennai Express* (2013), and very recent *Prem Ratan Dhan Payo* (2017), depict woman conforming to traditional role of a self-sacrificing individual. She has no intention to challenge the societal gender-based roles allotted to her. Male audiences gaze upon the female protagonists in these films as the ideal wife, and the female audiences identify themselves with this perfect image of an ideal Indian woman. Laura Mulvey analyses this activity of male and female audiences as 'Voyeuristic and Narcissistic' visual pleasures respectively. According to this allusion, the former is produced by looking at another person or situation as our object and the latter is derived by identifying with the figure in the image.

Patriarchy is both subversive and depressive in sharp contrast to the image of motherhood, which is a life force. However, when it comes to Indian cinema, women actors are marginalized to prevent them from performance or are coerced to underperform in comparison to the male actors. They are either worshipped as divine creatures or tamed by the male characters, if they act like shrews. They do not have much say in their own lives and are the puppets in the hands of male characters. In all women are mere showpieces in these films, represented as symbols of external beauty complimenting their inner beauty and perfection owing to care giving, self-sacrificing and nurturing nature. Mulvey in her research "*Visual Pleasure and Narrative Cinema*" argues that film is constructed around looks or gazes, which in turn shape editing and narrative, these looks are completely and eternally of men looking at women. Even when women are represented as working, they never occupy the positions of authority. This stereotyping of female gender in classical Indian cinema is what Claire Johnson (1973) calls a 'myth' of 'Woman'. Treated in Roland Barthes sign system as Johnson suggests, Cinema explains woman as everything that is not 'man' (p. 25). Working women play the roles of secretarial jobs, or bar dancers or bartenders or receptionists. *Tezaab* shows Madhuri Dixit as the only breadwinner of the family. Despite holding the financial reins, her father dominates and exploits her thus highlighting the patriarchal structure of the Indian society. Indian cinema has thus constructed this attractive, submissive doll like image of a woman who is nothing more than an object of desire for male and her only perfection lies in fitting in that image constructed for her.

In late eighties cinema saw an intrusion feminist concepts resulting in films like *Masoom, Jaane Bhi Do Yaaron, Ardh Satya, Arth, Khoon Bhari Maang* and *Umrao Jaan* to name a few. These films depicted the resistance of female characters towards their stereotypical handling by their male counterparts. In *Masoom*, Shabana Aazmi breaks the divine image of woman by not accepting the son born out of an illegitimate relationship of her husband Naseeruddin, outside marriage. Although, subversively and sans any explicit address, both male and female audience sympathized with the child and indirectly sided with the character of the husband, played by Nasir and unanimously realized the stubbornness of the character of the wife, played by Shabana for just one mistake by her husband. The movie ends with Aazmi conforming to the forgiving nature of an ideal female prototype. *Khoon Bhari Maang* also shows Rekha fighting all odds after she survives a deadly attack by the crocodiles in backwaters where her second husband Kabir Bedi deliberately shoves her with an intention to kill her. Initially a docile woman, she makes her comeback as a model and then strongly avenges all the wrong done by Bedi to her and to her children from her first husband. It is noteworthy here that in the first half Rekha is depicted as simple and not so beautiful widow of Rakesh Roshan. The birthmark on her face furthers her criteria of not fitting into the heroine like image. In the second half, the script, with the assistance of technological advancement, twists to transform Rekha into a glamorous heroine to the expectation of the target audience. *Jaane Bhi Do Yaron*, a comedy film shows the female characters in action. They are professionals in the field of journalism. *Umrao Jaan* — a landmark film of eighties shows Rekha despite being a courtesan lives life according to her own terms and conditions for some time but she also becomes the object of desire of the pimp in the brothel and cannot do much about it.

However, there are certain films depicting the working women as factory managers, civil servants, professors, and factory owners. All these roles are accepted in the film by the other characters as well as by the audiences as long as they can maintain a balance between their professional and domestic life. This image of a prefect woman pervades the typical Indian mentality. The professional skills of a woman play a secondary role as compared to her skills as a homemaker. Her perfection lies in how well she can manage her professional and domestic life without sacrificing any of her domestic roles. The best part is that the female actor is seen taking everything in her stride with a smile. She is accepted by her man as well as by the audiences only if she conforms to the image of an ideal and traditional Indian woman who should be meticulous in handling the gendered roles of cooking, cleaning and nurturing besides being professionally excelled.

Films like *Hum Dil De Chuke Sanam*, represent the female protagonist (Aishwarya Rai) displaying some courage to defy the family tradition. Her act of exchanging marriage vows while rehearsing her marriage with Sameer (Salmaan Khan) results in the banishment of Sameer (Salman Khan) and her marriage to Vanraj (Ajay Devgan). She shows passive resistance to her husband, who finally takes over himself the responsibility to help her in her quest to find her lost love, drives her by the hand all over the world, bears all the insults she throws at him and finally finds his wife's beloved. The film again is a flavoured version of the fairy tale where the prince in shining armour rescues the damsel in distress. The ball is again in the court of the male protagonist as the audience worships his glorified image in the film — a male who sacrifices his own desires and his wife as well to make the two lovers meet. Female protagonist finally after three long hours of hustle and bustle and resistance and boldness conforms to the traditional Indian society by choosing her husband over her lover. This is the type of woman male and female audiences identify with thus fulfilling voyeuristic, and narcissist visual desires.

The start of the current century saw some degree of transition in the screen space occupied by the female actors in terms of screen time and roles. While films like *Bulandi, Dhadkan, Hamara Dil Aapke Paas Hai, Pardesh, Kabhi Khushi Kabhi Gam, Chori Chori Chupke Chupke* and *Zubeida* confirm to the traditional gendered roles set aside to women there have been few women centric films like *Mardani, Revolver Rani, Mary Kom, Dangal, Kya Kehna, Lipstick under my Burkha* and *Kareeb Kareeb Single*. While the former again represent women as the carriers of family traditions and values, the means of procreator of human race and the desire of the male protagonist; the latter interrogate the day to day issues faced by 'the second sex' in the patriarchal society. Such movies can be treated as tools to sensitize the audiences of the female sensibility and are intended to hit the gender consciousness of both male and female audiences by breaking the objectionably distorted representations of women in commercial cinema. It is just similar to the issue of the fundamental rights that most of the people who do not even know what their fundamental rights cannot be expected to fight for them. These women-centric films in the Indian cinema thus act as the sensitization tools to tell the female audience of their desires and their basic rights. A handful of films can be called completely woman dominated, the best example of which is *Kahaani 1 and 2, Naam Shabana* and *Ghulaabi Gang*, where the female protagonist actually takes the entire action in her hands and dominates the screen time as well as the screen action in the film.

Women at Workplace: Indian Film Industry and Women

Brief idea of female representation in the film is required for the understanding of women in the Indian Cinema. The fact again cannot be denied that the Indian Film Industry is dominated by male gender and women only play the role of actors in the films. Talking about image of women actors in the film industry, Kaplan (1983) suggests that "all dominant images are basically the malconstructs" (p. 33). The Indian film industry has seen a negligible number of women behind the sets — as directors, screenplay writers, lyricists, stunt persons, and producers. Talking about the greater population of women in Bollywood — as actors, it cannot be denied that women are treated as commodities in the Film industry for the consumer audiences. The consumer gets uninterested by viewing a face over a long time and the supplier very well understands this demand, which accounts for the launching of many female new faces every year in the industry. The discussion furthers the thought put forth by John Berger (1972), "Men act, women appear. Men look at women; women watch themselves being looked at" (47). This thought put forward by Berger holds true for males in every capacity in the industry — males as actors, as directors, as technicians, as cameraman, as producers and as audiences. The story, the direction, the positioning of camera around woman's body the gaze of male characters all conspire to make woman actor nothing more than a spectacle to be gazed at.

Recently few women-centric films have been made and women have acclaimed better roles, emerging out as strong personalities but unfortunately, these films have not ended up with the box office collections they deserved. Number of tickets sold at the box office is the greatest factor towards making or marring the image of an actor. As Amit Rai (2009) observes, "The ticket circulation — as sign, as exchange value, as memento, as pass, as desiring micromachine — returns each actor to a differential field of potential" (p. 45). In a comedy show East India Comedy, Tapsee Panno raises this issue when she requests people to go to the theaters and watch *Naam Shabaana* where a woman acts rather being acted upon, before raising hue and cry about women not given strong roles. Other films released around *Naam Shabaana* were *Raess, Kaabil* and *Sultaan. Raees* had a budget of 127 crore and bagged 142 crore in the opening weekend itself and gets four stars out of five. *Kaabil* released in January 2017, earned a total box office collection of 133 crores.

Gender Wage Gap in Indian Cinema

Because of being locked out of the library, Virginia Woolf in her ground breaking essay *A Room of One's Own* plans to design a college for which it has become difficult to raise the funds. Woolf (1929) then interrogates "At the thought of all those women working year after year and finding it hard to get two thousand pounds together, and as much as they could do to get thirty thousand pounds, we burst out in scorn at the reprehensible poverty of our sex" (Part 1).

Despite equal pay for equal job rules, every industry shows disparity of salaries on various grounds. This disparity is predominant and more conspicuous on gender basis. This divergence has been greatly observed especially in the private sector, which definitely caters to a wider population as far as employment is concerned, women are paid way less as compared to males for performing the same job. To add to it there is perpetual harassment and exploitation. This vice has not spared the most important and predominant form of mass media — the film industry. Mark Wahlberg of Transformer Fame with handsome salary of 68 million dollars occupies the topmost rung in the ladder of world's highest paid actors released in August 2017. Other nine actors in the list are Dwayne "The Rock" Jhonson ($65 million); Vin Diesel ($54.5 million); Adam Sandler ($50.5 million); Robert Downey Jr. ($48 million); Tom Cruise (43 million); Shah Rukh Khan ($38 million); Salman Khan ($37 million) and Akshay Kumar ($35.5 million). Way down this ladder is seen Emma Stone topping the list of highest paid woman actors contended with just 26 million dollars.

The Global Wage Report 2016-2017, released by the International Labour Organization clearly reveals the worst levels of gender wage gap in India. While the Indian actors have made it to top ten highest paid list of actors in the world, the top Indian actresses do not even earn one-fifth of the salary earned by their male screen-partners. The value of male actors in the Indian film industry is kept at a lot higher bar as compared to the female actor having the similar amount of experience and talent. It is universally acknowledged that a commercial film does not work well without the presence of female stars. There are reasons for it, some of them not very highly regarded rather. People come to theatres for entertainment primarily. The entertainment is offered to them in the form of a plot, good song and dance sequences, beautiful face of the female actor and most often a sizzling item number. Had this not been the case, there would not have been instances of films sometimes becoming a box office hit just because of a single item number. It also accounts for the presence of an out of context item number in most of the contemporary films. In the films of earlier decades, these item numbers were the cabarets performed usually by the female actor in a negative role. People flocked in to watch the gliding female bodies and the sensibility of the audience has not changed much over the years. Inclusion of at least one catchy item song is a mandatory ingredient to produce a box office hit or more plainly — to sell a film. The question now arises is that if the presence of female actors is so important to get a film going then what accounts for this abnormal inequality in wages based on gender? Mulvey (1999) observes:

> The presence of woman is an indispensable element of spectacle in a normal narrative film, yet her visual presence tends to work against the development of a story line, to freeze the flow of action

in moments of erotic contemplation. This alien presence then has to be integrated into cohesion with the narrative (p. 837).

This clearly is an indicator of the fact that female actors and their respective positioning in comparison to their male counterparts in the Indian film industry is fraught with relative ambivalence, for being inevitably positioned in the state of flux between being the object of veneration and respect and as an object of sex. Behroz Gandhy and Rosie Thomas (1991) locate femininity in Indian context as very unique that fuels ambivalence; which is split in a complex manner between a 'pure' and a dutiful woman in sharp contrast to the traditional image of woman symbolic of strength and authority and worshipped by Indian men (110).

Let us look at the salaries paid to top women Bollywood actors. Priyanka Chopra of Miss World Fame (2000) joined the industry in 2003 with her debut in *The Hero: Love Story of a Spy*. With hits like *Mujhse Shaddi Karogi* (2004), *Andaaz* (2003), *Aitraaz* (2004), *Fashion* (2008) — which she won the National Film Award for the Best Actress, *7 Khoon Maaf* (2011), *Barfi* (2011), *Mary Kom* (2014) and *Bajirao Mastani* (2015) her present value per film is 8-9 crores. Whether it be Kashi Bai of *Bajirao Mastani*, a scintillating top model Meghna Mathur in *Fashion*, an autistic Jhilmil in *Barfi* or Sussanna Anna — Marie Johannes, each of her performances is matchless. An artist of such mettle, who has been in the industry for fourteen years, has earned a value of 8-9 crores for herself. In an interview with Glamour, Priyanka shares her experience of being told that "Female actors are replaceable in films because they just stand behind a guy anyway. . . . We were told we were too provocative or that being sexy is our strength . . ." (D'Cunha, 2017). Vidya Balan entered the Bollywood industry in 2005 with her acclaimed performance in *Parineeta*. She has bagged the credit for her unmatched performance in films like *Kahaani 1* and *2, Tumhari Sulu, Lage Raho Munna Bhai*, and *The Dirty Picture* — a biopic on Silk Smitha. Despite her acting talent, which is much better than the male actors are her value in terms of money, is much less compared to them. A research in the field of figures related to salaries of the popular actors in the Bollywood shows that Katrina Kaif earns 6-7 crores, Alia Bhat 4-5 crores, and Anushka Sharma earns 5 crores per film (Basu, 2016).

Male actors earn a far greater salary with Salman Khan charging about 60 crore, Shah Rukh Khan 40-50 crore, Amir Khan 50 crore, Akshay Kumar 40-45 crores, Hritik Roshan 40 crore, Ranbir Kapoor 25 crore, Ranvir Singh 20 crore, and Shahid Kapoor charges 18-20 crore per movie (freepressjournal.in). These statistics are evident of the huge gendered disparity in the Indian Film Industry. The veteran actress Waheeda Rehman in an interview stated that "... heroes got more money and their names appeared before the names of the heroines in the credit rolls. I do not know what it is about showbiz but here a man worships a man" (Somaaya, 2013:12). The reason for this disparity as explained by Natalle Robehmed, an associate editor at *Forbes* is the "role options for women and men":

> To me, that just comes down to roles. There are so many more roles available to men at which they can earn big pay days. . . . We need more, higher paying main roles that will obviously come with more female writers and Directors (Rothman & Korn, 2017).

Priyanka Chopra opened up about this disparity in pay cheques in an interview with Glamour stating "I was told that female actors are replaceable in films because they stand behind a guy anyway. I'm still used to being paid — like most actresses around the world — a lot less than the boys" (D'Cunha, 2017). Besides, the role and representation of women actors leading to their weak pay status, another factor contributing to this skewed ratio is that the women-centric films do not make as much box office collection as the male-centric ones. Tapsee Pannu, known for hits like *Pink* and *Naam Shabaana*, voices her thoughts in an interview in East India Comedy that there always have been pricing issues in the film industry and the reason she attributes to this is that not many people go to the theatres to watch women centric film resulting in the far less box office collection.

Gender-Age Gap

Om Shanti Om became a blockbuster with a star cast of Shah Rukh Khan paired with debut actress Deepika Padukone. The movie based on the theme of re-birth echoed an old Rishi Kapoor/Tina Munim starrer *Karz*. Despite the repeated story, the film was a big box office success. Born in 1965, Shah Rukh Khan entered the Industry in 1992 with *Deewana* as his debut film in which he was cast opposite 18-year-old Divya Bharti. Khan was 24 at that time which makes the age gap of 6 years between them. To add to this, Divya is cast as a wife and later a widow of forty-year-old Rishi Kapoor. Then came *Bazigar* starring Shah Rukh Khan with Shilpa Shetty and Kajol both almost a decade younger to him. Some women-actors with whom Khan has been repeatedly paired up are Juhi Chawla, Kajol, Priety Zinta, Rani Mukherjee and Deepika Padukone. Whereas Juhi is only two years younger to him, this age gap between him and his female cast has widened as his years grew in the industry. Kajol and Priety are ten years younger to the actor, Rani Mukherjee is thirteen years younger and Deepika tops this list by being 21 years younger to Khan. *Rab Ne Bana Di Jodi* — Romantic comedy by Aditya Chopra shows 43 year old Shah Rukh Khan opposite 20 years old Anushka Sharma in a marriage as well as a love relationship. This gender age gap is conspicuous in other actor pairs as well.

Salman Khan born in 1965 was 24 at the time of his debut film *Maine Pyar Kiya* and his female co-star Bhagya Shree was 20. His recent release is *Tiger Zinda Hai.* Twenty eight years of his journey from *Maine Pyar Kiya* to *Tiger Zinda Hai* (2017) saw an inverted graph of his age compared to his female co-star. In *Hum Aapke Hain Kaun* (1994) he was cast opposite Madhuri Dikshit — 24 who was two years younger to him. *Dil De Chuke Sanam* (1999) saw him opposite Aishwarya Rai — 8 years younger to him, *Hum Saath Saath Hain* shows Salman against Sonali Bendre 10 years younger to him, *Dabangg* (2010) shows Salman with Sonaakshi Sinha 22 years younger to him. Ready (2011) with Asin 20 years younger to Salman, *Ek Tha Tiger* (2012) with Katrina Kaif 18 years younger to him, *Sultan* (2016) brings him on screen opposite Anushka Sharma 23 years younger and *Tiger Zinda Hai* (2017) again with Katrina 18 years younger.

Other pairs, which deserve a notice in the case of gender age gap, are Akshay Kumar and Eliana D'cruz in *Rustom*, Sunny Deol and Kangna Ranaut in *I Love New Year*, *Policegiri* with odd pair of Sanjay Dutt and Prachi Desai. *Gabbar is Back* with Akshay again opposite Shruti Hasan, and in the recent movie *Toilet Ek Prem Katha*, he plays husband to very young Bhumi Pednekar. The gender age gap has persisted since the industry came into existence. *Dayavaan* shows Vinod Khanna opposite Madhuri Dixit and the couple share an age gap of 21 years. The decreasing order of the birth year of the female actors sharing the screen space with 75 year old Amitabh Bachchan can be charted out as Waheeda Rehman (1938), Ranjeeta (1956), Padmini Kohlapure (1965), Jaya Bhaduri (1948), Rekha (1954), Jaya Prada (1962), Sridevi (1963), Rani Mukherjee (1978), Nandita Das (1969), Tabu (1971) and Jiya Khan (1988).

Amir Khan (1965) first acted in *Qyamat Se Qyamat Tak* (1988) — a benchmark adaptation of Shakespeare's *Romeo and Juliet* in the role of

Raj (Romeo) with Juhi Chawla as Rashmi (Juliet). Further down his acting years his female co-stars included Karisma Kapoor (1974) in *Raja Hindustaani* (1996); Sonali Bendre (1975) in *Sarfarosh* (1999); Gracy Singh (1980) in *Lagaan* (2001); Kajol (1974) in *Fanaa* (2006); Asin (1985) in *Ghazini*; and Anushka (1988) in *PK* (2014). It is noteworthy that except Juhi Chawla all the actresses cast against him are almost a decade younger to him and sometimes even more. It is interesting to see that Anushka Sharma — his co-star in *PK*, shares her birth year with the year of the actor's first release *QSQT* and he was already 23 by that time.

In all these cases, the persistent increase in age gap between male and female stars, as the male star crosses his thirties is evident. While the male actors are climbing the success ladder at the age of 55 most of the female actors, retire usually by the age of 40. Even if they continue to work, they find it difficult to get a lead role occupying a prominent space on screen. It is interesting to see that as male stars grow older their on-screen female counterparts remain the same age. In all the cases discussed above one can see the advancing years of male stars from 45 to 55 whereas the female stars acting with them remain in the age bracket of 18 to 33. While most male actors are at the peak of their acting careers at the age of 40, most of the female actors find it difficult to find good and prominent roles in the films. This can be shown by reversing the age-gap equation between male and female actors. The actresses in the age group of forties and early fifties include Tabu (1973), Shilpa Shetty (1975), Karisma Kapoor (1974), Manisha Koirala, Kajol (1974), Madhuri Dixit, Juhi Chawla (1967), Sushmita Sen, Aishwarya Rai (1973) and Raveena Tandon. None of these actresses have ever been paired up with male actors like Tiger Shroff (1990), Varun Dhawan (1987), Aditya Roy Kapoor (1989), Ranbeer Kapoor (1982), and Ranvir Singh (1985) and Imran Khan (1983). Reema Lagoo and Sanjay Dutt share an age gap of one year and the actress has played mother to the actor in a couple of films. Do we need a further proof to prove the skewed gendered age gap in Bollywood.

Comeback After Marriage

The common practice among women is that they give a break to their careers when they get married or when they are in the family way giving rise to essentialist/existentialist debate. It has been commonly observed that in most of the cultures, if not all, man makes the choice and woman compromises hers. The picture becomes serious when women are committed in a marital relationship or have children. Bearing children is her essential aspect but raising them single handedly is a consequence of a gendered role. It is observed that most working women take a long break after marriage and after motherhood. A greater percentage of them do not resume work ever after this break. Even if they resume, conditions are very unfavourable for them. Employers usually do not prefer to hire them thinking that they would not be productive enough to meet the expectation of the company. Then arises the bargain and they are usually offered quite less salary as compared to her colleagues. Ultimately, the woman is at the receiving end at domestic as well as work front. This issue becomes graver in film industry where the value of a woman actor takes a drastic plunge and women actors find it difficult to make a comeback. If a woman actor signs up a fresh film after her marriage, it is tagged as a 'come-back' whereas no one has ever heard of such terminology in case of male actors. They keep continuing their job as it is. On the contrary, as has been discussed earlier their value incessantly increases with their experience in the industry.

Taking examples from the Bollywood — a seasoned actress Madhuri Dixit had to move to US after her marriage to a US-based doctor. After few years when she made a choice of returning to India and to Bollywood, her 'Comeback' project *Aaja Nach Le*, did not do well at box office. Aishwarya Rai of Miss World fame made her comeback with 'Action Replay'. The actress plays a lead role in the film opposite to Akshay Kumar, but the script had to time travel and characters were placed in an era almost 20 years behind. This device in a way created an illusion of Aishwarya in her twenties on screen. Kajol in her comeback film *Fanaa* is portrayed as a blind Kashmiri girl. The film worked wonders and Kajol was outstanding as usual. But, the question is would the scenario be the same if Kajol was portrayed in a romantic lead role as in *DDLJ* (*Dilwale Dulhaniya Le Jayenge*) or Aishwarya was portrayed as an actual 20 year old Bubbly girl. Would the audience accept that? Would the director cast them in such roles? The things do not stop here. The actresses, no matter how talented and beautiful they are have to face a staggering phase in their careers after marriage. After the 'comeback' also they just get a couple of offers after which their career graph shows a sharp decline. Most of the actresses usually are married by the time they are forty thus putting an end to their acting careers. Male actors are at the peak of their careers at the age of 40 and they keep climbing the success ladder even after they cross half a century of their age.

Casting Couch

The monstrous challenge faced by women in her workplace is sexual harassment in any form. Depending on the nature of the job or the workplace environment, it may include a variety of offensive activities. Lascivious comments on clothing or appearance, offensive and sexist joke, any form of physical contact, interference with an employee's ability to move, transmission of any material that is suggestive of sexual advances, watching porn or other objectionable material at workplace, playing sexually suggestive music or repeatedly requesting the employee out for a date or get-together are some of the usual sexual harassment situations women often find in a workplace.

The day of 75th Golden Globe Award will always be recounted as the most important day when Hollywood stars waged a war against sexual harassment at workplace. All the stars dressed in black explicitly exhibited their annoyance for sexual harassment at workplaces. There have been uncountable occurrences of established film producers and directors pestering young and vulnerable actors for sex in exchange of roles but the matter has always been a hush-hush affair. Nobody wishes to come to front and talk about it for various reasons. With the exposure of Harvey Weinstein's story of sexually exploiting a number of women, the film fraternity in Hollywood joined hand against this kind of misconduct at work places. Jennifer Lawrence — *the Hunger Games* star was made to do a "degrading and humiliating nude line-up" in the initial days of her career. Jane Fonda made revelation of losing her job once because she refused to sleep with her boss. About the Weinstein instance the TV presenter Myleene Klass revealed that he propositioned Klass with a sex contract including a confidential agreement emphasizing that she would not discuss about it with anyone. The fragile glass image of the Hollywood giant crushed down when this secret was revealed. Around 30 other established Hollywood actresses like Kate Beckimnsale, Emma Thomson, and Cara Delevigne made accusations about Weinstein sexual misconduct including three rapes after this episode. Actress Emma Thompson, revealed to *Sun* that this is "just the tip of the iceberg". About allegations, she commented, "They do not surprise me at all and they are endemic to the system" (Wootton, 2017).

Bollywood is not far behind in the cases of sexual abuse but people prefer to remain silent about the entire system. Everything is actually arranged so systematically that young people usually fall prey to it and then made to feel guilty about their own exploitation. When young and aspiring actors and actresses enter the industry with Bollywood dreams they are covertly or overtly trapped into such situations where they have to succumb to the sexual advances of the predators. They usually do not talk about it probably because somewhere they believe to have participated in the crime. After these budding actors taste the limelight, and become established actors they may feel it unnecessary to foil their image for which they have sacrificed and compromised a lot. In an interview to CNN News 18 editor Rajeev Masand, Vidya Balan, admits that people go through this hell and do not "want to be known for this controversy". Vidya recounts that the victims feel "that other producers would not give you work. . . . But it does seem like you speak about it, people would not want to work with you" (news18.com, 2017). Nobody has ever talked openly about his or her casting couch experiences in Bollywood. Rekha's recent Biography by Yasser Usman given an insight to this insidious creepy world by recounting that five minute long forced kiss which resulting out of the conspiracy of Kuljeet Pal, Director Raja Nawathe and actor Biswajit. Besides such tricks, there have been cases like forced rape scenes in reel and real.

The Dirty Picture cynically exploits this dark area of Bollywood. With bold and verbose Vidya Balan in the lead role, Silk Smitha's Biopic explores almost all the challenges faced by the women actors in the industry. Reshma does not get acclaim for her acting talent but is taken in immediately when she performs a sultry and erotic dance performance. In no time Reshma or 'Silk' earns name, fame and money. She is also cast opposite Suryakant — the legendary actor of South India who was idealized and admired by Silk when she was a child. This gives an insight to the actual picture in Bollywood about the very young actresses cast against aged actors. The film clearly shows multiple levels of the male gaze. The camera gazes at her body, thus objectifying it and commodifying it. Second level of gaze is the one by all male crew and cast present at the sets. Third level is the gaze of hero and the other male characters in the film within the film. Then there is the gaze of the audiences of the film within the film. The final level of gaze is that of actual real audiences watching the film *The Dirty Picture* in the Cinema Halls feasting their eyes with the slithering dance movements of Silk. These multiple levels of cinematic gaze objectify and commodity her turning her into a spectacle of 'to-be-looked-at-ness' (Mulvey, 1999).

Conclusion

The dominant cinema thus can be classified as misogynist and the film industry too is a binary construct with different sets of rules for different genders. The twentieth century medium of the masses is actually an agent — in fact the biggest agent enforcing symbolic patriarchy. While women acting in Cinema seem to have a shelf life, male actors continue to act ceaselessly. While women are the passive spectacles, the entire action revolves around the male actors giving an explanation as to why women actors are paid way less as compared to women. Apparently both male and female actors start to work at the approximate age of 24. While male actors are at the peak of their careers, most of the female actors cease to work at 40. The reasons for this abrupt end in their careers ranges from marriage to motherhood after which they make a comeback movie which happens to be their last or second last film in the lead role. There is no looking back for the male actors, after their entry into the industry. Actors such as Salman Khan, Shah Rukh Khan, Amir Khan, Akshay Kumar and Amitaab Bachchan are still at the top of their career ladders irrespective of their age. It is to be noted that all these actors are above 50 years of age. Without any doubt, they will keep getting cast in the lead roles for about a decade more and may be even after that with scripts twisted and framed to suit their ages as in case of Amitaab Bachchan. This brings to light the wide disparity in the retirement ages of male and female actors in the film industry. The actors get to work for about 15 to 20 years more as compared to the actresses of the same age or even lesser. More work means earning for a longer period in the terms of money as well as experience and value. Is it not a patriarchal construct reflected in the cinema industry that while the value of male actor increases with time that of the female actors shows a decline? Whatever be the workplace the challenges faced by women almost remain the same. It is time that all these challenges faced by working women be interrogated. Female stars have carved a niche for themselves each fighting against the existing power-politics nexus to raise important debate questioning this nexus and also the socio-political issues. Woman has been projected as a metaphor and woman actors have negotiated their stardom to construct the image in the cultural and historical space.

REFERENCES

Berger, J.; Dibb, M. & BBC Enterprises (1972). *Ways of Seeing*, London: BBC Enterprises.

Gandhy, B. & Thomas, R. (1991). Three Indian film stars, *Stardom: Industry of Desire*, London: Routledge Publications, pp. 107-131.

Johnston, C. (1973). *Women's Cinema as Counter Cinema*, Notes on women's cinema, SEFT, Glasgow: Screen 24-31.

Hall, A.C. (1998). *Delights, Desires and Dilemmas: Essays on Women and the Media*, Westport CT: Praeger.

Haskell, M. (1973). *From Reverence to Rape*, New York: Penguin.

Kaplan, E.A. (1983). *Women and Film: Both Sides of the Camera*, London: Metheun.

Mulvey, L. (1999). "Visual Pleasure and Narrative Cinema", *Film Theory and Criticism: Introductory Readings*, Eds. Leo Braudy and Marshall Cohen, New York: Oxford University Press.

Rai, A.S. (2009). *Untimely Bollywood*, New Delhi: Oxford University Press.

Rao, D.B. (2000). *Status and Advancement of Women*, New Delhi.

Soumaaya, B. (2013). *Talking Cinema: Conversation with Actors and Film Makers*, Noida: Harper Collins.

Tennyson, A. (1897). *The Princess*, New York: Charles E. Merrill. Retrieved from Questia.

Woolf, V. (1929). *A Room of One's Own*, eBooks@Adelaide. Web. 20 January, 2018.

Internet Sources

Basu, M. (2016, October 18). *Top 10 Highest Paid Bollywood Actresses.* Retrieved from *http://www.india.com/arts-and-cuture/top-10-highest-paid-bollywood-actresses-1493657/*

D'Cunha, S.D.D. (2017, August 30). *In India, the Gender Pay Gap Extends Even to Bollywood*. Retrieved from *https://www.forbes.com/sites/suparnadutt/2017/08/30/in-india-the-gender-pay-gap-extends-even-to-bollywood/"7977372f502b*

Rothman, M. & Korn, M. (2017, August 29). *Is the Pay Gap between Men and Women in Hollywood Growing?*, Retrieved from *http://abcnews.go.com/Entertainment/pay-gap-men-women-hollywood-growing/story?id=49376405*

Sonar, M. (2017, June 12). *Shah Rukh, Salman, Akshay: 10 of Bollywood's Highest Paid Actors and their Net Worth*. Retrieved from *http://www.freepressjournal.in/entertainment/shah-rukh-salman-akshay-10-of-bollywoods-highest-paid-actors-and-their-net-worth/1084037*

Vidya Balan Explains How She didn't Fall Prey to Casting Couch I Indian Showbiz Industry (2017, October 17). Retrieved from *http://www.news18.com/news/movies/vidya-balan-explains-how-she-didnt-fall-prey-to-the-casting-couch-in-indian-showbiz-industry-1559013.html*

Wootton, D. (2017, October 12). *He Revolted Me*. Retrieved from *https://www.thesun.co.uk/news/4672839/harvey-weinstein-myleene-klass-sex-contract/*

16

Women in Leadership: Barriers and Biases

Pratibha Pandey

Introduction

India once set aside as deprived and reluctant, is now one of the predominant and expeditiously mounting economies in the world. Yet, India's intensifying and awe-inspiring economic growth has a dark shadow looms reason being it is tangled with profound discrimination prevalent and other intimidation. This paradoxical framework draws attention to the necessity for proficient, adept and qualified workforce along with leadership to prolong India's augmentation and effectiveness. In India the aptitude, talent, aspiration and desire of females are essential to crusade development and growth in all sphere of human activity. Although women have already added much to India's gradient but also have more to interject to multifarious and maintainable Indian human capital pool. Females in India not only stand for or epitomize in top executives of formal leadership, but keep on steeping out in alteration from middle to top management roles thus creating all leaking pipeline of leadership. Leadership in India tend to be amalgamating with men, although research has already standardized that immeasurable shortfall by paying no heed to or underutilizing the female workforce. Tapping female leadership talent thus became commanding for subsistence and affordability.

Objectives

- To ascertain impediments hindering women manager's advancement to leadership positions.
- To examine the extent to which the challenges impinge on

female managers' performances and their progresses to leadership position.

* To suggest possible strategies that can be used to enhance women's participation in leadership position.

Barriers

Other prominent barriers to women's career advancement are lack of mentoring, networking opportunities, lack of transparency in roles and expectations, absence of a clear career path, unavailability of relevant platforms to upskill their expertise and exclusion from informal male-dominated networks.

As of today, the positive impact is evident with more women leaders driving strategy and framing policy, while women entrepreneurs become role models. If government agencies and the corporate world come together, it will not be long before India witnesses an era where there is a robust entrepreneurial network among women, fostering economic growth and sustaining business traction. Studies also reveal that women in leadership roles in an organization can make a transformational difference to its performance. An analysis of return on equity (ROE) data of top 100 Indian companies (BSE 100) by Randstad reveals that companies with women on their Boards have a positive impact on ROE.

Diversity in the Board is a business imperative. A government-mandated quota may help the cause of diversity as it provides a standard and uniform guideline. However, a quota may not help a company build depth or sustain the policy. If there is a mandatory need to fill seats, companies should be true to the intent and make appointments accordingly. Although, the quota for women directors is aimed at promoting diversity, the tenacity and rigour that women professionals of display, goes to show that merit will shine through even without reservations. Building a pipeline of women at the executive level is the need of the hour, and it can be achieved over a period of time through conscious and concerted efforts of both corporate and the government.

Barriers to Advancement

Why does this happen? Women with stellar performance records can be held back because they are not seen as having the potential to lead at a senior level. For example, the women CEOs on a global list of tops performing chief executives were nearly twice as likely as the men to have been appointed to the job from outside the company: women were less likely to emerge as winners in their own companies' internal CEO tournament. Furthermore, even when women are rated more highly than comparable male peers across a range of leadership behaviours, they are also rated lower than men on "envisioning", the dimension most closely associated with effective leadership at senior levels. Senior-level women suffer from this perception when appointments to top leadership positions are made. Catalyst research has found this especially to be true in cultures where vision is a top-rated characteristic of leadership. Exposure to female leaders can affect such stereotypes. An inspiring example of the benefits that women's increased role in leadership can offer comes from India where, in 1993, the constitution was amended to institute gender quotas for village leaders. Exploiting the random assignment of gender quotas to a third of the villages, Esther Duflo, Rohini Pande and collaborators found that continuing exposure to women leaders eliminated statistical discrimination by male villagers, impacting future generations' leadership aspirations, including teenage girls' educational outcomes and women's electoral gains. Women leaders also provided more public goods, in particular, clean water, than their male counterparts. If this can happen in as large and complex an "organization" as India, then surely today's business leaders can lead the way in the private sector with committed and concrete actions to close gender gaps in business leadership globally. Women today are still less likely than men to have the line experience required getting the top job. A 2011 McKinsey report showed that 62 per cent of senior women in the largest US corporations were in staff jobs, such as HR and Communications, that rarely lead to a CEO role; in contrast, 65 per cent of men on executive committees held line jobs. The World Economic Forum Corporate Gender Gap Report asked the top HR person in the largest companies of 20 OECD countries what percentage of the assignments considered to be business critical/important were currently held by women (e.g., key start-ups, turnarounds and line roles in key business units of markets).

Women's Barriers to Positions of Power

According to Cornell University, the "glass ceiling" is a metaphor first used by Nora Frenkiel in *Adweek* in March 1984 (Catherwood Library, 2005) to explain the subtle, invisible obstacles women face after they attain mid-management positions. They advance to the top of middle management but are unable to pass through this barrier. Media and contemporary messaging communicate that this glass ceiling is being shattered; the stark reality is that it still exists (Schmitt, Spoor, Danaher & Branscombe, 2009:56). Further, nuances of this restriction are surfacing in new forms, eliciting such terms as glass escalators (Eagly & Sczesny, 2009:30), slippers (Rudman & Heppen, 2003:1357), and cliffs (Ryan & Haslam, 2005:81). Another term more recently suggested for these barriers is the labyrinth, indicating the complicated, exhausting challenges that women must navigate on their way to senior roles (Guerrero, 2011:382). Although gains have been made in many employment areas, women remain significantly underrepresented in positions of power. Less than 16 per cent of corporate officers and board members of Fortune 500 companies are women. These positions have often come at a cost to women who do achieve them. These women carry such burdens as stereotyping, prejudice, sexual harassment, tokenism, and isolation (Barreto, Ryan & Schmitt, 2009:9). The glass ceiling is an easily applied metaphor for women's experiences. In real terms, however, the underlying causes of gender inequality in senior positions are less identifiable or well-defined. This chapter examines the barriers to women's advancement to senior positions and arranges them into four categories to clarify the complexities of why women hold few powerful roles in industry. They include structural issues in society and in corporate settings. They are demonstrated by prevailing perceptions of gender and leadership. They are presented in forms of prejudices and discrimination. Women's responses to these barriers also complicate the issue.

Women's Responses to Barriers

Women can perpetuate the barriers to their advancement by choosing to respond to difficulty in unhelpful ways. If a woman sees or experiences a barrier, she may respond by internalizing it inappropriately, by rationalizing it through sense making, or by avoiding the career altogether. Conversely, the perception that women do not advance because they shrink from opportunity, a choice termed the "ambition gap", is a myth (Lang, 2012, para 2).

When women experience discrimination in the workplace, particularly ongoing subtle forms of discrimination, they tend to internalize the incidents and take responsibility for what went wrong. This is because women in senior positions tend to hold to high standards of meritocracy, the belief that circumstances are largely a result of one's own actions (Barreto, Ellemers, Cihangier & Stroebe, 2009:110). The subtle discrimination that is more prevalent today lowers self-esteem. Women in these situations observe implied or vague barriers such as being ignored, overlooked, or resisted. When this happens, they try to figure out what went wrong and take personal responsibility for the incident. This approach does not address the underlying issue if their treatment comes from a colleague or if a superior is discriminating against them in subtle ways, such as not inviting them to a meeting, ignoring them in a conversation, or overlooking a suggestion. If a superior discriminates against them in blatant ways, on the other hand, such as making overt statements that women belong in certain roles or restricting educational development to men, the discrimination is easier to resist (Barreto, Ellemers, Cihangier & Stroebe, 2009: 109). Reduced confidence in their abilities perpetuates women's feelings of inferiority and creates a self-fulfilling effect.

Additionally, studies into women's response to breaks in the corporate contract show interesting facts on how women respond to barriers. Corporate contracts are the unwritten beliefs held by employees about what has been promised to them by their employers, such as increasing pay, job security, training, and promotion (Hamel, 2009: 235). Sense making involves the rationalizing of incongruent information and events (p. 235). Research has found that women, who are treated unfairly, particularly when the anticipated advancement or increased compensation is not actualized, will seek information, make attribution for the barriers, make sense of the incongruence, and then act in one of four ways. According to Hamel (2009:250), these actions are to leave quietly, leave while voicing their objections to the discrimination, remain at work and be silent, or remain at work and try to raise awareness to the problem. Although the latter is best to initiate potential change, it is also the most difficult and the least frequent choice. The vast majority of women, 90 per cent, leave quietly, which perpetuates any unresolved issues within their work environments. A perspective of this unwillingness to raise awareness about difficult work environments is flagged by Linda Robertson, a lawyer in Vancouver, who writes a blog about legal issues in Canada. In a post from November 15, 2010, she contends that women tend to foster harmony in the workplace and resist asking for raises so that they will not jeopardize their positions. She also discusses a gender bias in which a woman who advocates on her own behalf is seen by her colleagues as pushy and overbearing (Robertson, 2010, para 5). Finally, another way that women respond to barriers is by avoiding careers in which a higher rate of stereotyping or discrimination will occur. These tend to be male-dominated industries, particularly those that involve skills that are traditionally considered male strengths. Math and science careers are included in this category. Women who experience insecurity about or disparaging reviews of their ability to perform mathematical and scientific tasks choose careers that avoid these tasks (Zhang, Schmader & Forbes, 2009: 134). Many of these are lucrative careers, so women's absences from them contribute to the compensation gap between the genders. A recent argument that women do not advance because they do not try is called the "ambition gap", the perceived propensity for women to choose family before work or to shrink from opportunity. This argument has been discredited by *Catalyst*'s report entitled, "The myth of the ideal worker: Does doing all the right things really get women ahead? (Carter & Silva, 2011: 2). The study involved over 3,000 MBA graduates who stayed on a traditional career path and did not take leave for education, personal or family reasons. It summarized the myth that women did not ask for promotions with this statement, "Women were more likely than men to ask for a variety of skill-building experiences, to proactively seek training opportunities, and to make achievements visible, including asking for feedback and promotions" (p. 11). These actions were not, however, reflected in their advancement. The men and women in the research group who actively pursued advancement found different results. Twice as many men advanced to senior executive levels as women. Further, the researchers found little difference between the women who actively requested advancement and those who were less proactive in their efforts, unlike men who found significant advancement by asking for it (p. 11).

Conclusion

Although women are generally perceived to have made great strides towards equality in achieving senior positions, the fact remains that women still do not share equal representation in these roles. Executive women are atypical. Complex, pervasive and ongoing barriers limit the progress of millions of women who wish to move into positions of power. The structural, prejudicial, and discriminatory hurdles these women face is often subtle and misunderstood, creating a complex, pervasive, and multi-faceted labyrinth that thwarts any progress they may make. To correct this imbalance, corporations must distinguish the research from the myths and act accordingly.

Recommendations

1. Adjust hiring and promotion procedures to overcome gender stereotypes.
2. Requiring diverse slates. Most management and executive selections are made by considering a slate of qualified candidates whose qualifications and experience more or less match a carefully constructed formal job description.
3. Requiring diverse slates puts the responsibility on hiring managers and human resource professionals to identify a range of candidates and ensure that they are well prepared.
4. Evaluating multiple candidates simultaneously rather than individually. Gender stereotypes most frequently influence perceptions of task performance for those tasks commonly assumed to be gender-related (such as in math tasks where people tend to expect men to perform better, and verbal tasks where people expect women to do better), including leadership behaviours and characteristics.
5. Expunge subtle gender biases about what makes a leader from performance management and succession planning processes.
6. A more inclusive talent management system should gauge employees on actual results and potential, not simply characteristics subject to biased perspectives.
7. Give women stretch assignments that directly impact the bottom line. In addition to fostering a robust talent pipeline, stretch assignments have been linked by Catalyst research to increased career satisfaction and job commitment. More stretch assignments constitute a win-win for women.
8. Giving women assignments that will allow them to learn and prove themselves, many companies expect women to make it into senior management simply through formal mentoring and self-improvement courses. Women's assignments must become a top-if not the number one-priority.
9. Redesign mentoring programmes to focus on getting women into strategic business roles.

REFERENCES

Barreto, M.; Ellemers, N.; Cihangier, S. & Stroebe, K. (2009). "The Self-fulfilling Effects of Contemporary Sexism: How it Affects Women's Well-being and

Behaviour", in M. Barreto; M.K. Ryan & M. Schmitt (Eds.), *The Glass Ceiling in the 21st Century: Understanding Barriers to Gender Equality* (pp. 99-123), Washington, DC: American Psychological Association.

Barreto, M.; Ryan, M. & Schmitt, M. (2009). "Introduction: Is the Glass Ceiling Still Relevant in the 21st Century?", in M. Barreto; M. Ryan & M. Schmitt (Eds.), *The Glass Ceiling in the 21st Century: Understanding Barriers to Gender Equality* (pp. 3-19), Washington, DC: American Psychological Association.

Broughton, A. & Miller, L. (2009). "Women in Senior Management: Is the Glass Ceiling Still Intact?", *Is, Guc: The Journal of Industrial Relations and Human Resources*, 11(4): 7-23. *doi:10.4026/1303-2860.2009.0122.x*

Carter, N.M. & Silva, C. (2011). *The Myth of the Ideal Worker: Does Doing all the Right Things Really Get Women Ahead?*, Catalyst. Retrieved from *http://www.catalyst.org/knowledge/myth-ideal-worker-does-doing-all-right-things-really-get-women-ahead*

Catalyst (2007). *2006 Catalyst Census of Women in Fortune 500 Corporte Officer and Board Positions*, Retrieved from *http://www.catalyst.org/knowledge/2006-catalyst-census-women-corporate-officers-and-top-earners-fortune-500*

Cikara, M. & Fiske, S. (2009). "Warmth, Competence, and Ambivalent Sexism: Vertical Assault and Collateral Damage", in M. Barreto; M. Ryan & M. Schmitt (Eds.), *The Glass Ceiling in the 21st Century: Understanding Barriers to Gender Equality* (pp. 73-96), Washington, DC: American Psychological Association.

Collin, P.H. (2006). *Dictionary of Business*, London, UK: A & C Black.

Eagly, A. & Mladinic, A. (1994). "Are People Prejudiced against Women? Some Answers from Research on Attitudes, Gender Stereotypes, and Judgements of Competence", *European Review of Social Psychology*, 5:1-35.

Eagly, A. & Sczesny, S. (2009). "Stereotypes about Women, Men and Leaders: Have Times Changed?", in M. Barreto; M. Ryan & M. Schmitt (Eds.), *The Glass Ceiling in the 21st Century: Understanding Barriers to Gender Equality* (pp. 21-48), Washington, DC: American Psychological Association.

US Department of Labour, Federal Glass Ceiling Commission (1995). *Good for Business: Making Full Use of the Nation's Human Capital.*

17

Women in Cinema

Paramita Routh Roy

Well-being as an Oxymoron in the Stereotypical Existence of Women in Indian Cinema

With the stigmas and stereotypes doing the rounds in every nook and corner of the twenty first century concrete jungle, cinema has come a long way from making the stereotypes to breaking it with its gradual advancement in this tech-savvy era. From being only mere showpieces in the movies to gaining central position, civilization has witnessed the fluctuating representation of the second sex on the silver screens, be it in Hollywood, Bollywood or Tollywood. But how much of those women-centric frames have actually empowered this gender in reality is still the biggest question. Even if we find feminist voices being raised on screens through brilliant cinematography or direction, we have failed to resist them from falling prey to voyeuristic gaze — the item numbers in cinema stand as undeniable evidence to this fact. The so called 'Secondary Gender', which is objectified every second either through advertisements or cheap song lyrics, can hardly wish for their well-being in this profession. In the entertainment business women play a big role in attracting the audience gaze, but in the process they are the ones who are negatively promoted as nothing but sex objects to be used as lollipops to feed the eyes of the phallocentric audience. So, expecting the well-being of women in this profession is nothing but a joke. Using out of the context intimate scenes or baseless scantily dressed song sequences in movie trailers, have become the order of the day. When an intimate movie scene releases; it is the woman who is criticized for showing her bare body, when the male lead is appreciated for exposing his manliness on screen. So, this difference of treatment has become an integral part of this profession.

Pay scale differences, gender-politics and exploitation which has become synonymous with any profession, do not create an exception in case of the world of cinema. One thing which really bothers me is that; dark-skinned heroines are desperately made to look fair with layers of make-up in most of the cases and then they are trolled for not showing the real skin. The hypocrites never hum and haw before body shaming or even criticizing female actors for their looks as can be seen through uncountable YouTube video posts revealing the no makeup looks of them. In every step their dignity and self-confidence are broken through these heinous activities. I wonder why women in this film industry never protest to break the stereotypes and embrace their originality because their silence gives wind to this fire of biased yardsticks of judgement. Adding to all of these we stand witness to the fact that a married male actor never loses his popularity even after having kids while a female actor becomes an outcast in the industry. An actress who decides to marry has to face the question if she would continue her profession after marriage but on the contrary it is next to impossible to find a reporter asking the same question to the leading male actors of the Industry. Thanks to the emergence of women-centric movies which initiated a revolt with path breaking plots; that allowed the inhabitants of margins to taste the central position for few hours. Even after this, female movie directors are labelled as ultra-feminists and when any one of them expresses her views boldly without any inhibitions, she is tagged as lesbian — at least that is the one way the penis-bearers can show their authority, which is generally veiled under sophistication. The field of entertainment or cinema has several layers where women provide their inputs, starting from the female actors to the make-up artists or the assistants and every layer should be analysed in order to realize the nitty-gritty of the position of women. Observing from the angle of post-structuralism, we find that the centre of the structure is inhabited by the patriarchs while this centre give impetus to the formation of the marginalized section consisting of women as the binary opposite. Enjoying this exclusive ontotheological position, masculinity provides meaning to their binary opposite and that is the reason we find the roles of women to be marginalized in cinema. There are several instances where the movies portray a stereotyped gender role for a woman and that in turn results into pushing the feminine selves towards the periphery. A semiotic reading of any modern day cinema reveals that the existence and individuality of women is determined through the association of the male hero who provides meaning to her existence by accommodating her in his life through the institution of marriage. Being an ardent follower of popular culture it is very easy to notice that Hollywood movies provide a much liberal view of women's existence and identity in comparison to the sari-clad tantrum queens of Bollywood or Tollywood cinema. Movies like '*English Vinglish*' and '*Queen*' which illustrate the tale of women emancipation are overshadowed by endless phallocentric movies which revolves around the ups and downs of the male protagonist's life, where the female counterpart acts as a showpiece in accompanying the hero with an ever smiling face covered in designer wears. In Hollywood movies women are allowed to explore their sexuality and enjoy their rights by leading an independent life, but on the contrary it is tough to find such liberal unbiased movies in Bollywood, where showing off the midriff becomes a huge controversy. Patriarchs might claim that from the last few years Indian cinema has changed its angle of narration and its perspective by giving women much space than earlier. But can one or two movies create ripple in a system, which has been practicing an ideology from the days of yore? To make a difference and challenge the dominant ideology a strong ground for the alternative ideology should be formed through series of movies that will represent the voices of the marginality and give equal space to both the gender. Indian cinemas are made with a different perspective, either they project the life as it is or show the idealistic structure through the plot. And to illustrate on that, this idealistic representation is often peppered with biased signifiers which indirectly promote the subordination of the second sex in the hands of patriarchy. To satisfy the interest of a biased audience, the movies showcase such images so as to celebrate the softness and conventional role of woman. Throwing light over regional cinema becomes even more discomforting because it represents vulgarity and obscenity on a larger scale through the gender roles of women that they portray without even thinking about the effect it creates on the mindset of the society. Now-a-days, we have almost become attuned to the body shaming trolls that these female actors of regional cinema have to face every moment on social media platforms. Media being one of the most important instruments of the male-centric social structure assures the brilliant way of sustaining stereotypes, so, that they are not decentered from their power. One movie which did a great business in the market very recently is full of derogatory representation of women — *Judwa 2*, a sequel to the earlier version seems to be promoting the most controversial idea "Men will be Men" through the character of Varun Dhawan as he chases and disturbs the female lead to seek her attention.

She is indirectly molested and taunted; but at the end of the day she is seen dancing around the bush with him accepting his proposal. This objectification of female body as they are projected to be irresistible sex objects seems highly derogatory when read from the feminist ideology. This movie shocks us to the extreme as it is steeped with stereotypes and without even our notice establishes these biased thoughts within our unconscious. The fact that audience accept it whole heartedly denotes how blind the civilization is that they are unable to go beyond the veil and imbibe the conventions that they are watching for three hours. We find the mother behaving like that of Mrs. Bennet of Jane Austen's "Pride and Prejudice" to marry off her daughter to such a rich guy and settle her life. But we do not realize how unsettling this notion of settling a girl's life through marriage is at the cost of taking her independence. I wonder how this is possible for the audience which cherishes a movie like *Queen* to accept these stereotyped movies where more than the wish of the woman, the sexual urge of the man is seen to get satisfied. The Indian society which takes pride for its sensibility and education, claim their admiration for free spirited Hollywood movies. This brings us to question that people who are watching and going gaga over a movie or TV series like "Sex and the City" is the same bunch who are found clapping for biased cinematography, where a hero is glorified for the so called accepted manly behaviour of taking possession of a girl without even bothering about her consent. Various surveys done regarding this topic suggest that rape and molestation cases have increased in our society due to these things being glorified in the movies where we find the hero eve-teasing or touching the female actor without her consent. With more than half of the population swearing by cinema and the movie stars, it becomes even more important for the Film Industry to carefully select whatever they are going to present on screen. We find youngsters following every style that a hero adapts in a movie and, therefore, the onus remains even on the actors that how they are going to present themselves or what they are going to portray in front of the society.

The titles and taglines of the movies should not be left alone because as a teaser does, these titles also reveal what a movie is all about through smart terminology. When a semiotic reading of the movie titles are done, we find a chain of signifiers pointing towards one meaning that is the unique power of patriarchy and the subordination or marginalization of the women as the direct opposite to the centre. Naming few of them will make it clear that through what filters our consciousness go through as we render our senses to live the experience of three hours. Starting with '*Bajrangi Bhaijaan*', '*Raees*', '*Brothers*', '*Don*', '*Tiger Zinda Hai*', '*Bahubali*', '*Badrinath Ki Dulhania*', '*Jagga Jasoos*' to '*Poster Boys*', even if women in those movies had significant contribution, the name of those women protagonists never found their presence on the movie titles. What is even more surprising is that; faces of women are used on posters as key elements to attract the gaze of the common people, but the names of their characters are never given space by the marketing team. Throughout the poster the male protagonist is highlighted but as the industry knows it better that a movie cannot be sold depending fully on a man, they strategically reveal a clipping of the movie or a song sequence with a good amount of female skin being used as tropes; to increase the craze in the market. Although the well-trained and basically biased film critics applauded the movie '*Badrinath Ki Dulhania*' for celebrating the rights of women through the role of Alia Bhatt and subverting the conventions of making marriage an important thing in a girl's life, but what the title suggests is that the female protagonist is someone's wife and that becomes the sole identity for a girl. So in whatever way we try, it is actually tough for us to come out from the shells of preconceived notions as we were exposed to them from our childhood days. A child who grows up watching these movies gathers these as basic information of life and in course of time he or she tries to fit the gender roles that these movies promote. The girls aspire to become Cinderella, Rapunzel and then the idealist *Dilwale Dulhania Le Jaenge* type of brides. They are not allowed to think beyond that and for this only even when a *Piku* or *Simran* satisfy their souls, in their subconscious they are assured that these are only dreams which cannot be considered for achieving. Moreover, almost eight out of ten movies revolve around penis-bearers where the women are hardly given an important role to play. Women are shown in such a light that they are seen doing nothing except creating menace in the lives of others and thus contributing to the crisis in the movie. Therefore, the movies that create these notions that women create problems leading to the fall of men and have no other job, but to seduce men; give rise to the dominant phallocentric psychology. The item numbers in the movies have the same result upon our psychology as the population grasps the idea that women should always be available for their fun and entertainment and if not then it is fine to snatch her clothes in public as are shown in those songs. Women actors who dance in these songs containing derogatory lyrics never realize what effect that might create in the mindset of the society and how those cheap lines that disintegrates a woman's self-respect and integrity instrumentalises their harassments in public. If we carefully notice the language in which men tease women on roads, we might understand where this teasing dialectic has its origin. The common words that the eve-teasers use to comment upon a woman's body or her looks mostly belong to the film songs or dialogues. We often see a man calling a girl by names like '*chikni-chameli*', '*munni badnam hui*', '*laila*', '*sheila ki jawani*', '*baby doll*', '*jalebi bai*' and these names are enough to say how cinemas affect our psyche. As by natural instincts most of the people follow whatever is shown in the movies, as in the item songs male actors are shown enjoying the women attention and women actors seducing them, common people try to re-enact this by taunting women in public places. That satisfies their sexual hunger. With many women joining this entertainment field, there should have been a change in the way women are generally looked at, but until and unless these female stars speak against objectification, the ill effects of cinemas cannot be restricted. This does not mean that a woman has no right over judging how much skin she wants to show off on screen. She can do whatever she wants to but as a public figure she needs to make it sure that her work doesn't create negative perception on the minds of the common people. In the name of entertainment it is always the sexuality of women which is used and that creates a negative impact upon the society. In most of the commercial movies everything happens for women, around women and gives rise to the ill fate of the heroes who being a superman come out of the problems and even save distressed and helpless women. In reality women have made a place for themselves but still we find the civilization celebrating the damsels in distress themes movies where the six-pack bearers like that of the Google search engine have solutions for any problem. As we live under the assumption that modern Indian movies are empowering women's roles, that keeps us aloof from the truth that a greater section of movies that are made showcase the helplessness of women in the hands of male politics and they have no other option but to surrender themselves to those rowdy heroes who stalk them out at every step. We seldom come across a movie that celebrates matriarchy in totality. It is peculiar that commercial movies which actually revive the film industry with big hits depict the stereotyped happy endings where a woman agrees to marriage and motherhood. That is how happiness or completeness of a woman's life is illustrated and that undoubtedly gives rise to ever-existing biases. Is it mandatory for every woman to accept motherhood at the cost of their well-being and wishes? And if she chooses career over marriage does that lead to her transgression? These questions will keep haunting us till the day when we are successful in decentring patriarchy. In the century which is full of hypocrites, we stand witness to the reality where a movie like '*Befikre*' is highly criticized for portraying a free-spirited woman who has no inhibitions in smooching a guy or testing and being sure about her sexual compatibility with a guy before marrying him. Movies that enable us to see life in a new light and experience relationships that are against the clich (like the live-in relations), ultimately end in surrendering to the norms and getting social recognition. This is the problem with Indian movies that they shy away from making a point without thinking about what criticisms it might face. Indian cinema only thinks about making money and not about making a difference in the society and that is the reason no difference can be seen in the status of women in society or even in this Film Industry. Thus, the Indian movies actually confuse the audience by picturing an inhibition free life in one hand and showing the accepted standards on the other hand by making it as the final statement.

Well-being of women in the cinema cannot be analysed by only apparent observation of the gender roles that they are portraying on screen, but also by scrutinizing what reactions these women receive from the audience. How a gender role is reaching out to the society is more important than being satisfied with the mere increment of pay scale for women actors. When an actor like Kangana Ranaut spoke against the centered power, she faced trolls and criticisms everywhere. Her attempt at revealing the inner truths of the movie industry which nurtures the reality of casting couch even in the so called progressive twenty first century got very few supports but was hugely opposed by many. She was tagged as a mad woman when she tried to speak about a male actor who manipulated her and used her feelings towards him as a weapon to exploit her. There were more people who blamed her for the harassment she faced than the man who actually drove her to all of these just to save himself and maintain a clean picture in the society. The film industry being ruled by the flag bearers of patriarchy was so expected to corner her through several instances just because she dared to raise voice against the power. Therefore, the Film Industry, which claims itself to be the most progressive organization in the society makes us laugh out loud as it gives rise to such derogatory and heinous treatment to women. People believe that cinema is the mirror of the society, but, it is surprising that the picture this mirror is projecting in front of the civilization will make people identify themselves with stereotyped pictures, which can never prove good for the future generations.

Focusing on the statistics of female deaths and suicide rate of the people related to the Film Industry, it is evident how well they are treated by the industry. Shocking deaths of actors like Jiah Khan, Divya Bharti, Silk Smita, Parveen Bobi compel us to question the status of women actors in this industry. They succumbed under the depression which was to some extent caused by the society if not provoked by it. The constant pressure that an actor faces after giving few flop movies and the continuous judgement she has to go through are enough to make a person weak. A constant romantic or illegitimate association with the male actors that a female actor has to face disrupt the peace around her and pushes her into hell. They are burning evidences that how tough it is for women actors to survive in a field where they are constantly bitten under the boots of the biased media and society. We cannot turn a blind eye over the police reports that are made almost every day by women against the dirtiness of the Industry, which not only humiliates them sexually at every point, but also practices sexual harassments as any other normal job. Even if we consider that some reports come out to be false allegations, but still we cannot deny the truth of most of the reports. We live under an illusion that women who work in this industry get maximum protection from any crime done against her, but the truth is they are the ones most exposed to abuses and sexual violence as that news remain hidden under the red carpets. If a common woman thinks twice before reporting a rape case, a female actor has to think hundred times before taking that step as she knows the criminals are also under the limelight and it is all about power that will prove one to be wrong and the other to be right. There are maximum chances that the woman is hit with a defamation case due to the centralization of patriarchal power in the industry and even in the society.

Therefore, the question of equality between sexes in this entertainment industry bites the dust as the narrow mindsets are deep rooted within our unconscious and people shy away to take a step against the mainstream in fear of being judged. We live in such a society whose actions can never be predicted earlier — this is the society which created a fuss around the movie title of Sanjay Leela Bhansali's '*Padmaavat*' and forced to cover up the female protagonist's visible waist in a song sequence and at the same time these are the people who are celebrating the movie 'Padman' for dealing with the women question. I wonder if it is only because a male actor is standing up for the cause that the society is accepting it so easily, otherwise a woman would have been ridiculed if she spoke about her menstrual cycle openly. Just a few days back when the students of one of the leading Universities of India protested against the rape of a girl with slogans written on pads, they were brutally criticized and the female students were the ones who mostly were victims of the criticisms. When a male actor is standing for a cause of women emancipation, he is never ridiculed or judged as he is a part of the centre or the system, but when the same thing is done by a woman in a movie, she is tagged as feminist in a negative sense of the term. Presently social media is full with Padman Challenge posts and videos, but is it making any difference on our inner consciousness that still wants a black plastic bag to carry a pack of sanitary napkin? Will this campaign stop us from changing the TV channel when we are sitting with our family and a sanitary napkin is promoted in the advertisement? This brings us to the realization that these are nothing but marketing strategies of the film-maker who wants us to think that he or she is contributing towards rooting the progressive thoughts in the society through the pictures of click-happy Men with pads in their hands promoting equality of treatment of female problems. The Indian cinema can never progress in terms of establishing equality in the film industry until and unless the othering of women is stopped within its structure.

REFERENCES

Bahl, Vikas, director, *Queen*, 2014.
Bhansali, Sanjay Leela, director, *Padmaavat*, 2018.
Chopra, Aditya, director, *Befikre*, Yash Raj Films, 2016.
Culler, Jonathan D. (2011). *The Pursuit of Signs*, London: Routledge Publications.
Dhawan, David, director, *Judwa 2*, 2017.
Khaitan, Shashank, director, *Badrinath Ki Dulhania*, 2017.
Shinde, Gauri, director, *English Vinglish*, 2012.
Trivedi, Amit, director, *Padman*, 2018.

18

Women in Construction Industry

Pawan Kumar Mishra

Introduction

Construction industry is the backbone of a country as it creates the infrastructure necessary for economic and industrial growth. In India, it employs large number of skilled, semi-skilled as well as unskilled workforce due to its huge demand. The workforce employed in the construction industry has to face several hardships at the work since it is one of the hazardous occupations. Women workers are equally employed in this sector especially in unskilled category for sundry and manual works. They are working at various construction and project sites that are highly dangerous in nature and thus face several issues and challenges. Their major hardships are related to health, the work-life balance, safety at work, wage discrimination, harassment, and above all, working conditions as the biggest challenge.

Women employed in the construction industry in major cities are mostly unskilled labourers. They face serious problems related to their work environment, viz., wage discrimination, gender and sexual harassment, lower wages, health hazards, safety issues. Despite these problems, construction industry attracts female workers. Their skills are never upgraded to major skilled jobs in the construction industry like, mason, bar benders, carpenter, plumber, fabricator or painter etc. as they are allowed to perform only certain types of work and usually they assist the male workforce.

It is noted in the review of literature by the researchers that outside the agricultural sector, a significant and gradually increasing proportion of women workers are engaged in the construction sector (Shah, 2002). It is estimated that more than half of the 31 million construction workers in India are women (Government of India, 2008a:189). Women are employed in semi-skilled and sometimes in skilled jobs in other industries, but in the construction industry women are employed mostly as unskilled labourers (Jhabvala & Kanbur, 2002:7; Baruah, 2008). Today Indian sub-continent is the second fastest-growing economy in the world. The Indian construction industry has been playing a vital role in overall economic development of the country, growing at over 20 per cent Compound Annual Growth Rate over the past 5 years and contributing ~8 per cent to GDP.

Due to mechanization in the construction industry, liberalization of the Indian economy and the use of ready mixed concrete at construction sites, majority women workers are employed to carry the raw-materials for making concrete and placing the concrete manually. This also has resulted in the declining employability opportunities of the women workers. As per Jhabvala and Kanbur 2002 report, the estimated loss of employment due to mechanization of construction activities is about 1.5 million which is a significant number when the employment loss for the unskilled workers sectors are compared.

In today scenario, it is important that women employed in the construction trade are treated and provided equal opportunities on par with the male workers to take up the other skilled jobs like mason, plumber, carpenter and painter etc. so that issues like wage discrimination, gender bias can be eliminated which brings status of women workers in the construction trade on par with the other trades.

Objectives

The objectives of the present study were —

- To find out the major issues being faced by the women workers at construction sites like wage discrimination, working conditions, health hazards and safety issues through focus group studies and to find out why they should not be empowered to become skilled workers like masons, carpenters, plumbers and painters etc.
- To determine the willingness of women construction workers to become skilled workers and the willingness of men construction workers, contractors, construction and infra-structure companies to train and employ women as skilled workers like masons.

Literature Review

The review of literature is pertaining to some of the important articles and survey documented by various researcher regarding the construction industry and women's status. The focus of review is on the factors such as gender biasness, sexual harassment, family conditions of the women working in construction industry.

The variability in labour absorption in construction workers is much more pronounced for women than for men. It has often been noticed that whenever there is high demand for labour in this sector, the female employment rates is much higher than that of males. On the other hand, whenever there is any shrinkage in the workforce, female workers are the one who will be removed from the workforce than compared to males (Shramshakti Report). It appears that women construction workers form a buffer which provides the cushion to industry and as soon as the situation comes under the control they are shifted towards some other industry. The literature review is categorized into following sections to have an in-depth insight regarding discrimination of construction workers based on gender:

- Women's Employment.
- Gender Bias in Construction Sector.
- Wage Discrimination.
- Sexual Harassment at Workplace.
- Social and education context.
- Health Hazards.

Women's Employment

When it comes to female employment, however, the trends revealed by statistical analysis are more mixed. There have been some attempts to measure the intensity of work done by women in construction work as per the studies conducted by Madhok (2005) reported the status of women workers in the construction industry as under:

- In concreting, it was found that in 15 minutes, about 55 bundles, each weighing 7-8 kg., passed through the hands of women. In an 8-hour shift, therefore, an incredible 32,000 kg. Would have passed through a woman worker's hands.
- For masonry work, women carried 9-12 bricks (each weighing 2.5 kg.) on their head and moved with grace and skill along the scaffolding.

- While doing earth work women carried on their head 15 kg. of mud and walked 30 feet to deposit the mud and return. In an hour this was repeated 180 times. In an 8-hour shift a woman on average would have walked about 13 kms. carrying about 21,000 kg. of mud.
- While using a crowbar to dig into the earth, women would do this 15 times a minute, matching the efficiency of able bodied men.
- In curing, women were found carrying water in pots each weighing 8 kg., 15 times per hour to pour over concrete structures.
- In breaking *Jallis*, women used an iron hammer 52 times per minute and went on doing this for a 9-hour shift with a one-hour break in between (Girija & Geetha, 1989).

Gender Bias in Construction Sector

Women constitute half of the construction workers in India as semi-skilled/skilled jobs in other industries but in the construction industry, women are employed mostly as unskilled labourers (GoI, 2008a). They perform various unskilled jobs in the industry like cleaning building sites, carrying bricks, gravel, mortar and water up to the skilled carpenters and masons, irrespective of the number of years they worked, they are not upgraded from unskilled to skilled as males (Jhabvala & Kanbur, 2002; Baruah, 2008). This mindset has led to gender discrimination in this sector for work allocation and wage distribution (Suchitra & Rajshekhar, 2006). Such anti-women attitudes and discrimination further complicate the workplace culture of these women labour. They live very tough life and do not enjoy equality of status and social justice for which they actually deserve.

Wage Discrimination

Government fixed the wages for the unskilled and skilled labours for the public-sector unit as well as the private sector on the basis of work performed in terms of hours. But unfortunately, the industry works as in form of contract which provide the cost saving for government, which ultimately offer opportunity to the contractors to negotiate the wages. Males who are unskilled and skilled negotiate higher than female indicating gender biasness.

Women construction workers face discrimination in wages, as the contractors pay less than around 20 per cent wage to the women workers as compared to men workers. Women face discrimination on the job because even if they have the same skills as the men they are not given the same work. Thekedars act tough and do not pay wages regularly, handing out only enough for daily expenses and commuting. It is not safe for women to stand for a couple of hours at the naka. Thekedars and others eye them, harass them.

Sexual Harassment at Workplace

Sexual harassment is a serious problem for female construction workers. In a study it has been found that around 74 per cent of the respondents reported sexual harassment at workplace. Studies also revealed that insecure nature of employment, particularly for women, creates a vicious trap in which women are forced to please a subcontractor in order to get work. It is evident that the overwhelming majority of women in the industry are young, being between the ages of 16-40 years (Rai & Sarkar, 2012). A survey conducted in Punjab reported that of the respondents (55%) were in the age group of 21-30 years, followed by 37.50 per cent who were of 31-40 years (Bharara, K. *et al.*). Most of the workers are married. Women of these age group have the capacity to do hard work and easily harassed by the contractor. Thekedars and employers usually prefer to employ younger women whom they may exploit sexually. An extremity of demands of thekedars (contractors) can be estimated from the fact that to get employment, some of the older age workers force other poor young girls to please contractors; as in turn contractors has promised her to provide regular employment opportunity and 20 per cent extra commission on her wage for next whole year. Some reports state that they are exploited by thekedars both sexually as well as economically, many times such they face desertion of their own spouses and ultimately they loose the jobs.

Findings further noticed that despite the prevalence of such harsh and hostile work culture, low level of job satisfaction and unhealthy job relationship, construction industry overwhelmingly attract female labourers next only to agricultural sector. On the question why despite, such a hostile workplace, a large number of women folk take job at site?

There are several factors responsible for that, some of the factors are identified by the researchers in past which are family income, self-motives, social forces, season etc. The findings reveal that about 46 per cent of respondents reported that they do not have any other option, as they are widows or abandoned by their husband, or if husband is there, he is either drunkard or unemployed, therefore to meet the dire needs of family and to support children they have to take job at site. Another group (4%) is forced by poverty while 10 per cent are working to improve their economic status or helping other existing members of family in construction industry. Only 4 per cent of the female workers join the jobs at their own choice. It is largely noticed that on one hand where these womenfolk lack any particular skill, on another they are forced to work in unfavourable situations.

Social and Education Context

Based on three surveys of Delhi, Andhra Pradesh and Rajasthan, the picture emerges about women construction workers and their social context comes out as, *Harijans* and tribals are the largest groups represented, although they comprise only 15 per cent and 5 per cent of the Indian population respectively. It is apparent that the rural groups most likely to migrate in search of work are those who own the least land or are landless labourers. SC and ST are the largest landless groups in rural India, they also lack the skills as well other education. The construction industry is well suited for them according to their status, so, they are likely to comprise a significant section of construction workers. Ninety-six per cent of the construction workers in Delhi are *Harijan* migrant labourers from Rajasthan; *Harijans* and tribal together comprised 90 per cent of the Andhra sample, most of the women are young (average age 25) having joined the workforce before they reached their teens. Almost all are illiterate (*Construction Work in Women and Work: Continuity and Change*, Edited by Lebra, Paulson, Everett, Promilla & Co., 1984). Demographic picture has changed somewhat, with, for instance, more construction workers coming to Delhi from other states, comprising of Scheduled Castes and Tribes.

Health Hazards

The women workers at certain points were going through a number of job stresses like sexual harassment, being jobless, gender-based discrimination, proneness to different health hazards, physical problems, insomnia, nausea, headache, and other adverse outcomes. It is seen that at the work place they do not have any privacy for sanitation. Both male and female workers work together. Due to free mixing with the male co-workers they might get Sexually Transmitted Diseases (Tiwari & Gangopadhyay, 2011).

Specifically targeting to female construction workers, the impact of specific job stressors on women in the construction industry and the job stressors examined, were classified into areas of "Job/Task Demand", "Organizational Factors" and "Physical Conditions". Female construction workers differ from female workers in most other industries because their work setting is non-traditional. Therefore, in addition to the effects of classic job stressors that have been studied in women working in traditional jobs, there is possibility of very different perceptions of dominant job stressors and their levels of effect by female construction workers. It was also found that skill underutilization as well as having to over-compensate to prove oneself on the job were associated with psychological symptoms. While support from co-workers and supervisors did not moderate the association between control and gender-based harassment and discrimination, it did have a significant effect of job satisfaction (Goldenhar *et al.*, 1998).

Basic Rights of Women Workers

The I.L.O. formulated the following seven basic rights of women:

1. *The Right to Equal Pay*
    - ILO Convention No. 100,
    - Equal Remuneration, 1951 (in India).
2. *The Right to Equal Treatment*
    - ILO Convention No. 111,
    - Discrimination (Employment and Occupation) 1958 (in India),
    - ILO Convention No. 142; Human Resources Development, 1975.
3. *Maternity Protection, 1919*
    - ILO Convention No. 103,
    - Maternity Protection, (Revised), 1952 (in India).
4. *The Right to Combine Work and Domestic Responsibilities*
    - ILO Convention No. 156,
    - Workers with Family Responsibilities 1981.
5. *The Right to Paid Work*
    - ILO Convention No. 168.

6. *Employment Promotion and Protection, 1988*
   - ILO Convention No. 158,
   - Termination of Employment, 1982.
7. *The Right to Safe & Healthy Work Environment Free from Sexual Harassment*
   - Resolution on Equal Opportunity and Equal Treatment for Men and Women in Employment, 1985.

In the Indian constitution, Article 23 and 24 (i.e. Right against Exploitation), which are under the heading 'Fundamental Rights' and Article 39 Clauses (e) and (f) and Article 45, which are under the heading 'Directive Principles' of State Policy are covering the rights of women and children.

Recommendations

Studying the issues and resulting initiatives taken by different bodies, following recommendations are put forward:

- It is reported that in UK, one of the measures adopted by the government is to depute women in construction committees and portray women in construction as role models (Amaratunga *et al.*, 2006). Similarly, GoI should also look into deputing women in construction bodies and portray them as role models. This would encourage female students to take up a career in the construction industry.
- Since majority of the construction organizations are SMEs, industry level initiatives by government bodies or large organizations are required.
- Women should be involved in decision-making and they should handle departments that handle work of women staff and workers. Once they are in responsible positions their authority, responsibility or accountability should not be diluted (Chittibabu, 2007). Women can understand issues faced by other women better and can devise strategies for the same.
- Construction industry needs to change its working methodology, so, that flexible working hours could be implemented. This can be brought about by increasing computerization within the industry, reengineering the conventional method of working and creating virtual working environment. This would increase presence of women in managerial and senior positions.

- Building centres and similar grassroot level training agencies may appoint women organizers who could network with local communities in the catchment areas and educate families to encourage girls to go for training. Such trainings should be offered free of charge (Chittibabu, 2007).
- Contractors and Building-materials-manufacturing-Enterprises could be given incentives and administrative directives to give jobs to trained and skilled women (Chittibabu, 2007) and to provide services like mobile creches at sites.
- Workers' living area should be proper and hygienic. The facilities like good drinking water, toilets, bathrooms, and play ways should be available.
- For women workers, separate and safe space for living should be made available at all construction sites.
- Indian traditional dresses like saree could also be an inhibiting factor for women workers at site. Thus, at construction sites a standard dress code shall be for women and men workforce. This way they would not be differentiated from men in appearance and would be more comfortable in working at sites.
- There shall be more programmes of testing, certification and skill enhancement. These types of programmes are being run by Construction Industry Development Council to test the skills of the workers and recognize their skill levels. In these programmes, the skill enhancement provision is also available for semi-skilled and unskilled workers. The programmes should be available at each construction site.
- Construction workers welfare boards should act properly and effectively to implement the governments' welfare schemes to women workers.
- The law implementing agencies should work properly and effectively to implement laws of protection and welfare of women workers.
- A basic commitment should be given to adhere to labour standards and to insist that these are respected by all contractors and sub-contractors.
- Institutional participation on legislation and policy implementation on national level is necessary to improve the working conditions of women workers.
- Promotion and compliance of good practices in the industry should be always made.

- Training on health and safety should be carried out regularly.
- Compulsory employer's liability insurance to cover all workers on site should be implemented.
- Proper systems for risk management which include workers' participation should be maintained as an essential element.
- First aid and health services should be available at each site.
- Planning, co-ordination and operation of health and safety management system including training and workers participation are necessary.
- Initiatives to prevent the spread of HIV/AIDS and of other diseases should be taken on priority basis.
- There should be clauses in tenders to implement all these recommendations.

REFERENCES

Aadya & Kiran, U.V. (2013). "Occupational Stress of Women Workers in Unorganized Sector", *International Journal of Scientific and Engineering Research*, 4(3): 3-13.

Barnabas, Annette (2009). *Journal of International Women's Studies* Vol. 11: 2.

Bharara, K.; Sandhu, P. & Sidhu, M. (2012). *Issues of Occupational Health and Injuries among Unskilled Female Labourers in Construction Industry: A Scenario of Punjab State.*

Chen, Marty (2013). Harvard University, WIEGO Network.

Das, D.K. (1985). "Sex Discrimination against Female Workers in Unorganized Sector", *Indian Journal of Industrial Relations*, 21(2): 232-244.

Devi, Kalpana (2013). "Status of Female Workers in Construction Industry in India: A Review", *IOSR Journal of Humanities and Social Science (IOSR-JHSS)*, Volume 14, Issue 4 (Sep.-Oct. 2013): 27-30.

Girija, R. & Geetha, R. *et al.* (1989). *Socio-Economic Conditions of Construction Workers in Tamil Nadu*, Report submitted to ICSSR (Mimeo).

Jhabvala & Kanbur (2002). *Globalization and Economic Reform as Seen From the Ground: SEWA's Experience in India*, SEWA.

Kundu, Amitabh (2014). Ministry of Minority Affairs, Government of India Report.

Lebra, Paulson, Everett, Promilla & Co. (1984). "Construction Work", in *Women and Work: Continuity and Change.*

Madhok, S. (2005). *Report on the Status of Women Workers in the Construction Industry*, National Commission for Women, New Delhi.

Reddy, D.N. (1979). "Female Work Participation in India: Facts, Problems, and Policies", *Indian Journal of Industrial Relations*, 15(2): 197-212.

Richard, D.L. & Gelleny, R. (2007). "Women's Status and Economic Globalization", *International Studies Quarterly*, 51(4): 855-876.

Self-Employed Women's Association (2000). *Labouring Brick by Brick: A Study of Construction Workers.*

Tiwari, G. & Gangopadhyay, P.K. (2011). "A Review on the Occupational Health and Social Security of Unorganized Workers in the Construction Industry", *Indian Journal of Occupational and Environment Medicine*, 5(1).

PART III

Enhancing Well-being

19

Mindfulness

Shalini Sharma

Introduction

This chapter highlights the importance of mindfulness, an attribute of consciousness, in improving the psychological well-being of women. One of the major stressors of life for most of the individuals is worrying about future or getting stuck in the past leading to negative feelings like guilt, regret, resentment, grievance, anxiety, bitterness etc. A healthy state of mind requires one to focus one's attention in the present. However, day-dreaming, worries, excessive planning cause individuals to act mechanically — without conscious awareness, thus develop behavioural patterns which are unhealthy and mindless.

A disconnect between mind, body and heart is a very common and accepted way of being in the world for so many of us. Women of all age groups can be particularly prone to this as they have to balance and manage multiple roles, responsibilities and relationships at a given time. However, this can have serious effects on their physical and mental health, particularly their emotional well-being.

A number of psychological, philosophical and spiritual schools of thought have underscored the importance of quality of consciousness for the maintenance and improvement of well-being. An aspect of consciousness that has been much discussed and studied with respect to well-being is 'Mindfulness'. In simple terms it is construed as the state of being attentive to and aware of what is happening in the present. It helps one to train its mind to stop worrying about what has happened in the past or might happen and respond effectively to what is happening in the moment not only the events outside, but paying close attention to one's inner states like thoughts, sensations, feelings and emotions. This can promote well-being by facilitating self-regulatory behaviour and positive mental health.

Meaning of 'Mindfulness'

The term 'mindfulness' is a translation of the word *Sati* in Pali language, and has its roots in Buddhist traditions, though its origin stretch back at least as far as the third millennium B.C.E. as part of the Brahmanic traditions in the Indian subcontinent, from which Buddhism subsequently emerged (Cousins, 1996, cited in Lomas *et al.*, 2017:133). The term "mindfulness" is generally used to indicate both: (1) a state or quality of mind; and (2) a form of meditation that helps one to bring up and nurture this particular state/quality (Lomas *et al.*, 2017)

With respect to its first meaning, Kabat-Zinn (2003) defines mindfulness as "the awareness that arises through paying attention on purpose, in the present moment, and non-judgementally to the unfolding of experience moment by moment" (Lomas *et al.*, 2017:133). The main attributes of mindfulness include a pre-conceptual awareness and acceptance of experiences; flexible control of attention; a detached or unbiased receptivity to experience; and an inclination to the here-and-now (Brown, Ryan & Creswell, 2007a; Howell, 2008:773).

Nyanaponika Thera (1972) called mindfulness "the clear and single-minded awareness of what actually happens to us and in us at the successive moments of perception" (Brown & Ryan, 2003:822). Hanh (1976) defined mindfulness as "keeping one's consciousness alive to the present reality" (Brown & Ryan, 2003). However, 'paying attention' here indicates concentrating on what one is doing at the same time being aware of one's affective state, thoughts, and memories that arise in that moment, and also observing when the mind digress so that it can be refocused (Baer & Krietemeyer, 2006).

A central characteristic of mindfulness has been described as open or receptive awareness and attention (Deikman, 1982; Martin, 1997, in Brown & Ryan, 2003:822). Prof. Ronald, D. Siegel of Harvard Medical School concur the notion of non-judgement, and acceptance to the concept of mindfulness. He defines it "as awareness of present experience with acceptance" (Siegel, 2014). According to him there are three components of mindfulness: awareness, present experience and acceptance. Mindfulness requires training to devote our attention to our experience as it is occurring, moment by moment, with open-minded inquisitiveness and acceptance (Kabat-Zinn 1996, in Weare, 2014:4)

Shapiro, Carlson, Astin, and Freedman (2006) specified three components of mindfulness: intention (i.e. motivation for paying attention in this way; attention (i.e. the cognitive mechanisms through which said attention is enacted); and attitude (i.e. the emotional qualities with which one imbues one's attentive focus, like compassion) (Lomas *et al.*, 2017:133).

Mindfulness is also considered as a trait, as in, people differ in terms of level of mindfulness, some being more mindful than others. Higher levels of mindfulness is linked with good number of positive outcomes, including improved mental health, higher relationship satisfaction, and much better effective management of pain (Brown *et al.*, 2007). Trait mindfulness is strongly associated with greater subjective well-being (Baer *et al.*, 2008; Brown, Kasser, Ryan, Linley & Orzech, 2009; Falkenstrom, 2010, cited in Schutte & Malouff, 2011:1116).

Another way mindfulness is defined is as a meditational practice. Meditation refers to:

> "A family of self-regulation practices that focus on training attention and awareness in order to bring mental processes under greater voluntary control and thereby foster general mental well-being and development and/or specific capacities such as calm, clarity, and concentration" (Walsh & Shapiro, 2006:228, in Davis & Hayes, 2011:199).

As a meditational practice, mindfulness meditation, also refers to a diversified realm of mental activities, which share a common purpose of training the self-regulation of attention and awareness (Lomas, Ivtzan & Fu, 2015), with the aim of improving voluntary control of mental processes, thereby enhancing well-being (Walsh & Shapiro, 2006, in Lomas *et al.*, 2017:134). Its foundation lies on conventional mindful meditation but as a psychological concept is separate from spiritual beliefs and Buddhist practices (Kabat-Zinn 1982, cited in Khan & Zadeh, 2014:70). The term mindfulness meditation is often used interchangeably with Vipassana, a form of meditational practice that derives from Theravada Buddhism (Gunaratana, 2002; Young, 1997). Vipassana is also a Pali word for insight and clear awareness and carried out in a manner to gradually enhance mindfulness (Gunaratana, 2002 in Davis & Hayes, 2011:199). Mindfulness meditation came to be popular in the west notably through the efforts of Kabat-Zinn (1982), who utilized it for an innovative "mindfulness-based stress reduction" (MBSR) programme. There are number of interventions based on mindfulness meditation that will be discussed in the latter part of the chapter. It's important to know as of now the mechanism and process of mindfulness and how does it benefit the individual who practice it.

How Does Mindfulness Work?

(a) *Biological Changes in Brain and Body*

Studies of the biological basis of higher levels of trait mindfulness (e.g., Frewen *et al.*, 2010) propose that mindfulness is linked to differential brain activation during emotional processing (Schutte & Malouff, 2011:1116). Current developments in neuroscience have revealed that the structure and function of brain is not fixed from childhood, rather brain remains plastic and moldable throughout life. A large number of studies using brain imaging/MRI techniques and Randomized Control trials (RCT) methodology to inquire the impact of mindfulness are propounding that mindfulness training have a profound altering effect on the structure and function of the brain to enhance the quality of thought and feelings. Mindfulness meditation apparently reshapes the neural pathways thereby increasing the complexity and density of connections in centres associated with cognitive abilities (attention, self-awareness, introspection etc.) as well as emotion areas responsible for kindness, compassion and rationality. At the same time they tend to decrease the activity and growth in brain areas associated with negative emotions like anxiety, hostility, worry and impulsivity (Davidson & Lutz, 2008; Hölzel *et al.*, 2011a and b, in Weare, 2014:5).

Research evidence suggests that mindfulness meditation in comparison to concentrative forms of meditation (e.g., focusing on a mantra) arouse the middle prefrontal brain connected with both self-observation and meta-cognition more (Cahn & Polich, 2006; Siegel, 2007b) and also promote specific attentional mechanisms (Valentine & Sweet, 1999 in Davis & Hayes, 2011:199). Those who practice meditation for a long time, most noteworthy changes are observable in them, however, even short mindfulness interventions brings about clear and significant effects on brain functioning and performance (Hölzel *et al.*, 2011a, in Weare, 2014:5).

Research based on RCT have shown that subjects in a mindfulness meditation group had a significantly higher number of antibodies in the blood in response to an influenza vaccine as compared to those in the wait-list control group (Davidson *et al.*, 2003; Davidson & Lutz, 2008). A study using pre- and post-analysis found that twenty five minutes mindfulness meditation for five days by adults improved their immune-reactivity and led to decrease in stress hormone, cortisol (Hölzel *et al.*, 2011a, in Weare, 2014).

(b) *Personal-Psychological Changes*

Shapiro *et al.* (2006) contends that the main importance of mindfulness is that it entails a meta-mechanism referred as "re-perceiving". The three segments of mindfulness (intention, attention and attitude) integrate to bring about what is known as a "fundamental shift in perspective", in which "rather than being immersed in the personal drama or narrative of our life story, we are able to stand back and witness it" (p. 377) (Lomas *et al.*, 2017). This "standing back" referred to by Shapiro *et al.*, as "reperceiving" is also known as "decentring", defined as "the ability to observe one's thoughts and feelings as temporary, objective events in the mind, as opposed to reflections of the self that are necessarily true" (Fresco *et al.*, 2007, in Lomas *et al.*, 2017:134).

Those who practice mindfulness meditation report that over a period of sustained practice and training of mind they learn to focus their attention and consciousness in the present and accept their experience open mindedly as it is, rather than judging and typing it (as positive, negative, right-wrong etc.), by concentrating their attention on the felt physical sensations of the breath and the body to hold the wandering mind. Thoughts are perceived in a detached manner as mental events that come and go. This re-perception helps one to have control and reduce the habitual, mindless automatic mental activity including depressing thoughts, rumination, worrying and leads to less reactivity and impulsiveness, and a better ability to examine thoughts and emotions more objectively, to own them rather than deny or blame others. Conclusively, it can be remarked that meditational practice helps one to gradually come over and modify habitual mental sets and behavioural patterns leading to negative psychic states like stress, depression, frustration and promote positive mental states like compassion, calm, happiness, receptivity (Weare, 2014).

Mindfulness and Well-being

"Women have increased their participation in paid employment considerably during the past 30 years, but men have not increased their participation in housework to the same extent" (Evertsson & Nermo, 2004).

The statement holds true till the present time. The situation might appear better in metro cities, but a lot needs to be done to change the traditional gender-roles perspective. There is no denial of the fact that working women wear many hats and do much more multitasking than men. This might have a detrimental effect on their physical and mental health and overall sense of well-being.

Keyes (2005) regarded well-being as comprising three domains: *emotional well-being*, involving the combination of positive affect and life satisfaction; *psychological well-being*, constituting satisfaction with one's achievements and believing having a purpose in life and developing as an individual; and *social well-being*, including the quality of one's proclivity toward others (Howell, Digdan & Buro, 2010:419).

Researchers have contended that mindfulness does not only have a direct effect on well-being, but it is also an indirect predictor of well-being through its impact on enhanced self-regulated functioning (Brown & Ryan, 2003; Brown, Ryan & Creswell, 2007b; Shapiro & Schwartz, 1999, 2000 in Howell, Digdan & Buro, 2010:420). Shapiro *et al.* (2006) propounded that reperceiving/decentring has a positive impact upon well-being (in Lomas *et al.*, 2017:134). Mindfulness is regarded to be leading to high levels of well-being; particularly, mindfulness is believed to be directly enhancing well-being by adding fullness and richness to experience, and mindfulness is suggested to be indirectly promoting well-being by boosting healthy self-regulatory behaviour, including a heightened focused attention to, and acceptance of, one's personal needs or values and a developed capacity to behave in accordance with them (Brown & Ryan, 2003; Brown *et al.*, 2007a, in Howell *et al.*, 2008:773).

Mindfulness and Physical Health

There is a growing concern of the effects of women involvement in multiple roles on their physical and mental health. It has been observed that employment adds to the obligations of the women as it seldom gives a respite from their domestic duties of household management. Child bearing and rearing is also a huge responsibility that might take a toll on the physical health of women. A number of studies provide evidence for the beneficial effects of mindfulness meditation for varied physiological health problems. There is abundant research using the randomized control trial methodology (RCTs, involving comparison of two groups, one who receives the intervention and other not, with randomly distributed participants) showing the usefulness of mindfulness in decreasing a wide range of physical health problems including chronic pain, fatigue, cancer, heart disease, type-2 diabetes and psoriasis both in adults and youth (Baer, 2003; *Mental Health Foundation, 2010* in Weare, 2014:6).

Research evidence also indicates that mindfulness meditation leads to multiple health gains including increased immune functioning (Davidson *et al.*, 2003; see Grossman, Niemann, Schmidt & Walach, 2004, in Davis & Hayes, 2011:201). A study on mindfulness and physical health highlighted that mindfulness is associated with better cardiovascular functioning through a lower degree of smoking, greater physical activity, and a healthier body mass index (Loucks, Britton, Howe, Eaton & Buka, 2015). Furthermore, mindfulness has been positively linked with lower blood pressure, (Tomfohr, Pung, Mills & Edwards, 2015), successful weight loss for obese adults and improved eating behaviours [Rogers, Ferrari, Mosely, Lang & Brennan, 2017 (cited in Ackerman, 2017)].

Mindfulness-based stress reduction (MBSR) has been carried out for patients with a vast variety of chronic clinical ailments, as well among groups of relatively healthy individuals who have undertaken it to improve their abilities to cope with the significant stressors of daily life. Initial reports have indicated substantial benefits for individuals suffering from chronic pain, fibromyalgia, cancer, anxiety disorders and depression and the stresses of contexts as diverse as medical school and prison life (Arcari, 1997; Astin, 1997; Baime, 1996 in Grossman, Niemann, Schmidt & Walach, 2004:36). Results for effectiveness of MBSR for those suffering from chronic low back pain found that mindfulness enhanced patients' ability to function on their own, i.e. less dependence and experience of less back pain than treatment as usual (Cherkin, Sherman, Balderson, Cook, Anderson, Hawkes, Hansen & Turner, 2016 cited in Ackerman, 2017).

Mindfulness and Cognitive Functioning

To be able to function and perform to the fullest capability one requires optimum cognitive functioning like attention, memory, thinking, reasoning, decision-making, language etc. Though there is no consensus among researchers to say women are better multitaskers than men, but studies do point out that women multitask more often and multitasking negatively affects performance (Hamilton, *et al.*, 2010; Ophira *et al.*, 2010). One of the studies carried out at Michigan State University showed that women multitask 10 hours more per week than men and carrying out multitasking leads to increase in stress, negative emotions and work-life conflicts (Cabrera, 2016). This is also suggested to be the one of the reasons why women experience more stress than men given similar workloads.

It is also asserted that the more one multitasks the more difficult it gets one to carry out focused attention when it is required. Focused attention is not only important for better performance, but also for one's sense of psychological well-being. Low level of focused attention can also result in experiencing greater anxiety as our thoughts get us to worry about the future (Cabrera, 2016).

The practice of mindfulness meditation can help women to be pay attention to the present moment and enhance their sense of well-being by reducing stress levels.

Corcoran *et al.* (2010) propound that mindfulness meditation develops metacognitive awareness, reduces rumination by way of disconnection from persevering cognitive activities, and promotes attentional abilities through improvement in working memory; these cognitive benefits, consecutively add to effective emotion regulation strategies (in Davis & Hayes, 2011:200). In an experimental research, twenty beginner meditators participated in a ten day comprehensive mindfulness meditation retreat and were compared to a waitlisted control group on aspects like mindfulness, emotions, ruminative thinking and performance tasks for attention shifting, continued attention and working memory (Chambers *et al.*, 2008). The findings revealed that after the completion of the meditation retreat, the meditation group reported significantly higher self-reported mindfulness, reduced negative affect, less depressive symptoms, and low level of rumination as compared to the control group. Additionally, the meditation group had significantly better working memory capacity and comparatively greater capability to sustain attention during a performance task compared to the control group (Davis & Hayes, 2011).

Mindfulness may be helpful to healthy sleep-related functioning. Studies suggest that mindfulness-based interventions enhance sleep functioning (Winbush, Gross & Kreitzer, 2007), this is done by reducing arousal-producing and cognitive-distorting mechanisms (Ong, Shapiro & Manber, 2008; Yook *et al.*, 2008 in Howell *et al.*, 2010:419).

Mindfulness, Emotional Well-being and Psychological Health

Besides requiring to balance multiple roles — professional, familial, community — working women might have to deal with additional demands and challenges at work like role-stress, discrimination, gender bias, sexual harassment, daily hassles of commuting to work etc. This amplifies the level of stress experienced by women and inability to maintain work-life equilibrium may lead to feelings of guilt, low self-esteem and self-efficacy.

Mindfulness can help women to attain and maintain a positive state of mind, an acceptance of one's self and being comfortable with it. Mindfulness as a trait perspective assumes some people to be more mindful than others. Thereby people can be trained to be more mindful. A number of studies have shown dispositional mindfulness (the degree to which a person is mindful) to correlate positively with self-esteem, and self-acceptance (Thompson & Walz, 2008 in Weare, 2014:14). Women can be trained to develop their mindfulness as high level of mindfulness is correlated with significantly more positive affect, low negative affect, and higher life satisfaction (Brown & Ryan, 2003). It is shown that as mindfulness is improved as a result of interventions, like meditation training, well-being also tends to increase (Falkenstrom, 2010; Fredrickson, Cohn, Coffey, Pek & Finkel, 2008; Zautra *et al.*, 2008 in Shutte & Malouff, 2011:1116). Some research evidence also points out that higher levels of mindfulness are linked with more adaptive emotional functioning, termed as emotional intelligence (Baer, Smith & Allen, 2004; Brown & Ryan, 2003 in Shutte & Malouff, 2011).

Weinstein, Brown and Ryan (2009) proposed that more mindful individuals gave more positive stress appraisals and displayed a greater use of approach and a lower use of avoidance coping resulting in higher SWB. Studies have also showed that mindfulness has the capacity to lower negative emotional outcomes resulting from neuroticism (Barnhofer *et al.*, 2011; Feltman *et al.*, 2009). Neuroticism is believed to lead to mood spillover effects because of its association with rumination (Nolen-Hoeksema, Wisco & Lyubomirsky, 2008). Considering mindfulness intervention programmes can reduce ruminative thinking (Deyo, Wilson, Ong & Koopman, 2009), it seems possible that mindfulness will lower the effects of neuroticism on well-being (Wenzel *et al.*, 2015:69).

The positive effects of mindfulness at the time of pregnancy for reducing psychological distress, stress and anxiety are also supported by number of empirical studies. (Dunn *et al.*, 2012; Vieten & Astin, 2008). Virgili (2013) recently documented a meta-analysis measuring the effect of mindfulness for working adults, for lowering psychological distress, particularly stress, anxiety and depression. They analysed 19 mindfulness-based interventions, involving 1,139 participants. The findings revealed medium-to-large mean effect sizes for both before and after studies and control studies; an effect which sustained for follow-up of around 5 weeks, and was applicable to both short as well as longer interventions. There is a strong evidence for the effect of mindfulness on depression in adults (e.g. Segal *et al.*, 2012) and youth (e.g. Kuyken *et al.*, 2013). UK National Institute for Clinical Excellence recommends the eight week Mindfulness Based Cognitive Therapy (MBCT) course for repeated depression in adults. An investigation into the mechanism by which mindfulness works on depression is presently believed to involve its ability to help people develop a sense of space and objectivity related to their thoughts and assist them in detaching and loosening from the habitual, cyclical web of negative ruminative thinking (Segal *et al.*, 2012; Hölzel *et al.*, 2011b in Weare, 2014:11).

An experimental study by Manas *et al.* (2011) examined the effectiveness of mindfulness training to lower the levels of stress and sick leave taken by 31 secondary teachers, among which 16 formed the experimental and 15 the control group. Findings indicated significant decrease in levels of teacher stress and the number of days of sick leave, in addition to reduction in feelings of pressure and feelings of being demotivated and better coping in the experimental group in comparison to the control group (Weare, 2014:12).

Mindfulness and Social Well-being

Being embedded in social structures and communities, women face multiple challenges in meeting their social role and responsibilities. For women to experience a sense of well-being, requires, social integration or having a healthy relationship with one's family, society and community. Studies have also revealed mindfulness to be efficacious in relationship building, and predictive of higher sense of relatedness and interpersonal proximity (Brown & Kasser, 2005; Brown & Ryan, 2003 in Weare, 2014:14).

Many scholars in the field are trying to find the link between mindfulness and interpersonal behaviour and are examining concepts like mindful relating (Wachs & Cordova, 2007), mindful responding in couples (Block-Lerner, Adair, Plumb, Rhatigan & Orsillo, 2007), and mindfulness-based relationship enhancement (MBRE) (Carson, Carson, Gil & Baucom, 2006 in Davis & Hayes, 2011:201).

There is research evidence to support that trait mindfulness predicts a number of interpersonal issues and behaviours such as ability to manage relationship stress constructively, competence in identifying and expressing emotions to partner, relationship satisfaction, frequency of relationship conflict, level of negativity, and empathy (Barnes, Brown, Krusemark, Campbell & Rogge, 2007; Wachs & Cordova, 2007). Barnes *et al.* (2007) found that people with higher trait mindfulness expressed low level of emotional stress when faced with relationship conflict and reported low level of anger and anxiety during conflict discussion. Studies also show that mindfulness is inversely related to distress contagion and directly related with the ability to act with awareness in social situations (Dekeyser, Raes, Leijssen, Leyson & Dewulf, 2008 in Davis & Hayes, 2011:201).

Thus based on empirical evidence it is suggested that mindfulness safeguards against the emotionally distressing consequences of relationship conflict (Barnes *et al.*, 2007), is positively correlated with one's communication ability to clearly express oneself in social situations (Dekeyser *et al.*, 2008), and predicts relationship satisfaction (Barnes *et al.*, 2007; Wachs & Cordova, 2007). In addition to the above mentioned advantages, mindfulness also has some intrapersonal benefits like reduces reactivity, self-insight, morality, intuition, and fear modulation (Siegel, 2007b, 2009 in Davis & Hayes, 2011:201).

The above mentioned benefits relating to physical, psychological and social well-being is achieved and maintained by number of mindfulness based interventions, some of which are discussed below.

Mindfulness-based Interventions

Mindfulness meditation has been popularized in west by Kabat-Zinn who has developed a mindfulness-based stress reduction programme at the University of Massachusetts Medical Centre in 1979. In 1995, he came up with The Centre for Mindfulness in Medicine, Health Care, and Society. The beneficial effects of mindfulness based interventions in the area of physical and mental health are supported by plethora of research and have been discussed above. Some of the most popular mindfulness based interventions are outlined below:

Mindfulness-based Stress Reduction (MBSR)

MBSR was the first to be introduced mindfulness based programme for relieving stress and advancing physical-mental health and well-being of individuals. It involves 8-week course, which is structured in a class format in order for participants to learn and benefit from their collective experience. It is designed to be both educational and experiential, combining traditional Buddhist mindfulness meditation techniques (where participants learn to center their focus on the breathing and moving it towards an heightened awareness of other objects of attention like sensations, feelings, thoughts), simple *yoga* and stretching exercises, practices such as the 'body scan', in which participants concentrate on different areas of their body having mindful awareness and journal tasks to help participants integrate mindfulness into daily life.

The Centre for Mindfulness in Healthcare, Medicine and Society at the University of Massachusetts Medical School reports that, since its inception in 1979, more than 18,000 people have completed their 8-week course. The programme was conceptualized with the purpose of determining whether mindfulness and relaxation exercises can benefit people with chronic health issues like high BP, anxiety disorders and chronic pain. The intent is to promote overall well-being by helping individuals to focus their attention on their thoughts, feelings and internal states in the present (*Mental Health Foundation of New Zealand*, 2011).

During the meditation, participants engage in (a) body scanning, which includes non-judgemental awareness of sensations and feelings in different bodily parts; (b) meditation while sitting, where par-ticipants concentrate on breathing, at the same time having a non-judgemental awareness of any thoughts that crop up; and (c) *Hatha yoga* involving stretching exercises for strengthening and easing the musculoskeletal system (Cabrera-Caban *et al.*, 2016).

MBSR can be better discerned through the four processes suggested by Hölzel and colleagues (2011): (a) attention regulation, (b) body awareness, (c) emotion regulation, and (d) change in self-perspective (cited in Cabrera-Caban *et al.*, 2016:122). Generally, participants first learn attention regulation by the way of focused meditation, wherein they are cognizant of and pay attention to a given thought, feeling, or object. Over a period of time, with practice participants are able to focus attention for longer duration and are better equipped to filter out distractions of the mind. Another technique, body awareness, entails focusing attention on sensory experiences and breathing to help individuals to align their thoughts and feelings with the outside world. This is expected to result in better clarity (Marianetti & Passmore, 2009) and emotional intelligence (Keng *et al.*, 2011). The third process, emotion regulation, refers to the modification of emotional responses from impulsive reactivity to reflective thinking assisting participants in recognizing their experiences in an accepting, non-judgemental manner.

At the last, change in perception of the self refers to a transformation from a feeling of static-rigid self-perception to a more dynamic self-image. The belief here is when people feel less stasis about self they become more liberated and experience a more positive self-image (Flaxman & Bond, 2010, cited in Cabrera-Caban *et al.*, 2016:123).

The MBSR approach to teaching mindfulness has provided a framework on which many other interventions and therapies have been developed. Some of these are Mindfulness-Based Relationship Enhancement (MBRE), which develops interpersonal relationship practices for couples (Carson, Gill & Baucom, 2004); Mindfulness-Based Eating Awareness Training (MB-EAT) — an intervention developed specifically for binge-eating disorder (Kristeller, Baer & Quillian-Wolever, 2006); Mindfulness-Based Art Therapy (MBAT) (Monti *et al.*, 2006); and Mindfulness Based Childbirth and Parenting (MBCP), which prepares couples to effectively deal with issues related to upcoming birth, and trains them in intuitive attention, which forms the basis of a strong attachment relationship with the newborn child.

Mindfulness-Based Cognitive Therapy (MBCT) has its roots in the collective-based, eight-week programme MBSR, but was adapted by Zindel Segal, Mark Williams and John Teasdale (2002) to be used by individuals who were suffering from or had experienced repeated bouts of depression in their lives. It combines characteristics of cognitive therapy with mindfulness practices. MBCT is different from cognitive therapy as it involves non-judgemental acceptance of thoughts and feelings, rather than making an attempt to evaluate or modify the content of thoughts. This idea of perceiving the mind as a place of 'being' rather than 'doing' reduces rumination and helps depression-prone individuals to prevent approaching relapse. In their book *Mindfulness Based Cognitive Therapy*, Segal, Teasdale & Williams (2002) proposed that:

> "The ultimate aim of the MBCT programme is to help individuals make a radical shift in their relationship to the thoughts, feelings and bodily sensations that contribute to depressive relapse". It also aims to "help participants choose the most skillful response to any unpleasant thoughts, feelings or situations they meet".

The United Kingdom National Institute of Clinical Excellence (NICE) has recently promoted MBCT as an effective treatment for relapse prevention. Research has demonstrated that a number of people who have been clinically depressed three or more times (sometimes for

20 years or more) assert that undergoing the programme and learning these skills help to significantly lower the chances of depression to reoccur (National Collaborating Centre for Mental Health, 2009). [*Mental Health Foundation of New Zealand, 2011*]

Dialectical Behaviour Therapy (DBT)

Dialectical behaviour therapy (DBT) was developed by Marsha Linehan, as a cognitive-behavioural and mindfulness-based therapy for Borderline personality disorder (BPD). The essential dialect is between the contradictory forces of change and acceptance, i.e. accepting the things as they are, at the same time making an effort to improve them. In DBT mindfulness is learnt as a set of skills with the help of structured exercises. These involve observing, comprehending and engaging in one's present moment experience in a non-judgemental, singular focus and effective manner. DBT trains one in how to make use of the 'wise mind' — the latent ability to have clear awareness of one's thoughts and feelings. It was the first psychotherapy propounded to be effective in successfully treating BPD in controlled clinical trials, and it currently has a substantial evidence base, being regarded as one of the most effective treatments for BPD in terms of documented success rates.

Acceptance and Commitment Therapy (ACT)

Acceptance and Commitment Therapy (ACT) is a psychological intervention, empirically grounded, which aims to improve psychological flexibility in individuals by combining acceptance and mindfulness strategies, with commitment and behaviour change strategies. Psychological flexibility here means fully engaging with the present moment having full consciousness and based on what the situation entails modifying or persisting with the behaviour aligning with the person's preferred values. The therapy draws heavily from cognitive-behavioural framework, but differs in its dominant use of mindfulness exercises to help individuals in attaining flexibility. ACT is regarded by American Psychological Association as an empirically validated intervention for treating depression, as they listed it is as "an empirically supported treatment with modest research support status" (Mental Health Foundation of New Zealand, 2011).

The effectiveness of MBIs is undeniable based on the outcomes of meta-analytic studies, however, there are a number of methodological rigor issues that interferes in the global acceptance of MBIs as established psychotherapeutic interventions. The validity of MBI studies get limited by number of factors such as wide variations in MBI programme design; lack of adequate control for probable confounding factors; paucity of long-term follow-up data assessing the maintenance effects of MBIs; over-dependence on self-report measures etc. Questions have also been raised about the credibility and competence of MBI facilitators. Despite these criticisms mindfulness has witnessed a tremendous increase in popularity over the years and has carved a powerful niche in mainstream psychotherapy (Shonin, Gordon & Griffiths, 2013).

Psychological Assessment of Mindfulness

Having understood the effectiveness of Mindfulness based programmes on physical and psychological health of participants, it may be helpful to gain awareness about various assessment tools and questionnaires that have been developed to measure mindfulness. This is important for those interested to work in this area, and also to gain an insight about one's own mindfulness. Some of the questionnaires that measure mindfulness as a general, trait-like inclination to be mindful in day-to-day life are: Freiburg Mindfulness Inventory (Buchheld, Grossman & Walach, 2001), Kentucky Inventory of Mindfulness Skills (KIMS; Baer *et al.*, 2004), Mindful Attention Awareness Scale (MAAS; Brown & Ryan, 2003), Five-Facet Mindfulness Questionnaire (Baer *et al.*, 2006), Cognitive Affective Mindfulness Scale-Revised (Feldman, Hayes, Kumar, Greeson & Laurenceau, 2007), Toronto Mindfulness Scale-Trait Version (Davis, Lau & Cairns, 2009), Philadelphia Mindfulness Scale (Cardaciotto *et al.*, 2008), and Southampton Mindfulness Questionnaire (Chadwick *et al.*, 2008, in Keng, Smoski & Robins, 2011:3).

Some of these questionnaires conceptualize and assess mindfulness as a unifactor construct, i.e. based on a single factor. For example, the MAAS (Brown & Ryan, 2003) measures mindfulness as the general tendency to be aware of and attentive to daily life experiences, and uses a single factor structure of open/ receptive attention and awareness. There are other questionnaires which assess mindfulness as a multi-factor/multi-faceted construct. For example, the KIMS (Baer *et al.*, 2004) entails sub-scales that comprises of four mindfulness competencies underlined in DBT's framework: being aware of one's moment-to-moment experiences, detailing one's experiences in words, participation with awareness, non-judgemental acceptance of one's experiences.

Besides trait measures of mindfulness, state measures of mindfulness have also been developed to assess transient mindful states. These measures include the Toronto Mindfulness Scale (Lau *et al.*, 2006) and Brown and Ryan (2003)'s state version of the MAAS (in Keng, Smoski & Robins, 2011:3).

Conclusion

People of all age groups, gender orientation, societies can benefit from mindfulness based programmes. Research is abound with the positive impact of mindfulness on different aspects of an individual's being: physical, intrapersonal, interpersonal, and cognitive. However, research on beneficial effects of mindfulness for women is limited to prenatal (pregnancy) period and postnatal care. There is a need to relook at the importance of MBIs for both working and non-working women taking into account the uneven distribution of duties and responsibilities in majority of households. Although strict gendered division of labour has decreased across the world, yet women still do the lion's share of all housework (Evertsson and Nermo, 2004). Awareness needs to be spread about Mindfulness based interventions like MBSR, MBCT, DBT, ACT etc. for promoting physical, emotional and social well-being in women. To conclude, mindfulness based approaches for women represent an emerging area in the field, one with much potential promise.

REFERENCES

Ackerman, Courtney (2017). *The 23 Amazing Health Benefits of Mindfulness for Body and Brain. https://positivepsychologyprogram.com/benefits-of-mindfulness/*

Baer, R. & Krietemeyer, J. (2006). "Overview of Mindfulness and Acceptance Based Treatment Approaches", in R. Baer (Ed.), *Mindfulness Based Treatment Approaches* (pp. 3-27), Burlington: Elsevier.

Baer, R.A. (2003). "Mindfulness Training as a Clinical Intervention: A Conceptual and Empirical Review", *Clinical Psychology: Science and Practice*, 10: 125-143. *doi: 10.1093/clipsy.bpg015*

Baer, R.A.; Smith, G.T. & Allen, K.B. (2004). "Assessment of Mindfulness by Self-report: The Kentucky Inventory of Mindfulness Skills", *Assessment*, 11: 191-206.

Baer, R.A.; Smith, G.T.; Hopkins, J.; Krietemeyer, J. & Toney, L. (2006). "Using Self-reportassessment Methods to Explore Facets of Mindfulness", *Assessment*, 13: 27-45.

Baer, R.A.; Smith, G.T.; Lykins, E.; Button, D.; Krietemeyer, J. & Sauer, S. (2008). "Construct Validity of the Five Facet Mindfulness Questionnaire in Meditating and Non-meditating Samples", *Assessment*, 15: 329-342.

Barnes, S.; Brown, K.W.; Krusemark, E.; Campbell, W.K. & Rogge, R.D. (2007). "The Role of Mindfulness in Romantic Relationship Satisfaction and Responses to Relationship Stress", *Journal of Marital and Family Therapy*, 33: 482-500. *doi:10.1111/j.1752-0606.2007.00033.x*

Barnhofer, T.; Duggan, D.S. & Griffith, J.W. (2011). "Dispositional Mindfulness Moderates the Relation between Neuroticism and Depressive Symptoms", *Personality Individual Differences*, 51: 958-962.

Block-Lerner, J.; Adair, C.; Plumb, J.C.; Rhatigan, D.L. & Orsillo, S.M. (2007). "The Case for Mindfulness-based Approaches in the Cultivation of Empathy: Does Non-judgemental, Present-moment Awareness Increase Capacity for Perspective-taking and Empathetic Concern?", *Journal of Marital and Family Therapy*, 33: 505-516. *doi:10.1111/j.1752-0606.2007.00034.x*

Brown, K.W. & Kasser, T. (2005). "Are Psychological and Ecological Well-being Compatible? The Role of Values, Mindfulness, and Lifestyle", *Social Indicators Research*, 74: 349-368.

Brown, K.W.; Kasser, T.; Ryan, R.M.; Linley, A. & Orzech, K. (2009). "When What One has is Enough: Mindfulness, Financial Desire Discrepancy, and Subjective Well-being", *Journal of Research in Personality*, 43: 727-736.

Brown, K.W. & Ryan, R.M. (2003). "The Benefits of Being Present: Mindfulness and Its Role in Psychological Well-being", *Journal of Personality and Social Psychology*, 84: 822-848.

Brown, K.W.; Ryan, R.M. & Creswell, J.D. (2007a). "Mindfulness: Theoretical Foundations and Evidence for Its Salutary Effects", *Psychological Inquiry*, 18: 211-237.

Brown, K.W.; Ryan, R.M. & Creswell, J.D. (2007b). "Addressing Fundamental Questions about Mindfulness", *Psychological Inquiry*, 18: 272-281.

Buchheld, N.; Grossman, P. & Walach, H. (2001). "Measuring Mindfulness in Insight Meditation (Vipassana) and Meditation-based Psychotherapy: The Development of the Freiburg Mindfulness Inventory (FMI)", *Journal for Meditation and Meditation Research*, 1: 11-34.

Cabrera, Beth (2016). "Women Need Mindfulness Even More than Men Do", *Harvard Business Review, https://hbr.org/2016/06/women-need-mindfulness-even-more-than-men-do*

Cabrera-Caban, Enrique; Garden, Rebecca; White, Arianna & Reynoldson, Katelyn (2016). "Mindfulness-Based Interventions: A Brief Review of their Application to Graduate Student Strain", *The Industrial-Organizational Psychologist*, Vol. 53, Number 4: 121-127.

Cahn, B.R. & Polich, J. (2006). "Meditation States and Traits: Eeg, Erp, and Neuroimaging Studies", *Psychological Bulletin*, 132: 180-211. *doi: 10.1037/0033-2909.132.2.180*

Cardaciotto, L.; Herbert, J.D.; Forman, E.M.; Moitra, E. & Farrow, V. (2008). "The Assessment of Present-moment Awareness and Acceptance: The Philadelphia Mindfulness Scale", *Assessment*, 15: 204-223.

Carson, J.; Carson, K.; Gil, K. & Baucom, D. (2004). "Mindfulness-based Relationship Enhancement", *Behaviour Therapy*, 35: 471-494.

Carson, J.W.; Carson, K.M.; Gil, K.M. & Baucom, D.H. (2006). "Mindfulness-based Relationship Enhancement (MBRE) in Couples", in R.A. Baer (Ed.), *Mindfulness-based Treatment Approaches: Clinician's Guide to Evidence Base and Applications* (pp. 309-331), Burlington, MA: Elsevier.

Chadwick, P.; Taylor, K.N. & Abba, N. (2005). "Mindfulness Groups for People with Psychosis", *Behavioural and Cognitive Psychotherapy*, 33: 351-359.

Chambers, R.; Lo, B.C.Y. & Allen, N.B. (2008). "The Impact of Intensive Mindfulness Training on Attentional Control, Cognitive Style, and Affect", *Cognitive Therapy and Research*, 32: 303-322. *doi:10.1007/s10608-007-9119-0*

Cherkin, D.C.; Sherman, K.J.; Balderson, B.H.; Cook, A.J.; Anderson, M.L.; Hawkes, R.J.; Hansesn, K.E. & Turner, J.A. (2016). "Effect of Mindfulness-based Stress Reduction *vs.* Cognitive Behavioural Therapy or Usual Care on Back Pain and Functional Limitations in Adults with Chronic Low Back Pain: A Randomized Clinical Trial", *Journal of the American Medical Association*, 315: 1240-1249. *doi:10.1001/jama.2016.2323*

Corcoran, K.M.; Farb, N.; Anderson, A. & Segal, Z.V. (2010). "Mindfulness and Emotion Regulation: Outcomes and Possible Mediating Mechanisms", in A.M. Kring & D.M. Sloan (Eds.), *Emotion Regulation and Psychopathology: A Transdiagnositc Approach to Etiology and Treatment* (pp. 339-355), New York: Guilford Press.

Cousins, L.S. (1996). "The Dating of the Historical Buddha: A Review Article", *Journal of the Royal Asiatic Society* (Third Series), 6(1): 57e63. *http://dx.doi.org/10.1017/S1356186300014760.*

Davidson, R. & Lutz, A. (2008). "Buddha's Brain: Neuroplasticity and Meditation in the Spotlight", *IEEE Signal Processing Magazine*, 25(1): 176-174.

Davidson, R.J.; Kabat-Zinn, J.; Schumacher, J.; Rosenkranz, M.; Muller, D.; Santorelli, S.F. & Sheridan, J.F. (2003). "Alterations in Brain and Immune Function Produced by Mindfulness Meditation", *Psychosomatic Medicine*, 66: 149-152. *doi:10.1097/01.psy.0000116716.19848.65*

Davis, D.M. & Hayes, J.A. (2011). "What Are the Benefits of Mindfulness? A Practice Review of Psychotherapy-Related Research", *Psychotherapy*, Vol. 48, No. 2: 198-208.

Davis, K.M.; Lau, M.A. & Cairns, D.R. (2009). "Development and Preliminary Validation of a Trait Version of the Toronto Mindfulness Scale", *Journal of Cognitive Psychotherapy: An International Qaurterly*, 23: 185-197.

Deikman, A.J. (1982). *The Observing Self*, Boston: Beacon Press.

Dekeyser, M.; Raes, F.; Leijssen, M.; Leyson, S. & Dewulf, D. (2008). "Mindfulness Skills and Interpersonal Behaviour", *Personality and Individual Differences*, 44: 1235-1245. *doi:10.1016/j.paid.2007.11.018*

Deyo, M.; Wilson, K.A.; Ong, J. & Koopman, C. (2009). "Mindfulness and Rumination: Does Mindfulness Training Lead to Reductions in the Ruminative Thinking Associate with Depression?", *Explore*, 5: 265-271.

Dunn, Cassandra; Hanieh, Emma; Roberts, Rachel & Rosalind Powrie (2012). "Mindful Pregnancy and Childbirth: Effects of a Mindfulness Based Intervention on Women's Psychological Distress and Well-being in the Perinatal Period", *Arch Womens Ment. Health*, 15: 139-143.

Evertsson, Marie & Nermo, Magnus (2004). "Dependence within Families and the Division of Labour: Comparing Sweden and the United States", *Journal of Marriage and Family*, Vol. 66: 1272-1286.

Falkenstrom, F. (2010). "Studying Mindfulness in Experienced Mediators: A Quasi Experimental Approach", *Personality and Individual Differences*, 48: 305-310.

Feldman, G.; Hayes, A.; Kumar, S.; Greeson, J. & Laurenceau, J. (2007). "Mindfulness and Emotion Regulation: The Development and Initial Validation of the Cognitive and Affective Mindfulness Scale-Revised (CAMS-R)", *Journal of Psychopathology and Behavioural Assessment*, 29: 177-190.

Feltman, R.; Robinson, M.D. & Ode, S. (2009). "Mindfulness as a Moderator of Neuroticism-outcome Relations: A Self-regulation Perspective", *J. Res. Pers.*, 43: 953-961.

Flaxman, P. & Bond, F. (2010). "Worksite Stress Management Training: Moderated Effects and Clinical Significance", *Journal of Occupational Health Psychology*, 15(4): 347-358.

Fredrickson, B.L.; Cohn, M.A.; Coffey, K.A.; Pek, J. & Finkel, S.M. (2008). "Open Hearts Build Lives: Positive Emotions, Induced through Loving-kindness Meditation, Build Consequential Personal Resources", *Journal of Personality and Social Psychology*, 95: 1045-1062.

Fresco, D.M.; Moore, M.T.; van Dulmen, M.H.M.; Segal, Z.V.; Ma, S.H. & Teasdale, J.D., *et al.* (2007). "Initial Psychometric Properties of the Experiences Questionnaire: Validation of a Self-report Measure of Decentering", *Behaviour Therapy*, 38(3): 234e246. *http://dx.doi.org/10.1016/j.beth.2006.08.003.*

Frewen, P.A.; Dozois, D.J.A.; Neufeld, R.W.J.; Lane, R.D.; Densmore, M. & Stevens, T.K. *et al.* (2010). "Individual Differences in Trait Mindfulness Predict Dorsomedial Prefrontal and Amygdala Response during Emotional Imagery: An FMRI Study", *Personality and Individual Differences*, 49: 479-484.

Grossman, P.; Niemann, L.; Schmidt, S. & Walach, H. (2004). "Mindfulness-based Stress Reduction and Health Benefits: A Meta-analysis", *Journal of Psychosomatic Research*, 57: 35-43. *doi:10.1016/S0022-3999(03)00573-7*

Gunaratana, H. (2002). *Mindfulness in Plain English*, Somerville, MA: Wisdom Publications.

Hamilton, R., *et al.* (2010). "Being of Two Minds: Switching Mindsets Exhausts Self-regulatory Resources", *Organizational Behaviour and Human Decision Processes.*

Hanh, T.N. (1976). *Miracle of Mindfulness*, Boston: Beacon.

Hölzel, B.; Lazar, S.; Gard, T.; Schuman-Olivier, Z. Vago & Ott, U. (2011b). "How does Mindfulness Meditation Work? Proposing Mechanisms of Action from a Conceptual and Neural Perspective", *Perspectives on Psychological Science*, 6: 537. *DOI: 10.1177/1745691611419671.*

Hölzel, B.K.; Carmody, J.; Vangel, M.; Congleton, C.; Yerramsetti, S.M.; Gard, T. & Lazar, S. (2011a). "Mindfulness Practice Leads to Increases in Regional Brain Gray Matter Density", *Psychiatry Research Neuoroimaging*, 191(1): 36. *DOI: 10.1016/j.pscychresns.2010.08.006*

Howell, A.J.; Digdon, N.L. & Buro, K. (2010). "Mindfulness Predicts Sleep-related Self-regulation and Well-being", *Personality and Individual Differences*, 48: 419-424.

Howell, A.J.; Digdon, N.L.; Buro, K. & Sheptycki, A.R. (2008). "Relations among Mindfulness, Well-being, and Sleep", *Personality and Individual Differences*, 45: 773-777.

Kabat-Zinn, J. (1982). "An Outpatient Programme in Behavioural Medicine for Chronic Pain Patients Based on the Practice of Mindfulness Meditation: Theoretical Considerations and Preliminary Results", *General Hospital Psychiatry*, 4: 33-47.

Kabat-Zinn, J. (1996). *Full Catastrophe Living*, London: Piakus Books.

Kabat-Zinn, J. (2003). "Mindfulness-based Interventions in Context: Past, Present, and Future", *Clinical Psychology: Science and Practice*, 10(2): 144-156. *http://dx.doi.org/10.1093/clipsy.bpg016.*

Keng, S.; Smoski, M. & Robins, C. (2011). "Effects of Mindfulness on Psychological Health: A Review of Empirical Studies", *Clinical Psychol-ogy Review*, 31(6): 1041-1056.

Keyes, C.L.M. (2005). "Mental Illness and/or Mental Health? Investigating the Axioms of the Complete State Model of Health", *Journal of Consulting and Clinical Psychology*, 73: 539-548.

Khan, Zaynah & Zadeh, Zainab F. (2014). "Mindful Eating and Its Relationship with Mental Well-Being", *Procedia — Social and Behavioural Sciences*, 159: 69-73.

Kristeller, J.L.; Baer, R.A. & Quillian-Wolever, R. (2006). "Mindfulness-based Approaches to Eating Disorders", in R. Baer (Ed.), *Mindfulness and Acceptance-based Interventions: Conceptualization, Application, and Empirical Support*, San Diego, CA: Elsevier.

Kuyken, W.; Weare, K.; Ukoumunne, O.; Lewis, R.; Motton, N.; Burnett, R.; Cullen C.; Hennelly, S. & Huppert, F. (2013). "Effectiveness of the Mindfulness in Schools Programme: A Non-randomized Controlled Feasibility Study", *British Journal of Psychiatry. http://bjp.rcpsych.org/content/203/2/126.full.pdf+html.* Accessed 10th September 2014.

Lau, M.A.; Bishop, S.R.; Segal, Z.V.; Buis, T.; Anderson, N.D. & Carlson, L., *et al.* (2006). "The Toronto Mindfulness Scale: Development and Validation", *Journal of Clinical Psychology*, 62: 1445-1467.

Lomas, T.; Ivtzan, I. & Fu, C. (2015). "A Systematic Review of the Neurophysiology of Mindfulness on EEG Oscillations", *Neuroscience & Biobehavioural Reviews*, 57: 401-410. *http://dx.doi.org/10.1016/j.neubiorev.2015.09.018.*

Lomas, T.; Medina, J.C.; Ivtzan, I.; Rupprecht, S. & Eiroa-Orosa, F.J. (2017). "The Impact of Mindfulness on the Well-being and Performance of Educators: A Systematic Review of the Empirical Literature", *Teaching and Teacher Education*, 61: 132-141.

Loucks, E.B.; Britton, W.B.; Howe, C.J.; Eaton, C.B. & Buka, S.L. (2015). "Positive Associations of Dispositional Mindfulness with Cardiovascular Health: The New England Family Study", *International Journal of Behavioural Medicine*, 22: 540-550. *doi:10.1007/s12529-014-9448-9*

Manas, I.M.; Justo, C.F. & Martinez, E.J. (2011). "Reducing Levels of Teacher Stress and the Days of Sick Leave in Secondary School Teachers through a Mindfulness Training Programmes", *Clinicia Y Salud*, 22(2): 121-137.

Marianetti, O. & Passmore, J. (2009). "Mind-fulness at Work: Paying Attention to Enhance Well-being and Performance", in A. Lindley (ed.), *Oxford Handbook of Positive Psychology and Work* (pp. 189-200), Oxford, UK: Oxford University Press.

Martin, J.R. (1997). "Mindfulness: A Proposed Common Factor", *Journal of Psychotherapy Integration*, 7: 291-312.

Mental Health Foundation (2010). *Mindfulness Report*, London: Mental Health Foundation.

Mental Health Foundation of New Zealand (2011). *An Overview of Mindfulness-based Interventions and their Evidence Base*, Mindfulness Training Ltd. *https://www.mentalhealth.org.nz/assets/ResourceFinder/mindfulness-based-interventions-and-their-evidence-base.pdf*

Monti, D.A.; Peterson, C.; Shakin Kunkel, E.J.; Hauck, W.W.; Pequignot, E.; Rhodes, L. & Brainar, G.C. (2006). "A Randomized, Controlled Trial of Mindfulness-based Art Therapy for Women with Cancer", *Psychooncology*, 15(5): 363-373.

Nolen-Hoeksema, S.; Wisco, B.E. & Lyubomirsky, S. (2008). "Rethinking Rumination", *Perspectives on Psychological Science*, 3: 400-424.

Ong, J.C.; Shapiro, S. & Manber, R. (2008). "Combining Mindfulness Meditation with Cognitive-behaviour Therapy for Insomnia: A Treatment-development Study", *Behaviour Therapy*, 39: 171-182.

Ophira, Eyal.; Nass, Clifford & Wagner, Anthony, D. (2009). "Cognitive Control in Media Multitaskers", *Proceedings of the National Academy of Sciences*, Vol. 106, No. 33.

Rogers, J.M.; Ferrari, M.; Mosely, K.; Lang, C.P. & Brennan, L. (2017). "Mindfulness-based Interventions for Adults Who are Overweight or Obese: A Meta-analysis of Physical and Psychological Health Outcomes", *Obesity Reviews*, 18: 51-67. *doi:10.1111/obr.12461*

Schutte, Nicola. S. & Malouff, John. M. (2011). "Emotional Intelligence Mediates the Relationship between Mindfulness and Subjective Well-being", *Personality and Individual Differences*, 50: 1116-1119

Segal, Z.V.; Williams, J.M.G. & Teasdale, J.D. (2002). *Mindfulness-Based Cognitive Therapy for Depression*, First edition, London: Guilford.

Segal, Z.V.; Williams, J.M.G. & Teasdale, J.D. (2012). *Mindfulness-Based Cognitive Therapy for Depression*, Second edition. London: Guilford.

Shapiro, S.L.; Schwartz, G.E. & Bonner, G. (1998). "Effects of Mindfulness-based Stress Reduction on Medical and Premedical Students", *J. Behav. Med.*, 21: 581-99.

Shapiro, S.L. & Schwartz, G.E.R. (1999). "The Role of Intention in Self-regulation: Toward Intentional Systemic Mindfulness", in M. Boekaerts; P.R. Pintrich & M. Zeidner (Eds.), *Handbook of Self-regulation* (pp. 253-273), New York: Academic Press.

Shapiro, S.L. & Schwartz, G.E.R. (2000). "Intentional Systemic Mindfulness: An Integrative Model for Self-regulation and Health", *Advances in Mind-Body Medicine*, 16: 128-135.

Shapiro, S.L.; Carlson, L.E.; Astin, J.A. & Freedman, B. (2006). "Mechanisms of Mindfulness", *Journal of Clinical Psychology*, 62(3): 373-386. *http://dx.doi.org/10.1002/jclp.20237.*

Shonin, Edo; Gordon, William. Van & Griffiths, Mark. D. (2013). "Mindfulness-based Interventions: Towards Mindful Clinical Integration", *Front Psychol*, 4: 194. *doi: 10.3389/fpsyg.2013.00194*

Siegel, D.J. (2007b). *The Mindful Brain: Reflection and Attunement in the Cultivation of Well-being*, New York: Norton.

Siegel, D.J. (2009). "Mindful Awareness, Mindsight, and Neural Integration", *The Humanistic Psychologist*, 37: 137-158.

Siegel, R.D. (2014). *The Science of Mindfulness: A Research-based Path to Well-being*, Virginia, USA: The Great Courses Publication.

Speca, M.; Carlson, L.E.; Goodey, E. & Angen, M.A. (2000). "Randomized, Wait-list Controlled Clinical Trial: The Effect of a Mindfulness Meditation-based Stress Reduction Programme on Mood and Symptoms of Stress in Cancer Outpatients", *Psychosom Med.*, 62: 613-22.

Teasdale, J.D.; Segal, Z.V.; Williams J.M.G.; Ridgeway, V.A.; Soulsby, J.M. & Lau, M.A. (2000). "Prevention of Relapse/Recurrence in Major Depression by Mindfulness-based Cognitive Therapy", *J. Consult. Clin. Psychol.*, 68: 615-23.

Thera, Nyanaponika (1972). *The Power of Mindfulness*, San Francisco, CA: Unity Press.

Thompson, B.L. & Waltz, J.A. (2008). "Mindfulness, Self-esteem, and Unconditional Self-acceptance", *Journal of Rational-Emotive and Cognitive-Behaviour Therapy*, 26(2): 119-126.

Tomfohr, L.M.; Pung, M.A.; Mills, P.J. & Edwards, K. (2015). "Trait Mindfulness is Associated with Blood Pressure and Interleukin-6: Exploring Interactions among Subscales of the Five Facet Mindfulness Questionnaire to Better Understand Relationships between Mindfulness and Health", *Journal of Behavioural Medicine*, 38: 28-38. *doi:10.1007/s10865-014-9575-4*

Valentine, E.R. & Sweet, P.L.G. (1999). "Meditation and Attention: A Comparison of the Effects of Concentrative and Mindfulness Meditation on Sustained Attention", *Mental Health Religion & Culture*, 2: 59-70. *doi:10.1080/13674679908406332*

Vieten, C. & Astin, J. (2008). "Effects of a Mindfulness-based Intervention during Pregnancy on Prenatal Stress and Mood: Results of a Pilot Study", *Arch. Womens Ment. Health*, 11: 67-74.

Virgili, M. (2013). "Mindfulness-based Interventions Reduce Psychological Distress in Working Adults: A Meta-analysis of Intervention Studies", *Mindfulness. DOI10.1007/s12671-013-0264-0.*

Wachs, K. & Cordova, J.V. (2007). "Mindful Relating: Exploring Mindfulness and Emotion Repertoires in Intimate Relationships", *Journal of Marital and Family Therapy*, 33: 464-481. *doi:10.1111/j.1752-0606.2007.00032.x*

Walsh, R. & Shapiro, S.L. (2006). "The Meeting of Meditative Disciplines and Western Psychology: A Mutually Enriching Dialogue", *American Psychologist*, 61(3): 227-239. *http://dx.doi.org/10.1037/0003-066X.61.3.227.*

Weare, K. (2014). *Evidence for Mindfulness: Impacts on the Well-being and Performance of School Staff*, Mindfulness in Schools Project, In association with University of Exeter.

Weinstein, N.; Brown, K.W. & Ryan, R.M. (2009). "A Multi-method Examination of the Effects of Mindfulness on Stress Attribution, Coping, and Emotional Well-being", *Journal of Research in Personality*, 43: 374-385.

Wenzel, Mario; Von Versen, Christina; Hirschmller, Sarah & Kubiak, Thomas (2015). "Curb Your Neuroticism — Mindfulness Mediates the Link between Neuroticism and Subjective Well-being", *Personality and Individual Differences*, 80: 68-75.

Winbush, N.Y.; Gross, C.R. & Kreitzer, M.J. (2007). "The Effects of Mindfulness based Stress Reduction on Sleep Disturbance: A Systematic Review", *Explore*, 3: 585-591.

Yook, K.; Lee, S.H.; Ryu, M.; Kim, K.H.; Choi, T.K. & Suh, S.Y. *et al.* (2008). "Usefulness of Mindfulness-based Cognitive Therapy for Treating Insomnia in Patients with Anxiety Disorders: A Pilot Study", *Journal of Nervous and Mental Disease*, 196: 501-503.

Young, S. (1997). *The Science of Enlightenment*, Boulder, CO: Sounds True.

Zautra, A.J.; Davis, M.C.; Reich, J.W.; Nicassario, P.; Tennen, H. & Finan, P. (2008). "Comparison of Cognitive Behavioural and Mindfulness Meditation Interventions on Adaptation to Rheumatoid Arthritis for Patients with and without History of Recurrent Depression", *Journal of Consulting and Clinical Psychology*, 76: 408-421.

20

Enhancing Subjective Well-being in Women through Workplace Belongingness

Shagufta Afroz and *P.S.N. Tiwari*

Introduction

Women workers in India are faced with lot more challenges than their counterparts in the other countries. Besides of so many efforts from past years, female section of society is deprived in comparison to male sections. They are not given the first priority in social and economic decisions in her own family. According to United Nations Development Programmes (UNDP) report, women are involved in doing 76 per cent work of world, still they are socially and economically deprived. They receive only 10 pèr cent of the universal income and have 1 per cent part in global asset. This discrimination also persists in their workplace in unorganized sectors. In informal sections women workers do not get same wages for same nature of work for same hours done by men. They are exploited at workplace. There are a number of problems faced by women in their working career.

Where established social norms are challenged by women going out to work they may face gossip and stigma within their own communities or worse — verbal, sexual and physical abuse. And men can also face stigma as a result of women going out to work — where it challenges their traditional roles as bread-winners for example. Where women are able to take on paid work they are still expected to undertake the bulk of unpaid work in the home caring for the young, old and the sick. This role is vital but is undervalued and means that women are more likely to be time poor and overburdened which can affect their overall health and well-being. It also means that they are less likely to achieve better paid, secure jobs.

A gender bias creates an obstacle at the recruitment stage itself. If a male and female are competing for a post and have the same qualifications, many-a-times it is seen that the job goes to the male the reason being the age old thinking and in-built conviction that women are capable of less work than men or are less efficient than men. This skewed approach governs the injustice of unequal salaries and wages for the same job.

Sexual harassment, molestation, eve teasing etc. are some very common problems women face at their workplace. What is the reason for this? Just because they are 'women' or just because they are 'working' and 'independent' and are challenging men in every field? Harassment in the workplace emerges as one of the five top critical issues. Nearly one-third of women interviewed admit to having experienced harassment, although more than 60 per cent do not report it. Indian women are the most likely to speak up (53%), a clear change of attitude since the fatal attack of a female student on a bus in Delhi in 2012.

Ego of the male counterpart is also a problem in the advancement of women. Men do support women to go out and work. But once she starts doing extremely well or earns a larger pay package than her male counterpart, the 'ego' comes in the way in some cases. These men find it difficult to accept the progress and achievement of women whether she is his wife or colleague.

The review of literature shows that more focus is on married working women than on unmarried working women (Karl, 2009). Murthy, G.K. (2013) advocates for more facilities to women in the workplace. Suggesting that ". . . it is an important part of development strategy as well as an act of social justice". Dashora (2013) is of the opinion that "participation of women in workplace is essential for the development and population planning".

Wentling (2003) showed that the twin role of the women causes tension and conflict due to her social structure which is still more dominant. In her study on working women on Delhi, she has shown that "traditional authoritarian set-up for Hindu social structure continue to be the same basically and hence women face problem of role conflict change in attitude of men and women according to the situation can help to overcome their problem". In short the major issues and problems that women face in their workplace includes unequal pay, security, sexual harassment, lack of proper family support, deficient maternity leave etc. these problems directly and indirectly leads to decrease women well-being and enhances the level of stress, depression and lack of self-confidence. Because of the above said problem the women feel less belong to their workplace. When that sense of belonging is lacking in a workplace, employees feel threatened in a way that is akin to physical pain. The result? "Anxiety, avoidance of tasks and uncooperative or even undermining behaviour". Having a sense of belonging is a common experience. Belonging means acceptance as a member or part. Feeling that you belong is most important in seeing value in life and in coping with intensely painful emotions. When an employee has a sense of belonging in the workplace, it connotes ownership. You belong therefore you own. Not property but something more meaningful. You own responsibility. You have a sense of autonomy that enables you to act for the good of the organization. Not because you have to, but because you want to but the need to belong is often overlooked in the workplace.

The stress that comes from feelings of social isolation can lead to detrimental physical and mental effects, including a reduction in higher level cognitive functioning and problem solving abilities. It can also give rise to feelings of apathy, anxiety, and even antagonism in some cases.

Having a sense of belonging is particularly important for female and minority employees. A recent Stanford study looked at the effect of social marginalization on women entering predominantly male fields, such as STEM. It found that negative performance issues for these individuals could often be attributed to a lack of inclusion and feelings of isolation from not being part of the larger demographic group.

It is well known in the literature that a strong sense of belongingness improves quality of life overall by enhancing workplace performance, happiness and motivation to achieve other goals. While many motivation theorists recognize that belongingness is an important psychological drive it is also often inappropriately considered as a minor background process (DeWall, Baumeister & Vohs, 2008). This is indeed the case with respect to the hierarchy of needs and social identity theories which regard these processes as unconscious drives to obtain esteem needs. DeWall *et al.*, (2008) found that there were significant links between self-regulation and social acceptance; specifically that rejection or lack of social acceptance inhibited self-regulatory performance. Self-regulation is the internal cognitive process that allows us to maximize effort, maintain persistence, balance accuracy and speed as well as assess potential mistakes during task performance (DeWall *et al.*, 2008). Self-regulation is a crucial cognition for work performance as well as daily function. Impairment of this cognition is detrimental to success in occupational life. Another study conducted by Cockshaw and Shochet (2010) also found substantial associations between depression and lack of belongingness in the workplace; specifically that lack of social acceptance in the workplace increases depressive symptoms. This finding is consistent with belongingness theory which would suggest that this is an emotional pain consequence resulting from lack of belonging. The findings of the literature suggest that social acceptance and belongingness are fundamentally important for having a successful work life. There are limitations to these studies, however, Cockshaw and Shochet (2010) suggest that their study had not considered the opposite direction of the casual influences between depression and belongingness; they had not considered that existing depression could have influenced perceptions of social acceptance. Furthermore, DeWall, Baumeister and Vohs (2008) suggested that their findings contradict some existing theories of belongingness motivation which would otherwise suggest that lack of belongingness would in fact have a positive effect of self-regulatory performance as an attempt to seek social acceptance. Replication of these studies with compromises to these limitations is required; however, the findings are a significant contribution to understanding the importance of belongingness and how it affects work performance. The review of literature shows that there are many studies on the relationships of well-being and belongingness as Walton (2007) concludes that a feeling of belonging to a country, region, and local community can influence people's sense of identity and the extent to which they participate in society. Belongingness can provide people with considerable social support, which directly promotes happiness and health. Indeed, hundreds of studies have documented that social support has beneficial effects on the cardiovascular system, the endocrine system, the immune system, and even on gene expression (Cacioppo & Patrick, 2008; Uchino *et al.*, 1996). Being social excluded seems to have a negative impact on all people, even when people are rejected by those who they vilify (Williams, 2007).

Against the above backdraft, the present chapter aims to point out the significant role of workplace belongingness on the subjective well-being of working women because the literature lacks the studies on working women in Indian context having emphasis on workplace belongingness to enhance the sense of belonging to workplaces to reduce the harmful impacts of the problems a women faces in her working life which leads them to feel lower well-being. Subjective well-being (SWB) is defined as "a person's cognitive and affective evaluations of his or her life" (Diener, Lucas & Oshi, 2004). Subjective well-being (SWB) refers to how people experience the quality of their lives and includes both emotional reactions and cognitive judgements. Due to the dual role played by the working women, they are twice as likely as men to experience a major depressive episode. Shyam and Yadav (2004) concluded that males score higher on general well-being than females.

Following are the specific objectives of this chapter:

- To explore the impact of workplace belongingness (low and high) on Subjective well-being and its dimensions as well.
- To explore the correlation between workplace belongingness and subjective well-being.

Method and Procedure

Research Design

The present research work is primarily exploratory correlational in nature. By using bivariate correlation analysis, the association between two variables has been checked. The obtain data was subjected to One way ANOVA to check the significance of Workplace belongingness (high and low) on subjective well-being and its dimensions.

Sample

This field study was conducted on relatively a heterogeneous sample of 199 working women belonging to rural and urban settings of Eastern Uttar Pradesh. The age range of the subjects was 27 to 45 years. The participants varied in terms of Education Level, Socio-economic Status and Occupation.

Tools

- *Workplace Belongingness Motive Scale* — Belongingness motive scale developed by Afroz, S. and Tiwari P.S.N. (2017). The scale consist 27 items. The scoring pattern is Likert's five points ranging from 5-Highly agree to 1-Highly disagree. The Cronbach's alpha of the scales was found to be 0.85. Gutman Split-Half Coefficient was found to be 0.87. The higher score on this scale denotes to the higher level of belongingness to workplace whether the lower scores indicate the lower level of belongingness at workplace.

- *Subjective Well-being Scale*—It was developed by Roop Nagpal (1985). This scale consists of 82 items, 9 items out of 82 are choices to respond. The manner of scoring is 4 to 1. This measurement assess eight psychological social components of subjective well-being: (1) Positive affect, (2) Negative affect, (3) Mental Mastery over self and Environment, (4) Rootedness and belongingness, (5) Structural and Cohesive aspect of family, (6) Density and social network, (7) Security in health and socio-economic status, (8) Expectation achievement harmony.

Procedure

The above mentioned questionnaires were compiled in order as follows: 27 items workplace Belongingness Motive scale, 82 items Subjective well-being scale. The "personal data Sheet and Informed Consent Form" consisted of the demographic information about the participants followed by an informed consent. Participants were explained the purpose of the study, eligibility criteria, the voluntary nature of participation and the procedure participants would be involved in. After this information, the potential participants were asked to indicate whether they agree to participate in the study, individuals who did not want to participate in the study were thanked for their time.

The psychometric tests were administered to participants individually. Instructions related to each scale were clearly explained to each participant and their queries (if any) were attended appropriately. After completion of the test, scoring was done using the manual of tests. Extreme group strategy was used to identify the high and low workplace belongingness group. The scores above Q3 were considered as high and below Q1 as low workplace belongingness group. The obtained scores were then subjected to One way ANOVA and Correlation analysis for results.

Results

To obtain the results, the data was subjected to One-way ANOVA with low and high level of workplace belongingness as independent variable and subjective well-being with its dimension as dependent variables. In addition to the result section, a bivariate correlation was performed between workplace belongingness and different dimensions of subjective well-being. The results are presented through Table 20.1.

TABLE 20.1: Means and SDs of Subjective Well-being with Its Dimension as a Function of High and Low Workplace Belongingness

Variables	*Level of Workplace Belongingness*	*M*	*SD*	*N*
Subjective well-being overall	High	181.04	9.68	107
	Low	144.75	5.072	92
Positive affect	High	36.99	4.97	107
	Low	29.15	4.75	92
Negative affect	High	33.12	6.33	107
	Low	36.75	7.91	92
Mastery over self and environment	High	22.96	4.37	107
	Low	21.77	4.85	92
Rootedness and belongingness	High	21.95	3.24	107
	Low	15.18	3.51	92
Structural and cohesive aspect of family	High	13.51	1.99	107
	Low	13.33	2.31	92
Density and social network	High	15.96	2.10	107
	Low	14.23	2.58	92
Security in health and socio-economic status	High	10.51	2.22	107
	Low	9.03	3.05	92
Expectation achievement harmony	High	14.77	2.22	107
	Low	13.21	2.79	92

It is evinced by Table 20.1, that women having higher sense of belonging to their workplaces has scored higher (M = 181.04) on the level of subjective well-being overall in comparison to the women having lower (M = 144.75) sense of belonging to their workplaces. Furthermore, in all the dimension of Subjective well-being, the women with higher sense of belongingness exceed the women having lower sense of belongingness except the Negative affect in which the result is opposite to that of the other dimensions.

TABLE 20.2: Summary of One Way ANOVA for Subjective Well-being and Its Dimensions as a Function of Low and High Workplace Belongingness

Source of Variance		*SS*	*df*	*MS*	*F*
(1)	(2)	(3)	(4)	(5)	(6)
Subjective well-being overall	Between groups	70354.50	1	70354.50	
	Within groups	12281.10	197	62.34	28.55
Positive affect	Between groups	1877.99	1	1877.99	
	Within groups	7670.86	197	23.71	79.22
Negative affect	Between groups	278.20	1	278.20	
	Within groups	9946.67	197	50.49	5.51

(Contd.)

TABLE 20.2 (*Contd.*)

(1)	(2)	(3)	(4)	(5)	(6)
Mastery over self and environment	Between groups Within groups	32.39 4662.06	1 197	32.39 21.13	1.533
Rootedness and belongingness	Between groups Within groups	1353.86 2234.63	1 197	1353.86 11.34	19.35
Structural and cohesive aspect of family	Between Groups Within Groups	1.67 910.54	1 197	1.67 4.62	0.361
Density and social network	Between groups Within groups	3.49 1074.06	1 197	3.49 5.45	0.640
Security in health and socio-economic status	Between groups Within groups	13.30 1369.63	1 197	13.30 6.95	1.914
Expectation achievement harmony	Between groups Within groups	13.30 1230.24	1 197	9.58 6.25	1.535

Note: $P < 0.01$

To ascertain the impact of workplace belongingness on subjective well-being and its various dimensions, one way ANOVA was performed and the summary is presented in Table 20.2, which evinced that High and Low workplace Belongingness groups significantly differed on level of positive affect [F (1,197) = 79.22, $p < 0.01$], negative affect [F (1,197) = 5.51, $p < 0.01$], Rootedness and belongingness [F (1,197) = 119.35, $p < 0.01$] and overall Subjective Well-being [F (1.197) = 128.55, $p < 0.01$].

TABLE 20.3: Inter-correlation between Workplace Belongingness and Subjective Well-being with Its Dimension

Variables	*Workplace Belongingness*
Subjective well-being overall	0.548
Positive affect	0.317
Negative affect	– 0.095
Mastery over self and environment	0.146
Root and belong	0.434
Socio-economic status of family	0.005
Density and social network	0.088
Security in health and socio-economic status	0.201
Expectation achievement harmony	0.083

The correlation (Table 20.3) shows that workplace belongingness positively correlated with subjective well-being overall, Positive affect, Mastery over self and environment, Rootedness and belongingness and Security in Health and Socio-economic Status.

Discussion

The chapter aimed to point-out the role of workplace belongingness in the well-being of working so that the so many problems face during their job which directly and indirectly harms the well-being of women can be reduced with the help of enhancing the sense of belongingness to their workplaces. The result showed that the two groups — High and low workplace belongingness, significantly differed on the level of subjective well-being. The high belongingness group showed having more subjective well-being in comparison to low belongingness group. On the dimension of Positive affect, rootedness and belongingness, the high belongingness group was higher than that of low belongingness group. Furthermore, the Negative affects were found more in the low belongingness group and less in high belongingness group. This result is incongruent with the result of correlation analysis which also revealed that higher sense of belonging to workplace leads to having higher sense of well-being. In a study Afroz S. and Tiwari, P.S.N. (2017) found workplace belongingness as one of the strong predictors of well-being and Quality of life. A sense of belongingness positively correlates with high level of self-esteem also. Of course, when a person notices that he is being liked and cared by the group which he values; helps his self-esteem enhancement. His/her level of confidence increases because of self-exposure and commitments by group members to him. This perceived sense of security helps a lot to increase self-esteem and confidence. People with greater perceived social support enjoy greater self-esteem. The need to belong has its effects in the workplace. They seek the approval of their leaders, bosses, and other employees in order to be accepted. Researchers found that belongingness increased cooperative behaviour among employees. When the leaders influence followers by bringing awareness to the collective unit and strengthening the feeling of belonging and that enhances employees' compliance. Organizational citizenship behaviours are employee activities that benefit the collective group without the individual gaining any direct benefit. Helping is a huge component of organizational citizenship behaviours because helping involves voluntarily assisting others with problems that are work-related and preventing other issues from arising. Task performance is enhanced and supported when the acts of helping in a work environment are established and evident. Ronald J., Burke; Mustafa Koyuncu and Lisa Fiksenbaum (2010) examine the relationship of the perceived presence of organizational practices designed to support women, career advancement and their work attitude and satisfaction and their psychological well-being. Five organizational experiences were considered — Negative attitude towards women, equal treatment, support, career barriers and male standards. Women reporting more supportive organizational experience and practices were more engaged in their work; more job and career satisfied and indicated greater levels of psychological well-being.

A sense of belongingness increases a person's willingness to assist others in the group by the group rules. Belongingness and group membership encourages social groups with motivation to comply, cooperate, and help. Cohesive work groups show more consideration, report positive relationships within the group and elicits more organizational citizenship behaviours. Also, an already cohesive and collective group will make people more inclined to comply with the rules of the workplace. Some people help each other in return for a future expected favour; however, most workings help because it is the "right" thing to do or because they like their leaders so much and wish to express this likeness. People are more receptive to a leader who provides a clear sense of direction and inspiration with the promise of a better future. Workers who feel more isolated in the workplace feel the need to belong even more than those who are not isolated because they are missing that collective feeling of unity. A workplace functions better as a collective whole. As the result showed and well documented in the literature that a strong sense of belongingness to workplace also improves to QOL and SWB of employees' indirectly because directly it provides the employees with better job performance, a chance to know what exactly their goals are, better communication to their leaders or managements. With the recognition of the importance of social needs such as belonging, you can create a positive culture that avoids triggering the threat response and encourages the reward response employees that find their environment supporting social needs such as belonging have significantly improved enjoyment and performance. When the brain is the reward state, employees perceive more options to solve problems, are more insightful, collaborate better and have higher performance overall. When employees feel a sense of belonging and identification with the organization, they are naturally motivated to help it succeed. Here are some suggestions to improve the sense of belonging at workplaces:

- One of the major problems is sexual harassment of women at workplaces due to which women feel unsafe and less belong to their workplaces. This must be stopped anyhow. There can be formation of complaint committee which will keep the privacy of the employee complaining and investigate the competent independently. This step would make the women felled secure and fit to their workplaces.

- The offices should provide high quality and affordable childcare and elder care for their women employees. Though women have excelled in every walk of life, it is also true that the job of care taking of child and other elder members of family is granted as their responsibility. They have to deal with this dual responsibility. This step of providing childcare and elder care will add more freedom and sense of belongingness to their workplaces.
- They should make be Paid maternity and paternity leave; though this facility is already in the government sectors, it should be facilitating in private sectors also.
- There should be facility of safe picking-up and dropping up for women employees in offices. Especially in those offices where women have to work till evening and night. This will make a sense of security in women employees and enrich them with the felling that their organization cares for them.
- The women should have a right to request part time work but only in secure conditions.
- Comprehensive job protection for pregnant workers.
- Equal wages must be given to women for the same work, a man does.
- Formalize flexibility and work life balance policies.
- Encourage mentorship and sponsorship of women.
- Education campaign for women employees for their rights.

REFERENCES

Afroz, S. & Tiwari P.S.N. (2017). "Development of a Multidimensional Scale of Belongingness Motive", *Scholars Journal of Arts, Humanities and Social Sciences*, 5(8B): 878-883. *DOI: 10.21276/sjahss.*

Afroz, S. & Tiwari P.S.N. (2017). *Motive to Belong and Is Behavioural Consequences*, Thesis. D.D.U. Gorakhpur University, Gorakhpur, pp. 130-131.

Cockshaw, W. and Shochet, I. (2010). "The Link between Belongingness and Depressive Symptoms: An Exploration in the Workplace Interpersonal Context", *Australian Psychologist*, 45(4): 283-289.

Dashora (2013). "Problems Faced by Working Women in India", *International Journal of Advanced Research in Management and Social Sciences*, 2(8): 82-94.

DeWall, C.N.; Baumeister, R.F. & Vohs, K.D. (2008). "Stated with Belongingness? Effects of Acceptance, Rejection, and Task Framing on Self-Regulatory Performance", *Journal of Personality and Social Psychology*, 95(6): 1367-1382. *Doi: 10.1037/a0012632.*

Diener, E.D. & Oishi, S. (2004). "Are Scandinavians Happier than Asians? Issues in Comparing Nations on Subjective Well-being", in: Frank Columbus (ed.), *Asian Economic and Political Issues*, Vol. 10. Hauppauge, New York: Nova Science, pp. 1-25.

Karl, M. (2009). "Inseparable: The Crucial Role of Women in Food Security Revisited", *Women in Action*, No. 1: 8-19.

Murthy, G.K. (2013). "Women and Corporate Leadership in Indian Perspectives", *IRACST. International Journal of Research in Management & Technology*, 2(4): 377-382.

Ronald J.; Burke, Mustafa Koyuncu & Lisa Fiksenbaum (2010). "Organizational Practices Supporting Women's Career Advancement and their Satisfaction with Life and Well-being in Turkey", *Women in Management Review*, 21(8): 610-624.

Shyam, R. & Yadav, S. (2004). *General Well-being of Relocated and Home Based Elderly: Need for Developing Indigenous Model for Institutional Care*, National Seminar, D.E.I. Deemed University, Agra.

Walton, G.M. & Cohen, G.L. (2007). "A Question of Belonging: Race, Social Fit, and Achievement", *Journal of Personality and Social Psychology*, 92(1): 82-91.

Wentling, R.M. (2003). "The Career Development and Aspiration of Women in Middle Management Revisited", *Women in Management Review*, 18(6): 311-324.

21

A Study of Conscientiousness and Subjective Well-being of Working Women

Harendra Sharma

Introduction

Conscientiousness

Most individuals learn how to manage their desires, and the inability to resist impulses and temptations during the course of development. The basis of conscientiousness is self-control, but there are some individual difference in the self-control processes of planning, organizing and carrying out tasks. Those people who have a high level of conscientiousness, they are purposeful, strong-willed, and determined sometimes few people become great musicians or athletes without having a reasonably high level of conscientiousness. Conscientiousness is an aspect of what was once called character, high conscientiousness scorers are scrupulous, punctual and reliable. Low scorers are not necessarily lacking in moral principles, but they are less exacting in applying them, just as they are more lackadaisical in working toward their goals. There is some evidence that they are more hedonistic and interested in sex (McCare & Costa, 1986).

They are some differences between a conscientious male and a conscientious female. A conscientious male is reasonably efficient and generally sensible and rational in making decisions but a conscientious female is perceived as being reasonably efficient and generally sensible and rational in making decisions. A conscientious male is moderately neat, punctual and well organized and reasonably dependable and reliable in meeting his obligations. He has a moderately high need for Achievement, but the can also set work aside for recreation. He is average in self-discipline. He is reasonably cautious and generally thinks things through before acting. A conscientious female is described as moderately neat, punctual and well organized. There are some similarities between a highly conscientious male and a highly conscientious female. A male and a female who have a high level of conscientiousness adhere strictly to their ethical principles. They have high aspiration level and strive for excellence in whatever they do. They are determined, persistent, and able to force themselves to do what is necessary.

But there is a difference between a highly conscientious male and female. A female is reasonably cautious and generally thinks things through before acting, deliberates and think things carefully before acting.

Subjective Well-being

All people want good life. If asked about the features of good life, "Happiness" is one common preferred thing in every life. People have desired the criteria of a good life. Such as loving others, pleasures or self-insight. Another idea about a good life is that people themselves. Every person has a subjective definition of his/her life. And this subjective definition is a way determines that his/her life is worthwhile. Every person himself determines a standard of what is good or happy life. This very approach of subjective definition of good life is called "Subjective Well-Being" (SWB). SWB includes both cognitive and affective evaluations of their lives by people. The experience of few unpleasant and may pleasant emotions will lead to plenty of SWB. Moreover, when people get interesting activities to engage with their lives. SWB should not be confused with a valuable life, however, because their are many other features which determine objectively good life, but SWB refers to people's own evaluation of their lives.

Every person himself determines a standard of what is good or happy life. This every approach of subjective definition of good life is called "Subjective Well-being (SWB)". Subjective well-being is multidimensional and many different factors interact to determine the well-being of individuals. These factors include, personal and environmental stressors and resources, coping styles as well as demographic variables such as race, gender and socio-economic class. Gasper (2002) points out, the term well-being is a concept or idea referring to whatever is assessed in an evaluation of a person's life situation or being. Gender differences in the normal range of SWB show a somewhat different picture. In most studies, women consistently report more negative emotions than men (Costa *et al.*, 2001; Hansson *et al.*, 2005). William, Shonin, Sumich, Sundin and Griffiths (2013) show that the participants who received Meditation Awareness Training (MAT) showed significant improvements in psychological well-being and dispositional mindfulness over controls. MAT may increase emotion regulation ability in higher education students with issues of stress, anxiety, and low mood. Individuals receiving training in mindfulness meditation may benefit by engendering a broader, more ethically informed, and compassionate intention for their mindfulness practice. The flinging indicated that awareness is positively correlated with well-being.

P. Dadlani, Markopoulos, and Aarts (2009) in their study showed the need to transcend momentary awareness of commotion, or mundane activities and to focus long-term trends in their elderly parents' well-being. In a study of one hundred HIV positive clients, done by Carson and Green (1992) spiritual well-being (SWB) and hardiness in HIV positive patients were assessed. Kobasa (1979) reports that persons who are either HIV positive or who have diagnosis of ARC (AIDS related complex, which is no longer used) or AIDS have a positive relationship between SWB and hardiness, and persons who are either HIV positive or who have a diagnosis of ARC or AIDS have a positive relationship between existential well-being (EWB) and hardiness. Skomorovsky and Sudom (2011) have found that hardiness is associated with greater psychological well-being and lower levels of stress.

Bruck and Ceci (1999) in their study found that encoding or retrieval high-anxious participants would be predicted to perform more poorly than low anxious participants in an eyewitness paradigm involving memory recall. Victims who have high misinformation suggestibility have a lot of problems (anxiety, low performance, sadness, more mental problems, fear, helpless, unhappiness, discrimination, negative emotion and negative changing lifestyle) more than who have low misinformation suggestibility. A study by Hoosen and Jacqui (2011) focuses on HIV/ AIDS, global trends, global funds and delivery bottlenecks. Globalization affects all facets of human life, including health and well-being. The HIV/AIDS epidemic has highlighted the global nature of human health and welfare and globalization has given rise to a trend towards finding common solutions to global health challenges.

World over there is a concern for studying positive aspects of behaviour. The negative behavioural aspects have been over-emphasized. People are directed towards positive aspects of behaviour. An increasing

and such theories would be theories of subjective well-being and quality of life. Further studies reveal that people adapt to most of the conditions very quickly. For example such, Dinere and Fujita (1996), found that in less than three months the effects of many major life events (e.g. being forced or promoted) lost their impact on SWB. A social manifestation of adaptations contained in Mayer's (2000) discussion of income and SWB over the past five decades. People's desire increase as their income rise and they therefore, adapt to higher levels of income, with the net increase in SWB.

Research in the area of subjective well-being have identified two conceptual facts of well-being. The emotional aspect consisting of independent positive affective and negative affective components (Diener & Encous, 1984) and cognitive judgement aspect of life satisfaction (Andrews & Withey, 1976).

Aim of the Study

The current exploratory study was conducted with two main aims:

1. To investigate the subjective well-being in the two groups Doctors and Engineers.
2. To make an effort to find out that how conscientiousness correlations with subjective well-being.

Hypotheses

1. Well-being would be not significant in the two groups Doctors and Engineers.
2. There will be close relationship between conscientiousness and well-being.

Method

Participants

There were 40 participants in the present study. They were divided into two groups Doctors and Engineers. The age group was between 35 to 45 years.

Measures

Two measures were taken in the present study.

I. Conscientiousness Scale

The scale was made by Costa and McCrae, Digman and Takemoto-Chock (1981). Costa and McCrae developed a scale in which they identified 5 main traits of personality. Conscientiousness is one of them. There were 48 items of conscientiousness was a five point scale that included strongly Disagree, Natural, Agree, Strongly Agree. Answers were awarded scores of as 0 to 4. Positive items were scored 4 while negative items were scored 0.

In the conscientiousness scale there were 6 dimensions and each dimension had 8 items. The items were based on these six dimensions. The six dimensions were as follows —

1. *Competence:* I am known for my prudence and common sense.
2. *Order:* I would rather keep my options open than plan everything in advance.
3. *Dutifulness:* I try to perform all the tasks assigned to me conscientiously.
4. *Achievement:* I am easy going and lackadaisical.
5. *Self-Discipline:* I am pretty good about pacing myself so as to get things done on time.
6. *Deliberation:* Over the years I have done some pretty stupid things.

II. Subjective Well-being Questionnaire

The scale contained 82 items. It was a short form of the questionnaire made by **Dr. Rup Nagpal and Dr. Helmul Sell (1985)**. It included 130 items. The reduced form of the questionnaire was suggested by **Bacha Inang (2001)**. The scale includes eight areas which were perceived as being related or parts of well-being.

1. *Subjective Well-being — Positive Affect:* It includes items on specific life concerns such as health, education, work, standard of living, family and friends as well as some items reflecting the perception of well-being in an overall perspective.
2. *Subjective Well-being — Negative Affect:* Most the items here were inverse of the questions relating to positive affect. These intended to elicit the general unhappiness and higher worries or regrets about particulate life concerns.
3. *Mental Mastery over Self and Environment:* The exercise of mental mastery may also be an important area.

4. *Rootedness and Belongingness:* It includes, the perception of sharing value, beliefs and qualities of inner life which form a special dimension of well-being.
5. *Structural and Cohesive Aspects of the Family:* It is anticipated that structural aspects of family life and democratic functioning in the family may be related to each other and may have substantial impact on well-being.
6. *Density of Social Network:* Such items tends to cover this area were meant to elicit information on perceived being from the social networks other than the family group.
7. *Security in Health and Socio-economic Crisis:* Such items were meant to cover the respondents feeling of security in the cases of various crisis situations.
8. *Expectation Achievement Harmony:* Such items were meant to explore the area of well-being thoughts of as particularly important. The extent to which long term expectations in life had been met by actual achievement.

Procedure

All participants of the present study were contacted individually. Participants were asked to respond on a five-point scale questionnaire. There were two groups of participants — 20 Doctors and 20 Engineers. After making the formal rapport with them, they were introduced about the scale and they were given the following instructions:

1. *Instructions:* This questionnaire contains 48 statements. Please read each item carefully and circle the one answer that best corresponds to your agreement or disagreement. Circle "SD" if the statement in definitely false or if you strongly disagree.

   SD D N A SA

   There are no right or wrong answers. Describe yourself honestly and state your opinions as accurately as possible".
2. *For the second scale (SWB) the following instructions were given:* "People are different. They live in a variety of situations and they do not feel the same way about life and the world around them. From a practical viewpoint, it is important to know how different persons fell with regard to their day to day concerns such as their health, family, work etc. Such knowledge is necessary if an improvement in the quality of life of people is to be brought about.

This is a questionnaire on how you feel about some aspects of your life and about your life as a whole. Each question may be answered by any one of the given categories by putting a circle (O) around the number which seems to represent your feelings best. For example, in the first question if you feel you general health is very good and you feel physically fit, please put a circle around the response 'very good' (1). At times you may find that your feelings are not represented perfectly by any one of the given response categories. In such cases, just choose the one closest to what you think.

You may find that some questions appear repetitive. Nonetheless, please answer them all. You do not need to have your answers agree with each other.

This questionnaire may appear rather long to you. But if you work as fast as you comfortably can, you will find that it does not really take very long to fill in.

All information given by you will be treated as confidential and will be used only for research purposes".

Subjects were contacted and requested to complete a set of questionnaire. Instructions were imprinted on it. Afterwards filled questionnaires were collected. Subjects were thanked for their support. After collecting all of the data the results were analysed.

Results

The scores of all three variables measured are given in the Table 21.1. Tables are made on the basis of score of each variable, which shows the dimensions scores along with their suitable. The results of the statistical are also shown in tables.

TABLE 21.1: Scores obtained by Each Group A (Doctor), B (Engineer) on Conscientiousness

Sl.No.	*Dimensions of Conscientiousness*	*Group A*		*Group B*	
		Scores	*Mean*	*Scores*	*Mean*
1.	Competence	463	23.15	434	21.70
2.	Order	397	19.85	410	20.50
3.	Dutifulness	527	26.35	488	24.40
4.	Achievement striving	447	22.35	408	20.40
5.	Self-discipline	404	20.20	394	19.20
6.	Deliberation	440	22.00	456	22.80
Overall Conscientiousness (Grand Total)		**2678**	**133.90**	**2590**	**129.50**

Table 21.1 shows the scores and mean values of conscientiousness in all two groups. The first thing which is visible in this table is that the scores of the Doctors (Group A) (2678) is high. With the mean value (133.9) while the mean score of Engineers (Group B) is 129.5. The scores of two groups are slightly different from each other. The dimension-wise scores of all has shown some variations. In the first dimension Doctors have got the high mean score 23.15 than that of group B that is 21.70. While on the second dimension of order the mean score of Engineers is high (20.50) in comparison with the score of Doctors (19.85). On the third dimension of dutifulness Doctors have got higher mean score 26.35 while group B is on 24.40. On the fourth dimension slightly high score (22.35) while group B have obtained (20.40). On the fifth dimension self-discipline the score obtained by Doctors (20.20) is slightly different from the scores obtained by Engineers (19.70). And lastly on the sixth dimension deliberation the mean value of Doctors is slightly low than that of mean value obtained by Engineers. The results are shown in Table 21.2.

Table 21.2 shows that correlation between conscientiousness and SWB in the Doctors is high. It shows that Doctors are more conscientious and their SWB high. It also shows that there is no correlation between conscientiousness and SWB in Engineers.

TABLE 21.2: Coefficients of Correlations between Conscientiousness and SWB in Doctors and Engineers

	Conscientiousness		*SWB*		*Correlation*	*Level of Significance*	*df*
Doctor	Total Mean	2682 134.1	Total Mean	3186 159.3	743	0.01 0.549 High correlation	38
Engineers	Total Mean	2606 130.3	Total Mean	3202 160.1	0.096	Not significant	38

The difference between many sub-dimensions are also clearly visible. These dimensions are first, third, fourth. To see the significance between both groups on these sub-dimensions *t* value was calculated. *t* value of the first sub-dimension (competence) is 1.21 which is significant at 0.10 level.

The value of the third dimension (Dutifulness) is 1.55 which is significant at 0.10 level and the *t* value of the fourth dimension (Achievement Striving) is 1.80 which is significant at 0.05 level.

TABLE 21.3: *t*-test between both Groups on Sub-dimensions Conscientiousness

Group	*Dimension*	*Total*	*Mean*	*t-value Level*	*Significant*	*df*
Doctor		463	23.15			
vs.				1.21	0.10	18
Engineers	Competence	434	21.70			
Doctor		527	26.35			
vs.				1.55	0.10	18
Engineers	Dutifulness	488	24.40			
Doctor	Achievement	447	22.35			
vs.				1.80	0.05	18
Engineers	striving	408	20.40			

Table 21.4 shows the scores obtained by each group of SWB. Dimension-wise there is slight difference between each group. The mean value of Doctors (36.10) on the first dimension positive affect of SWB is higher than the Engineers (34.80). On the second dimension SWB Negative affect both were about to similar with the mean value of Doctors (25.10) while Engineers have obtained a little high score (25.90). On the third dimension Mental Mastery over self to Environment, Engineers (27.40) in comparison with Doctors (26.00). On the fourth dimension Rootedness Belongingness both were about to similar the mean value of Doctor (18.30) and Engineers (18.25). On the fifth dimension structural to cohesive aspect of family, Doctors obtained (14.45) while Engineers are on (14.20). On the sixth dimension Density of social Network there is slight difference between both mean values the scores, Doctors are (13.30) and Engineers obtained (14.35). On the seventh dimension security in health and socio-economic crises, Engineers have obtained the score (11.95) while Doctors are on (11.35). On the last dimension Expectations-Achievement harmony, Doctors are obtained a little high score (14.40) than that of Engineers (13.60).

TABLE 21.4: Scores obtained by Each Group A (Doctor), B (Engineer) on Subjective Well-being

Sl.No.	*Dimensions of SWB*	*Group A*		*Group B*	
		Scores	*Mean*	*Scores*	*Mean*
1.	Subjective well-being positive affect	722	36.10	696	34.80
2.	Subjective well-being negative affect	502	25.10	518	25.90
3.	Mental mastery over self to environment	520	26.00	548	27.40
4.	Rootedness and belongingness	366	18.30	365	18.25
5.	Structural to cohesive aspect of family	289	14.45	284	14.20
6.	Density of social network	266	13.30	287	14.35
7.	Security in health and socio-economic crises	227	11.35	239	11.95
8.	Expectation achievement harmony	288	14.40	272	13.60
	Overall SWB (Grand Total)	**3180**	**159.00**	**3209**	**160.45**

There is little difference between the overall SWB in both groups. Group A (159.00), Group B (160.45).

TABLE 21.5: Coefficients of Correlations betw3en Conscientiousness and SWB in Doctors on Sub-dimensions

Group	*Dimension*	*Mean Value*	*Correlation Value*	*Significance Level*	*df*
Doctor	Competence *vs.* SWB	23.15 159.30	0.230	Not significant	38
Doctor	Dutifulness *vs.* SWB	25.95 159.30	– 0.550	Not significant	38
Doctor	Achievement striving *vs.* SWB	22.35 159.30	– 0.425	0.01	38

TABLE 21.6: Coefficients of Correlations between Conscientiousness and SWB in Engineers on Sub-dimensions

Group	*Dimension*	*Mean Value*	*Correlation Value*	*Significance Level*	*df*
Engineers	Competence *vs.* SWB	21.7 160.1	– 0.190	Not significant	38
Engineers	Dutifulness *vs.* SWB	24.4 160.1	– 0.480	Not significant	38
Engineers	Achievement striving *vs.* SWB	20.4 160.1	– 0.130	Not significant	38

To see the dimension-wise difference between conscientiousness and SWB in Doctors and Engineers correlation was calculated. Which is negatively significant.

Discussion

The aim of the present study was to investigate the conscientiousness in doctors and engineers and their subjective well-being of working women. Investigator also tried to find out the factors which contribute to conscientiousness and SWB of these people. Subsequent researches have consistently reported, however, that five robust factors — Neuroticism (*Vs.* Emotional Stability), Extraversion (or surgency), conscientiousness (or Dependability), Agreeableness, and openness (or

Imagination, intellect, or culture) are sufficient to represent the underlying structure of personality (Borgetta, 1964; Fiske, 1949; Norman, 1963; Tupes & Christal, 1992).

Costa and McCrae (1991) have found the negative relationship of well-being with Neuroticism, but there was a positive relationship between extraversion and well-being. So this investigator also tried to see the relationship between other personality factors like conscientiousness with well-being.

In order to measure these factors two groups of (A) Doctors and (B) Engineers were contacted. Their scores on conscientiousness and SWB were obtained. The highlights of the results are:

Tables 21.1, 21.2 and 21.3 show the scores of each group on conscientiousness along with its sub-dimensions. It shows that the mean scored conscientiousness in doctors is high. The score of Engineers is slightly less on conscientiousness was calculated separately for both groups of respondents. The score of conscientious more conscientious. But what factors are responsible which cause high conscientiousness in this group and comparatively low in group B. There are some social factors which contribute in conscientiousness in both groups. On various dimensions the scores obtained show that competence of doctors is higher as compared to engineers. It includes positive aspects of personality. Table 21.1 also depicts that the score of doctors on the dimension Dutifulness is high. It shows their feeling of responsibility. Another sub-dimensions have slight differences between both groups. There are only three sub-dimensions which show the increasing conscientiousness of doctors.

To see the difference between both groups on the sub-dimension of conscientiousness *t*-tests were computed. Competence is one of them and other sub-dimensions are — Dutifulness and Achievement Striving *t* value was computed on these dimensions, which was significant. The *t* value of dutifulness is significant at 0.10 levels and Achievement striving is significant at 0.05 level. The present results show that doctors are more dutiful, more competent and have achievement striving and they have more conscientiousness.

Table 21.4 shows the mean scores of each groups on SWB. It also shows that the groups of engineers on SWB are slightly higher in comparison to the scores of Doctors what factors are responsible, which cause high SWB. What factors are responsible which cause high SWB? Now, if scores on various are examined dimension positive affect of doctors is high from group B. It includes frequency and intensity of pleasant emotions. Table 21.4 also shows that another sub-dimension on which doctors scored higher, is the feeling of security and health in socio-economic about any type of health related or socio-economic crisis. Also their scores are high on expectations achievement harmony which means that they have achieved what they desired in their lives. There are three sub-dimensions on which the doctors have scored more which have gave rise to their overall SWB. The scores of other sub-dimensions are not very much different in both groups.

To see the difference between conscientiousness and SWB of Doctors and Engineers correlation were calculated. The correlation between conscientiousness and SWB in doctors are more conscientious because they are connected with human lives. So, their SWB was found to be higher. But, there is no correlation found between conscientiousness and SWB in Engineer. It shows that group is not conscientious for their work. There are some social factors which contribute for their low conscientiousness. It is possible that the aim of life of engineers are to earn money. They do not bother about the means of earning. Whether money is being earned through legitimate or illegimate means, does not trouble them. There are, however, some individual differences which were found in the present study. There are some differences between both groups on the sub-dimension of conscientiousness. Dutifulness is one of them. Correlation was calculated on this dimension, which was negatively significant.

Tables 21.5 and 21.6 show the correlation between conscientiousness and SWB in both groups. The correlation between conscientiousness and SWB in doctors is highly significant. But no correlation was found between conscientiousness and SWB in engineers. The score obtained by both groups on SWB show that engineers have obtained a little high value from doctors. What factors are responsible which cause high SWB. Now, if scores on various are examined the dimension. Subjective well-being positive affect of doctors is high from group B. It includes frequency and intensity of pleasant emotions. Table 21.4 also shows that another sub-dimensions on which doctors scored higher, is the feeling of security and health in socio-economic crisis. They are secure when it is questioned about any type of health related or socioeconomic crisis. Also their scores are high on expectation achievements harmony which means that they achieved what they desired in their lives. There are three sub-dimensions on which the doctors have scored more which have gave rise to their overall SWB. The scores of other sub-dimensions are not very much different in both groups.

To see the difference between conscientiousness and SWB of Doctors and Engineers correlations were calculated. The correlation between conscientiousness and SWB in doctors was highly significant. It shows that doctors are more conscientious because they are connected with human live, so their conscientiousness was found to be higher. But there is no correlation was found between conscientiousness and SWB in engineers. It shows that engineers are not conscientiousness for their work. There are some social factors which contribute for their low conscientiousness. It is possible that the aim of life of engineers are to earn money. They do not bother about the means of earning. Whether money is being earned through legitimate or illegitimate means; does not trouble them. There are, however, some individual differences which were found in the present study. There are some differences between both groups on the sub-dimension of conscientiousness. Dutifulness is lone of them. Correlation was calculated on this dimension, which was negatively significant. But, the correlations on two sub-dimensions — competence and achievements striving were higher as compared to engineers.

From the results of the present study it has been found that there is no direct relationship between conscientiousness and SWB even as regards profession, there is direct relationship between conscientiousness and SWB as visible and found in the group of Doctors. The result of the study shows the direct relationship between conscientiousness and SWB in engineers. The aim of life of engineers is to earn money, but doctors are conscientiousness because of being related with human lives while engineers are not. It is comment on the socio-political climate of our nation.

The results are also show that the correlation between the sub-dimension achievement striving and SWB is negatively significant. It can be said that doctors want to gain higher achievement in their lives, that is why they are not very much conscious about their SWB. Probably this is the main factor that contribute the low SWB of doctors in comparison to engineers.

Women who score in this range work toward their goals in a deliberate manner, they have relatively high reliable and carry through on commitments they make. They have good self-discipline and take their obligations seriously. Individuals low in conscientiousness are often unwilling to undertake the work of psychotherapy and may even be more likely to miss appointments. They also have a low toleration for frustration, so, they find it difficult to fact their problems squarely.

These are some relevant theoretical, postulations on which results can be explained. However, to the extent that any theory claims to specify, which factor may increase the level of subjective well-being, two things are necessary. First thing is that the relationship between conscientiousness and well-being itself is not clearly specified and always it is logical to think that these two may not be positively correlated. Because a person might easily compensate for work dissatisfaction elsewhere than work and have an overall good well-being. Secondly, in subjective well-being the implication is 'subjective' that certainly means that individual differences. The factors which relate the perception of well-being is irrespective of internal factors. So, this is a crucial determinant of SWB.

REFERENCES

Andrews, F.M. & Withey, S.B. (1976). *Social Indicators of Well-being*, New York: Plenum.

Andrews, M.F. & Robinson, P.J. (1991). "Measures of Subjective Well-being", in J.P. Robinson; P.R. Shaver & L.S. Wrightman (eds.), *Measures of Personality and Social Psychological Attitudes*, San Diego: Academic Press, Inc., pp. 61-111.

Borgatta (1964). "The Structure of Personality Characteristics", *Behavioural Science*, 9(8): 17.

Bruck, M. & Ceci, S.J. (1999). "The Suggestibility of Children's Memory", *Annual Review of Psychology*, 50: 419-439.

Cacioppo, J.T.; Gardner, W.L. & Bernston, G.G. (1999). "The Effect System has Parallel and Integrative Processing Components: From Follows Function", *Journal of Personality and Social Psychology*, 76: 839-855.

Carson, V.B. (1992). *Prayer, Meditation, Exercise, and Special Diets: Behaviours of the Hardy Person with HIV/AIDS*, University of Maryland School of Nursing, Baltimore.

Carson, V.B. & Green, H. (1992). "Spiritual Well-being: A Predictor of Hardiness in Patients with Acquired Immunodeficiency Syndrome", *Journal of Professional Nursing*, 8(4): 209-220.

Costa, P.T.J., *et al.* (2001). "Gender Differences in Personality Traits Across Cultures: Robust and Surprising Findings", *Journal of Personality and Social Psychology*, 81: 322-331.

Costa, P.T. Jr. (1991). "Clinical Use of the Five Factor Model: An Introduction", *Journal of Personality Assessment*, 57: 393-398.

Costa, P.T. Jr.; McCrae, R.R. & Dye, D.A. (1991). "Facet Scales for Agreeableness and Conscientiousness: A Revision of the NEO Personality Inventory", *Personality and Individual Differences*, 12: 887-898.

Diener, E. (1984). "Subjective Well-being", *Psychological Bulletin*, 95(3): 542-575.

Deiner, E.; Horwitz, J. & Emmons, R.A. (1985). "Happiness of the Very Wealthy", *Social Indicators — Research*, 16: 263-274.

Deiner, E.; Sapyta, J. & Suh, E. (1998). "Subjective Well-being is Essential to Well-being", *Psychological Enquiry*, 9: 33-37.

Deiner, E. & Suh, E. (1999). "Societies We Live in: International Comparisons", in D. Kahneman; E. Dinener & N. Schwartz (Eds.), *Well-being: The Foundations of Hedonic Psychology* (pp. 434-452), New York: Russell Sage Foundations.

Deiner, E.; Wolsic, B. & Fujita, F. (1994). "Physical Attractiveness & Subjective Well-being", *Journal of Personality and Social Psychology*, 69: 120-129.

Eid, M. & Diener, E. (1999). "Intra Individual Variability in Affect: Reliability, Validity and Personality Correlates", *Journal of Personality and Social Psychology*, 76: 66-676.

Fiske, D.W. (1949). "Consistency of the Factorial Structures of Personality Rating from Different Sources", *The Journal of Abnormal and Social Psychology*, 44: 329-344.

Gasper, D. (2002). "Is Sen's Capability Approach an Adequate Basis for Considering Human Development?", *Review of Political Economy*, 14(4): 435-461.

Hansson, A., *et al.* (2005). "Well-being in an Adult Swedish Population", *Social Indicators Research*, 74: 313-325.

Kobasa, S.C. (1979). "Stressful Life Events, Personality and Health: An Inquiry info Hardiness", *Journal of Personality and Social Psychology*, 37: 1-11, web of Science.

Myers, D.C. (2000). "The Funds, Friends, and Faith of Happy People", *American Psychology*, 55: 56-67.

Norman (1963). "Toward an Adequate Taxonomy of Personality Attributes: Replicated Factor Structure in Peer Nomination Personality Ratings", *The Journal of Abnormal and Social Psychology*, 66(6): 574-583.

P. Dadlani; P. Markopoulos & Aarts (2009). *Intertwining Implicit and Explicit Awareness of Well-being to Support Peace of Mind and Connectedness*, Department of Industrial Design, Eindhoven University of Technology, P.O. Box 513, Den Dolech 2, Eindhoven, 5600 MB, The Netherlands.

Skomorovsky, A. & Sudom, K.A. (2011). *Role of Hardiness in the Psychological Well-being of Canadian Forces Officer Candidates*, Defence Research and Development Canada, Department of National Defence, 101 Colonel By Drive, Ottawa, ON K1A OK2, Canada.

Tupes, E.C. & Christal, R.C. (1992). "Recurrent Personality Factors Based on Trait Rating", *Journal of Personality*, 60: 225-251.

Veenhovenrn (1994). *Correlates of Happiness: 7,836 Finding from 603 Studies in 69 Notions, 1911-1994*. Unpublished Manuscript, Erosmus University, Rotterdam Potteram, The Nitherlands.

William, V.; Shonin, Sumich; Sundin, A. & Griffiths, M. (2013). *Meditation Awareness Training (MAT) for Psychological Well-Being in a Sub-Clinical Sample of University Students: A Controlled Pilot Study*, Purchase on Springer.com.

22

Resilience as a Coping Weapon for Stress among Working Women

Shoaib Hasan and *P.S.N. Tiwari*

Introduction

In modern era the role and prominence of the women have been changed enormously. At the present time, Indian women's exposure to educational opportunities is substantially higher than it was some decades ago, especially in the urban setting. This has opened new vistas, increased awareness and raised aspirations of personal growth. With increasing female education and more liberty for their rights and privileges, women's attitude towards their stereotyped role is changing. Now-a-days, women play different role which are leading to stress and poor mental health problem in their lives. Rajasekhar and Sasikala (2013) argued that employed women face stress due to family responsibilities, job insecurity, workplace culture and high demand of job performance. They also determined that effective management of stress involves preparing role occupants to understand the nature of stress, directing stress for productive purposes, and making role occupants' to understand their strength and equipping them to develop approach strategies for coping with stress.

Problems of Working Women

Acceptance as Working Professionals

Most Indian men are yet to come to terms with the fact that women are also capable of working with them, shoulder to shoulder, in any field or professional sphere. They still visualize women as individuals who should be in charge of the kitchen and other domestic affairs.

Work is either seen as a temporary evil for women whose husbands do not earn enough, or the domain of women who do not "know their place". As a result, Indian working women do not get the respect they require from their male colleagues in the workplace.

Balancing Work-Family Life

No matter how high their position or designation is in the office, women in India are still viewed as the family manager back home. They are expected to return home at a certain time, cook, clean and take care of family affairs.

In fact, men who help out around their house are often the butt of jokes by their male friends. This makes life extremely stressful for women who have little help around the house and have to do it all.

Travelling for Work is Not Acceptable

One of the problems faced by married working women is that they cannot travel or go on tours without having to answer uncomfortable questions by most of their friends and family. This is especially true for married women, who also have a flourishing career. Their professional obligations often depend on the support and understanding of family members.

A married man can go on long official tours outside his home city, without raising eyebrows and questions from his family members and peers, but his equally-successful wife would face disapproval. As a result, women often have to opt out of jobs than involve travel or settle for not being promoted as a result.

Safety of Working Women

The "nosey questions factor" aside, there is still the concern for safety of working women who need to travel on official business. Women travelling out of their home city for work trips are considered vulnerable and an easy target to fulfil the lewd intentions of their chauvinist male colleagues. Checking into a hotel alone is one of the problems faced by working women, even if the trip is purely official. Many hotels refuse to allot a room to a single woman (under strange pretexts) because of their own safety concerns or if a woman decides to stay alone, she is viewed with suspicion.

Unequal Pay

One of the raging topics of discussion in the context of problems faced by working women (not only in India, but also in many other countries) is that of equal pay. Legally, a woman is entitled to get the same salary as their male colleagues for the same kind of work done by them. However, gender discrimination is rampant as many companies still do not adhere to these guidelines and pay women less than their male colleagues.

Discrimination at Workplace

However, Indian women still face blatant discrimination at their workplaces. A major problem faced by the working women is sexual harassment at the work place. Further, women employees working in night shift are more vulnerable to such incidents. Nurses, for example, face this problem nearly every day. There is nothing that is done in hospitals to tackle and address the danger they face. Such blatant disregard of current Indian laws is one reason why sexual harassment at the workplace continues to increase.

Also, Indian women are often deprived of promotions and growth opportunities at work places, but this doesn't apply to all working women. A majority of working women continue to be denied their right to equal pay, under the Equal Remuneration Act, 1976 and are underpaid in comparison to their male colleagues. This is usually the case in factories and labour-oriented industries.

Makowska studied psychosocial determinants of stress and well-being among working women and found significance of the work-related stressors was evidently greater than that of the stressors associated with the family function, although the relationship between family functioning, stress and well-being was also significant. Research has shown that the more juggling incidents per day, the better her chances for having low satisfaction at the end of the day (Williams & Suls, 1991) and the chances for experiencing stress buffering effects increases. In addition, Repetti *et al.* (1989) reported that women who do not get their spouse support in household management are also experiening high level of stress.

Stress in work place can be regarded as any negative, stressful or difficult situation of hardship that is encountered in the occupational setting (Jackson *et al.*, 2007). The changing and modernization of the current working environment have had employees work longer hours. Work stress can be defined as the negative effects on the worker's physical and emotional health as a result of the mismatch between the worker's capabilities, resources or needs and the requirements of the job (NIOSH, 1999). Stephen Palmer and Kristina Gyllensten (2005) noticed, multiple roles, lack of career progress, discrimination and stereotyping are the factors that create stress among the women. They confirmed that women reported higher levels of stress as compared to men. In addition DeMeis and Perkins (1996) discussed that women are still considered responsible for the majority of household labour and management, child care and elder care and employed women work to the equivalent of two full time jobs. The dual roles of the working women are leading to stress in their lives. This makes employed women experience strain on their time and energy (Hughes & Galinksy, 1988; Kenney & Bhattacharjee, 2000). Similarly, Ansuman, Adithya and Madhulita (2014) determined that maximum number of women is suffering from poor mental health. According to them home and workplace atmosphere played a major role in deciding mental health status of women. Furthermore, this study is a comparison in the degree of occupational stress experienced by married and unmarried working women. The study reveals that married women are experiencing more stress than unmarried women, and the stress is explained in terms of traditional trends, demands of society and more roles and responsibilities assigned to them as a mother, wife and homemaker (Nagina, 2009). This statement is also supported by Kodavatiganti and Bulusu (2011) and said that women educators face comparatively higher level of stress than men counterparts. The stresses amongst the academicians are caused because of lengthy working hours, scarce resources and classrooms that are over filled. The study accomplishes that moderate level of job stress and quality of life was found among majority of the respondents.

Balaji (2014) studied various factors which could lead to work family conflict and the stress undergone by women employees. He concluded that married women employees experience work family conflict due to the number of hours worked outside the home, flexible or in flexible working hours, size of the family and number of dependents of the family. These factors have unembellished consequences for the psychological distress and well-being of married working women.

Sussanna (2012) identified high psychological demands; job strain and low job control are associated with increased stroke risk in working women.

Bhuvaneshwari (2013) revealed that stress in married working women is caused due to various family and official commitments, harassments at work place, working for long hours and improper work life balance. These factors lead to stress in working women such as prolonged headaches, hypertension and obesity. She also concluded that stress can be relieved from balancing work and family, from institutional support, by spending time with the family and performing physical exercises.

Stephen (2005) discovered work overload, uncooperative patients, criticism, negligent co-workers, lack of support from supervisors, and difficulties with physicians are the factors that cause stress among the nurses. They also suggested that interventions to reduce stress might improve interpersonal and motivational aspects of job performance.

Dr. A. Chandra and Balaji Kishore (2015) studied the relationship between self-esteem and stress, the factors that create stress among gold collar employees in Chennai city and the effect of stress on the health of the employees. Their study revealed that most of the female married employees are experiencing high level of stress as compared to men and unmarried employees. From the data it is concluded that there is no significant relationship between self-esteem and stress.

Again this study is done by Ramanaiah and Subramanian (2008) on gold collar employees of Chennai city to know the level of stress they are experiencing. According to them the employees are under high level of stress and there exists a negative relationship between marital status and stress. They concluded that stress among female employees is due to role isolation; inter role distance and role overload.

It simply seems that women are generally hectic and more stressed than men and that they disguise more roles and are constantly rushing towards goal fulfillment. Researchers from The University of Arizona's School of Family and Consumer Resources decided to find out. They took a sample of 166 married couples and had each participant maintain a daily diary over the course of 42 days, where they recorded their daily stressors. The results indeed indicated that women reported a greater amount of "high distress" days and fewer distress-free days than men. Interestingly, the differences in levels of stressful days were due to women experiencing more onsets of "distress episodes" (having stress response triggered), rather than being more likely to continue in a distressed state from one day to the next. In other words, women did not hold onto their stress more; they just experienced more episodes of being stressed (Elizabeth Scott, M.S., 2010).

For the purposes of this chapter, we refer to resilience as the ability of an individual to adjust to adversity, maintain equilibrium, retain some sense of control over their environment, and continue to move on in a positive manner. It is therefore an active process that Giordano (1997:1032) describes as "a shifting balance between vulnerability and resilience". If equilibrium is maintained, an individual can theoretically manage any situation that comes along. Thus, I argue that developing personal resilience can reduce vulnerability.

Resilience is a scientific term that applies to materials that have the capacity to return to their original shape after being bent or stretched. Over time, however, we have come to apply the term to people as well. People who have the ability to recover readily from illness, depression, defeat, or other kinds of adversity. Resilience has been defined as the capacity to withstand, regulate and cope with ongoing life challenges and succeeds in maintaining equilibrium despite negative effects from stress (DiCorcia & Tronick, 2011; Montpetit, Bergeman, Deboeck, Tiberio & Boker, 2010; O'Neill & Dias, 2007; Schetter & Dolbier, 2011).

The American Psychological Association (2014) defines resilience as "the process of adapting well in the face of adversity, trauma, tragedy, threats or even significant sources of stress (*para. 4*)". While this definition is useful, it does not reflect the complex nature of resilience. Determinants of resilience include a host of biological, psychological, social and cultural factors that interact with one another to determine how one responds to stressful experiences.

For many women, resilience is a strength considered essential. Both women and men need resilience to deal with difficulties in life. But, women often need more resilience than men to overcome traditional obstacles placed in their way, in order to advance in the business world. Too many women, however, are not aware of the amount of resilience they do possess. An individual who adapts well to stress in a workplace or in an academic setting, may fail to adapt well in their personal life or in their relationships.

Resilience plays the significant role of a defensive factor, protecting the individual's psychological being and increasing positive changes when coping with stressful situations (Dolbier, Jaggars & Steinhardt, 2010; Kinman & Grant, 2011). It seeks to promote and maintain health and avert illness (Muller, 2009). Recent literature has progressively shifted focus to study resilience in the context of overcoming everyday moderate stress instead of chronic stresses like abuse and discrimination as it is also perceived as a stressor that may negatively impact an individual (DiCorcia & Tronick, 2011; Lazarus & Folkman, 1984).

Gail M. Wagnild, Ph.D., is founder of the Resilience Centre and a national expert on resilience, and she says that when you know your capacity for resilience, it gives you the confidence to deal with whatever life throws at you. Being resilient helps you to cope in variety of different ways, be they personal, professional, or social.

Some Features that Build Resilience

Psychologists believed that individuals can develop and strengthen personal resilience through developing strategies for reducing their own vulnerability, and the personal impact of adversity in the workplace. Tugade and Fredrickson (2004) suggest that everyone has resilience potential, but its level is determined by individual experiences, qualities, the environment and by each person's balance of risk and protective factors. Protective factors help individuals to achieve a positive outcome regardless of the risk (Tusaie & Fredrickson, 2004).

The literature review acknowledged a number of factors that either build or impede resilience in working women.

Personal Qualities

Internal resources were identified in the literature as a major contribution to women resilience. Toth's (2003) study with refugee women suggests that personal qualities such as optimism, adaptability and perseverance helped them to cope and survive. A belief in one's own inner strength to deal with life's challenges (Brough, Gorman, Ramirez & Westoby, 2003) a positive attitude, and having hope for a good future helped working women to cope (Khawaja, White, Schweitzer & Greenslade, 2008). The determination to cope was seen as a component of taking control, rather than being a victim (Gorman, Brough & Ramirez, 2003). Shakespeare-Finch and Wickham's (2009) study suggests that looking ahead to the future strengthens people's resilience. One participant in the study stated: "I am going to lay a good foundation for me, for my children, for my family" (Shakespeare-Finch & Wickham, 2009:38). Similarly, a study with the 'Lost Boys of Sudan' identified that an acceptance of the situation and refocusing on the present and the future helped some of the boys to cope (Luster, Qin, Bates, Johnson & Rana, 2009).

Becoming More Reflective

Theories of adult learning recognize the importance of reflection to learning (Larson & Brady, 2001; Wilson & Kiely, 2002). Reflection is a way of developing insights and understandings into experiences, and of developing knowledge that can be used in subsequent situations. In reflection, concrete experience is used as a catalyst for thinking and learning. Journaling can be a useful reflective strategy (Giordano, 1997). Writing about an experience is known to be useful, in that the writer ascribes meaning to events (Jackson, 2000). Thus, new understandings and insights can arise for the writer through the act of writing. For example, experiencing consistently negative emotional responses about a person, place or thing can be very illuminating, and may be a catalyst for reflection and exploring ways of adopting more positive responses to particular situations, people and events.

Support

Social support has been identified as a significant component in resilience, and the maintenance of relationships is a component of social support (Tusaie & Fredrickson, 2004). Separately from personal qualities being linked to working women resilience, external forms of support were also prominent in the construction of resilience. A number of qualitative studies highlighted the importance of family (including extended family), friends, and community in boosting resilience process. Support included both the mutual processes of giving and receiving support. In a qualitative study, Bosnian women cited the support received from their spouses, children and family as a key factor in building their resilience. As one participant stated: "once you have family you cannot give up, you have to stay strong for them" (Sossou, Craig, Ogren & Schnak, 2008:378). Likewise, qualitative studies conducted in Australia also confirmed support and its relationship to resilience (Schweitzer, Greenslade & Kagee, 2007). Apart from receiving support from friends and family, people also utilized their own ethnic community to help them cope and adjust to their new way of life (Schweitzer *et al.*, 2007). Mixing and having a strong attachment with their ethnic peers, helped people to cope with resettlement, and was associated with significantly "greater levels of well-being in the psychological, social and environmental domains" (Correa-Velez, Gifford & Barnett, 2010:1404).

Lenette, Brough and Cox's (2012) qualitative research with single women found resilience building is connected to "person-environment interactions", rather than being linked to static, individual-inner traits. Moreover, the women's narratives suggest resilience is underpinned by a dynamic process which is fluid, contextual and constructed continually throughout ordinary, day-to-day processes involving challenges and opportunities. Pulvirenti and Mason's (2011) study with service providers working with working women experiencing violence, also confirm that resilience is a process rather than a fixed inner personal characteristic. Moreover, the service providers argue such essentialist individualized notions of resilience can be used by governments to reduce their social responsibility in providing services and resources, and this can lead to blaming an individual for their current circumstances (Pulvirenti & Mason, 2011). Furthermore, the service providers suggest that the women's resilience is constructed in an environment of external support, not just from friends, and within their own ethnic communities, but their resilience is conditional upon the assistance of the wider host community (Pulvirenti & Mason, 2011). These studies suggest resilience moves beyond the essentialist notion of resilience that resides within an individual alone, an inner trait, to encompass personal qualities that also interact within a social context. This equates to the concept of social construction that argues that knowledge and understanding about the world comes from exchanges between people in their social, cultural and historical context (Payne, 2005). Thus, human meanings made from such interactions "are never singular, individual or simply subjective, never outside the social, but have shared inter subjective meaning within the cultural nexus of power and knowledge" (Brown & Augusta-Scott, 2007:9).

Developing Emotional Insight

There is increasing literature on the importance of emotional intelligence (EI) in the workplace. In broad terms, EI is the ability to understand one's own emotional needs, and have insight into the emotional needs of those encountered in the workplace (Daly *et al.*, 2004). Understanding one's own emotional needs and reactions gives insights into how to cope with stress and adversity and can help spawn ideas for different ways of coping in the future (Bright, 1997; Giordano, 1997). Furthermore, as discussed earlier, positive emotions can assist in developing resilience (Fredrickson, 2004; Tugade & Fredrickson, 2004), and so developing insight into negative and positive emotions could be a beginning step in strengthening personal resilience. Giordano (1997) suggests journaling and self-reflection as strategies for enhancing emotional insight, as does McGee (2006).

Building Positive Fostering Professional Relations and Linkages

Building positive professional relationships is essential for working women. This is the network that becomes a professional support system. We each need a network of people who can be called upon for guidance and support when needed. It is especially important to develop systems with people outside the immediate work area. These coworkers can provide authentication and take on the role of sounding board, especially at times when tensions are running high in the workplace and when seeking such support within their own workplace may expose individuals to unnecessary vulnerability. Professional networks should include relationships that are nurturing in nature. Ideally, all collegial relationships would have some degree of nurturing, but this is often not the case. Everyone needs to be nurtured sometimes and it is important to foster these nurturing relationships. Actively seeking particular relationships, such as a mentoring relationship, can provide nurses with the opportunity to enter into mutually beneficial supportive and nurturing relationships (Daly *et al.*, 2004).

Mentorship has been alluded to in the literature in relation to building healthy relationships to protect children at risk and promote resiliency (e.g. Gilligan, 1999; Benard & Marshall, 2001; Joinking, 2003). From the perspective of nursing, McGee (2006) notes the benefits of guidance and support from colleagues and the need to nurture traits of resiliency in the self, students and co-workers.

Accomplishing Life Balance

A number of writers define the importance of feelings of connectedness, achieving life balance and having an 'anchoring force' in life (Giordano, 1997:1033). Tusaie and Fredrickson (2004) acknowledge the importance of "a belief system that provides existential meaning, a cohesive life narrative and an appreciation of the uniqueness of oneself" (p. 4) for having high levels of resilience. Regardless of spiritual beliefs, it is important to participate in a range of healthy activities outside one's professional life. These activities should ideally include those that are physically, emotionally and spiritually nurturing. In this way, it is possible to retain some balance in life, in working women very demanding career such as nursing.

Thinking and Coping Styles

Psychologist and executive coach Naomi Harrison states that, "The way you think about challenges can help you build resilience and well-being at work".

Harrison recommends practicing the following strategies to build resilient thinking:

- Think about what is working well. This can help problems seem smaller and empower you to act.
- Remind yourself of previous accomplishments — both big and small. For example, ask yourself: When have you had success coping dealing with a problem in the past? What did you do that made it successful? Can you use any of those strategies to the current issue? This type of thinking can help increase your confidence and help you feel empowered.
- Break issues into smaller chunks and smaller goals. Smaller goals make it easier to see progress and can motivate you to persist through challenges.
- Focus on what is in your control and act on that.
- Be prepared for mistakes or setbacks to happen. When mistakes happen, see them as problems to be solved and shift your attention to working out how to overcome the issue.

Religiosity and Spirituality

Religion and spirituality are strongly identified as another major factor contributing to refugee people's resilience. Several studies have shown that religion in its various forms is linked to enhancing a person's psychological and physical well-being (Green & Elliot, 2010). For example, a study with 62 young orphaned participants suggested that Buddhist spirituality promoted resilience in children in many ways: it offered them "structure, encouraged cognitive restructuring, acceptance of the trauma, cultivated a sense of control and the rituals promoted integration in the broader community" (Fernando & Ferrari, 2011:70). Schweitzer *et al.* (2007) suggests a belief in God helped people regain control and meaning in their lives. Another study found some refugee people resigned themselves to the situation, and believed fate was out of their hands and in God's hands (Khawaja *et al.*, 2008). Spirituality gave other refugee people strength: whether it was a belief in a "higher power, calling on dead relatives or something deep inside", spirituality assisted refugee people to cope through hard times (Sossou *et al.*, 2008: 378).

Maintaining Positivity

By definition, adversity is not a positive phenomenon. However, adversity and hardship often do have some positive aspects. Resilient people are able to draw on some form of positive emotion even in the midst of stress and hardship (Fredrickson, 2004; Tugade & Fredrickson, 2004). Bright (1997) provides a list of elements of resilience. She identifies optimism as a key component and in this way concurs with Tugade and Fredrickson (2004) in identifying positive emotions as important. In addition to optimism, Bright associates factors such as autonomy, empowerment, emotional awareness and self-care as important in developing resilience. Optimism and the capacity to see the range of future possibilities that events carry with them are aspects of maintaining a positive outlook (Bright, 1997). Resilient people are able to see the positive aspects and potential benefits of a situation, rather than being continually negative or cynical. Positive emotions and laughter are associated with beneficial physical and emotional outcomes (Tugade & Fredrickson, 2004), and Bonanno (2004, 2005) suggests that positive emotion and laughter can decline levels of adversity-related stress by reducing negative emotions.

Even in this day and age, there is an inflated adage — bought into by many, dictating that men are definitely the stronger sex. There are obviously varying degrees and definitions for the word 'strength'. Physiologically speaking, men are typically stronger — when you are talking about raw brute strength than their female counterparts are. (But NOT always, as we know of some pretty strong women in this world).

But when it comes to mental, emotional, and psychological strength — the picture of a women breaking down into sappy puddles at the first hint of strife in their lives, is quickly becoming nothing more than a ruse. Women are not only able to defy obstacles, but have an uncanny and creative ability to overcome the odds, deal with drastic life changes and find solutions to problems in an unpredictable world that is seemingly changing the way society looks at a woman. Truth is, we should never underestimate the strength and resilience of a woman!

For instance, often when things in life do not go as planned or roadblocks are hit such as; getting passed over for a job, getting pregnant unexpectedly, raising a child alone, suffering through the loss of a spouses job, the family home burns down, a car accident, health issues within the family — it is so often the steadfast woman who is holding all things together. When it comes to keeping calm and moving on, today's woman has become the jack of all trades, dealing with levels of stress from the family level to the professional level. Today women are strong and resilient and should never be underestimated. Their strength lies in their ability to bounce back, to lead, be creative and yet do all the things a man can do. That said they still have the compassionate and caring side that cares for the sick, raises our children and keeps families together.

Devastatingly, the review point to the importance of promoting positive behaviour, identifying and minimizing risks, enlightening the relationship of resilience with other aspects, and developing intervention programmes that incorporate support network resources. Empirical studies have primarily focused on at risk females who are physically and mentally ill, abused, psychologically vulnerable and maladjusted, while little is known about females who are considered physically and mentally healthy. It will be interesting to study more on working mothers and female in resilience studies to observe the interplay between work stress and resilience, especially working mothers who play multiple roles.

REFERENCES

Ahern, N.R. (2006). "Adolescent Resilience: An Evolutionary Concept Analysis", *Journal of Pediatric Nursing*, 21: 175-185.

American Psychological Association (2009). *Working with Refugee Children and their Families: An Update for Mental Health Professionals*. Retrieved April 15, 2011, from *http://www.apa.org/pubs/info/reports/refugees-health-professionals.pdf*

Ansuman Panigrahi; Adithya Prasad Padhy & Madhulita Panigrahi (2014). "Mental Health Status among Married Working Women Residing in Bhubaneshwar City: A Psychological Survey", *BioMed Research International*.

Asbring, P. (2001). "Chronic Illness — A Disruption in Life: Identity-transformation among Women with Chronic Fatigue Syndrome and Fibromyalgia", *Journal of Advanced Nursing*, 34: 312-319.

Balaji, R. (2014). "Work Life Balance of Women Employees", *International Journal of Innovative Research in Science, Engineering and Technology*, Vol. 3, Issue 10.

Barnes, G. (1999). "Divorce Transitions: Identifying Risk and Promoting Resilience for Children and their Parental Relationships", *Journal of Marital and Family Therapy*, 25: 425-441.

Benard, B. (1991). *Fostering Resiliency in Kids: Protective Factors in the Family, School and Community*, Northwest Regional Educational Laboratory, Portland.

Benard, B. & Marshall, K. (2001). *Big Brothers/big Sisters Mentoring: The Power of Developmental Relationships*, Resilience Research for Prevention Programmes, 1-8. National Resilience Resource Centre, Centre for the Application of Prevention, Technologies University of Minnesota, Minneapolis.

Bhuvaneshwari, M. (2013). "A Case Study on Psychological and Physical Stress Undergone by Married Working Women", *IOSR Journal of Business and Management*, Vol. 14(16): 38-44.

Bonanno, G. (2004). "Loss, Trauma and Human Resilience: Have We Underestimated the Human Capacity to Thrive After Extremely Aversive Events?", *American Psychologist*, 59: 20-28.

Bonanno, G. (2005). "Clarifying and Extending the Construct of Adult Resilience", *American Psychologist*, 60: 265-267.

Bonanno. G.; Wortman, C.; Lehman, D.; Tweed, R.; Haring, M.; Sonnega, J.; Carr, D. & Nesse, R. (2002). "Resilience to Loss and Chronic Grief: A Prospective Study from Pre-loss to 18-months Post-loss", *Journal of Personality and Social Psychology*, 83: 1150-1164.

Bright, J. (1997). *Turning the Tide*, London: Demos Publishers.

Brough, M.; Gorman, D.; Ramirez, E. & Westoby, P. (2003). "Young Refugees Talk about Well-being: A Qualitative Analysis of Refugee Youth Mental Health from three States", *Australian Journal of Social Issues*, 38(2): 193-208.

Brown, C. & Augusta-Scott, T. (Eds.) (2007). *Narrative Therapy: Making Meaning, Making Lives*, London: Sage Publications.

Chandra Mohan, A.; Balaji, K.D. & Kishore Kumar, T. (2015). "An Empirical India", *Abhinav: National Monthly Referred Journal of Research in Commerce and Management*, 2(5).

Cline, D.; Reilly, C. & Moore, J. (2003). "What's Behind RN Turnover? Uncover the 'Real Reasons' Nurses Leave", *Nursing Management*, 34: 10-53.

Coleman, M. & Ganong, L. (2002). "Resilience and Families", *Family Relations*, 51: 101.

Collins, M.C. (1996). "The Relation of Work Stress, Hardiness, and Burnout among Full-time Hospital Staff Nurses", *Journal of Nurse Staff Development*, 12: 81-85.

Correa-Velez, I.; Gifford, S. & Barnett, A. (2010). "Longing to Belong: Social Inclusion and Well-being among Youth with Refugee Backgrounds in the First Three Years in Melbourne, Australia", *Social Science & Medicine*, 17(8): 1399-1408. *doi:10.1016/j.socscimed.2010.07.018*

Daly, J., Speedy, S. & Jackson, D. (2004). *Nursing Leadership*, Elsevier Australia, Marrickville, N.S.W.

Darbyshire, P. & Jackson, D. (2005). "Using a Strengths Approach to Understand Resilience and Build Health Capacity in Families", *Contemporary Nurse*, 18: 211-212.

Dashora, K.B. (2013). "Problems Faced by Working Women in India", *International Journal of Advanced Research in Management and Social Sciences*, 2(8): 82-94.

DiCorcia, J.A. & Tronick, E. (2011). "Quotidian Resilience: Exploring Mechanisms that Drive Resilience from Perspective of Everyday Stress and Coping", *Neuroscience & Biobehavioural Reviews*, 35(7): 1593-1602. *http://dx.doi.org/10.1016/j.neubiorev.2011.04.008*

Dolbier, C.L.; Jaggars, S.S. & Steinhardt, M.A. (2010). "Stress-related Growth: Pre-intervention Correlates and Change Following a Resilience Intervention", *Stress & Health: Journal of the International Society for the Investigation of Stress*, 26(2): 135-147. *http://dx.doi.org/10.1002/smi.1275*

Edward, K. (2005). "The Phenomenon of Resilience in Crisis Care Mental Health Clinicians", *International Journal of Mental Health Nursing*, 14: 142-148.

Esche, C. & Tanner, E. (2005). "Resiliency: A Factor to Consider when Facilitating the Transition from Hospital to Home in Older Adults", *Geriatric Nursing*, 26: 218-222.

Fernando, C. & Ferrari, M. (2011). "Spirituality and Resilience in Children of War in Sri Lanka", *Journal of Spirituality and Mental Health*, 13(1): 52-77. *doi: 10.1080/19349637.2011.547138*

Flach, F. (1980). "Psychobiologic Resilience, Psychotherapy and the Creative Process", *Comprehensive Psychiatry*, 21: 510-519.

Flach, F. (1988). *Resilience: Discovering a New Strength at Times of Stress*, New York: Fawcett Columbine.

Fredrickson, B. (2004). "The Broaden-and-build Theory of Positive Emotions", *Philosophical Transactions of the Royal Society London B Biological Sciences*, 359: 1367-1377.

Gantner, Rose, *Women and Resilience*, Senior Director of Health Promotion, UPMC Work Partners, UPMC Insurance Services Division.

Gilligan, R. (1999). "Enhancing the Resilience of Children and Young People in Public Care by Mentoring their Talents and Interests", *Child and Family Social Work*, 4: 187-196.

Giordano, B. (1997). "Resilience: A Survival Tool for the Nineties", *Association of Perioperative Registered Nurses Journal*, 65: 1032-1036.

Gorman, D.; Brough, M. & Ramirez, E. (2003). "How Young People from Culturally Diverse Backgrounds Experience Mental Health: Some Insights for Mental Health Nurses", *International Journal of Mental Health Nursing*, 12(3): 194-202. *doi: 101140527.*

Green, M. & Elliot, M. (2010). "Religion Health and Psychological Well-being", *Journal of Religion and Health*, 49(2): 149-163. *doi: 10.1007/s10943-009-9242*

Gu, Q. & Day, C. (2006). "Teachers Resilience: A Necessary Condition for Effectiveness", *Teaching and Teacher Education*.

Harvey, S.; Blouin, C. & Stout, D. (2006). "Proactive Personality as a Moderator of Outcomes for Young Workers Experiencing Conflict at Work", *Personality and Individual Differences*, 40: 1063-1074.

Hodges, H.F.; Keeley, A.C. & Grier, E.C. (2005). "Professional Resilience, Practice Longevity, and Parse's Theory for Baccalaureate Education", *Journal of Nursing Education*, 44: 548-554. *http://psychcentral.com/blog/archives/2013/03/10/why-are-women-so-stressed-in-the-workplace/ http://www.psychology.org.au/assets/files/stresstipsheet.pdf*

Hunter, A. & Chandler, G. (1999). "Adolescent Resilience", *Journal of Nursing Scholarship*, 31: 243-247.

Hutchinson, M.; Vickers, M.; Jackson, D. & Wilkes, L. (2006). "Workplace Bullying in Nursing: Towards a More Critical Organizational Perspective", *Nursing Inquiry*, 13: 118-126.

Jacelon, C. (1997). "The Trait and Process of Resilience", *Journal of Advanced Nursing*, 25: 123-129.

Jackson, D. (2000). *Understanding Women's Health Through Australian Women's Writings: A Feminist Exploration*, Unpublished Doctoral Thesis. Flinders University of South Australia, Australia.

Jackson, D.; Clare, J. & Mannix, J. (2002). "Who would Want to be a Nurse? Violence in the Workplace: A Factor in Recruitment and Retention", *Nursing Management*, 10: 13-20.

Jackson, D.; Mannix, J. & Daly, J. (2001). "Retaining a Viable Workforce: A Critical Challenge for Nursing", *Contemporary Nurse*, 11: 163-172.

Joinking, A. (2003). *Building Resilient Families*, Australian Social Policy Conference, University of NSW, Sydney, Australia.

Judkins, S.; Arris, L. & Keener, E. (2005). "Programme Evaluation in Graduate Nursing Education: Hardiness as a Predictor of Success among Nursing Administration Students", *Journal of Professional Nursing*, 21: 314-321.

Karuna Kodavatiganti & Viswanadham Bulusu (2011). "Stress Indicators and Its Impact on Educators", *SIES Journal of Management*, 7(2): 88-96.

Kelley, T. (2005). "Natural Resilience and Innate Mental Health", *American Psychologist*, 60: 265.

Khawaja, N.; White, K.; Schweitzer, R. & Greenslade, J. (2008). "Difficulties and Coping Strategies of Sudanese Refugees: A Qualitative Approach", *Transcultural Psychiatry*, 45(3): 489-512. *doi:10.1177/1363461508094678*

Kinman, G. & Grant, L. (2011). "Exploring Stress Resilience in Trainee Social Workers: The Role of Emotional and Social Competencies", *British Journal of Social Work*, 41(2): 261-275. *http://dx.doi.org/10.1093/bjsw/bcq088*

Kitano, M. & Lewis, R. (2005). "Resilience and Coping: Implications for Gifted Children and Youth at Risk", *Roeper Review*, 27: 200-205.

Kulig, J.C. (2000). "Community Resiliency: The Potential for Community Health Nursing Theory Development", *Public Health Nursing Management*, 17: 374-385.

Larson, D. & Brady, E. (2001). "Learning Stories of Our Own", *Adult Learning*, 11: 13-15.

Laursen, E. & Birmingham, S. (2003). "Caring Relationships as a Protective Factor for at Risk Youth: An Ethnographic Study", *Families in Society*, 84: 240-246.

Lazarus, R.S. & Folkman, S. (1984). *Stress, Appraisal and Coping*, New York, NY: Springer Publishing Company.

Lenette, C.; Brough, M. & Cox, L. (2012). "Everyday Resilience: Narratives of Single Refugee Women with Children", *Qualitative Social Work*, 11(5): 1-17. *doi: 10.1177/1473325012449684*

Lowinger, Jocelyn, *Resilience in the Workplace*.

Luster, T.; Qin, D.; Bates, L.; Johnson, D. & Rana, M. (2009). "The Lost Boys of Sudan: Coping with Ambiguous Loss and Separation from Parents", *American Journal of Orthopsychiatry*, 79(2): 203-211. *doi: 10.1037/a0015559*

Luthar, S. & Cicchetti, D. (2000). "The Construct of Resilience: Implications for Interventions and Social Policies", *Development and Psychopathology*, 12: 857-885.

Luthar, S., Cicchetti, D. & Becker, B. (2000). "The Construct of Resilience: A Critical Evaluation and Guidelines for Future Work", *Child Development* , 71: 543-562.

Makikangas, A.; Kinnunen, U. & Feldt, T. (2004). "Self-esteem, Dispositional Optimism, and Health: Evidence from Cross-lagged Data on Employees", *Journal of Research in Personality*, 38: 556-575.

Makowska, Z. (1995). "Psychological Characteristics of Work and Family as Determinants of Stress and Well-being of Women: A Preliminary Study", *International Journal of Occupational Medicine Environmental Health*, Vol. 8, Issue 3: 215-222.

McGee, E. (2006). "The Healing Circle: Resiliency in Nurses", *Issues in Mental Health Nursing*, 27: 43-57.

McVicar, A. (2003). "Workplace Stress in Nursing: A Literature Review", *Journal of Advanced Nursing*, 44: 633-642.

Montpetit, M.A.; Bergeman, C.S.; Deboeck, P.R.; Tiberio, S.S. & Boker, S.M. (2010). "Resilience as Process: Negative Affect, Stress, and Coupled Dynamical Systems", *Psychology & Aging*, 25(3): 631-640. *http://dx.doi.org/10.1037/a0019268*

Motzer, S.; Hertig, V.; Jarrett, M. & Heitkemper, M. (2003). "Sense of Coherence and Quality of Life in Women with and Without Irritable Bowel Syndrome", *Nursing Research*, 52: 329-337.

Muller, R. (2009). "The Importance of Resilience to Primary Care Practitioners: An Interactive Psycho-Social Model", *The Australian Medical Journal*, 1(1): 1-15. *http://dx.doi.org/10.4066/amj.2009.23*

Murray, C.L.; Gein, I. & Solberg, M. (2003). "A Comparison of the Mental Health of Employed and Unemployed Women in the Context of a Massive Layoff", *Women and Health*, 37(2): 55-72.

Neill, J.T. & Dias, K.L. (2001). "Adventure Education and Resilience: The Double-edged Sword", *Journal of Adventure Education & Outdoor Learning*, 1(2): 35-42. *http://dx.doi.org/10.1080/14729670185200061*

Parse, R. (1998). *The Human Becoming School of Thought: A Perspective for Nurses and Other Health Professionals*, Thousand Oaks, CA: Sage Publications.

Patterson, J. (2002). "Understanding Family Resilience", *Journal of Clinical Psychology*, 58: 233-246.

Payne, M. (2011, 2005). *Humanistic Social Work: Core Principles in Practice*, Chicago: Lyceum Books.

Polk, L. (1997). "Toward a Middle-range Theory of Resilience", *Advanced Nursing Science*, 19: 1-13.

Pulvirenti, M. & Mason, G. (2011). "Resilience and Survival: Refugee Women and Violence", *Current Issues in Criminal Justice*, 23(1): 37-52.

Rabkin, J.; Remien, R.; Katoff, L. & Williams, J. (1993). "Resilience in Adversity among Long-term Survivors of AIDS", *Hospital and Community Psychiatry*, 44: 193-200.

Rajasekhar & Sasikala B. (2013). "An Impact of Stress Management on Employed Women", *Language in India*, 13(4).

Ramanathan, T.; Ramanathan, M. & Rajendran, G. (2014). "Research Reviews on Stress among Working Women in IT Field", *International Journal of Scientific and Research Publications*, 4(9).

Ramaniah, G. & Subrahmanian, M.U. (2008). "Stress among Gold Collar Employees in Chennai City", *Management and Labour Studies*, 33(4).

Repetti, R.L. *et al.* (1989). "Employment and Women's Health: Effects of Paid Employment on Women's Mental and Physical Health", *American Psychologist Association*, 44(11): 1394-1401.

Rew, L.; Taylor-Seehafer, M.; Thomas, N. & Yockey, R. (2001). "Correlates of Resilience in Homeless Adolescents", *Journal of Nursing Scholarship*, 33: 33-40.

Rutter, M. (1985). "Resilience in the Face of Adversity: Protective Factors and Resistance to Psychiatric Disorder", *British Journal of Psychiatry*, 147: 598-611.

Rutter, M. (1999). "Resilience Concepts and Findings: Implications for Family Therapy", *Journal of Family Therapy*, 21: 119-144.

Schaefer, K. (1995). "Struggling to Maintain Balance: A Study of Women Living with Fibromyalgia", *Journal of Advanced Nursing*, 21: 95-102.

Schetter, C.D. & Dolbier, C. (2011). "Resilience in the Context of Chronic Stress and health in Adults", *Social and Personality Psychology Compass*, 5(9): 634-652. *http://dx.doi.org/10.1111/j.1751-9004.2011.00379.x*

Schweitzer, R.; Greenslade, J. & Kagee, A. (2007). "Coping and Resilience in Refugees from the Sudan: A Narrative Account", *Australian and New Zealand Journal of Psychiatry*, 41(3): 282-288. *doi:1080/00048670601172780*

Shakespeare-Finch, J. & Wickham, K. (2009). "Adaption of Sudanese Refugees in an Australian Context: Investigating Helps and Hindrances", *International Migration*, 48(1): 23-46. *doi: 10.1111/j.1468-2435.2009.00561.x*

Sharma, V.K.; Trakroo, M.; Subramaniam, V.; Rajajeyakumar, M. & Bhavanani, A.B. *et al.* (2013). "Effect of Fast and Slow Pranayama on Perceived Stress and Cardiovascular Parameters in Young Health-care Students", *Int. J. Yoga*, 6: 104-110.

Shirom, A. (2004). "Feeling Vigorous at Work? The Study of Positive Affect in Organizations: Emotional and Physiological Processes and Positive Intervention Strategies", *Research in Occupational Stress and Well-Being*, 3: 135-164.

Shiva, G. (2013). "A Study on Work Family Balance and Challenges Faced by Working Women", *IOSR Journal of Business and Management*, 14(5): 01-04.

Silberberg, S. (2001). "Searching for Family Resilience", *Family Matters*, 58: 52-57.

Simonik, T. (2015). *Reflections on Hope and Recovery*, National Eating Disorder Information Centre. Retrieved April 20, 2015.

Sossou, M.; Craig, C.; Ogren, H. & Schnak, M. (2008). "A Qualitative Study of Resilience Factors of Bosnian Refugee Women Resettled in the Southern United States", *Journal of Ethnic & Cultural Diversity in Social Work*, 17(4): 365-385.

Stephen Palmer & Kristina Gyllensten (2005). "The Role of Gender in Workplace Stress: A Critical Literature Review", *Health Education Journal*, 64(3): 271-288.

Strachota, E.; Normandin, P.; O'Brien, N.; Clary, M. & Krukow, B. (2003). "Reasons Registered Nurses Leave or Change Employment Status", *Journal of Nursing Administration*, 33: 111-117.

Sussanna Toivanen (2012). "Social Determinants of Stroke as Related to Stress at Work among Working Women: A Literature Review", *Stroke Research and Treatment*, Hindwai Publishing Corporation, Vol. 2012.

Tedeschi, R. & Calhoun, L. (2004). "Posttraumatic Growth: Conceptual Foundations and Empirical Evidence", *Psychological Inquiry*, 15: 1-18.

Todis, B.; Bullis, M.; Waintrup, M.; Schultz, R. & D'Ambrosio, R. (2001). "Overcoming the Odds: Qualitative Examinations of Resilience among Formerly Incarcerated Adolescents", *Exceptional Children*, 68: 119-139.

Toth, J. (2003). *Resilience: The Experience of Immigrant and Refugee Women*, Master Thesis, University of Manitoba, Manitoba Heritage Thesis Database. Retrieved April 12, 2011, from *http://mspace.lib.umanitoba.ca/handle/1993/3801*

Tugade, M. & Fredrickson, B. (2004). "Resilient Individuals Use Emotions to Bounce Back from Negative Emotional Experiences", *Journal of Personality and Social Psychology*, 86: 320-333.

Tusaie, K. & Dyer, J. (2004). "Resilience: A Historical Review of the Construct", *Holistic Nursing Practice*, 18: 3-10.

United Nations High Commissioner for Refugees (UNHCR) (2009). *Facts and Resources*. Retrieved April 12, 2011, from *http://www.unhcr.org/pages/49c3646c4d6.html*

Williams & Liane, M. Kurina (1991). *health.bsd.uchicago.edu/members/kurinaLia/kurina_socialstructure.*

Wilson, A. & Kiely, R. (2002). *Towards a Critical Theory of Adult Learning/Education: Transformational Theory and Beyond*, Annual Meeting of the Adult Education Research.

www.azadindia.orgConference, Raliegh, NC.

www.graph.co.uk

www.workingwomensforum.org

www.wscpedia.org

Index